Live from Number 10

by the same author

Sources Close to the Prime Minister
with Peter Hennessy and David Walker
(Macmillan)

Live from Number 10

The Inside Story
of Prime Ministers and
Television

MICHAEL COCKERELL

faber and faber
LONDON · BOSTON

First published in 1988
by Faber and Faber Limited
3 Queen Square London WC1N 3AU

Printed in Great Britain by Mackays of Chatham PLC,
Chatham, Kent

British Library Cataloguing in Publication Data
Cockerell, Michael
Live from number 10: the inside story
of Prime Ministers and television.
1. Television and politics—Great Britain
I. Title
320.941   PN1992.6
ISBN 0-571-14757-7

For Bridget

Contents

List of Illustrations

Acknowledgements

I owe a great debt to Sally Doganis, who was my producer for BBC TV's two fiftieth anniversary programmes, *Television and Number 10*. She unearthed Winston Churchill's secret screen test from an attic where it had been gathering dust for over thirty years and has probably watched more archive programmes of prime ministers than any other woman alive. Despite this, her flair and originality have never waned.

The doyenne of British political television, the late Grace Wyndham Goldie, left an unrivalled collection of documents and memoranda to which I have had full access. I have also drawn on papers from Number 10 Downing Street.

Over the years I have had the privilege of talking about television to every modern prime minister from Harold Macmillan to Margaret Thatcher, either at Number 10 or after they left. When I quote what they have told me on the record, I put it in the present tense: thus 'Ted Heath says' or 'Harold Wilson remembers'. I have also had long sessions with many prime ministerial aides – among them, the late William Clark, the late Sir John Colville, Lord Deedes, Lady Falkender, Joe Haines, Sir Donald Maitland, Barry Day, Tom McNally, Harvey Thomas, and others who prefer not to be publicly acknowledged. I am most grateful to all of them, as well as to broadcasters and broadcasting chiefs, including the late Leslie Mitchell, Sir Geoffrey Cox, Michael Peacock, Stanley Hyland, John Grist, Alan Protheroe, Sir Ian Trethowan, and the late Sir Hugh Greene.

My thanks to many others from the BBC and ITV companies who helped make this book possible: Tim Slessor, George Carey, Will Wyatt, Peter Pagnamenta, Stephen Lambert, Cecilia Coleshaw, Peter Ibbotson, Peter Richardson, Jeff Walden and Maya Even.

At Faber and Faber, my editor Will Sulkin was a constant source of encouragement and good advice while Jo Egerton is an inspired picture researcher. My agent Ed Victor is king of the cajolers and Mike Dale nursed me through the teething troubles of my first word processor: my son William uncomplainingly accepted its temporary take-over of his bedroom.

I owe a special debt to four people who struggled through the early manuscript – my father Professor Hugh Cockerell; my wife Bridget; the former Director of BBC Television Programmes, Brian Wenham, and the

Professor of Politics at Nottingham University, Dennis Kavanagh. Their advice was immensely encouraging and valuable. Every error and interpretation of events is of course my own responsibility.

Michael Cockerell
London, April 1988

Introduction

Mrs Thatcher is not Bob Hope. She makes few jokes during her public performances; her occasional one-liners are provided by speech-writers. But on television, in the summer of 1984, the Prime Minister had a whole studio audience falling about with laughter. In answer to the question, 'Do you ever relax?' she responded: 'I am always on the job.' Mrs Thatcher was clearly taken aback by the audience's delighted howl and then began to laugh herself – without ever looking as if she understood what the joke was. This was the highlight of a pretty bizarre television programme.

Before it went on air, a warm-up man had regaled the studio audience with a series of risqué stories and insights into the world of show business. He had instructed the audience when to applaud and encouraged loud laughter. All this was standard light entertainment procedure; what was unusual were the 'two special guests' that London Weekend Television proudly announced for that night's *Aspel and Company*. One was 'the singer, composer and superstar', Barry Manilow. The other was Mrs Margaret Thatcher, the first serving British Prime Minister ever to appear on a TV chat show.

'Cue applause,' the studio director in the gallery demanded into the ear-piece of the floor manager. The audience promptly clapped their hands off and the orchestra played the signature tune especially composed for the BBC newsreader turned TV-personality, Michael Aspel. The Prime Minister, wearing a shimmering maroon silk dress, entered stage right. With shoulders slightly hunched, she bustled across the space-age set. 'You are a very seasoned television performer, do you still feel nervous when you appear?' asked Aspel. 'Oh, I am not a professional and I am not a seasoned performer. I always feel nervous because we are on with you professionals,' beamed Mrs Thatcher with a glowing smile she had never produced in a television studio before.

The timing of the Prime Minister's appearance in such tinselly surroundings was not a matter of chance. The miners' strike was at its height. For weeks violent images of pitched battles between police and pickets had been filling the news bulletins. Although the opinion polls showed that a large majority blamed the miners' leader Arthur Scargill for the violence, the Government was becoming increasingly concerned at Scargill's recitative against the intransigence of an uncaring and dictatorial Prime Minister. Mrs Thatcher's publicity advisers calculated that she would benefit from appearing on a programme which concentrated on her human side as a wife and mother. 'I just think that women have a special capacity to cope,' she told Aspel, 'they manage to cope with the home, they manage to cope with the job, they manage to cope with bringing up children, they manage to cope with any emergency. And I'm no different from anyone else.'

It was all a world away from the way television had first started in Britain in 1936. The idea that the small screen would develop into the most potent of all means for a prime minister to influence the voters seemed laughable. 'Television won't matter in your lifetime or in mine,' the editor of the *Listener* told a young BBC producer fifty years ago. The fledgling service was closed down for the whole of the Second World War and, when it restarted, did everything possible to keep out of politics. There was no reporting of any politically controversial subject. And the television news itself was made so bland and timeless that a recording of Monday's newsreel would be repeated verbatim the following Wednesday.

'Why do we need this peepshow?' Winston Churchill asked as Prime Minister in 1951. He was never to give a TV interview. But by 1953, Churchill had come to recognize the power of television and took lessons, in strictest secrecy, to learn its techniques. The oratorical devices that served so well in Parliament and at great public meetings, he discovered, were ill-suited to the informality of home viewing. Since Churchill, prime ministers have struggled with varying degrees of success to come to terms with the small screen.

Like pensioners puzzling over word processors, elderly men sought to master new technologies. 'Coming into a television studio is like entering a twentieth-century torture chamber,' said Harold Macmillan, 'but we old dogs have to learn new tricks.' In fact, both the politicians and the broadcasters were groping in the dark with a medium neither side properly understood and were making up the rules as they went along. Some party leaders – like Mrs Thatcher in her early days – behaved towards television like an African tribesman faced with a white man's camera; she seemed convinced it would take her soul away.

With the help of highly skilled media advisers, successive prime ministers have over the years sought to deploy ever more sophisticated techniques of political persuasion and image projection on television. They have regarded their performances as crucial to their election chances. Tensions between the government of the day and broadcasters seeking to challenge established authority became inevitable.

Conservative and Labour prime ministers alike have been convinced that the BBC was ineradicably biased against them. Churchill said that the Corporation was 'honeycombed with Communists'. But Harold Wilson insisted that some of the top men at the BBC were card-carrying Tories engaged in a conspiracy to bring him down. Over the years Number 10 has turned its guns with increasing ferocity on the citadels of television: at first on the BBC alone but later on ITV as well.

The results of these battles to control what is transmitted have been highly significant for the public: most people now receive most of their political information and impressions from television. But the electronic images Churchill's successors have projected – of themselves and their governments – have very often been far removed from their real political lives at Number 10. And the broadcasters themselves, while loudly proclaiming their robust independence, have sometimes been willing participants in prime ministerial charades made especially for television.

Every modern prime minister has hated, loved or feared television. Some have done all three. This book tells the story of the relationship between the two sides – a tragi-comic tale of good intentions, mutual misunderstandings and bitter recriminations.

With the televising of the Commons, which Mrs Thatcher strenuously resisted, the Prime Minister will be on public display as never before. She is determined to be the star of the new political show. And her Government now promises the biggest upheaval in television's history – with a profusion of new channels from the sky, the ground and from under the earth. As a result, the Prime Minister herself faces unprecedented fresh battles to control what she describes as 'the most powerful form of communication known to man'.

CHAPTER I

No Politics, Please

'Winston Churchill never looked at television, and he was not going to be televised himself if he could possibly help it.'
Sir John Colville, Churchill's
private secretary

Mrs Thatcher's desire to keep sex and violence off the air matches the restrictive instincts of her predecessors at Number 10 – except that the subject they felt had no place on the screen was politics. In the early years of television there was no coverage of elections nor of any controversial subject due to be debated in the coming fortnight. 'It would be a shocking thing to have the debates of Parliament forestalled on this new robot organization of television,' declaimed Winston Churchill. For the first fifteen years after the start of television the BBC's own Directors-General did not even have a set in their homes. In that way at least they were different from the very first of the TV premiers.

The Labour Prime Minister, Ramsay MacDonald, was some way ahead of his time. In 1930 he had a set installed in Number 10 Downing Street. This might have seemed somewhat eccentric: the start of the world's first television service was six years away. But MacDonald was not doomed to long evenings by the fire watching a blank screen. His fellow Scot, John Logie Baird, was already experimenting with closed-circuit demonstrations of his new invention and vigorously lobbying the Government to be allowed to go public.

The early programmes MacDonald watched on his Baird Televisor in March 1930 included Gracie Fields singing 'Nowt for Owt' and a Pirandello play, *The man with the flower in his mouth*. Later that year televisors went on sale to the public, price 25 guineas. Ramsay MacDonald wrote to Baird: 'When I look at the transmissions, I feel that the most wonderful miracle is being done under my eye. You have put something in my room which will never let me forget how strange is this world – and how unknown.'

Five years later, MacDonald's National Government – he was Prime Minister with the Conservative leader, Stanley Baldwin, his deputy – decided that the BBC should start the world's first high-definition television service. Transmissions began in November 1936 with a song from a

I

chanteuse named Adèle Dixon: 'A mighty maze of mystic magic rays is all about us in the blue'. But there was little to suggest the new medium would become the most powerful form of political communication ever invented. The early programmes featured a pantomime horse, a bus driver explaining how he had constructed a model of Drake's ship, the *Golden Hind*, dancing girls and a fifteen-minute introductory talk by the Postmaster-General, Major the Hon. G. C. Tryon. The programmes were introduced by Leslie Mitchell, chosen as television's first announcer from 'a shortlist of 590 handsome young men' and soon dubbed the 'TV Adonis'. There were also two 'announcer hostesses', Elizabeth Cowell and Jasmine Bligh, selected from over a thousand applicants for their 'pleasing mezzo voices, charm, tact and ability to appeal to both sexes'.

The first programmes had tiny audiences. There were only four hundred TV sets in the country and reception was limited to within thirty miles of London. The radio critic of the *Listener* at the time was a sharp-minded young woman who was later to become a most formidable figure in developing the relationship between Prime Ministers and television: Grace Wyndham Goldie. She remembered that in the early days the people working in television were 'almost completely ignored – by the public, by the politicians and by the BBC itself'. In his autobiography, the BBC's first Director-General, Sir John (later Lord) Reith failed to mention the inauguration of television. Reith was a radio man. Television to him – insofar as he bothered to think about it at all – meant trouble. The problem was that it depended on pictures.

Under Reith, the BBC had built its reputation on the spoken word. Since wireless transmissions began in 1922, words had to be treated with formality and reverence: hence Reith's instruction that radio announcers wear dinner jackets for evening broadcasts. Pictures could compromise the BBC's high standards in two different ways. First, the new people coming into television were largely from the movies, the music hall and the theatre – different worlds from the Corporation created by the gaunt Calvinist. Second, visual images would be unnecessary distractions from the high purposes of the carefully scripted radio talk. The new medium was bound by definition to be empty-headed and trivial; show business would replace sobriety.

It did not occur to the BBC's first Director-General that future prime ministers would want to have anything to do with television – that the flickering images from Alexandra Palace in 1936 presaged the blazing battles to come between his successors and Number 10 for control of the small screen. But Reith did know from his own experience how attractive the power of the airwaves was to the politicians. He had from the start fought to establish for radio his own version of independence from political control.

The first major test of strength between the fledgling BBC and the Government had come during the General Strike of 1926. It set the pattern for future relations between the two sides. The main protagonists both saw themselves as men of destiny: John Reith of the BBC and Winston Churchill, the Chancellor of the Exchequer. In the General Strike, Churchill was in charge of Government propaganda. With the Fleet Street printers out, there were no national newspapers and Churchill, a former journalist, produced a daily sheet called the *British Gazette*. He wanted to commandeer the BBC to broadcast further propaganda against the strikers. 'It would be monstrous not to use such an instrument to the best possible advantage,' Churchill insisted in Cabinet. The two men of destiny were set on a collision course.

To the Chancellor's intense anger, Reith insisted that the BBC could not be used as an instrument of crude government propaganda. Instead the Corporation would put out 'authentic, impartial news' – which to Reith had a rather limited definition. He helped the Prime Minister, Stanley Baldwin, write the broadcast that Baldwin made in the middle of the strike. And neither the Labour party leader, Ramsay MacDonald, nor any of the strike leaders was allowed on the air. As Reith put it at the time, faced with the threat of direct control by Churchill, 'it would be inadvisable for us to do anything that was particularly embarrassing for the Government'.

Reith knew that, by law, the Government could give him orders about what to broadcast. Or it could take over the BBC completely. He succeeded in pre-empting Government action – at a price. For some strikers the BBC had become nothing more than an official mouthpiece: the British Falsehood Corporation. Churchill himself developed a profound antipathy for Reith and a distaste for the BBC that was to intensify over the years with the coming of television. In the meantime radio had established itself as a source of power and politicians became increasingly anxious to use it for their own ends.

By the time television began in 1936, radio was recognized as a prime means of electioneering. From the first the Conservatives had shown much greater interest and skill in using radio for their general election broadcasts than either Labour or the Liberals. Churchill and Baldwin had quickly taken to the microphone. The *Daily Express* judged that Churchill achieved 'a note of extraordinary intimacy with his audience' in a 1929 broadcast. But on the new medium of television, in the three years up to the Second World War, there was only a single appearance by a prime minister.

In September 1938, Neville Chamberlain was about to fly back from his talks with Hitler in Munich. A young producer in the BBC's new Outside Broadcast department, Ian Orr-Ewing (later to become a Conservative MP,

3

then a peer) hurriedly checked to see if one of the two mobile camera vans was available. 'I found out that the Prime Minister was due to land at four o'clock and I said, "Don't you think we should get down to the aerodrome to welcome him?" There was an OB van free and I got permission to take it to Heston aerodrome.'

Chamberlain's return home was televised live. Many of his successors were to follow in his footsteps – down from aeroplane steps to the waiting TV cameras. (And in the case of James Callaghan forty years on it would prove a significant political mistake.)

'We had got the cameras on the roof at Heston,' remembers the BBC engineer, Keith Edelstein, 'I held the microphone and this funny old man came out of the aeroplane waving a piece of paper.' Chamberlain's prop was aimed at the cinema newsreel cameramen and the press photographers. But the tiny television audience was the first to hear that the famous piece of paper signified 'peace in our time'. 'I wish that were true,' muttered the young BBC TV commentator at Heston: but Richard Dimbleby kept his scepticism off the air. *The Times* reported that the coverage of Chamberlain's return had 'a quality of history in the making that no other outside broadcast has equalled'.

A week later on television's only and occasional current affairs programme, *News Map*, the cartoonist and writer, J. F. Horrabin, analysed the significance of Chamberlain's visit with the BBC's foreign correspondent. It was a rare moment of seriousness on pre-war television. Much more typical was the weekly *Picture Page* introduced by Leslie Mitchell: among those interviewed, according to the programme's producer, were 'a fairy, a monkey, a string of onions, a Bond Street model, a sword swallower, an Alsatian dog and a Siamese cat [presumably for balance], a tray of muffins, a box of herrings and a silkworm'.

The first televised prime ministerial statement had a shelf-life of less than twelve months. 'Peace in our time' came to an end on 3 September 1939. In Britain, television was the first casualty of the Second World War. Chamberlain believed the TV transmitters would make ideal homing beacons for enemy planes. On 1 September, BBC engineers received a telephone call from the Postmaster-General's office ordering them to stop transmitting immediately. The final scene of the first age of television was a cartoon of Mickey Mouse imitating Greta Garbo. 'Ah tink ah go home' were the last words before the screens suddenly went blank. There was no closing announcement and viewers were given no explanation why they had been left alone.

'The world's first high-definition television service was halted on the threshold of certain success,' lamented the *BBC Handbook* for 1940, 'we throw a glance nowadays at the blank screens of our receivers and remember when they held us like a spell. And we ask with Keats, "Was it a vision, or a waking dream?" ' It was to be seven years before the dream machine was reconnected. In the meantime, the skills of the TV engineers were needed for the development of radar.

It was to be a radio war and one which again brought Churchill and Reith into collision. Their clashes would colour the Tory leader's attitudes both to the BBC and to television, when transmissions began again in 1946. At the start of the war, Reith had been given the task of reconciling the conflicting demands of security and truth. He had resigned from the Corporation in 1938, claiming he was not fully stretched. Now Reith achieved a life-long ambition and became a Cabinet minister. Chamberlain put him in charge of the newly formed Ministry of Information. It was not a happy appointment. In the early months of 1940, Reith came up against his old adversary. Churchill was First Lord of the Admiralty and believed the new Information Minister was collaborating with the Corporation against the war effort. In fact Reith was unsuccessfully attempting to impose a system on the BBC, which would have brought it under direct government supervision. But the Corporation was resisting the plans and Churchill claimed it was 'an enemy within the gates, doing more harm than good'.

Within two days of becoming Prime Minister in May 1940, Churchill removed Reith from the Information Ministry, and subsequently demoted him to the Ministry of Works. 'There he stalks, that Wuthering Height,' the Prime Minister would remark of the now embittered former Director-General, who believed his leadership talents were being wantonly ignored at the moment of destiny.

The war gave Churchill the opportunity to make full use of his skills as a radio broadcaster: skills he had had little opportunity to sharpen on the BBC in the previous decade. Churchill had been a rebel Tory, opposed to his Party's official line and particularly hostile to Chamberlain's appeasement policy. Reith had decreed that there was no place on the airwaves for Party dissidents and Churchill's broadcasts were confined to lucrative appearances on American radio. Churchill had come to hate the BBC and had not forgiven its first Director-General. But now the tables were turned.

As the nation's war leader, Churchill was able to demand access to the microphone when he liked. While Chamberlain had considered closing down the BBC 'because people wouldn't have time to listen', Churchill knew different. His stirring broadcasts became a highly effective weapon of war. But his attitude to the BBC did not change, even though the Corporation's authority had grown steadily throughout the war. In the most fraught and difficult circumstances of all, the BBC had retained its independence: it had successfully resisted the understandable impulses of the politicians – notably Churchill – to turn it into an arm of straightforward government propaganda to help the war effort and keep up morale.

Radio had a good war. It established itself as the most powerful of all agencies of information and the one most sought after by the politicians. When radio's tiny television cousin came back on to the scene in 1946, there was virtually no one at the top, either in Westminster or Broadcasting House, who recognized its political growth potential – and that it would help to make and break future prime ministers.

Leslie Mitchell, the man who had inaugurated pre-war television was the first face on the post-war screen. 'As I was saying, before I was so rudely interrupted,' he began when the service was resumed in June 1946. Clement Attlee, the Labour Prime Minister, and Winston Churchill, now leader of the Opposition, were united with the BBC's Director-General, Sir William Haley, in their agreement on what part television should play in the coverage of politics. None. Haley, a newspaperman by training who was later to become editor of *The Times*, said he felt TV was totally unsuitable as a forum for political discussion, debate or presentation of the news. He did not even own a set. Attlee took the conservative view that it would have been better if television had never been invented. It was nothing more than an idiot's lantern. Churchill, who retained his profound distrust of the BBC, agreed.

Sir John Colville, who was first Attlee's private secretary, and then Churchill's, said of the two men's attitude to television: 'It was out of their ken altogether. They belonged to a generation which considered a politician should make his mark in the House of Commons. And of course their speeches were much more widely reported in the press than the equivalent would be today. They did not really consider television a means of political communication at all.' When the BBC offered both men the chance of making a TV broadcast in 1948, they turned it down flat. 'When I was very young,' explained Churchill, 'if one said something in one's constituency which might have led to trouble if it was spread abroad, nothing happened. Now one has to weigh every word knowing all the time that people will be listening all over the country. It would be intolerable if one also had to consider how one would appear – what one would look like all over the land.'

Churchill had a second reason for rejecting the BBC's proposal. He told his doctor and confidant, Lord Moran: 'They are honeycombed with Socialists – probably with Communists.' The minutes of the regular meetings between the BBC and the political parties in the first six years after the war reveal Churchill's almost obsessive belief that 'a nest of Communist sympathizers' had infiltrated the Corporation. And he was fed with ammunition by Conservative Central Office. Forty years before the anti-BBC campaign led by the Party Chairman, Norman Tebbit, the Tories had set up a special unit to monitor the Corporation. It was the brain-child of a young brigadier with a distinguished war record who had become the Tories' first ever Head of Broadcasting – John Profumo. Subsequently he would be the central figure in the first political scandal to be widely covered by television.

Profumo told the author: 'I wanted to keep an eye on left-wing bias at the BBC. I couldn't think how we could do it. Whenever we wrote to Haley, the Director-General, he would say that we should look not just at one programme but at the whole lot. I decided to put an advertisement in the *Daily Telegraph* saying that I was looking for long-term patients in hospital who had a radio – or if they didn't, we would give them one. When people replied, we asked if they would agree for a small payment to listen to the programmes we chose and then write to a box number. We appointed six monitors. And each week we would have a monitoring conference at Conservative Central Office on the day the *Radio Times* was published and we would select the programmes to be monitored. We would say "that chap looks left-wing" and we wanted to see whether his broadcasts were biased. I still remember one programme – about tapestries of all things. The commentary said something like: "to think these tapestries hang on the walls of the rich and they were woven in the humble hovels of the peasants." I suppose creative young people are left-wing. But as a result of our efforts we made a great deal of headway with the BBC – it had its effect. The whole thing came full circle with Mr Tebbit's activities, don't you think?'

The efforts of Profumo's monitoring group were concentrated almost entirely on the radio: in the years after the restart of television there was virtually no politics on the small screen. Much of the mixture was exactly as before. 'Hello, do you remember me?' asked the 'announcer hostess' Jasmine Bligh on the night the service reopened. Mickey Mouse playing Greta Garbo followed. Early programmes included Muffin the Mule, Continental Cabaret and the excitements of live outside broadcasts from a wholesale dry cleaners and a paper plate factory. 'Should one of the main events of Monday night's viewing have been the cooking of whitebait?' lamented the television critic of the *Evening Standard*.

For the first eighteen months of the resumed service, television news faithfully followed the dictates of Sir William Haley: pictures had to be avoided at all costs. 'Otherwise,' said the Director-General, 'the necessity would arise to subordinate the primary functions of news to the needs of visual presentation. Any such subordination would prejudice all sorts of values on which the BBC's great reputation for news has been founded.'

Until 1948, an anonymous radio announcer read the news for television behind a picture of the BBC clock. That year, with many misgivings, the Corporation started a television newsreel. It so lacked topicality that the same edition went out twice a week. And, even as late as 1953, the retiring Chairman of the BBC, Lord Simon, was able to proclaim: 'There is surely not the least possibility that television newsreels will ever replace news on sound. A great majority of items are of such a nature that they cannot now or ever be shown visually.'

Sir William Haley and the other top BBC officials at Broadcasting House believed that the Corporation's reputation depended on scrupulously avoiding all political controversy. Their problem was that a number of producers in the television department of Alexandra Palace felt that political controversy would be the stuff of good programmes. Such a divergence of views was to become familiar to many of Sir William's successors. But for the first decade after the war, the BBC had an institutionalized arrangement with the political parties to keep television out of politics. It was known as the Fourteen Day Rule; under it no subject that was certain or even likely to be debated in the House of Commons in the next fortnight could be discussed on television.

Both Attlee and Churchill were staunch defenders of the Fourteen Day Rule. 'It would be shocking to have debates in this House forestalled time after time', Churchill proclaimed in the Commons, 'by expressions of opinions by persons who had not the status and responsibility of MPs.' And even MPs themselves were barred from appearing because of the Fourteen Day Rule. The Rule had first been drawn up between the BBC and the political parties as a measure of war. It was renewed by mutual consent in 1947. And, almost in the manner of prisoners who kiss the chains that bind them, the BBC's senior officials seemed willingly to embrace the restrictions. But in the newly formed Television Talks department at Alexandra Palace producers like Grace Wyndham Goldie bitterly resented the Rule, although they felt powerless to change it.

General elections were also a forbidden zone for television. The BBC suggested to the political parties that they might like to use television in the 1950 campaign for their own election broadcasts, as happened on radio. Attlee, Churchill and the Liberal leader, Clement Davies, unanimously rejected the idea. According to George Barnes, who rejoiced in the title of BBC Director of the Spoken Word, 'every effort was made to interest them, but the matter in their view did not even admit of argument.' The BBC then decided it would be far too risky for there to be any reporting at all of the election campaign on television or radio. This was partly a matter of a highly restrictive interpretation of the Representation of the People Act and partly a fear of becoming involved in political controversy. In 1950 the BBC prided itself on pre-empting any charge of unfairness or partisanship during the campaign by avoiding any mention at all of the election. It was only after the polls had closed that the BBC dared to refer to the fact there had been a campaign. Grace Wyndham Goldie was put in charge of the first ever television general election results programme.

She discovered a young Oxford postgraduate, David Butler, who had no television experience but had great enthusiasm and knowledge of British elections, to help present the programme. Studio staff in gym shoes trained in dashing from one studio to another to bring the results in fast. The top BBC officials from Broadcasting House looked on the whole enterprise with disdain and trepidation. 'Instructions came pouring in from Broadcasting House,' wrote Mrs Goldie in her book, *Facing the Nation*. There had never before been running comment on election results as they came in. It had to be very careful and factual. There was to be absolutely no prediction. The Head of Television Programmes, Cecil McGivern, was highly unenthusiastic about the whole project. He considered that the results should be left to radio and that political matters were unsuited to a visual medium. His view was widely shared at Alexandra Palace, Broadcasting House and in Westminster. McGivern's only suggestion about the results programme was that there had to be an outside broadcast from Trafalgar Square, 'which might give the occasion a little humanity'.

In the event the results programme was very successful. According to Mrs Goldie, the only mistake was going to Trafalgar Square. The results were flashed on a giant display screen in a confusingly different way from those in the studio and they were 'interspersed with crude cartoons of political figures at which the crowds roared with laughter, but which we could not show because they were political comment'. From those small beginnings – of David Butler with his students and their slide rules – has grown the great ritual of today's results programmes: by far the biggest and costliest single-night exercise that television ever mounts.

Emboldened by the success of the results programme, the one man at Alexandra Palace who did believe passionately in focusing the cameras on politics now initiated the first-ever regular current affairs programme. Norman Collins was the Controller of Television and, in a variety of roles over the next decade, was to be central to the developing relationship between prime ministers and the small screen. In March 1950, Collins began *In The News*, which featured four panellists in a studio discussion. Ironically, because of the restrictions of the Fourteen Day Rule, they were scarcely allowed to discuss any political matters that were actually in the news. Despite this, the programme was an instant success and the panellists became the nationally Famous Four: the rebellious Conservative MP Bob (later Lord) Boothby, the left-wing Labour MP Michael Foot, the Oxford don A. J. P. Taylor and a former Independent MP, W. J. Brown. The party leaders' reaction to *In the News* was to become standard over the years when faced with a controversial political programme. They sought to draw its sting.

The party Whips, who were responsible for liaison with the BBC, insisted that they should have the right to nominate the panellists. It was intolerable that people like Foot and Boothby, maverick figures on the fringes of their parties, be given a platform. The BBC should choose solid, respectable representatives of mainstream party opinion. The Whips provided the names of the MPs they wanted to appear. Under pressure, the BBC submitted – while insisting that they should retain the right to choose whom they wanted. Only one of the Famous Four would appear at a time. New political faces went on the air, including the young Labour MP, James Callaghan, who was subsequently to become Prime Minister with more television experience than any of his predecessors. One name suggested by Conservative Central Office was 'a very bright girl, young, under thirty, very good-looking with a first at Oxford – Mrs Margaret Thatcher'. But she was only an unsuccessful parliamentary candidate and was not invited to appear.

The creation of *In the News* was matched by the start of another kind of political television. In the years ahead it would lead to weeks and months of agonizing by the parties and their leaders and to hours of tedium for the viewers: party election broadcasts began. Attlee had won the 1950 election with a majority of just six. It was clear there would soon be another general election. When it came in October 1951, the parties agreed with the BBC that they would make a small step towards putting the campaign on the screen. There was still to be no coverage on the news nor on *In the News*, which was to be suspended during the campaign. But there were, for the first time, to be three party election broadcasts on television.

The series was opened by the octogenarian Liberal, Lord Samuel, who more than twenty years earlier had made one of the first radio party politicals. His television broadcast was not an unqualified success. He sat alone in the studio and read from a fifteen-minute script, scarcely ever looking up at the camera. It was a live broadcast and there were no modern devices, like the autocue or the teleprompter, to enable Lord Samuel to look straight at the camera while reading off a hidden screen. He overran the agreed time slot and was cut off in mid-peroration when he inadvertently gave the producer the pre-arranged signal that he had finished. As the *Glasgow Herald* put it at the time – it was a broadcast that 'made no concessions to the viewing public at all'.

The Conservative broadcaster the following day did not walk naked into the TV studio. The Tories had prepared long and hard for their television début. They had chosen as the star of their first TV party political, not the Leader, Winston Churchill, but his debonair heir-apparent, Anthony Eden. Eden had decided that he would not, as Lord Samuel had, attempt to speak straight to the camera – one of the more difficult television techniques for untrained public figures to acquire. With some experience of appearing on American television, Eden proposed that the party political should take the form of an interview. The problem was to find the right person to ask the right questions.

The public relations officer at Conservative Central Office, Colin Mann, had a bright idea. Why not ask Leslie Mitchell if he would agree to do the interview? Mitchell, the first television announcer, had conducted over three thousand interviews and was still one of the best-known faces on the BBC. 'I was sitting in my office minding my own business when a telephone call came through,' Mitchell told the author shortly before he died in 1986. 'It was Anthony Eden. He asked if I would be interested in being his interviewer in the Conservatives' election broadcast. He told me later that I obviously had a very large television following, which was why he wanted me: to increase his own audience.'

The broadcast was to be acclaimed a triumph for Eden. *The Times* stressed Eden's spontaneity and sincerity. The *Daily Telegraph* said that 'Eden had mastered the natural manner which is the secret of an effective TV appearance and used no notes. It was an unqualified success.' The *Daily Mirror* reported that 'Eden had knocked the TV bogey for six'. And the *Daily Express* proclaimed: 'Hail to Anthony Eden, the scriptless wonder. He needed no cues.' In fact, contrary to the press reports, the whole broadcast had been carefully contrived and rehearsed; all the spontaneity and sincerity was synthetic.

The arrangements for the interview had been made in total secrecy. Once Mitchell had agreed to appear, the Conservatives' chief publicity officer, Mark Chapman-Walker, wrote to him: 'It is absolutely *essential* that no whisper get out to the effect that you will be participating in the broadcast.' It was arranged that Mitchell should meet Eden at Warwick Castle, the home of the Conservative deputy leader's nephew. There, with the aid of two tape recorders they attempted a spontaneous interview. 'In answer to my first question,' said Mitchell, 'Eden replied, "that is a very good question, but first I'd like to talk about another aspect." He wanted all my questions put in a different order and to raise different points.' Eventually Eden handed Mitchell his standard campaign speech and said: 'I will record this for you and then you can interpolate your questions back in London.'

Mitchell did not think much of the idea but agreed to try. He was up all night replaying Eden's speech again and again and adding a question which would cue each new passage. 'But there was no way of enlivening it,' said Mitchell, 'it was dead as mutton.' The Conservatives meanwhile had put out a press statement promoting the broadcast: television's best-known interviewer would be putting to Anthony Eden the questions that the public had raised in the campaign. But at 7 a.m. on the day of the broadcast. Mitchell telephoned Chapman-Walker to say that the interview could not work and he would have to pull out. Chapman-Walker rushed round and on hearing the tape exclaimed: 'My God, it's awful.' Mitchell suggested that Central Office issue a statement to say that he had suddenly broken his leg and offered to stay out of sight for the coming weeks. But Eden thought differently.

He had arrived back that morning on the overnight sleeper from Edinburgh and went straight round to Mitchell's house. 'I gather I was not much good,' said Eden. 'What do you want me to do?' He sat down with Mitchell and for the next two hours they worked out with a tape recorder word for word what each of them should say and in what order. That original tape recording still exists. The two men spoke with similar clipped, upper-class accents and Eden himself sometimes sounded confused as to which were the questions and which his answers. 'And then who says that about the cost of living, you or I?' he asked Mitchell at one point. Finally they agreed on the exact form the interview should take. Mitchell had the whole of the proposed interview transcribed and Eden proceeded to learn it by heart. He was not to be the last future prime minister to place himself completely in the hands of a television professional.

That night Leslie Mitchell introduced the first-ever Conservative election broadcast on television: 'Good evening, I would just like to say first that, as an interviewer, and as what I hope you will believe to be an unbiased member of the electorate, I'm most grateful to Mr Anthony Eden for inviting me to cross-question him on the present political issues. I would like, too, to feel that I am asking those questions which you yourselves would like to ask in my place. Well now, Mr Eden, with your very considerable experience of foreign affairs, it's quite obvious that I should start by asking you something about the international situation today, or perhaps you would prefer to talk about home. Which is it to be?'

Eden replied that while the voters were naturally enough preoccupied with the international situation there were some formidable domestic problems whose seriousness, he felt, had not yet been understood by the voters as a whole. 'Really, that's interesting, which are they?' asked Mitchell. The interview continued in that vein. 'I wonder, sir, whether I may introduce a question which I'm sure will infuriate you, but since I'm here presumably for that reason: it has often been said in recent times that the Conservative party is a war-mongering party. Is there a shred of truth in that or is there not?' On cue, Eden bristled: 'I do resent that question.'

Mitchell dined at Eden's home in Mayfair that night. The interviewer assured the Tory deputy leader that the broadcast had been a resounding success. It was a verdict echoed by Winston Churchill, who telephoned Eden with his congratulations. And the next morning the *Daily Telegraph* TV critic enthused: 'It was without question the most successful television appearance of any politician that I have seen either in Britain or in the United States.' There was one dissenting voice, although it was kept private at the time. Under the agreement with the parties the BBC provided a producer and studio facilities for the election broadcasts. The producer who was responsible for getting the programme on to the air, although she had no say in its content, was Grace Wyndham Goldie. 'It was a terrible programme, of course,' said Mrs Goldie later, 'but you see the parties couldn't have awkward questions asked. Politicians couldn't use scripts. Everything was live, there was no recording. The politicians were terrified of saying something that could be used by the whole world. So they had all these things totally rehearsed. And they hired nice kind interviewers to put the questions they were told to ask, that the parties wanted answered.'

One of the features of the Eden broadcast was the use of a device that was to become standard in television political programmes – the TV graphic. Eden produced a graph which purported to show that the cost of living had risen very sharply under six years of Labour rule. The first-ever Labour election broadcast the following day used the same figures as Eden but produced a graph showing the cost of living rising considerably less steeply. The Labour broadcast was presented by Christopher Mayhew, the former MP who had lost his seat in the 1950 general election and had moved into television. He was the first of what was to become a long line of electronic hybrids: the politician turned broadcaster, later to be followed by the broadcaster turned politician. In the Labour broadcast, Mayhew vehemently attacked Eden's graphic as gross distortion. 'Just as Crippen was the first criminal to be caught by the wireless, so Eden is the first political criminal to be exposed by television,' claimed Mayhew.

Eden's cod interview and battle of the graphs set the style and tone for future party political broadcasts. They demonstrated the kind of television that politicians produce when left to their own devices.

Apart from the three party election broadcasts, there was no television coverage at all of the campaign. Churchill's 'Whose finger on the trigger?' speech which dominated the newspaper headlines did not receive a single mention on the BBC. But once the polls had closed, Grace Wyndham Goldie attempted to build on her experience of the previous election and mount a more elaborate results programme. 'We found a long thing like a pig trough,' remembers Mrs Goldie's production secretary, Rosemary Gill, 'and we prepared caption cards for all 633 constituencies with every permutation and combination of how the results could come out. One caption artist wrote the whole lot – six thousand or something. At the other end of the studio was another caption artist with a step-ladder and a pot of black paint. We didn't even have Magimarkers in those days. When the results came through we scrabbled through our pig trough, found the appropriate card, pencilled in the figures, gave them to a caption artist who slopped the wet paint on and we took turns to rush them to the next-door studio and put them on an easel.' It was a world away from advanced computer graphics, although thirty-six years on Peter Snow's performance in front of the BBC's election night battleboard would have some of the same manic intensity.

On 26 October 1951, Winston Churchill was back as Prime Minister. Although he accepted that Eden's broadcast might have contributed to his election victory, Churchill remained convinced that television had no real part to play in politics; in any case, at the age of seventy-eight, the Prime Minister felt he was far too old to start to learn the techniques of the new medium. 'Winston Churchill never looked at television,' said his private secretary, Sir John Colville, 'and he was not going to be televised himself if he could possibly help it. He hated the lights, he hated the glare and he hated the heat.' But Churchill's last period of office was to transform his view of the political potential of television. And it was to end with the Prime Minister arranging for his own secret TV screen test in Number 10 Downing Street.

CHAPTER 2

This Thing they call TeeVee

*'In those days, so few people knew anything about television that
in the kingdom of the blind the cock-eyed man was king.'*
William Deedes, former Conservative MP

After a year back in Downing Street, Winston Churchill was coming to
recognize the power of television. In January 1953, he sailed on the *Queen
Mary* for an official visit to America. As the liner steamed into New York
harbour, the Prime Minister spoke to the TV cameras. It was a very rare
event. There had been no television during his wartime premiership and
throughout his second term in office, from 1951–5, Churchill never gave a
television interview. But in the Verandah Grill of the *Queen Mary*, flanked
by his wife, his daughter and his son-in-law, Christopher Soames, the Prime
Minister told the American networks: 'This television has come to take its
place in the world. As rather an old-fashioned person, I have not been one
of its principal champions, but I don't think it needs any champions, it can
make its own way. And it's a wonderful thing indeed to think that every
expression on my face at this moment may be viewed by millions of people
throughout the United States.' The Prime Minister paused for effect. 'I
just hope the raw material is as good as the means of distribution,' he added
to the laughter of his family and the cameramen. To their delight, Churchill
then produced his V-sign before being whisked off to his limousine.

Back in Britain, Churchill's senior Cabinet colleagues were slowly
beginning to shed their disdain for television; instead they were coming to
regard it as a powerful weapon of political propaganda. The Conservatives'
first Head of Broadcasting, John Profumo, was now an MP and had been
on a special trip to study the American presidential campaign of 1952. 'I
saw that television was making an enormous political impact,' says Profumo.
'The real impression General Eisenhower and his Vice-Presidential candidate, Richard Nixon, made on the public was through TV. And the
Americans were much cleverer in their election propaganda than we were.'
Profumo produced a report for the Tory Party Chairman, Lord Woolton,
arguing it was 'absolutely essential to get all our people on all the programmes
we can: my view was that television was the real thing'. Woolton sent the
report on to the Prime Minister. Churchill was impressed. He made

Profumo a junior minister and leading politicians began to appear on the screen.

Rab Butler, the Chancellor, gave the first ever TV interview about the Budget. And in March 1953, the political parties reached agreement with the BBC that for the first time outside a general election they should be allowed their own programmes. 'There now follows a party political broadcast . . .' was the accepted introduction. Over the years it was the signal in millions of homes throughout the land that it was time to put the cat out, make the tea, go to the lavatory or switch off the set. But the political parties prepared their early broadcasts with the highest of hopes that they would magically convert large sections of the electorate overnight.

The first party political broadcast starred the Secretary of State for Housing and future Prime Minister, Harold Macmillan, as well as a fresh-faced Tory MP and former *Morning Post* reporter, William Deedes. The producer for the BBC, which was to provide studio facilities and put the programme on the air, was Grace Wyndham Goldie. Churchill followed the preparations for the broadcast in detail. The Conservatives' chief publicity officer, Mark Chapman-Walker, told Mrs Goldie: 'The Prime Minister is taking a great interest in the programme and wants to try out the technical tricks of television.' The Conservative party planned to put on a highly elaborate programme. And they spent weeks preparing for the broadcast.

Macmillan insisted he did not want the whole programme to be done by what he called a 'stooge interviewer', as Leslie Mitchell had been for Anthony Eden in the Tories' election broadcast two years earlier. Nor, however, did he want to face any hostile questions. The Conservatives decided that the programme would be a fast-moving affair, with numerous clips of film, still pictures and camera captions. The draft script bore the mark of many hands, including Macmillan, Churchill, Lord Woolton, Deedes and publicity officers at Central Office. Mrs Goldie said: 'I was soon alarmed by the unrealistic complications which the Conservatives were planning to introduce.' She felt they were being far too ambitious and she would not ask professional broadcasters to attempt the complicated cueing of pieces of film that was proposed. The Conservatives said that the programme was an experiment and they were prepared to see it flop. Mrs Goldie responded that if it flopped the BBC would be blamed. There were many anguished meetings and attempts to simplify the script.

Macmillan was determined to make a personal success of the broadcast. As he admitted to knowing nothing about television, he was disposed to listen to Mrs Goldie's suggestion. He also accompanied William Deedes to Conservative Central Office at Abbey Gardens in Westminster for training

on how to appear on television. The two officials in charge of TV acclimatiz-
ation were Peter Kneebone, who had been on a BBC training course, and
the Party's newly appointed television officer, Winifred Crum-Ewing – the
Tories' double-barrelled answer to Grace Wyndham Goldie. 'Oh, it was
all frightfully earnest,' remembers Deedes. 'They reckoned rightly that
nobody knew anything about television and so they had what they called a
"mock box" and you sat in front of it. It was a square wooden box made to
look like a television camera and it had a sort of lens at the end and you
were made to feel you were being filmed and you were put through your
paces. In those days so few people knew anything about television that in
the kingdom of the blind the cock-eyed man was king.'

At last came the great day. Macmillan and Deedes had to be on parade
at ten in the morning at the former Gaumont British film studios in Lime
Grove, West London, the new headquarters of the Television Talks
department. The programme was due to go out live some ten hours later:
five of the twenty minutes were on film; the rest of the highly complicated
programme was live. Mrs Goldie proved herself a very hard task-mistress
in the hours of rehearsals that followed. 'We were locked in by the BBC for
practically the whole of the daylight hours,' says Deedes, 'and I found myself
in the middle between Mrs Goldie who wanted to produce good television,
Conservative Central Office who wanted to produce a piece of Party
propaganda and Mr Macmillan who wanted to sell houses. The whole thing
was hilarious, it was amateur night.

'Teleprompt hadn't been invented so it was like learning a school play,'
continues Deedes. 'We had to learn every line by heart and pick up each
other's cues. And when we'd rehearsed it about thirty-seven times and
Macmillan would say for the thirty-seventh time in response to one of my
questions, "I am very glad you raised that", one tended to feel it may have
lacked spontaneous appeal for the audience. Every now and then we felt we
had got it bang right and Mrs Goldie approved, the Central Office man
would say "you've left out a figure" and Mrs Goldie would say: "Whose
broadcast is it anyway, yours or mine?" Macmillan was the only person that
Mrs Goldie didn't get cross with. All the rest of us got scolded from time
to time for slackness, inattention, failing to memorize, looking down at the
paper – which was forbidden.'

The demands of the new medium stirred in Harold Macmillan memories
of his service as a Guards' officer at the Somme almost forty years earlier.
Says Deedes: 'Just at the end of rehearsals, Mrs Goldie said to us, "I think
you two should have a rest before you go on air." And we went downstairs
to the basement in Lime Grove and were put into a couple of bunks just to
sleep under a blanket for half an hour or so. And Macmillan muttered in

the dark: "This reminds me very much of the trenches." ' From then on, Macmillan was to spend many testing hours of his political life in the trenches of television.

The first-ever party political broadcast outside an election opened with Deedes telling the audience that they were watching an experiment but one that the Conservatives felt they should pioneer: 'I hope you will think we were right.' Deedes managed to appear relaxed and confident but Macmillan came over as a stilted, old-fashioned figure. 'This ordeal was quite new to me. It was like going over the top,' said Macmillan, 'I gradually was to become inured to the need for these performances, although I always suffered from extreme nervousness and never became at all expert.' In fact Macmillan was to become the most skilled of television performers and, even on his début, he managed a flash of urbane humour. When Deedes asked him about housing progress in Scotland, Macmillan replied that he was not directly responsible for Scotland which had its own Secretary of State: 'But we work together like brothers and, indeed, we might well do so, for we are brothers-in-law.'

'The public reactions to the broadcast were amazingly favourable,' says Deedes. 'People said it all looked very good, though on the night it looked to us like chaos.' The *Sunday Express* claimed the Tories had found a new TV star in Macmillan. 'At moments he might have deputized for Uncle Mac of *Children's Hour* he was so patiently informative. Just before the broadcast a make-up girl had given him a light dusting of the brownish-yellowy powder used for TV. When he spoke about Opposition statements that his housing programme would collapse like a pack of cards, viewers were shown a pack of cards collapsing. Nothing was left to chance for the broadcast. It proves that our politicians have become TV-conscious.' Macmillan wrote to thank Deedes after the programme and ended his letter: 'we have embarked on a great adventure, my friend.' Mrs Goldie's view of the broadcast, as it had been of Eden's pre-election programme, was scathing. 'The broadcast had that curious air of falsity that clings to party politicals: it was impossible to believe it. The parties did not want to use television in those days – and in my view they still don't – to inform the public,' she said twenty years later, 'they just wanted to put forward a piece of propaganda to influence the public's attitude.'

The first party political broadcasts came at a time when the BBC was gradually edging towards greater coverage of politics on the screen, though it was still greatly restricted by the Fourteen Day Rule. Mrs Goldie had begun a programme called *Press Conference* on which Cabinet ministers were starting to appear; in each case they had to seek Churchill's permission to broadcast. Later in 1953, a new magazine programme began that was over the years to become a powerful vehicle for politicians. It was called *Panorama*. Like almost all new studio ventures, it made a dismal début. The first editions were a *mélange* of light musical items and gentle discussions about such subjects as 'the poor wearing quality of nylons'. *Panorama* was a perfect example of what was wrong with TV, claimed the *Sunday Times*. But in the early summer of 1953, television's public standing was transformed overnight.

On 2 June, Queen Elizabeth II was crowned in front of the TV cameras. Churchill had done his utmost to keep the Coronation off the screen. He shared the view of the Duke of Norfolk who, as Earl Marshal, was responsible for the arrangements for the Coronation and of the Archbishop of Canterbury that television and the people who worked in it were vulgar; that the cameras would be intrusive and their presence would place too great a strain on the young Queen. The Coronation Arrangements Committee decided that television should be barred from the Abbey and Churchill's Cabinet endorsed the decision.

It was a bitter blow for the BBC. From the first the Corporation had, on Reith's instructions, dedicated itself to covering Royal events. One of the first outside broadcasts by the infant television service in 1937 had been the Coronation of George VI, with cameras mounted outside the Abbey. Reith had calculated that a link between the monarchy and the BBC – the oldest and newest institutions of the State – could help protect the Corporation from attacks by the Government. To attempt to reverse the Cabinet's ban on Coronation coverage, the BBC mounted a formidable lobbying operation. The press began to campaign for cameras in the Abbey and some Cabinet ministers had second thoughts. But what decided the matter was the Queen herself. Sir John Colville, who had been her private secretary when she was Princess Elizabeth and had then become Churchill's principal private secretary in Downing Street, told the author: 'The Prime Minister went to the Queen and said that the general feeling in the Cabinet was that the Coronation should not be televised. To which the Queen said, effectively, "Rubbish. It shall be televised. All this expense and everything done for this great occasion, it should be seen by people everywhere." And when Churchill came back from Buckingham Palace he said to me: "After all, it is the Queen who is being crowned and not the Cabinet. And if that is what she wants it shall be so." '

The Cabinet then endorsed the decision that the Coronation should be televised – on one condition. The cameras had to be kept at least thirty feet away from the Queen in order, as Churchill put it, 'that no more intimate view be given than was available to the average person seated within the Abbey'. Peter Dimmock, the BBC's senior outside broadcasts producer then went to the Abbey to demonstrate how unobtrusive the cameras could be. 'I put a two-inch lens into the camera and placed it thirty feet away and showed them. What they didn't know and what I knew was that on the day I would use a twelve-inch lens and get the Queen in close up.'

The Coronation broadcast was regarded as a triumph for the BBC and had a powerful effect on the nation's political leaders. First, there was the size of the audience. Sales of television sets had soared and twenty million people watched the broadcast, twice as many as heard it on the radio – the first time that the TV audience had exceeded sound for a major national occasion. 'A large number of the opinion-leading class, who had hitherto not bothered with television, were astonished to see how good it was,' wrote Peter Black in his history of the BBC. 'Television became and stayed the nation's most powerful popular mass medium and in the minds of the politicians and other social leaders the most influential. Whereas before the Coronation the BBC had some difficulty persuading the eminent to appear, now it had some difficulty keeping them off.'

Television had come of age. Churchill was now persuaded that it was an ideal medium for political pageantry. He recognized that the televised Coronation had both played on the viewers' emotions and bestowed a popular aura on the nation's ruler. The Prime Minister determined to exploit for himself grand ceremonial on the small screen. In 1954, he agreed that for the first time the cameras should be allowed into Parliament – a decision that would have been unthinkable before the Coronation. There was to be live transmission from Westminster Hall of the spectacular celebrations laid on for Churchill's eightieth birthday. And that evening, the BBC sought to entice the Prime Minister to make his first appearance especially for television.

Grace Wyndham Goldie recounted in *Face the Nation* that she enlisted the help of Churchill's wartime Chief-of-Staff, General 'Pug' Ismay. Together they compiled a programme of tributes on film and in the studio from the Prime Minister's friends and colleagues all over the world. Mrs Goldie wanted to ensure that Churchill watched the programme and then spoke on it live. But she did not want to disrupt his life at Number 10 and there was in any case no evidence that he ever watched television there. With the co-operation of the Chancellor, Rab Butler, Mrs Goldie installed cameras in Number 11 Downing Street. And she requested Lady Churchill to try to persuade her husband both to watch the programme and to do so in the Chancellor's residence.

As the programme began, to her immense relief Mrs Goldie saw on her monitor at Lime Grove the Prime Minister shuffling into the room where both the cameras and the television set were. He slumped into an armchair in front of the screen. But as the programme went on, both Mrs Goldie and her producer at Downing Street, an ebullient former press officer called Huw Wheldon, suddenly developed a feeling of dread in the pits of their stomachs. Churchill had remained absolutely motionless in his armchair throughout the first twenty-five minutes of the broadcast. Wheldon became absolutely convinced that he had achieved an awful first; he was the producer of a programme which a prime minister had died watching.

'Like an ancient tortoise, Churchill neither moved nor responded,' recalled Mrs Goldie. 'It was impossible to believe that he knew in the least what was happening. But when Lady Violet Bonham Carter, at the end of her message, said: "Courage, that is your greatest gift to those who know you", I watched unbelieving on my gallery monitor the ancient head move slowly from side to side in a gesture of negation and tears roll slowly down the leathery cheeks. Only we in the gallery saw this incredibly moving spectacle. And we were filled also with professional relief. He was registering something after all. As the programme ended everyone round the mahogany table in the studio, gay with its candles and champagne, rose to their feet and raised their glasses. Ismay said: "Prime Minister – Happy Days." And Churchill coming suddenly to life, like a statue from the stone age taking on humanity, started to speak.'

The Prime Minister addressed the camera directly. 'I have been entranced by the thrilling panorama you have presented to me of so many of my cherished friends who have been given an opportunity of expressing their feeling of kindness to me and the memories that they have. I am fortunate indeed to have met these men and women and to have worked with them in the years of struggle through which we have passed. I am grateful that modern science has enabled me on my birthday to receive in this amazing manner their friendly greetings and good wishes.'

Churchill's first special television appearance in Britain symbolized the fact that he and his Ministers were gradually coming to terms with the new medium. The Tory party's television officer, Winifred Crum-Ewing, had followed John Profumo on a special trip to study how American politicians used television. Conservative Central Office had taken the unprecedented step of buying a television set for her to watch at home. (In those days virtually no politicians had sets, though they had strong ideas about television; while today they all have sets which they virtually never watch but still have strong ideas about television.) And in the autumn of 1954 the BBC for the first time was allowed to televise the Conservative Party Conference. The Labour party in the midst of the Bevanite split had refused the cameras entry.

It was to be Churchill's last conference as Leader. As Grace Wyndham

Goldie was feverishly editing the extracts of the Prime Minister's speech she planned to use, she received a telephone call from his private secretary. Churchill wanted to be reassured about one specific part of his speech. He had stood up to a huge ovation and had scarcely begun to speak when he faltered. The audience had become anxious. It was known that the Prime Minister had been seriously ill and it appeared he might collapse on the platform. His two sons-in-law, Duncan Sandys and Christopher Soames, were behind him. They moved forward to his support and one of them handed him a glass of water. The Prime Minister drank it, raised the glass towards the hall, smiled broadly and then said with perfect timing: 'You didn't think I could drink this, did you?' There was a roar of laughter. Mrs Goldie had decided to include the incident in that night's conference report and was concerned that the Prime Minister might want it dropped. She need not have worried. His secretary said on the telephone: 'You see, Mr Churchill had prepared this occasion very carefully and so he didn't want it to be missed on television.'

From the Prime Minister down the Conservatives had become camera-conscious: they were well ahead of Labour in recognizing the potential benefits of coverage. The Tories' publicity men had arranged for the Party's most attractive women to be seated behind Churchill for his conference speech, although the effect had been somewhat spoiled by one Cabinet minister's wife who had seemed to be asleep through most of the speech. Back at Conservative Central Office Mrs Crum-Ewing stepped up her TV training for ministers and MPs on the Party's mock box. 'The odd thing was that those who looked good on the mock box were often disastrous in the studio and those who flunked the mock box sometimes came out frightfully well in real life,' remembers William Deedes. 'It wasn't until we got to the genuine studios that we discovered that we had to unlearn almost all that we had been taught. There was a world of difference between what Central Office conceived to be the atmosphere of a television studio and actually coming into the prestigious BBC studios in Lime Grove.'

Today Deedes, with the benefit of twenty-twenty hindsight can afford to laugh at the mock box. But at the time ministers, in their terror of television, regarded Mrs Crum-Ewing as an electronic alchemist who would magically transform them into pure gold on the small screen. It was to her that Winston Churchill himself turned, in utmost secrecy, when he decided that he wanted to see whether he could learn to master the techniques of television and use them to his political advantage. For his first two years back in Downing Street, the Prime Minister had reacted to the TV cameras in the manner of a seventeenth-century aristocrat who did not want the vulgar mob to stare at him. He would either walk straight past the television cameras or put his hand over the lens if they came too close. But the success of the Coronation broadcast had convinced him that he could no longer just ignore television; it was not going to go away. In 1954, he arranged for Mrs Crum-Ewing to give him a TV screen test in Number 10 Downing Street. She and the television cameraman were instructed to keep the whole proceedings absolutely confidential; for over thirty years they succeeded in keeping the secret.

Churchill, wearing a black jacket and spotted bow tie, sat at his desk with a microphone rigged above his head. Mrs Crum-Ewing gave the Prime Minister his cue to start. 'I have come here, not to talk to you and certainly not to enable you to spread the tale all over the place,' growled Churchill, 'but just to enable me to see what are the conditions under which this thing they call TeeVee is going make its way in the world. I am sorry, I must admit, to have to descend to this level, but we all have to keep pace with modern improvements and it is just as well to see where you are in regard to them. There is no point in refusing to move with the age and therefore I have consented to come and have this exhibition, which is for one person and one person only. And only one person is to judge what is to be done with this. I am that person. There you are, here you see me [Churchill spread his arms out wide], there is no other in this business.

'Of course it may be that a great future of political life is opening to the world through the medium of television. It will be a great relief to the people looking at all the comics and so forth, now and again to get a real streak of serious thought and inspiration to them and receive this all free, gratis and for nothing, or thrown in between the advertisements on the wonderful shows they are going to offer to the world. For my part, I am merely experimenting and reconnoitring – finding out what it is like. And I am bound to say that, while I am very much obliged to those who are helping me in the matter, I'm not at all an enthusiast. If I were an enthusiast, oh, I should be adopting an entirely different method of approach.'

Churchill then read out an extract from one of his speeches on the desirability of holding a summit conference. And he ended by reciting a poem which he said he had learned forty years earlier from *Punch*.

> Beside the water in St James's Park,
> I stretched myself to rest beneath this old tree,
> But can't, for all the cackle, squeak and squawk,
> Of these 'ere ducks and suchlike blooming poultry.
> These fowls have nowt to do, but fill themselves with buns,
> Thrown to them by blooming nuns.

Mrs Crum-Ewing left Downing Street clutching the film negative of the screen test. She had it developed in strictest secrecy and laid on a special showing for the Prime Minister at his country home. Churchill hated it: 'I should never have appeared on television,' he said. In fact, he comes over very powerfully in the film. His bulldog face matched the shape of a television screen and his eyes sparkled, but the Prime Minister decided that television was not for him. He was in any case nearing the end of his time in office. And he had already set in train the most radical change in the structure of television, which he had sardonically described in his screen test as the promise of wonderful shows between the advertisements.

From the time Churchill had returned to power in 1951, a group of Conservative backbenchers had mounted a persuasive campaign to bring the BBC's monopoly over television to an end. 'A single TV programme imposed on the country from London is too powerful a weapon of propaganda to leave lying about,' argued a leading member of the group, the former BBC producer Ian (later Lord) Orr-Ewing. The Broadcasting Study Group's prime mover was John Profumo. He was part of a highly skilled lobbying operation that was to lead to the creation of ITV and to have profound effects on television's coverage of politics. It was a long and bitter campaign. At first Churchill seemed totally opposed to the idea of commercial television. 'Why do we need this peep-show?' he asked. 'There was also vitriolic opposition from the BBC,' says Profumo. 'Haley, the Director-General, came to the House and he was livid. I was sent for by various BBC Governors and they tried to lobby me. But we young Turks really wanted a new channel: we pushed and pushed.' One of Profumo's allies was the Deputy Chief Whip, Edward Heath. 'I am not a viewer, so I am not biased,' said Heath in 1952, 'but I think it might be good if you had competition for the BBC.'

The arguments used by Profumo's Young Turks were threefold. First, it was ideologically good to break any public monopoly and introduce genuine competition; second, advertising on television would stimulate the consumer economy and, third, it would be one in the eye for the BBC. Many Tories remained convinced that the Corporation was ineradicably biased against them and had somehow helped lose Churchill the 1945 election. And a row over a television play called *Party Manners* in 1950 had fuelled Profumo's campaign.

The Conservative belief in the left-wing nature of the BBC was matched by Labour's conviction that the Corporation was the voice of the Establishment. Prime ministers would over the years have a series of rows over specific programmes which they claimed showed political bias. But *Yesterday's Men* and *Real Lives* were long into the future when *Party Manners* caused the first major political kerfuffle. By today's standards, it was a mild comedy which suggested that some politicians on the Left feather their own nests.

The Labour party was outraged and made a bitter complaint; what was at issue was whether the play would be shown again the following week, as scheduled. The *Daily Herald*, Labour's official newspaper, demanded that 'this crude, silly and insulting comedy should not be repeated'. The Chairman of the BBC Governors, Lord Simon, gave in to the pressure; he ordered the repeat of *Party Manners* to be cancelled. Simon claimed that the fact he was a member of the Labour party was irrelevant to his decision. To many Tories, the incident was all the proof they needed that the Corporation was nothing but a left-wing fifth column, with a card-carrying Socialist at its head. The Chairman of the Tory party, Lord Woolton, said later that the cancellation of the programme in response to Labour party pressure was what convinced him that the BBC's monopoly had to be ended.

But the Corporation was not going to surrender its privileges without a fight. Ranged behind it were the Church, the film and theatre industry, the Labour party, the TUC and half the Cabinet. 'For the sake of our children we should resist commercial television,' proclaimed the Archbishop of York. 'In that subtle way that is unique to this island,' wrote *The Economist*, 'it was not so much stated as taken as self-evident that only cads would want to have advertising on the air.' Among the cads were most Tory backbenchers, some Cabinet ministers, the advertising industry, City and entertainment interests, Lord Nuffield, A. J. P. Taylor, Valerie Hobson (soon to become Mrs John Profumo), Rex Harrison and Somerset Maugham.

Outside the Commons, the leading organizer of the campaign for commercial television was Norman Collins. He had been Director of BBC TV until he resigned in 1950, claiming that the top officials at Broadcasting House were implacably hostile to the development of television. Collins set up one of the first modern pressure groups under the guise of a company called High Definition Films. His chief target was the Prime Minister. But Churchill remained contemptuous of the prospect of commercial television which he took to calling 'a twopenny Punch and Judy show'. Says Profumo: 'Churchill wasn't keen. He thought the whole idea of breaking the BBC's monopoly would be unpopular and rather unnecessary.' But the Prime Minister's old antipathies towards the Corporation were re-awakened by the entry into the campaign of Lord Reith.

The former Director-General initiated a debate in the House of Lords on the future of broadcasting. In a fury of Calvinist rhetoric, Reith went over the top. He declaimed that commercial television would be an unmitigated disaster in England – 'like dog-racing, smallpox and bubonic plague'. Churchill dictated a draft reply to Reith saying he found his arguments 'ill-considered and odd', adding for good measure: 'I have never forgotten how wrong you were about the General Strike.' The next day Churchill told his doctor, Lord Moran: 'I first quarrelled with Reith during the General Strike. He behaved quite impartially between the strikers and the nation. I said he had no right to be impartial between the fire and the fire brigade.'

The Prime Minister's continuing resentment against his old adversary coupled with the arguments of the Profumo and Collins pressure groups had helped hose away Churchill's doubts about the wisdom of removing the BBC's protected status. 'I am against the monopoly enjoyed by the BBC,' Churchill told Moran, 'for eleven years they kept me off the air. They prevented me from expressing views that proved to be right. Their behaviour has been tyrannical.' In the summer of 1952, Churchill announced in the Commons that after serious study he had decided in favour of a second channel.

At a meeting in the Reform Club, Norman Collins euphemistically christened the new baby 'independent television'. In the spring of 1954, Parliament passed the bill setting up the new Authority. Although the Opposition leader, Clement Attlee, pledged that his party would abolish ITV, the mould had been broken. Television in Britain would never be the same.

The ending of the BBC's monopoly would have a dramatic effect on the relationship between broadcasters and politicians. And, just as the Corporation was issuing memos to its staff full of fighting talk about defeating the commercial enemy, a new man was moving into Number 10. Anthony Eden, for so long the heir-apparent, became Prime Minister with a totally different attitude towards the cameras from Churchill. Eden liked television. He believed he was good at it and he was determined to shape it into a totally new instrument of prime ministerial power.

CHAPTER 3

The First Television Election

'Any of the election telecasters on either side can lose the election in five seconds.'

Randolph Churchill, 1955

'No two men have ever changed guard more smoothly,' said Sir Winston Churchill of his hand-over to Sir Anthony Eden. On 6 April, the BBC television's *News and Newsreel* reported the event in fulsome terms. 'And now we are going to show you film of some of the main stages in this great day for Sir Anthony,' enthused the anonymous newsreader. 'From his home in Carlton Gardens this morning Sir Anthony came out in morning dress. Photographers and cameramen were there to catch the Foreign Secretary's famous smile.' The film showed Eden bound for the Palace in his black Daimler. 'He kissed hands on his appointment and came out. Now it is the smile of Her Majesty's first minister.' The BBC provided many details of the new Prime Minister's comings and goings that day, his luncheon arrangements and his changes of clothing; but there was not a mention of his policies nor any attempt to interview him. Despite the efforts of Grace Wyndham Goldie, the top officials of the BBC still regarded the Corporation as above politics. And most leading politicians regarded themselves as above television. But the new Prime Minister had other ideas.

After just a week in Number 10, Eden called a snap general election; the Conservatives' term of office still had eighteen months to run. He wanted to be the first Prime Minister to announce his decision to go to the polls in a 'ministerial broadcast' on television. But the BBC said he could not. Under Churchill and Attlee both political parties had consistently refused the BBC's offer of television time for broadcasts by ministers on matters of national interest. Attlee said it would turn politicians into entertainers while Churchill, as Prime Minister, could not accept that the Opposition should have a right of reply if the broadcast was politically controversial. Under the agreement with the political parties, 'ministerials' could only be made on radio. Eden, not for the first time, was furious with the BBC. He had been similarly frustrated the previous year when, as Foreign Secretary, he had demanded to make a television broadcast of his own devising and had turned down the alternative of appearing in the regular *Press Conference* programme.

27

As Prime Minister, Eden reasoned that he should have the right to address the nation on television whenever he wanted. He determined that if he won the election, he would change the rules. In the meantime he intended to make use of television in the campaign.

Four years earlier, Eden had been the star of the Tories' first and only party election broadcast on television during the 1951 campaign. But by 1955, things had changed. The parties had now had the experience of almost a dozen party political and Budget broadcasts and had overcome their initial telephobia. The Conservatives and Labour agreed with the BBC that they would each have three broadcasts of their own: two of fifteen minutes and one of half an hour. Exaggerated hopes and fears built up in the parties. Winston Churchill's son, Randolph, wrote: 'It can be truly said of the election telecasters on either side that any of them can lose the election in five seconds.' In the view of the press and the politicians, this was to be the first television election.

By now, over a third of the population had television. But would the BBC this time feel it dare venture any coverage of the campaign – which was to be the last before the start of ITV that autumn? The Conservatives' television officer, Winifred Crum-Ewing, wrote in a note to ministers: 'during an election period the Corporation is extremely careful to avoid broadcasting any political matter which might have an influence or bearing on the result of the polling.' She felt sure the Tories could rely on the Corporation to maintain 'this admirable policy'. Mrs Crum-Ewing was right. There was once again to be no reporting of the campaign. In addition, the BBC warned all comedians not to make jokes on politics and it dropped a scheduled undergraduate debate on science and religion. 'This was carrying neutrality to the point of castration,' remarked one critic. With television providing no independent information, the parties' own broadcasts took on special significance.

Eden welcomed this. He believed he was good on television and wanted to ensure that he would himself be the star attraction of the Tories' broadcasts. 'I attached first importance to television as a medium,' Eden said later. He decided that he would appear in the last two of the three broadcasts. The opening programme would be devoted to the Government's achievements and introduced by the Foreign Secretary, Harold Macmillan, who had appeared in the first party political broadcast two years earlier. To help produce the broadcasts, the Tories had hired Roland Gillett, who had just been appointed programme director of the newly formed ITV company, Associated Rediffusion. He had worked in American television; with far greater resources and the experience of being on the air while the BBC was closed down for seven years from 1939, the US system had advanced technically a long way ahead of Britain. Gillett was the first example of what was to become over the years a growing trend in British politics: the 'media adviser' called in for his special television expertise by the parties. It was a field in which the Conservatives were always to lead the way until Neil Kinnock's 1987 election campaign.

The BBC took great exception to the hiring of Gillett: this was a vote of no confidence by the Tories in its traditional production methods. There was, in addition, a delicate problem of protocol. In an effort to curtail the poaching of staff, the Corporation had decreed that no one from one of the new commercial TV companies could enter its premises. A *frisson* of anger went through the BBC's senior officials when Gillett turned up at Lime Grove with Macmillan. But they bit their tongues. Worse was to follow when they learned what Gillett planned. Leonard Miall, head of the Television Talks department and the BBC's man in overall charge of putting out the parties' election broadcasts, remembers: 'Gillett thought our style was far too static. What was required in a television talk was "flow"; there had to be a great deal of movement. He had therefore worked out that Harold Macmillan would first be seen leaning rather nonchalantly with his elbow on a scenery mantelpiece. He would then walk over to a chair, talk to a different camera, move to another chair and talk to a third camera.'

Next Gillett wanted Macmillan to pick up a money box painted with figures showing how little the people had been able to save under the previous Labour government. Macmillan was then to walk over and place it on top of a larger money box with numbers showing that under the Conservatives personal savings had been thirty times as great. The first money box was a child's metal one; the second was to be thirty times the size. After the controversy that had surrounded the cost of living graphs in Eden's first election broadcast four years earlier, it had been agreed that the parties should produce their own graphics and props. The Tories had given detailed instructions to a private scenery designer on the exact dimensions of the large box. Unfortunately he had misunderstood. He had built it not thirty times as big as the original, but thirty times bigger in each direction. It was thus 27,000 times the volume of the smaller one and was the size of an executive desk. It arrived in the studio, on the night of the live broadcast, only shortly before Macmillan did. Two men were required to carry it up into the studio and rest it on trestles.

'Gillett was hideously embarrassed,' says Miall, 'and he asked whether it was possible for the BBC's workshop quickly to produce an alternative. I told him we hardly had time to draw one let alone construct one. I said, however, that provided he would be prepared to sacrifice a certain amount of Macmillan's precious "flow" we might be able to make the adjustment electronically.' Miall agreed to show the small money box in close-up and the huge money box in a separate wide shot. In that way the vast disparity in size would be less obvious. but, Miall told Gillett, it was essential that Macmillan did not attempt to put the small box on the huge one or viewers would spot the trick. Gillett agreed, but he had another problem. He had invited journalists into the studio immediately after the programme; they would spot the difference. The BBC had to get rid of the outsize box immediately the programme was over. Miall said this would be impossible; it had taken two strong men a great deal of time and effort to bring it into the studio, there would not be time. Instead Miall instructed his assistant to pocket the small money box the moment the broadcast ended. The journalists were somewhat surprised at the size of the larger money box and asked vainly where the other one had got to.

The broadcast was not regarded as a great success. Halfway through the programme, Macmillan told the audience: 'Now I've got just a few more things to say to you and since I have been pretty busy recently I have made a few notes to help me.' He then put on his glasses, looked at his notes and took off his glasses. 'Oh yes,' he smiled, 'things are getting better. We have got the whole thing in our hands. There is a wonderful future before us.' In his study of the 1955 election David Butler noted: 'it was the most lukewarmly received of the Conservative TV programmes. Macmillan, who seemed ill at ease, made plain the difficulties of delivering a rehearsed monologue on television.' Macmillan himself said: 'My performance was weak and jejune. I had to give a talk of a few minutes to be followed by a film which, although rather childish, was not perhaps altogether ineffective.' The film, entitled *Onward from Success*, had been specially shot by Winifred Crum-Ewing. Until two days before the broadcast, she had hoped that Churchill himself would take part in it; it would have been his début in a party political broadcast. But he refused after seeing the film. Randolph Churchill claimed that it was because his father thought that a shot of a slum lavatory in the film was in bad taste.

Eden decided that the second of the broadcasts would feature himself flanked by leading members of his Cabinet. The programme was a copy of the BBC's *Press Conference*. 'We were to appear', said Eden, 'with a panel of ten newspaper editors who would ask us questions of which we had not been advised in advance.' But an incident at Lime Grove almost kept the Prime Minister off the air. Two days before the broadcast a mentally deranged man had managed to find his way into the studios and been escorted out. Security was tight when the Prime Minister and his Cabinet colleagues arrived. 'The rehearsals did not go well,' remembers Leonard Miall, 'they had far too large a cast. During the camera line-up, when the equipment was left to settle down, this vast crowd of editors, Cabinet ministers and Central Office advisers repaired to a densely packed hospitality room. At one point, Sir Anthony Eden wished to escape from the hubbub in order to practise his opening remarks to camera. After visiting the men's lavatory he noticed that the commissionaires' locker room opposite was empty and so slipped inside. A commissionaire then came in and headed for his locker. Seeing the back of a man walking along muttering, he exclaimed, "Gosh, one of those loonies has got in again." 'The commissionaire was about to lock the intruder in the room and switch out the lights, when he suddenly recognized the Prime Minister.

Eden had learned his lines well. His hair, his tie and his voice were all elegantly silky as he addressed the camera. The Prime Minister introduced his Cabinet colleagues who were to answer the newspaper editors' questions. 'We haven't of course the least idea what the questions are going to be,' Eden said and added with a winsome smile: 'I only hope we shall know the answers.' In fact, the ministers had been given a pretty good idea of the questions in advance as almost all the editors' newspapers supported the Conservatives. One exception was the editor of the *Daily Mirror*, Hugh (later Lord) Cudlipp. Which sort of Toryism, he asked, did the Prime Minister favour: the more humanitarian style which supported the welfare state or the Toryism of the big majority – of slums, neglected housing needs and massive unemployment? Eden answered in a relaxed manner that he supported 'an intelligent progressive Toryism which would try to build on what had been achieved in the past three and a half years'. David Butler felt that the programme lacked bite but 'the team answered smoothly, as men well-briefed, long in office and with an air of authority which no Opposition leaders, however skilled, could match.' Eden himself thought the programme 'fairly successful – although both questions and answers were apt to go on too long'.

The Prime Minister tried to ensure that he saw all the Labour party's election broadcasts. In the days before video cassette recorders, this meant catching them as they went out live. 'I watched them as far as I could, despite the calls of the campaign,' said Eden, 'for it is a useful part of one's own preparation to see one's opponents perform. The Opposition did not, I think, make good use of their television time.'

The Labour broadcasts had been fraught with even more problems than the Tories'. For the previous three years, two enthusiastic young men had urged the Party leadership to take television seriously and plan the election broadcasts in advance. One was Christopher Mayhew, who had appeared in the first Labour election programme in 1951 and had considerable experience as a television reporter.

In a paper he prepared for the Party, Mayhew suggested: 'We might consider giving attractive and representative personalities from the rank and file one and a half minutes each of straight talking. Their statements could be worked out in close collaboration with an experienced writer and broadcaster. The idea would be, not so much to put party arguments across (viewers will know all the important arguments already thanks to *In the News*) as to give a convincing demonstration of the friendliness, honesty and wisdom of the Labour people.' It could have been Labour's 1987 campaign organizer, Bryan Gould, also briefly a television reporter, talking. Mayhew had from the earliest days grasped what has come to be regarded as one of the essential features of television: that it is a medium of impressions rather than analysis, a powerful means of portraying personality but not of conveying abstract arguments. The programme based on Mayhew's recommendation was called *Meeting the Labour Party*. According to the *Listener*'s television critic: 'We were invited to fall in behind a painstakingly ordinary candidate for conversion as he went about calling on Labour party members to ask them why he should join. There was an amusing unanimity of readiness to bid him goodbye. "You know the way out?" The housewife, the farmer and the miner spoke up well. Someone had decided that the nursing sister's excruciating Sloane Street vowels would give tone to the appeal. I doubted that.'

The other young MP who had tried to galvanize Labour towards television was a former producer in the BBC Overseas Service, Anthony Wedgwood Benn (as he was then known). In a report to the newly formed Broadcasting Committee he had urged the Party radically to 'revise its assessment of the importance of broadcasting propaganda so as to take into account the new situation created by the size of television and radio audiences'. Labour should study new techniques as a matter of urgency and it was essential to set up their own rehearsal studios at party headquarters to match the Tories' mock box. Benn warned; 'Without doubt the Conservatives are well advanced in their plans for making full use of television for political purposes.' They believed that the effectiveness of public meetings was now largely ended, they had sent an emissary to study the American presidential elections in 1952 and Central Office had made a special film on TV techniques. And Benn added ominously: 'They are building up a network of TV cells consisting of party members willing to have open house for their friends and neighbours when programmes are shown.' The Labour party took no notice of Benn's warnings. One result was that their election broadcasts in 1955 ranged from the soporific to the chaotic. They featured a future and a former Prime Minister.

The campaign opened with Clement Attlee and his wife in a studio mock-up of his home sitting room at Cherry Cottage, complete with a blazing fire (it was mid May). The interviewer, Percy Cudlipp, began: 'Mr Attlee, you are off tomorrow on your twelve-hundred-mile tour by motor car, that must mean you still have some faith in spite of television in the old-fashioned public meeting.' Mr Attlee sucked his pipe. 'Um, I think there's a good deal, you know, to the public meeting. After all, a candidate likes to see his audience. And I think the electors like to see their candidates. And after all, too, you can't heckle on television, while you can at a public meeting, I had an extremely good one at Blaydon the other night.' This was by far the Labour leader's longest answer. His responses became monosyllabic as an increasingly desperate Cudlipp tried to think up new questions. According to Tony Benn, who produced the programme for the Labour party, Cudlipp had been given twenty-eight questions for the fifteen-minute broadcast, but he used them up after five minutes. Attlee's technique for discountenancing a hostile interviewer might have been highly effective, but he was using it against his own side. David Butler believed the broadcast was Labour's least inspired of the campaign: 'Mr Attlee neither said anything new, nor anything old in a new way.'

The second Labour broadcast featured a future Prime Minister, Harold Wilson. He had scarcely appeared before on television in Britain. The BBC regarded him as a follower of the left-wing Aneurin Bevan and kept him off the main current affairs programme, *In the News*. Michael Foot filled the BBC's Bevanite quota. Wilson's first television experience had come in America where he had been interviewed by the redoubtable Ed Murrow. 'He gave me three pieces of advice for appearing on television,' remembers Wilson. 'Never attack a man for his race, as race; never attack a man for his religion, as religion; and never sweat on TV.' In Labour's 1955 election broadcast Wilson was unable to obey Murrow's third law of television.

The programme was called *Your Money's Worth* – the theme that has dominated party political broadcasting from Eden's début to today. The idea was to show how fast the cost of living was rising for the average family. Its two presenters were to look like a married couple sitting together in a room with large-spotted wallpaper. The husband-figure was Harold Wilson who had managed to retain his reassuring Yorkshire accent, despite his years as an Oxford don, a Whitehall civil servant and a Cabinet minister. His small-screen wife was Edith Summerskill, who chaired Labour's National Executive Committee and was to provide the women's angle. But another eminent Labour figure very much wanted to appear in the programme – the Party's General Secretary, Morgan Phillips.

'Morgan had been pressing the idea of a "mystery voice" that would shout in the middle of the programme: "What are you going to do about it?" ' said Tony Benn, the Labour party's producer. 'We thought he had dropped it, but two days before the programme he rang to say that he proposed to insist on the idea and wished to be the mystery voice himself. This thoroughly put the wind up us all and I contemplated ringing Attlee in Scotland to ask him to forbid this lunatic idea.' For the BBC, Leonard Miall tried to persuade Phillips that viewers would be bound to think that the unexplained intervention must have come from one of the TV camera crew. Phillips' reaction was 'to hell with the BBC', he would come and be the mystery voice in any case, said Benn. 'Edith and Harold quite happily agreed that this was mad and they would not have anything to do with it. This was tactfully conveyed to Morgan, who did not in fact appear.' But there were many more troubles ahead.

The plan was to have a range of products in the studio: identical piles of butter, cheese, sausages, bacon, as well as other food and clothing, placed side by side. There would be two sets of markers to show how prices had risen dramatically in four years since the Conservatives came to power. Edith Summerskill was to stick the Labour price label into the first pile and the Tory label into the second. But it did not work out quite as simply as that. The young Labour production secretary for the broadcast, doing her first job from university, was Marcia Williams. She was later to become Harold Wilson's political secretary and to be made Lady Falkender. Her memories of the broadcast remain vivid: 'We had a wonderful tableau of dairy products. And during the rehearsals Edith would say, "now here we have cheese that has gone up by so much" and she would plonk the marker straight into the butter, and then she would put the marker for the butter straight into the cheese. And by the time they had said to her, "Edith start again", we would go through two or three more rehearsals. And under the studio lights the butter was melting, the cheese was sort of dribbling and the whole thing was a scene of utter chaos.'

'The last hours before the broadcast are hard to describe so great was the confusion,' says Benn. He had been attempting to persuade Edith Summerskill to drop the seductive manner she adopted for the cameras and appear more down to earth, but with no success. 'In a crowded studio the Co-op man was balancing his jars of jam,' Benn continues, 'Edith insisted on simpering and the script was changed every two minutes. The producer for the BBC, Donald Baverstock, didn't know if he was coming or going. At every run-through we overran by up to six minutes. It was therefore with sinking hearts and Edith full of gin that we approached transmission. By then, those of us who were involved were incapable of assessing our work. After all her coaching, Edith returned to the seductive voice and Harold brought in all the points he had promised to cut and a lot of new ones that had just occurred to him. The cameras forgot to photograph the great display of clothes and the programme was running about five minutes behind time.

'At about this time the studio manager signalled to Edith to hurry up. She therefore butted in on Harold with a bit about the family and said "good night" very firmly. Harold however was not to be put off so easily. He had been deprived of two good points and proposed to insert them even at this late hour. "Don't forget that Labour stands for . . . " came his insistent voice behind a rising volume of music and shots of motor cars going down Chiswick High Road. We thought it would never end,' said Benn. When it finally did, the first on the telephone to Benn in the hospitality room was Morgan Phillips. The Labour General Secretary raged that he and the entire staff at Transport House agreed it was the worst programme ever done by any political party. Phillips proposed to protest to the Governors of the BBC at what he described as the 'sabotage' of the broadcast. The normally ebullient Benn was cast into gloom. Then he had a second call from a fellow member of the Labour Broadcasting Committee, William Pickles, the LSE lecturer and regular broadcaster. 'William said it was the best programme he had ever seen. His only criticism was that the music behind Harold Wilson's voice had been a little too loud, but the idea was excellent. That was the general reaction. None of the press tumbled to the shambles that had occurred.'

Conservative Central Office recognized the programme's impact as it received a flood of calls demanding answers to Labour's charges. But from that day on, Wilson vowed that he would never again allow himself to be so vulnerable in a television studio. Says Lady Falkender: 'We said we must come to terms with this and work out exactly what we can do with television. One or two of our people had some experience, but in the main we knew nothing about it – absolutely nothing.' Wilson determined to learn how to become an effective performer. He was to apply himself so diligently that he would arrive at Downing Street nine years later with more television skills than any of his predecessors. But in 1955, it was Eden who was showing what good use a Prime Minister could make of television.

As the election campaign reached its climax, Eden had to decide on the Tories' final broadcast. 'How was it to be used?' he wrote in his memoirs five years later. 'I knew what I wanted to do, but I was not sure that I dared. This was to speak direct to the British people without company and without script. This sounds simple enough now, but at the time nothing of the kind had ever been attempted and, if it were to flop, the consequences on our electoral fortunes could be serious. The Opposition were not risking a lone appearance by any of their leaders. Encouraged by Mark Chapman-Walker,

Lord Woolton's brilliant assistant in propaganda matters, I made the attempt.'

Winifred Crum-Ewing suggested to Eden that he should make use of a new invention she had seen in America, called a teleprompter. It would enable him to read a script from a hidden screen in front of the camera. But there was a major drawback. Mrs Crum-Ewing's son, Humphrey, who worked as her assistant, says: 'In those early days we realized that anyone who read the teleprompter gave the appearance of having extraordinary rolling eyes that looked as if they were seasick. So, after trying it out, we decided that the Prime Minister could not use it, because it made him look completely mad.' In the end, Eden settled for large cue cards with notes on them, placed discreetly out of the viewers' sight. His broadcast was live. It was the first time a prime minister had ever spoken directly to the voters in a fifteen-minute television solo. And it set the pattern for future election campaigns.

Eden regarded the broadcast as a high-risk gamble. It paid off. 'We were watching the one man among the party leaders who is a television star,' commented the *New Statesman*'s diarist. 'I suspect after last Saturday's appearance that those members of his party who are all for jockeying him out of office, as soon as decency permits, are now thinking again.' In his study of the election, David Butler wrote: 'By common consent the greatest *tour de force* among the television broadcasts was the final one by Sir Anthony Eden. Without any tricks or visual devices he talked directly to the viewers for a quarter of an hour in genuinely extempore fashion. He won universal praise for the way in which he managed to convey a sense of calmness, optimism, decency and competence. Labour fully conceded the supremacy of the Prime Minister's final broadcast.'

Eden had been the first party leader to fight an election campaign in the modern style. 'I gave television and radio first preference and reduced the number of public meetings,' he said. Between five and six million people watched each of the parties' election broadcasts – a quarter of the electorate. Surveys showed that most viewers preferred the Conservative programmes, which might have been because more Tories had sets. But more of the public had gained a better direct impression of what Sir Anthony Eden looked and sounded like, than it had of any previous prime minister in history.

Eden pushed up the Conservative majority from 17 to 60. He was now Prime Minister in his own right and planned further showings of his televisual charms. He was going to use the cameras to speak to the country whenever he thought fit. And he was determined to strengthen political control over television. But the ground was already shifting under his feet.

In her report to Eden on the election, Mrs Crum-Ewing described how she had set up a network of experts to monitor everything broadcast by the BBC throughout the campaign. 'No bias of any kind was reported during the election period,' she wrote. This was hardly surprising. Apart from the parties' own broadcasts, there had been no coverage of the campaign of any kind. *The Economist* commented: 'As usual the purity of intention behind the BBC's rules must be applauded with politeness rather than enthusiasm; these slightly ludicrous election arrangements are inevitable so long as the monopoly in broadcasting remains.' But within six months of Eden's election victory, commercial television began.

The new independent stations – and in particular the national news service, ITN – would soon dramatically alter the relationship between the broadcasters and the politicians. The BBC's treatment of ministers and their 'shadows' veered between the deferential and the sycophantic, especially in its news programmes. The Corporation had also willingly accepted many legal and other restrictions, like the Fourteen Day Rule and the ban on election reporting. The new stations did not feel bound by the same constraints and inhibitions. Television politics was about to enter a completely new era. For the first time the Prime Minister himself was in the van of change. But Sir Anthony Eden was to discover that the BBC, which had seemed afraid even to bark during a general election campaign, still had pretty sharp teeth when the Prime Minister wanted to turn it into his lapdog.

CHAPTER 4

Those Communists at the BBC

'I felt ashamed that the BBC had not been able to provide the Prime Minister with more suitable surroundings in which to make so momentous a broadcast.'

Grace Wyndham Goldie

Sir Anthony Eden had the vanity of a handsome man. Like the Duke of Windsor, he had been a model of male elegance for thirty years and had even given his name to a style of gentleman's hat. Television enabled millions of people to judge for themselves the looks and charm of the new Prime Minister. He liked having his face on the small screen; for him TV was a wonder drug. Other leading members of his party had feared or scorned the cameras, but Eden had made use of them in the 1955 election campaign and had emerged triumphant. Now he proposed to turn television into a tool of government. He saw no reason why he should not appear whenever he saw fit and say exactly what he wanted to say. This was after all what happened in other great democracies.

Two months after becoming Prime Minister, Eden and other Western leaders went to a summit meeting with the Russians in Geneva. To help him with his television appearances, Eden had just appointed as his press secretary an experienced BBC presenter, William Clark. 'At the summit, Eden found himself sitting next to President Eisenhower who fairly regularly made nationwide broadcasts on American television,' Clark told the author. 'Then he sat next to the French Prime Minister, Edgar Faure, who about once a fortnight gave TV broadcasts explaining his policies to the nation. Eden discussed with me about setting up the same kind of thing in Britain. He wanted to use television as a new instrument, a new weapon for national unity and purpose.'

Eden's idea found some sympathy at the highest levels of the BBC. Why should the Prime Minister not be able to address the nation, on what was rapidly becoming the most important medium of communication, on his own terms? After all, top BBC men added *sotto voce*, the Government sets the licence fee and there is no point in gratuitously offending its leading member. After lengthy negotiations, the Government and the BBC reached agreement. The Prime Minister and leading members of the Cabinet should have the right to make 'ministerial broadcasts' on television, as they already could on radio, about matters of national importance. The Opposition could seek a right of reply, if it considered the broadcast controversial. But whether the reply was granted depended on a highly abstract set of rules. Eden's Cabinet colleague, Rab Butler, likened them to medieval theology. And, in the coming year, interpretation of the rules was to become the subject of the most acrimonious row between the Prime Minister and the television authorities.

But at the start, Eden was well pleased with the new agreement and immediately took advantage of it. He talked directly to the camera about the visit of the two Soviet leaders, Bulganin and Khrushchev, to Britain. He had discussed with the young director from the BBC, David Attenborough, what sort of shirt to wear and whether he should have his moustache trimmed. Convinced that his smooth skills as a diplomat and his personal charm translated themselves well on to television, Eden would begin his broadcasts, 'my friends' – despite the fact that the majority of the electorate had voted against him. The beauty of ministerials, as he saw it, lay in what did not happen. First the Opposition had no automatic right of reply; second no one shared the screen with him. There was no interviewer to put awkward questions, no leading him into areas he preferred to ignore. Instead he could say what he wanted, when he wanted and in exactly the way he wanted.

For Eden's first ministerial, the urbane old Etonian had insisted on the unlikeliest of helpers. Johnny Day was a BBC studio technician who gloried in his thick Cockney accent and use of rhyming slang. A fortnight before Eden's ministerial, Day had been the floor manager for a Budget broadcast by the new Chancellor, Harold Macmillan. 'When Mr Macmillan came in, there were a lot of people in blue suits saying "yes Chancellor, no Chancellor",' remembers James Cellan-Jones, the assistant floor manager. 'But Johnny Day said to Macmillan: "Right cock, over 'ere. Boys, give me a piece of Duke of York" and on the marvellous blue carpet he scrawled a band of white chalk. "Right, that's where you put your daisy roots. Now you look at that camera and you go 'blah, blah, blah'. Then they've got a caption, you look at it and go 'blah, blah, blah' again. Right?" A mesmerized Macmillan simply nodded and did it. Later Anthony Eden sent in a request, "Can John Day be present when I do my broadcast?" '

Eden was happy to use all the BBC's technical expertise – however unconventional – to improve his own performance. He saw ministerial broadcasts as the ideal way of appearing: by talking directly to the people he would strengthen both his personal links with them and his own authority. But he had no intention of allowing television to develop into a forum on which the policies of his government would be critically examined. The

Fourteen Day Rule, which prohibited discussion on television of any subject likely to come up in Parliament the following fortnight, buttressed his position.

When Eden became Prime Minister, the Rule remained the biggest inhibition on the development of television's political coverage. But it was now coming under fierce attack. On one edition of *In the News* the Chairman, Dingle Foot, described the Rule as 'a lunatic restriction'. His panel agreed. In a rare display of unity between the press and television, a campaign against the Rule began. In July 1955, the BBC announced it proposed to abandon the Rule altogether – unless ordered otherwise. This was a direct challenge to Eden and his government. The new commercial television stations would be coming on air in a few months' time; already their representatives were declaring that they did not feel bound by a provision that was antiquated and undemocratic. Eden feared that if the Rule were scrapped, television would move in exactly the opposite direction from the one he wanted. Controversial political matters, which the Cabinet was discussing privately, would become the stuff of public debate. That was unthinkable. There could be no question of television producers or interviewers setting the political agenda. When the Fourteen Day Rule came up for debate in the Commons, Eden's immediate predecessor spoke in his new role as the most distinguished backbencher of all. Sir Winston Churchill put the Prime Minister's case in a way that was bound to appeal to the House: 'It would be a shocking thing to have the debates of Parliament forestalled on this new robot organization of television and BBC broadcasting.' The rights of MPs had to be protected 'against the mass and against the machine'. The ex-Prime Minister, Clement Attlee, supported Churchill. The Labour leader had no time for television: he had been on one visit to Lime Grove and, according to Grace Wyndham Goldie, had 'sat obstinately silent and disapproving and departed as coldly as he had come'.

Following the debate, the Postmaster-General, Dr Charles Hill, issued a formal instruction to the BBC. From being a gentlemen's agreement, the Fourteen Day Rule now had the force of law. 'Break this law!' demanded Michael Foot in *Tribune*, and urged the BBC's Director-General, Sir Ian Jacob, to risk being 'despatched to the Tower'. Sir Ian declined the invitation. The Government made it clear that Hill's ukase would apply not just to the BBC but to the new independent television stations. It appeared that coverage of politics on the screen would remain highly restricted and docile. Edenvision seemed to have won a famous victory. In fact, the Fourteen Day Rule had only a short lifespan ahead. The following year it would be swept away in the biggest political convulsion to hit Britain since the war. And in the meantime, a number of other developments were already slowly working against the Prime Minister's view of television as a medium for illustrated Government press releases.

One was *Panorama*. At the start of 1955 it was still a lightweight fortnightly mixture of musical items and non-political discussions. But the BBC decided that it had to put on a programme that would compete with the promised tougher approach to politics of the new independent companies. *Panorama* was about to be killed off but Grace Wyndham Goldie decided that the name was worth salvaging, although she would completely change the content. Four days before the much-publicized launch of ITV in September 1955, the new weekly *Panorama* began. It was to be 'a magazine of informed comment, quality and significance: television's window on the world', with a new presenter, Richard Dimbleby.

Over the years, *Panorama* would become a major platform for leading politicians from the Prime Minister downwards. From the first, Dimbleby gave the relaunched programme style and authority; it soon built up an audience of eight million. There were already signs of a new, aggressive form of interviewing from *Panorama*'s bow-tied, bespectacled first reporter – Woodrow Wyatt. He was a former Labour MP. 'I introduced a different type of questioning from the hitherto deferential "Yes Sir/No Sir" approach to the important by the BBC interviewer,' wrote Wyatt in his memoirs. 'None of the people interviewed seemed to me more awesome than many I had been used to dealing with on level terms for eleven years.' But Wyatt's technique was reserved almost exclusively for foreigners. In its early editions the new *Panorama* treated British politicians with considerable caution and remained hemmed in by the restrictions of the Fourteen Day Rule.

Only when Parliament was not sitting could there be more uninhibited coverage of politics. In autumn 1955, the BBC for the first time had cameras at both main party conferences. The Labour party had reluctantly followed the Tories' example of the previous year, but insisted that just one morning of the Conference could be shown. On the eve of the appointed day, Dr Edith Summerskill, who was chairing the Conference, warned the delegates that TV cameras would be present the next morning and they would doubtless find the light and heat intolerable. 'There were boos and hisses throughout the hall,' remembers Leonard Miall, BBC television's Head of Talks. 'Next morning Dr Summerskill was there in dark glasses and a wide-brimmed hat. Most of the others on the platform were similarly protected. They looked rather like stereotyped gangsters.' In fact, the BBC's lights had been on throughout the whole of the previous day's session. To many suspicious delegates this was the first example of what was to become a long catalogue of the Corporation's devious behaviour towards them.

The Conservatives allowed the cameras in for the whole of their proceedings. At that time the leader himself would never arrive at the conference until it was almost over. He would make a triumphal entrance on the last afternoon and then deliver his address to the faithful. Anthony Eden was determined that this should be the highlight of the television coverage. The man presenting the BBC's conference programmes was the political journalist, Geoffrey Cox (later knighted), Assistant Editor of the *News Chronicle*. Cox had been a newspaperman almost all his professional life, but a single incident during the Prime Minister's speech convinced him of the power of television. 'Eden was speaking under very powerful lights and the ranks of Tory ladies and gentlemen behind him felt they were being half-broiled and half-blinded by the lights. I could see that one of the formidable Tory ladies of the day, Lady Davidson, was coping with this heat by fanning herself with her programme.' Cox and his producer were concerned as they watched their monitor about the distracting effect of Lady Davidson's fan. They felt the white blur behind Eden was spoiling his speech. They changed the focus on the camera and the size of the shot, but it did not work. Finally they sent a message and watched it being passed from hand to hand until it finally reached Lady Davidson. 'When she read it,' says Cox, 'I could see on the monitor the look on her face. First it was fury, then it was the indignity of having been told to stop fanning herself and then, suddenly, a quite different look came over her face. One of resignation. She saw there was nothing she could do about it. She put down her programme. I realized at that moment the power of television. A medium that could defeat the Lady Davidsons of this world could defeat anything; I realized then that the TV era had arrived.'

Within three months of the Conference, Cox had forsaken Fleet Street for the editorship of Independent Television News. He was to become one of the most influential figures in changing the relationship between prime ministers and television. Aidan Crawley, a former Labour MP and junior minister had started ITN in 1955 and had decided to bring some of the techniques of American television news to Britain. ITN would not be a pale shadow of the BBC. The news would be read not by anonymous men; but by named *newscasters* who would help write it themselves and would become authoritative figures in their own right. (Three weeks before ITN came on the air, the BBC had finally allowed its newsreaders to be seen, although it still could not bring itself to name them.)

But the biggest change that Crawley wanted to bring about was in television's attitude to politicians. At that time, says Sir Ian Trethowan, who was one of ITN's early newscasters and later became BBC Director-General, 'BBC interviews with British politicians were uncritical, verging on the fawning'. Most interviews were about ministerial visits – normally conducted at a sea- or airport. 'Is there anything you would care to say, sir, about the results of your visit?' the gentlemanly BBC reporter would ask. The minister would turn to the camera and deliver his prepared statement.

Aidan Crawley wanted none of that. He knew from his own experience in the Commons that ministers were perfectly used to a rougher and tougher approach. He was determined to bring it to television. 'Crawley laid down that we should not be beholden to politicians, not go cap in hand to them as the BBC did,' said Reginald Bosanquet, one of ITN's first reporters: 'The obsequiousness of BBC staffers no doubt stemmed from the fact that they were in a sense civil servants, paid for out of public funds and on a lower grade than Cabinet ministers. Crawley said that we had no need to adopt a similar servile attitude.' The man Crawley chose to make his beliefs flesh was a young radio producer who had trained as a barrister – Robin Day. According to his own description, Day was a 'grim, uncongenial, bespectacled type'. Soon after he was hired he walked into the ITN offices and met his formidable new studio director, Diana Edwards-Jones. 'She said to me "who the hell are you?" And I said "I am a newscaster" and she said "God Almighty, can't they do better than that?" '

From that bad day, the callow newscaster was quickly to establish himself as an abrasive interviewer. One television critic wrote of his early efforts: 'In the studio, Mr Day puts his blunt, loaded questions with the air of a prosecuting counsel at a murder trial. As he swings back to face the cameras, metaphorically blowing on his knuckles, one detects the muffled disturbance as his shaken victim is led away.' Few people saw these first interviews. Independent television was confined to London when it started and even there most people's sets had not been converted to receive it. Leading politicians were not among Day's earliest victims; in those days they did not come into news studios. But Day was developing techniques that he would subsequently use with great effect even against prime ministers.

ITN's less deferential approach to politicians was evident in its filmed reports. Sound cameras went with Duncan Sandys, the Housing Secretary, when he visited the East End. While the BBC still used mute cameras, ITN's recordist picked up the salty exchanges between Sandys and disgruntled Cockney council tenants. In such reports ministers began looking less like remote authority figures. ITN reporters would also turn up at airports and press conferences to ask much more pointed questions than ministers had ever received from the BBC. 'Politicians and public men were asked the questions that needed answering, not "stooge questions" that the Great Men were graciously disposed to answer,' says Robin Day. ITN also banned the BBC practice of presenting lists of questions in advance to ministers, who would then learn and rehearse their answers. 'This change made it an interview on the broadcaster's terms not those of the person questioned,' says Geoffrey Cox, 'but many politicians disliked the proposed change and all public relations officers hated it.'

Ministers took a long time to accept the change. A turning point came when Duncan Sandys was moved from Housing to the Ministry of Defence. Reginald Bosanquet went for a press conference given by the new Defence Secretary. 'The BBC, being the senior service, were given the first television interview with Sandys. They had furnished him with written questions and one by one he answered them,' said Bosanquet. When his turn came, Bosanquet was admonished by the Ministry's public relations men for not having supplied a list of questions, but replied that ITN did things differently. After considerable hesitation, Sandys agreed to an unscripted interview. According to Bosanquet's account, Sandys was so pleased with the result that he called the BBC back and demanded to do his first interview again, unscripted. 'We were running what was virtually a training school for our elder statesmen and politicians, weaning them away from the era of using the BBC as a quasi-official outlet for what they felt the public should be allowed to know, which made boring television.' Bosanquet's was an accurate description of the way much of BBC news operated but in the current affairs department at Lime Grove a more questioning approach towards politicians was already emerging.

By the summer of 1956 two contradictory strands had developed in the relationship between the Prime Minister and television. On the one side, Eden had control of the airwaves for ministerial broadcasts on what he deemed to be matters of national importance, and the Fourteen Day Rule kept most political controversy off the screen. Against that, *Panorama* and ITN were developing a more robust and sceptical style of political coverage and were increasingly unwilling to transmit the Government line unquestioningly. These cross-currents swept the Prime Minister and the broadcasting authorities to head-on collision, when the most momentous political crisis since the war suddenly hit Eden's Cabinet. The Prime Minister went into battle on two fronts: against his enemies abroad and against the BBC at home.

When Colonel Nasser nationalized the Suez Canal in July 1956, Eden decided that he would use television as his prime means of rallying the people behind him. He wanted to apply the lessons he had learned from the Second World War to Suez. Just as Churchill had inspired the nation with his brilliant wartime radio broadcasts – so Eden would be the first Prime Minister to do so through the screen. With his lifetime experience of foreign affairs, Eden had no doubts that Nasser had to be treated as another Hitler or Mussolini. The young Foreign Secretary had resigned in protest against Chamberlain's policies in 1938, now he planned to tell the country that to seek to appease a dictator was the highest form of folly. Eden arranged to come to the television studios on 8 August.

The broadcast was not a happy experience for Eden, who was often nervous and self-conscious as he went on air. The BBC's new Television Centre building was not yet completed and all its larger studios were needed for regular programmes. Eden with his wife and his entourage arrived at Lime Grove on a hot August night. The BBC had laid on iced champagne. Grace Wyndham Goldie, who was to produce the broadcast for the BBC, felt that Eden looked strained and ill that night. She took the Prime Minister up to a tiny studio normally used by the continuity announcer. To reach it, he had to climb three flights of concrete steps lit by naked bulbs. The studio itself was dusty and stifling hot. It was draped with thick velvet curtains to drown out the noise of underground trains from the Metropolitan line that ran outside. 'I felt ashamed,' said Grace Wyndham Goldie, 'that the BBC had not been able to provide a prime minister with more suitable surroundings in which to make so momentous a broadcast.'

In the studio, Eden suffered from a problem that was to affect many prime ministers on television: whether or not to wear glasses. Most men reach Downing Street in late middle age, at the earliest, and prefer not to be seen wearing their reading glasses for fear of looking old to the voters. Vanity was not Eden's sole reason for wanting to broadcast bare-faced. He feared that to be seen wearing glasses in public would give the impression that he was on the wane and without the physical and mental toughness needed to stand up to the youthful Nasser. He had always managed to avoid appearing bespectacled on television before by learning his scripts by heart. But this time days of anxious deliberations and careful weighing of phrases had gone into his script, with changes being made up to the last minute. Eden felt he could not afford to get a word wrong.

He began rehearsals without his glasses. 'He was a victim of the belief that you had to look the audience straight in the eye – never take your eye off them,' said his press secretary, William Clark, 'because there were millions of people out there watching your every move.' But he found he had to keep looking down at his script and even though it had been written in specially large type, he still could not read it properly. 'So he had to put his glasses on,' said Clark, 'and he was convinced that "those Communists at the BBC" were deliberately shining the lights in his eyes. Like Churchill, Eden thought the BBC was infiltrated with Communists. He had picked up the old man's prejudices having been his number two for so long.'

With the lights glinting on his horn-rimmed glasses, Eden finally made his live broadcast, stumbling occasionally over his words. His target was the new Egyptian Hitler. Nasser could not be allowed to get away with his actions: 'With dictators you always have to pay a higher price later on, for their appetite grows with feeding.'

Although resentful at the BBC for the conditions in which he had to broadcast, Eden believed he had succeeded. The nation seemed united in his support. The Labour Opposition, under its new Leader Hugh Gaitskell, did not seek to exercise its right of reply. Unlike Attlee, Gaitskell was convinced of the political importance of television. But in the early days of the Suez crisis, he was completely behind Eden and fierce in his denunciation of Nasser. Only as it became more likely that the Prime Minister intended to back his televised denunciation of Nasser with military force did Gaitskell's position change. As Labour moved into outright opposition to the Government, so the problems of balance and fairness faced by the television authorities mounted. And Eden's prolonged battle with the BBC began.

Round one came later in August over a proposed TV appearance by the Australian Prime Minister, Sir Robert Menzies. Eden believed that following his own broadcast a distinguished elder statesman should come on television and effectively issue a call to arms. His first thought was to use Churchill, but then he decided on Menzies. Over lunch at Number 10, Eden arranged with Menzies what he would say. 'I had no doubt that his television broadcast would be welcome,' said Eden and instructed his press secretary, William Clark, to tell the BBC to make the necessary arrangements. But the BBC feared that its coverage was becoming unbalanced. Eden had made a minsterial broadcast on television, then the Foreign Secretary, Selwyn Lloyd, had made one on radio and the Opposition was now pressing for its view to be heard. The BBC decided that Menzies would effectively be the third Government spokesman in a row and turned him down. William Clark broke the news to the Prime Minister. 'I rang Eden on the scrambler and his reply or something else burned out the telephone. He demanded I go straight over to Chequers. I was there at the speed of light. Eden simply exploded with wrath. When I finally picked myself up from the ceiling, I was able to say that I felt I shouldn't do any more: it was really up to him to take it up with the BBC.'

Eden professed to feeling totally unable to understand the BBC's decision. He discounted the fact that both he and Selwyn Lloyd had already broadcast – referring dismissively to his own Foreign Secretary as 'some other speaker who shared my point of view' – and he described the refusal to invite Menzies as 'insulting to a Commonwealth Prime Minister'. He was not content to let the matter rest and, to his good fortune, he had a special personal contact at the highest level of the Corporation. The Chairman of the Board of Governors was Sir Alexander Cadogan, who had spent most of his professional life in the Foreign Office and had ended up as Permanent Secretary under Eden. Churchill had appointed him BBC Chairman three years earlier. Cadogan was also a director of the Suez Canal company and, according to his biographer, 'shared Eden's view of Nasser as an unscrupulous demagogue of paranoiac tendencies'. Now Eden rang Cadogan to insist that Menzies appear on television. 'Cadogan was devoted to Anthony Eden,' says Harman Grisewood, who was the Chief Assistant to the BBC's Director-General. 'All his inclinations as an old civil servant were to do what the Prime Minister of the day felt was in the national interest. It was a natural inclination for him to give in to the pressures.' According to William Clark, 'Throughout the Suez crisis Eden used the telephone as an instrument of persecution on poor old Alex Cadogan, who did not know how to refuse calls from the Prime Minister.' It achieved Eden's purpose over Menzies. Cadogan reversed the BBC's original decision, which he privately described as 'nonsensical'.

Menzies was invited to make a ministerial broadcast. The producer was an intense twenty-five-year-old Wykehamist – already marked out by the BBC in the manner of the Civil Service as a high-flyer – Alasdair Milne. He and Grace Wyndham Goldie had gone to make arrangements for the programme in what she described as 'the bottle-littered bedroom in the Savoy Hotel of the Australian Prime Minister's public relations officer'. In his broadcast, Menzies echoed Eden's words: 'to leave our vital interest to the whim of one man would be suicidal'. Eden found Menzies' broadcast 'admirable' and wrote secretly to Churchill: 'The BBC is exasperating me by leaning over backwards to be what they call neutral and to present both sides of the case, by which I suppose they mean our country's and the Dancing Major's.'

Once Eden had finally decided that he was going to use force to take back the Canal from Nasser, he had no doubts about the BBC's proper role. He wanted the Corporation to become an arm of war. 'He really believed that anything that was said pro the enemy and any questioning of the motives, legality and the rightness of our cause were acts of sabotage and treason,' said William Clark. He passed the Prime Minister's views on to Harman Grisewood, who was effectively running the BBC in the absence at a broadcasting conference in Australia of the Director-General, Sir Ian Jacob. A week before British troops went into action Grisewood was summoned to the Ministry of Defence. He was shown the War Room and told that Eden planned to introduce all the apparatus of wartime censorship. 'This created a great difficulty for the BBC because it was not a national war in the sense of the Second World War,' said Grisewood. 'The country was very deeply divided. The people had a right to hear the arguments of the Government and the Opposition – of those who opposed the whole venture altogether.'

The Prime Minister naturally saw things very differently. He felt that the television companies, and in particular the BBC, were purposely seeking to destroy national unity by showing anti-war demonstrations and interviewing critics of his policies. 'Are they enemies or just socialists?' the Prime Minister demanded of William Clark. The press secretary noted in his diary Eden's growing 'passion and determination to teach the BBC a lesson' and that Cabinet ministers were 'looking up the rules to see how they could control broadcasting'. Eden was also greatly concerned that the BBC's overseas radio service both reported his critics' views and carried extracts from editorials in newspapers like the *Manchester Guardian* and the *News Chronicle* that were opposed to the use of force. He felt that such broadcasts would undermine the morale of British troops waiting at Mediterranean bases to go into action. 'Eden believed', said Harman Grisewood, 'that once our forces were involved, we were fighting the Queen's enemies. There was no more to be said.' As he shaved and dressed, Eden would hold early morning meetings with Clark and fulminate against the BBC. 'Eden's worries resulted in innumerable schemes to discipline the BBC,' said Clark, 'I tried to make clear to the Corporation just how near to an explosion relations with the Prime Minister were getting.'

In his Number 10 office towards the end of October, Clark passed on a specific warning to Harman Grisewood: 'William told me that the Prime Minister had instructed the Lord Chancellor to prepare an instrument which would take over the BBC altogether and subject it wholly to the will of the Government. The next I heard was that Eden had found the draft inadequate and the Lord Chancellor had been asked to prepare something stronger.' Grisewood did not know where to turn. With the Director-General still in Australia, the logical person to consult was the Chairman, Sir Alexander Cadogan. But he had already made his attitude clear to Grisewood. 'Cadogan said to me one day, twirling his moustaches and looking very impressive indeed, "Can you imagine how dispiriting it would be for our boys" – that was the phrase used at the time – "to go into action having heard that the leader of the Opposition opposes the war altogether. Of course we should suppress anything of that kind." I think that had I passed Eden's threat on to him he would have said: "Oh yes, I think that's a jolly good idea. I think the BBC ought to be taken over in wartime like that." '

Grisewood was still trying to decide how best to react to Eden's threat, when the whole Suez affair reached its climax. BBC television once again came directly into the Prime Minister's line of fire. On 31 October, following the Israeli attack on Egypt, Eden's government ordered the bombing of Egyptian airfields; it was the obvious prelude to an invasion to recapture the Canal. The Prime Minister insisted that he should make another television appearance to rally the public behind military action. 'He felt that the rules about ministerial broadcasts did not really apply to prime ministers,' said William Clark. 'Eden wanted to put the national point of view. He would appear as the summation of our national interests without the right of reply by the Opposition, which he felt ought not to be in opposition at all.' What Eden wanted above all, according to Harman Grisewood, 'was that the mantle of Churchill should now enwrap him. And he would appear on the screen as a war leader, supported by the nation, the father of the people, the hero of the hour.'

It was the first broadcast live from Number 10. After the previous botch at Lime Grove, William Clark had persuaded the BBC to install a special coaxial cable in Downing Street. All his life, Eden assured viewers, he had been a man of peace. He was still the same man, but Britain had no alternative but to intervene militarily 'to put out the forest fire' of the fighting between Egypt and Israel. The Labour leader, Hugh Gaitskell, watched the broadcast at the home of the Editor of ITN, Geoffrey Cox. 'Gaitskell lived only a couple of blocks away from my home in Hampstead. He had no television set. I received a telephone call: could he come round and listen to Eden on mine? He did so.' Immediately Eden's broadcast ended, Gaitskell rang the BBC demanding to exercise his right of reply to Eden on television the following evening. To his intense fury, the Labour leader came up against the 'medieval theology' of the rules that had been agreed by the political parties and the BBC over ministerial broadcasts.

Under the rules, the Opposition could request a right of reply, if it considered a ministerial broadcast controversial. If the Government did not accept this, it was up to the BBC to act as a kind of television ombudsman: it had to assess the polemical level and 'exercise its own judgement' whether to grant a right of reply. This guaranteed that, with feelings running high, the BBC would be pitched into the party political arena. When Gaitskell rang requesting the right of reply, the BBC told him he had first to take it up with the Government through 'the usual channels' – in other words, the Whips' Office. The Government Chief Whip was Edward Heath: 'Eden had asked me to say that it was not right for Gaitskell to reply to his broadcast. Eden was Prime Minister and he had a right to address the whole country when we were at war.' Heath claimed that Eden's broadcast had been as uncontroversial as possible and rejected Gaitskell's request.

Gaitskell then rang Harman Grisewood in high dudgeon insisting that he be given the right to reply. The BBC was being crushed in a political vice. On the one side, an increasingly jumpy and splenetic Prime Minister was seeking ways to take the Corporation over and keep dissenting voices off the air. On the other, the Leader of the Opposition was demanding with menaces the right to attack the Prime Minister on television, with our troops about to go into battle. But Cadogan refused to make up his mind, telling Grisewood he was going to bed. Two hours later, at one in the morning, Gaitskell was on the telephone again angrily demanding that Grisewood wake Cadogan at once for a decision. The Opposition leader was in no way mollified when Grisewood volunteered to tell him the Chairman's ruling 'at a Christian hour' in the morning.

Eventually Cadogan decided that Gaitskell should be allowed to broadcast. It was a decision that further enraged Eden and did nothing to placate Gaitskell, who felt he was only receiving what was his by right. With British troops due to go into action at first light the next morning, Gaitskell's broadcast did nothing to stiffen their morale. He sought to widen the divisions in the Tory party, appealing 'to those Conservatives who like us are shocked and troubled by what is happening. . . . Only one thing now can save the honour and reputation of our country. Parliament must repudiate the Government's policy. The Prime Minister must resign.' It was the first time television had ever shown an Opposition leader demanding a prime minister's resignation.

William Clark immediately rang Grisewood to pass on Eden's instruction that the more inflammatory parts of Gaitskell's broadcast should not be included on the BBC's Arabic Service. But it was all too late: the broadcast had already been transmitted simultaneously to the Middle East. And the Anglo-French invasion of Suez was in any case doomed to débâcle as the Americans opposed it. In the Commons the following week, a group of Conservative MPs launched an acrimonious attack on the whole of the BBC's coverage of Suez charging that there had been deliberate distortions in news bulletins, press reviews and other current affairs programmes; presentation of the crisis had been biased by omission, exaggeration, the use of voice, tone and an unrepresentative choice of people for interview. Tory MPs were to repeat the same sort of charges during the Falklands crisis nearly thirty years later. As our troops go into battle, the first casualty is often the BBC.

Grace Wyndham Goldie, who produced Gaitskell's and both of Eden's Suez broadcasts, was herself at the receiving end of many of the pressures on the BBC from the politicians. 'Most governments at moments of international or national stress would like to be in control of broadcasting and ensure that only their own policies are heard, by suppressing those of the Opposition,' said Mrs Goldie. 'This is peculiarly likely to happen when governments are convinced they are acting wisely and in the national interest. Suez is a salutary warning of the lengths to which a political party may go when in power to prevent the broadcasting of any opinions but its own.' Despite the formidable pressures and threats against it from the Prime Minister, the BBC managed to maintain its independence – just. Had the crisis gone on much longer, or had Eden emerged victorious, it might well have been a different story.

Suez had two other main effects on the relationship between the broadcasters and the politicians. For the first time in a major crisis a prime minister had used television rather than radio or the press as the main means of addressing the nation: it marked the start of a growing trend. And it was to mean that prime ministers would appear to the voters as both more human and more vulnerable figures – concerned, like Anthony Eden with his glasses, almost as much about what they looked like, as what they said. Suez also swept away the Fourteen Day Rule. With the crisis dominating parliamentary business every day for weeks on end, the television companies decided completely to ignore the Rule. The Prime Minister had enough battles on his hands already with the BBC to seek to enforce it. As the Suez crisis ended the Government suspended the Rule – at first for six months, then indefinitely.

By today's standards, television coverage of Suez was minimal. In the first days of the crisis, the only film available of the Canal were aerial shots taken during the Second World War by the Central Office of Information. And though Eden spoke directly to the cameras twice in four months, he did not answer a single question on television. 'It is extraordinary to think that throughout the Suez crisis he was never interviewed in the way that prime ministers are interviewed on television nowadays – quite toughly,' says Sir Ian Trethowan. At the time of Suez, Trethowan was the Lobby correspondent of the *News Chronicle*. Although his newspaper's editorial line was strongly opposed to Eden's policy, Trethowan himself was pro-Suez. When William Clark resigned as the Prime Minister's press secretary immediately after the cease-fire in November, Eden offered the job to Trethowan. The future Director-General of the BBC might have been able to bring his own presentational skills to the service of the beleaguered Prime Minister, but he declined the offer – 'mainly because I have never believed that journalists convert well into PR men, but I was rather touched.' Doubtless Trethowan also perceived that Eden's days at Downing Street were numbered.

Two months after ordering British troops into Suez, Anthony Eden resigned. He was convinced that television, which he had been the first Prime Minister to seek to use as a tool of government, had in the end been used against him and contributed to his downfall. The man who took over had also been one of the Tories' earliest TV performers. But unlike Eden, Harold Macmillan disliked appearing on television. His début in 1953 had reminded him of the trenches in the First World War. He had turned down a request to appear on the BBC general election results programme in 1955, telling the producer: 'I don't think I look very good on that thing and I don't want to have any more to do with it.'

But in the next seven years, Harold Macmillan was to become highly skilled as a television performer and extremely adept at presenting the cameras with the favourable images of himself and his government. He came to Downing Street in January 1957 with the Conservatives in total disarray. Suez had split the Party and many Tories had already written off the next general election. Within two years, Macmillan would transform the Government's political prospects; his use of television was a major factor in the transformation. From his initial fear and loathing of the TV cameras, he became a master of the medium. As Macmillan put it himself: 'This old dog has had to learn new tricks.'

CHAPTER 5

Old Mac's new TV tricks

*'People of my age were brought up on the hustings. Now with
television, it is like playing lawn tennis and there isn't anybody
to hit the ball back from the other side of the net.'*

Harold Macmillan

Before Harold Macmillan, no one had ever heard of a prime minister's TV
image. He was the first to project one. Yet on the day he reached Number
10, Macmillan felt he could ignore television altogether. He had become
Prime Minister against the expectation of almost all the press. In those days
'the customary processes of consultation' by which the new Tory leader
would emerge were simply handled. The Lord Privy Seal, Lord Salisbury,
had consulted each of his fellow members of the Cabinet with the exception
of the outgoing Prime Minister, Anthony Eden, and of the two main
candidates to succeed him – Rab Butler and Harold Macmillan. 'Well,
which is it – Wab or Hawold?' Salisbury had asked in his aristocratic drawl.
Hawold it was. And that evening the new Prime Minister took his Chief
Whip, Ted Heath, to dine at the Turf Club, without imagining that the
television cameras would follow them.

'Unhappily,' said Macmillan, 'the news was obtained by some source or
another and as we came out our way was barred by all the usual paraphernalia
of press and television to which I had not yet become accustomed. I thought
that my guest and I were entitled to a bottle of champagne and some game
pie. The food, the drink, and above all the place were seized upon with
avidity as the symbols of a reactionary regime.' Over the years, Macmillan
would turn his Edwardian sense of style and his patrician manner to his
political advantage. His first night as Prime Minister was a graphic reminder
that from now on he would always be on parade: that he would have to come
to terms with the medium of television, which he neither liked nor trusted.

Six days after becoming Prime Minister, Macmillan made his first
television broadcast. It was a far from happy experience. After the humiliation of Suez, the Tory party was at its lowest ebb since 1940. Macmillan
had decided to keep Selwyn Lloyd, the most obvious scapegoat for Suez,
on at the Foreign Office where he returned, according to *The Economist*,
'down a long, cold arch of raised eyebrows'. That decision together with

the bad publicity over the Prime Minister's dinner with Heath had already helped persuade a number of Tory MPs – and even some of his own Cabinet colleagues – that Lord Salisbury had received the wrong answer to his question. Macmillan feared his government might only survive for a few weeks. He felt that to try to steady both his party and the country he had to make a ministerial broadcast on television, much as he would have preferred otherwise.

His first problem was how he could best get his message across. Macmillan had become an effective public speaker, relying on notes which he wrote on cards in the style of a psalm – with the key words and phrases indented. He wanted to use this method for his first broadcast as Prime Minister. 'At this time,' said Macmillan, 'the techniques of television were still primitive and even the most consummate politicians were not yet expected to be consummate actors. The chief problem appeared to be whether one should learn the statement by heart and deliver it as from the stage, or whether one should speak from a text – a method which had its own pitfalls, especially on any foreign issue. I proposed to the expert advisers who organized the performance that I should behave perfectly naturally and not be ashamed to look down at notes from time to time. This however was then regarded as a great breach of decorum.' The Prime Minister's expert advisers included Charles Hill, the Postmaster-General and former 'Radio Doctor', George Christ from Conservative Central Office, described by Macmillan as 'a man with real genius – a brilliant political journalist who was already an intimate friend and valued colleague', and Harold Evans, his press secretary (later knighted and no relation to the former Editor of the *Sunday Times*), who became a shrewd image-builder. They were able to offer the Prime Minister a way out of the dilemma over his notes.

Harold Macmillan should become the first prime minister to use the new machine – which TV presenters and newsreaders now relied on – the teleprompter. His script would be reflected by a series of mirrors, invisible to the audience, which would enable the Prime Minister to read it while looking straight at the camera. Eden's advisers had rejected the teleprompter as it made him roll his eyeballs and look demented; now Macmillan found other disadvantages. 'First, being very short-sighted, I could not see it; second if I could just manage to read the words by screwing up my eyes, I presented the appearance of a corpse looking out of a window.' In the end, for his first broadcast, Macmillan hit upon his own version of a technique that newsreaders have developed over the years. He would try to read the words off the teleprompter but would also regularly look down at his notes. The newsreaders look down solely to appear more natural; the Prime Minister consulted his psalm-style notes because he could barely read the teleprompter and, like Eden at the time of Suez, did not want to put his reading glasses on in public. In his broadcast, Macmillan called for an end to defeatist talk about Britain being a second- or third-class power: 'What nonsense. This is a great country and do not let us be ashamed to say so . . . There is no reason to quiver before temporary difficulties. Twice in my lifetime I have heard the same old tale about our being a second-rate power, and I have lived to see the answer.'

The producer of the ministerial broadcast for the BBC was a voluble Welshman who had won an MC in 1944, Huw Wheldon. He was unimpressed by the Prime Minister's performance. Immediately after the broadcast, Wheldon had a meeting with Harold Evans, and the Chief Whip, Ted Heath. 'I held out very strongly', wrote Wheldon afterwards in a confidential report to the BBC, 'that the Prime Minister's script as written was totally inadequate. I pointed out that it could not be spoken by one human being to another without embarrassment to both parties.' Wheldon then went on to read out the script in his histrionic style to Evans and Heath, who were very disturbed by the demonstration. 'They acknowledged that the Prime Minister could not possibly have read the script as it stood to any group of people in the world,' said Wheldon. 'It was not a question of changing words here and there. Fundamentally it is a question of not taking the job seriously. It seems to me this convention in ministerial broadcasts of speaking sentences into a camera which no human being could possibly speak directly to a postman, or a professor or a housewife or a child is made all the worse by the use of the teleprompter, which allows the whole statement to be given in much the same way as a press communiqué.'

Wheldon's remonstrations had a powerful effect. Macmillan realized he would have to take television seriously. Unlike Eden, who had thought his own good looks and charm would translate themselves on to the screen without effort, Macmillan was prepared to think about television. At the age of sixty-two, the Prime Minister realized he had to alter the techniques of public speaking that had served him throughout his political life. 'People of my age were brought up on the hustings where something comes back to you from the audience all the time,' said Macmillan in an interview after he retired. 'Now with television, it is like playing lawn tennis and there isn't anybody to hit the ball back from the other side of the net; nothing comes back. And it took me a long time to learn – I think I got a little better towards the end – and I remember someone once said to me "there will be twelve million people watching tonight". And I just had the sense to say to myself, no, no, no, two people – at the most three. What you have to remember is that on television you are talking to two people – that is quite different from talking to two thousand people. It is a conversation, not a speech. And those politicians who didn't learn that continue to make speeches into it; it is not effective.'

It was to take Macmillan a long time before he learnt the difficult art of speaking informally into a television camera. Much of his early practice was conducted at London Airport. 'It had become the major gateway through which politicians, from the Prime Minister downwards, increasingly came and went,' says the former Editor of ITN, Sir Geoffrey Cox. 'A great many pioneering interviews were done in the incongruous setting of the VIP lounge at London Airport; it was hung with an extraordinary series of curtains, which made it look like a sitting room in a seaside boarding house. But ministers tended to speak a great deal more freely there than would have been the case if we had ever let them get back into Whitehall. It became the setting where television interviewing stretched its fledgling muscles.' The growth of television coincided almost exactly with the growth of air travel.

Macmillan himself became the first of the jet-age prime ministers; he flew further and more often than any of his predecessors. He was the subtle father of shuttle diplomacy. And he discovered that there was nothing television liked so much as a peripatetic premier. 'Genuine political activity as distinct from amateur theatricals is hard to televise,' said John Whale, then an ITV reporter, 'so journeys by heads of government are very useful to television. They are international relations made visible.' At every airport, Macmillan would find the cameras waiting for a statement or an interview from him; there was no escape from the VIP lounge lizards of television.

'Television and jet aeroplanes, these are the things that have made the life of a modern prime minister almost impossible,' Macmillan half-jokingly complained in a speech, 'because it is in airports that television chooses to lurk. You go by sea, you go by road, you go by rail, nobody bothers you very much. But if you go by air, there it is – that hot, pitiless, probing eye. After fourteen hours of travel you get off the airplane, wanting only a shave and a bath – oh no, you are cornered. The lights in your eyes, the cameras whizzing. You put up your hand to shade your eyes and the next day there you are in the *Daily Clarion* looking weary, old, worried, over a caption which implies you are past it. Alternatively, you pull yourself together and you try to look young and buoyant. You say something which you think will be apposite and enlightening. And what happens? Why, in the editing your carefully chosen phrases are all boiled down to fifty seconds and focused on the aggressive question to which you fumbled the answer. You can't win.'

It was in fact through an airport television appearance that Macmillan first began to win over the public. In January 1958, just a year after taking office, the Prime Minister suffered a shattering political blow. The whole of his Treasury team resigned – Peter Thorneycroft, whom Macmillan had chosen to replace himself as Chancellor, along with his two deputies, Enoch Powell and Nigel Birch. They were prototype monetarists seeking to curb the expansionist Macmillan. To lose one Treasury minister could be accounted a misfortune, but for all three to go at once was a calamity. Macmillan came into his Private Office at Number 10 that morning to rehearse the show of nonchalance he intended to produce for the television cameras at London Airport the following day. According to his private secretary, John Wyndham (later Lord Egremont), 'the Prime Minister put on a studied act, affecting to ignore the resignations and spending an inordinate time discussing slowly and calmly any amount of trivialities, occasionally ringing a bell for a secretary and dictating a totally unimportant letter.'

Macmillan was due to fly out on a tour of the Commonwealth. In a show of solidarity for the TV cameras, the whole of the Cabinet, including his new Chancellor, Derrick Heathcoat-Amory, had arrived to see him off from the airport. First the Prime Minister had to talk about the resignations. 'In speaking to the TV and press,' Macmillan later admitted, 'I made a carefully prepared statement: I referred to some recent difficulties at home which had caused me a little anxiety. However, I thought the best thing to do was to settle these little local difficulties. I was conscious of seeking to minimize the crisis.' To refer to the unprecedented resignation of the whole of his Treasury team as 'little local difficulties' was a masterpiece of understatement. It was exactly in keeping with the impression of calm that Macmillan had sought to create from his first day in Downing Street – to contrast with the frenetic unpredictability of Eden's final days.

Macmillan had banned his driver from using the special horn in the prime ministerial car which Eden had insisted should continuously sound his advance. Political journalists reported, after a Lobby briefing by Harold Evans, that the Prime Minister was so coolly in control that he found time each night to read Trollope. And Macmillan produced a motto for his Private Office: 'Quiet, calm deliberation disentangles every knot.' It was all part of a carefully created image of 'unflappability'. In fact, Macmillan was a highly emotional man, who would suffer agonies of nerves and was sometimes physically sick before big speeches or television performances. But he was a good enough actor to hide them in public. He had first adopted an air of nonchalance – known as the Balliol manner – to cover his shyness at Oxford more than forty years earlier. And throughout his public life he had retained a theatrical façade, which was now serving him well on the new medium of television.

Macmillan's style, mannerisms and personality were on more public display than those of any previous prime minister. Television's coverage of politics was expanding as the early restrictions and inhibitions were disappearing. Macmillan himself had given the process impetus. The Fourteen Day Rule had been suspended for an experimental period of six months after Suez; in July 1957, the Prime Minister announced in Parliament that he was suspending the Rule indefinitely. One of the taboos on the close-up coverage of politics was ended and a second was now coming under critical scrutiny.

The weekend after Macmillan had flown away from his little local difficulties to his Commonwealth tour, a secret conclave of the most senior figures in politics and broadcasting met at Nuffield College in Oxford. Rab Butler, Home Secretary, and Ted Heath, the Chief Whip, were there for the Conservatives; Hugh Gaitskell, the Party leader, and Tony Wedgwood Benn for Labour; and Jo Grimond, the Liberal leader, along with the Directors-General of the BBC and ITA and other political broadcasters and academics all attended. They were discussing whether television should be allowed to cover elections. They felt the subject was so sensitive that they prepared a totally anodyne statement for the press, if it found out about the meeting: 'Some politicians and other public figures are staying in the College this weekend to take part in a discussion on the problems of public information in a democracy.' The participants were too coy to bring themselves to mention the word television.

At the meeting, two of the most experienced political broadcasters, David Butler and Robert McKenzie, challenged the received BBC wisdom that only by total abstention could the Corporation guarantee impartiality during an election campaign. 'If that were true, suicide would be the only route to total impartiality,' said Butler. The politicians could see some advantages to themselves if they agreed to television coverage of elections but, according to the minutes of the meeting, 'it was feared that a great expansion might lead to confusion in the minds of the public and, while some participants thought they should proceed with caution, others said there was only a choice between a blackout and a spotlight.' Within days of the academic discussion, the television authorities and the politicians had a real live test case.

There was to be a by-election in the Lancashire town of Rochdale. This was the heart of the territory, tagged Granadaland, of the most politically adventurous of the new ITV stations. No Granada representative had attended the Nuffield meeting and the company now decided that Rochdale was the ideal place to break the taboo on election coverage. The BBC thought differently and put out a statement which announced grandly: 'We do not intend to depart from our usual practice in by-elections that we do not influence voters nor report the campaigns in news bulletins.' Granada was contemptuous of the BBC's continuing self-denying ordinance on election coverage: 'This extraordinary lacuna is best explained by John Reith's belief that some things were best left to God and others to the State,' said Granada's Denis Forman (later knighted), who was to become the company's Chairman. Granada determined to test the belief that election coverage was illegal under the 1949 Representation of the People Act – as did ITN.

Rochdale, a Conservative marginal seat, was a crucial test of support for Macmillan's government. Unlike the BBC, ITN felt it could not ignore the by-election: its Editor, Geoffrey Cox, sent a film crew to Rochdale. The scenes of the candidates walking around the constituency and knocking on doors appear very familiar today. At the time, Cox feared they would land him in jail. He was subject to dark threats that at any moment his crew might be arrested. But Cox went ahead with the first television by-election report. 'We called the bluff of the political parties and people found that the sky did not fall in and the Attorney-General did not issue a writ,' said Cox.

In its report, ITN described what the three candidates stood for, but Cox felt he could not go so far as to show them actually speaking. In part, this was an act of sensible caution. The Liberal candidate at Rochdale had been until a few weeks earlier an ITN newscaster – Ludovic Kennedy. A number of politicians had already turned into television broadcasters; he was the first to attempt the reverse transformation. ITN did not want to be accused of promoting Kennedy or of giving him, an experienced broadcaster, an unfair advantage over the other two candidates. Granada did not have the same concerns. 'After wrestling with the law and with the political parties, we at last gained sanction for a broadcast in which the three candidates were allowed to present their views for a precisely timed period on television,' said Denis Forman. Granada followed this with a press conference programme in which the three candidates were questioned by local journalists. On polling day there was a record turn-out – nearly 81 per cent of the electorate.

'The televoter is born,' wrote Kenneth Allsop in the *Daily Mail*, 'here is proof in dramatic, simple figures that overnight Rochdale has changed the nature of democratic politics. Theorizing may now end. Television is established as the new hub of the hustings.' In the by-election the Conservatives were pushed into a bad third place. Harold Macmillan calculated that the Liberals, who came a close second to Labour, had picked up sixteen thousand votes direct from the Conservatives. He attributed this, in part, to Ludovic Kennedy's television prominence: 'the Liberal candidate represented the new and coming power in British political life'. The Prime

59

Minister realized that the ending of the taboo on election coverage meant that the new and coming power would for the first time play a major independent role in the next general election campaign – whenever he decided to call it. No longer would the parties have the screens to themselves for their election broadcasts and no longer could the politicians rely on television to maintain a discreet silence about the course of the campaign. A greater spotlight than ever before would fall on the Prime Minister himself; the histrionic Harold Macmillan was not unhappy at the prospect.

In the meantime, he had decided to make full use of television to build up his standing in the eyes of the electorate. 'Macmillan was well aware'. said an early biographer, Anthony Sampson, 'as Baldwin had been with the wireless thirty years before, that the new medium gave him a unique chance to by-pass the Press Lords and project himself – and nobody else – to the nation.' The chief problem was how best he should deal with little local difficulties. He knew that on his return from his six-week Commonwealth tour, in February 1958, he would be expected to answer questions at London Airport about the calamitous Rochdale defeat two days earlier. He decided to filibuster. 'Before any of us had a chance to ask the Prime Minister anything,' said Reginald Bosanquet who was there for ITN, 'he had taken out his prepared notes and launched himself on an old-fashioned type of speech to the TV cameras. It was a comprehensive review of his impressions of the Commonwealth countries he had visited. My heart not only sank but almost disappeared. He went on and on until eventually our cameraman said: "Christ, we're running out of film." I felt the time had come to interrupt – no easy decision to make.'

'Sir,' said Bosanquet, 'as time is short, could we question you on a domestic matter which I think is uppermost in our minds at the moment?' 'If you must,' Macmillan protested. Bosanquet then asked how much of a setback the Rochdale result was. Macmillan replied that he had not had the opportunity to discuss it with his colleagues; he was disappointed but not discouraged. And the Prime Minister, wearing the Guards' tie that he normally put on in time of trouble, added: 'after all, in war or politics a single engagement does not settle a whole campaign. I propose to go on and do our job.' 'Mr Gaitskell has said that your job is to resign.' 'I've heard leaders of the Opposition say that before,' replied Macmillan with a smile, 'in fact I think I have said it quite often myself. It is what you might call common form.'

It was the first time that a political leader had ever had to explain away a bad election result in an airport interview. But Macmillan was not unhappy with his performance; he agreed a week later to take part in a programme which would ensure that the relationship between television and prime ministers would never be the same again. Until that time no British premier had ever been interviewed in a TV studio. Their appearances had been limited to brief airport news interviews and to party political or ministerial broadcasts, which they controlled. Now Macmillan had effectively agreed to walk naked into the studio: he had accepted an invitation to appear on the BBC *Press Conference* programme and three days later on ITN's *Tell the People*.

The BBC gave him an easy ride. The format of *Press Conference* with three journalists asking questions was an early example of a rule that television producers have continued to ignore: the greater the number of interviewers, the less effective the questioning. Macmillan was asked almost exclusively about his Commonwealth tour and was able to reproduce much of what he had prepared for his airport filibuster. *The Times* described Macmillan's questioners as 'a restrained group'. ITN determined on a completely different approach. Macmillan would be interviewed by Robin Day alone, who would not confine himself to the Commonwealth. He planned to ask about the future of the Foreign Secretary, Selwyn Lloyd – a question dominating the political press. Lloyd had become target number one for many Conservatives – particularly after an inept parliamentary performance shortly before the Macmillan interviews.

The Prime Minister arrived at Television House and was delighted to find that, like him, the ITN producer was wearing a Guards' tie. Macmillan was taken up to the studio, where Robin Day was waiting for him. 'As the cameras were being lined up,' says Day, 'Mr Macmillan derived considerable amusement from the seating arrangements. He complained that whereas he was sitting on a hard, upright seat, I was enthroned behind the table in a comfortable swivel chair with well-padded arms.' This, said Mr Macmillan, seemed to symbolize the new relationship between the politician and TV interviewer. He felt as if he were 'on the mat'. Day offered to swap chairs. 'Not at all, not at all,' said Macmillan, 'I know my place.'

With his horn-rimmed glasses and spotted bow tie, Day had already become a familiar television figure. His forthright style of questioning, developed in his short time at the Bar, contrasted sharply with the deference that was still the norm among BBC news reporters. 'How do you feel, Prime Minister,' asked Day, 'about the criticism which has been made in the last few days – in Conservative newspapers particularly – of Mr Selwyn Lloyd, the Foreign Secretary?' Macmillan's answer was unsurprising. He felt that Selwyn Lloyd was a very good Foreign Secretary who had done his work extremely well. 'If I did not think so, I would have made a change. I do not intend to make a change simply as a result of pressure. I don't believe that is wise. It doesn't accord with my idea of loyalty.'

Day's question brought him a great deal of notoriety. The *Daily Telegraph* wondered 'whether the Prime Minister should have been asked what he thought of his Foreign Secretary before a camera which showed every flicker of the eyelid. Who is to draw the line at which the effort to entertain stops?' The *Daily Mirror* claimed that Macmillan had absolutely no alternative but to defend Selwyn Lloyd: 'What else *could* he say about his colleague? Mr Robin Day by his skill as an examiner has been responsible for prolonging in office a man who probably doesn't want the job and is demonstrably incapable of doing it. The Idiots' Lantern is getting too big for its ugly gleam.' The *Daily Express* described the interview as 'certainly the most vigorous cross-examination a prime minister has been subjected to in public'.

Ted Heath, the Government Chief Whip, complained to ITN. 'He was angry about Day's question on Selwyn Lloyd and felt we had broken the Queensberry Rules in putting it,' said Geoffrey Cox, 'but we were at that stage engaged in changing the Queensberry Rules – that there should be no inhibition on any issue in the public mind that was put to a politician who had come into the studio.' In his memoirs published in 1971, Macmillan did not mention Day by name, but said he had been asked 'a somewhat truculent question by one of the new class of cross-examiners which has since become so popular'. But despite its truculence the question had not come as a surprise to Macmillan, who had worked out his answer in advance. Robin Day says: 'As it happens, I know the Prime Minister expected a question about his Foreign Secretary and was fully prepared to defend him.'

Day's encounter with Macmillan set the pattern for future prime ministerial interviews on television. The seating arrangements in the ITN studio, which Macmillan had noted so wryly, symbolized the unblushing emergence into the limelight of the belligerent inquisitor. But often the blood on the studio floor would turn out to be only tomato ketchup. Over the years Robin Day was to ask many good questions of prime ministers; he was to get many fewer good answers.

Macmillan emerged from the Robin Day interview with his political reputation enhanced. The *Yorkshire Post* reported: 'Tories will be delighted with the Prime Minister's TV success. Certainly he is no longer just a House of Commons man.' 'He made a tremendous personal impact,' says Day, 'I later heard that he referred to this interview as the first time he had really mastered television.' The Prime Minister had regarded television as a painful necessity for a modern politician – to be avoided whenever possible. Now he was beginning to realize both that he was becoming good at it and that it was working to his political advantage. Three months after his encounter with Robin Day, he agreed to an interview with the doyen of American television, Ed Murrow. It was a great success. Both the BBC and

ITV transmitted the Murrow interview with Macmillan. Opinion polls taken after it showed that the Prime Minister's personal popularity had increased dramatically. 'The Prime Minister appeared relaxed, easy and genial, every inch the favourite fireside politician,' said the *Spectator*. 'A master of urbane conversation – the Premier in fine form,' was the *Manchester Guardian*'s headline.

'Some commentators were kind enough to regard the improvement in our political fortunes as partly due to this interview,' said Macmillan later. 'At that time the appearance of political leaders, which has now become an almost daily feature of the television programmes, was rare and perhaps correspondingly important. At any rate this discussion seemed to have a considerable effect on the public and my stout defence of the greatness of our country and its role in the world was perhaps received with all the greater satisfaction by my many listeners because it was in tune with their deepest feelings.'

The Prime Minister was learning that his style was well suited to a television interview. No longer did he need to appear like a corpse at a window screwing up his eyes to read the teleprompter. In a studio interview he had to look at the person asking the questions rather than directly into the camera. And he was able to make use of the skills as a wit and raconteur he had developed over the years, at the clubs and dining tables of political London. Macmillan was the most clubbable of prime ministers: a member of the Athenaeum, Bucks, the Beefsteak, the Carlton, Pratt's and the Turf – to say nothing of the House of Commons. Now he was discovering that his nights in St James's had been ideal training for the studio interview: his mastery of the aside, the understatement and throw-away line all translated well to the screen. A television audience could not be addressed like a public meeting but it could and should be treated like an intimate dinner companion.

By the middle of 1958 the Prime Minister's abilities on the screen mattered more than ever. The number of homes with TV sets had risen to seven in every ten compared to under one in ten at the start of the decade. According to the opinion polls, television had become the prime source of news and political information for most of the public. And television's coverage of politics was expanding. ITV had started *This Week* to match *Panorama* and the BBC had begun *Tonight*, a daily magazine programme with a populist approach. To counter the liveliness of ITN, even the fusty BBC news was being shaken up by its iconoclastic new Editor-in-Chief, Hugh Carleton Greene. 'There was some sort of rule that news about the Royal Family had to come first,' said Greene. 'And there was a joke going round that a favourite opening for a television news bulletin would have been: "Yesterday, the Queen Mother did something or other." ' Greene wanted to end the BBC's role as the voice of the Establishment – it was to become instead 'the gadfly on the body politic'. There was to be more politics on the air and more politicians subject to searching and sceptical questioning.

Macmillan would increasingly be centre stage. He was determined to make the most of the new opportunities and polish his image with the voters – especially as there would soon have to be a general election. 'The Prime Minister was completely alert to the niceties of presentation, whether in content, style or timing,' said Harold Evans. 'He thought about them deeply and was usually a jump ahead of the rest of us.' Macmillan was now able to display a flair for showmanship to millions at home and on a world stage. Jet travel had increased the scope for personal diplomacy and on his foreign trips, he calculatedly made himself the focus of the cameras' attention. William Deedes, who had appeared with Macmillan in the first ever party political broadcast and was to become his chief publicity adviser, said: 'He entered into the part on television. It was exactly to him like charades in a country house where you all put on funny clothes and funny hats and did an act; that's why he got into the spirit of it.' The Prime Minister never had a better opportunity to put on a funny hat than when he went to Moscow at the start of 1959.

No Western leader had visited the Soviet Union since the end of the Second World War. To the chagrin of the Americans, Macmillan decided that he would take on the role of leader of the alliance and attempt personally to set up a summit conference with the Russians. Accompanied by a press and television corps of over a hundred, Macmillan arrived at Moscow Airport. He walked down the steps of his Comet wearing a twelve-inch-high white fur hat that was guaranteed to catch the TV cameras' attention. 'That wonderful, wonderful hat', the BBC's former political editor, Tommy Thomson, wrote in the *Daily Mail*, 'did more in ten minutes today for Anglo-Soviet relations than diplomatic exchanges do in a month.' In fact, in his eagerness to present an eye-catching picture, Macmillan had given inadvertent offence to his hosts. His white hat was national dress in Finland and not regarded as the most tactful of headgear for Moscow. But as Robin Day, who was covering the visit for ITN, said, 'this was the picture of the year'.

The Soviet Leader, Nikita Khrushchev, mixed charm with insults throughout the trip – which seemed at times doomed to end in humiliation for Macmillan. But the Prime Minister behaved with grace under pressure and television helped him emerge from Moscow with his reputation as a statesman enhanced. On the final night of his visit, he was allowed to make an uncensored broadcast on Soviet television. 'It was a strange feeling', said Macmillan on his return, 'speaking to perhaps millions and millions of people – each phrase translated as you spoke – and feeling perhaps you could get into the minds of people that you had never seen and could never see some picture of what we are like at home.' The British press – both Labour and Conservative – described Macmillan's Moscow broadcast as a triumph: the people of Moscow had learned more from Macmillan in ten minutes than their own leaders had ladled out to them in ten years.

Macmillan's visit ended with a news conference in Moscow's Hall of Journalists. Robin Day chose the occasion to ask the Prime Minister about the date of the general election. 'Unfortunately,' says Day, 'Mr Macmillan must have taken the question as implying that his Moscow visit had been undertaken for electioneering purposes. He delivered a crushing rebuke in front of three hundred reporters. "That is a question from the wrong man in the wrong place." I was well and truly slapped down.' Macmillan returned to London with nothing more tangible to show than an agreed communiqué that his visit had made 'a valuable contribution to understanding between the two sides'. But television coverage of the Moscow trip had greatly enhanced his prominence with the public at the expense both of his Cabinet colleagues and of the Opposition leader, Hugh Gaitskell. Macmillan was able to present himself as prepared to fly anywhere in the cause of world peace – even at the risk of rebuff. A sharp rise in his opinion poll rating showed that 51 per cent of the population regarded him as a statesman; only 20 per cent felt the same about Gaitskell. Nearly thirty years later Margaret Thatcher, a great admirer of Macmillan's style, would follow his example and arrange a much-televised visit to Moscow in the run-up to a general election.

In 1959, the left-wing cartoonist Vicky attempted to deflate the flying premier with irony. But his ironic depiction of 'Supermac' – like Nye Bevan's of 'Macwonder' – rebounded and the image of an all-powerful Prime Minister began to take hold. 'Already decent Tories hang around outside Number 10 Downing Street', mocked the *New Statesman*, 'hoping that Mr Harold Macmillan will touch them and cure their warts. Soon they will be thinking of him not as a human being at all, but as a spirit dwelling on some height.' It was an impression Macmillan was seeking to enhance with the aid of the TV cameras. His flying visits to world capitals were coupled with his identification at home as the Prime Minister of affluence.

In the spring of 1959 he encouraged his Chancellor to take ninepence off the standard rate of income tax, in the biggest give-away budget ever. Having lifted the restrictions on hire purchase, Macmillan was presiding over an unprecedented consumer boom. Encouraged by commercial television, more families were buying cars, washing machines, refrigerators and TV sets than ever before. And for the first time in British politics, the Conservatives were using the new techniques of television advertising to promote the Party and its leader like a commercial product. Lord Hailsham, the rumbustious Tory Chairman, had appointed the advertising agency, Colman, Prentis and Varley, to run a sustained poster and press campaign. The agency targeted young working-class voters. One idealized picture showed a young family cleaning the new car together and another a mother and children eating tea from a well-stocked table while their father watched television. The slogan was: 'Life's better with the Conservatives – Don't let Labour ruin it'.

The advertising campaign had started in 1957 and was part of the most prolonged build-up to a general election ever seen up to that time in British politics. It reached its climax in 1959. In the first nine months of the year, before the Prime Minister announced the date of the election, the Conservatives spent a quarter of a million pounds – then an unprecedented sum by British standards – on press and poster advertising. In the same period, the Prime Minister was regularly on the TV news. He followed his Moscow trip with visits to other European capitals and to Washington. These were interspersed with frequent forays into carefully chosen marginal constituencies at home. Conservative Central Office organized throngs of Tory supporters to cheer the Prime Minister and present a picture of popularity. And in August 1959, just before Macmillan called the election, he mounted his own television spectacular.

The programme came live from Number 10 and starred the Prime Minister and the American President. Macmillan had prevailed on President Eisenhower, an intimate since wartime days, to change his itinerary and include Britain in his tour of continental Europe. The Prime Minister met the President at London Airport and the two men were driven off together in an open car through cheering crowds; the journey to London took two hours. As the victorious Commander of Allied Forces fourteen years earlier, General Eisenhower was a popular figure in Britain. The Prime Minister wanted to make use of that popularity. He invited BBC cameras into Number 10 for a television exclusive and spent hours rehearsing with the President. 'The whole house has been filled with technicians and workmen of all kinds,' Macmillan noted in his diary on 31 August, the day of the broadcast. 'I was nervous about my televised discussion with the President because it would be almost impossible to steer between dangerous indiscretions and mere trivialities.'

The programme began with the BBC announcing in awed tones over a picture of the exterior of Number 10: 'Tonight the President of the United

States is the guest of honour at a dinner party in 10 Downing Street. The President and the Prime Minister are together in the State Drawing Room where the BBC television service now joins them.' Macmillan and Eisenhower, both wearing dinner jackets, sat in armchairs opposite each other. The Prime Minister, with his bow tie tucked under his collar in a style that was to be much imitated by young blades in months to come, began: 'Well, Mr President, I want to start by saying how much we all welcome you here. In the seventeen years of our friendship we have had many frank talks together, and I think we can have a frank talk here at Number 10.' 'Well, Harold,' replied the President, 'let me tell you right away and tell all those good people out there, who have been so kind to me and my party, that we are mighty glad to be back visiting again this lovely country.'

With both men discreetly consulting their notes, the President pronounced that Anglo-American relations had never been stronger and they discussed the possibility of a summit meeting with the Russians. The Prime Minister recalled his Moscow visit earlier in the year and was hopeful; the President less so. On cue, after twenty minutes of the live broadcast, Macmillan said: 'Well, Mr President, I think our time is rather drawing to an end. We mustn't go on too long. But I would like to say – and I know I speak on behalf of every man, woman and child in this country – how very glad we are to have you with us and we welcome you here. And now we have got our guests and among them, I am happy to say, we have Sir Winston Churchill.' The President and Prime Minister then walked towards the adjoining room where the doors were opened by a footman. Viewers saw the dinner guests, who had been watching the conversation on specially installed television sets, break into applause.

In his diary that night, the Prime Minister noted: 'It is all over. The discussion wasn't bad, although we were both nervous. The first account from viewers seems to be – enthusiastic.' Macmillan had succeeded in his aim of projecting himself as a national leader above party politics, on the friendliest first-name terms with the popular American President. He was also the first prime minister to realize how effectively his official home could be used for television. His successors were to follow his example and invite the cameras to film carefully staged happenings behind the normally closed doors of Downing Street, when they thought it electorally advantageous to do so. And the TV authorities, ever grateful for entrée, would happily present viewers with the illusion of access to genuine political events.

Macmillan received good press reviews of his performance with Eisenhower, which would no doubt today have been dubbed 'The Mac 'n' Ike Show'. The Prime Minister denied that he had arranged the President's visit for his own electoral purposes, but admitted it had been a happy coincidence. And exactly a week after he had shown the voters how close his relationship was with the leader of the Western world, Macmillan called the general election. As a result of ITV's breakthrough the previous year at Rochdale, television was no longer a total abstainer from election reporting. Granada offered all candidates in the North a minute and a half each, either at mid-afternoon or late at night, to state their case. 'A very large number of candidates appeared in the *Marathon* programmes, but very few people watched,' said Granada's Denis Forman. 'Who could have foreseen in those artless earnest programmes the beginnings of the great television election machine?'

Faced with the opportunity of covering the election for the first time, the BBC threw caution at the screen. It cancelled the popular, topical *Tonight* programme for the whole of the campaign, and kept all politicians, from the Prime Minister downwards, off *Panorama* and *Press Conference*. Instead it mounted a series of *Hustings* programmes with local audiences questioning party spokesmen. The BBC allowed the three major political parties to select both the audiences and the spokesmen. As two-thirds of the audience was automatically opposed to each of the platform speakers, the resulting programmes were so noisy and rumbustious that it was to be fifteen years before the political parties agreed to appear with voters in a studio again. ITN decided to mount a ten-minute nightly campaign report, but immediately ran into severe practical problems.

Both Macmillan and Gaitskell were due to launch their campaigns with major speeches on the same night. The ITN Editor, Geoffrey Cox, arranged to film the two speeches and proposed to run them at exactly the same length. Unfortunately, he had troubles with the Gaitskell speech: the film was still being processed when the programme ended. 'All we could offer was silent coverage of the Labour leader arriving in Bristol for the meeting,' says Cox. 'The contrast was marked. Harold Macmillan was seen and heard, vigorous, confident and witty against a background of cheering supporters. A silent, overcoated Hugh Gaitskell hurried along a station platform to be greeted by a handful of supporters.' Cox apologized profusely to the Labour party and promised he would do better the next day. He arranged for two cameras and two sets of lights to cover Gaitskell's meeting which, conveniently, was in London. As he was preparing the programme, Cox received a telephone call from George Ffitch, his reporter at the Gaitskell meeting. 'I don't know whether to laugh or cry when I tell you this,' said Ffitch. His film crew had managed to blow all the lights at the meeting as Gaitskell arrived, 'so not only is there no film, there's no meeting either.'

By now the Labour party, long deeply suspicious that ITN and the rest of commercial television were creatures of the Conservatives, had become convinced of a conspiracy to sabotage its election campaign. Cox promised the Party that Gaitskell's third speech would be handsomely covered by ITN; he would personally ensure that nothing went wrong. But lightning struck thrice. The dispatch rider, who was racing to London with film of the Labour leader's speech, skidded off the icy road. He ended in a ditch and the can snapped open, exposing the negative and making the film useless. Cox was in utter despair – fearing all manner of retribution from the Labour party. 'This time I knew no amount of explanations or apologies could meet the situation. Whatever the reasons behind the screen, we were not giving the public a fair picture of the election.' In desperation he turned to the BBC. By chance the Corporation's Head of News, Waldo McGuire, was an old colleague. Cox rang McGuire and pleaded for a favour: could he possibly have a copy of the BBC's film of Gaitskell's speech? McGuire obliged and ITN's editor breathed again.

With today's electronic technology, Cox's problems would not have happened. Gaitskell's speech would be instantly available for transmission, as he made it – no film, no negative, no labs, no processing, no dispatch riders. (Of course, TV high technology is by no means trouble-free: 'to err is human, it takes a computer to really screw things up' is the legend posted in many television control rooms.) But the scarce and primitive technical resources available in 1959 dictated the way both BBC news and ITN covered the campaign. Both sides concentrated almost exclusively on the party leaders – a pattern that was to be followed in subsequent elections, even as technology advanced. 'Because film cameras with sound were relatively scarce in 1959, television news editors were bound to give priority to coverage of the main speech of the day by the party leaders,' says Geoffrey Cox. 'Night after night the leaders were heard as well as seen on the screen, whereas lesser but still prominent figures might appear only in silent film sequences. Harold Macmillan's genial confidence and Hugh Gaitskell's searing earnestness, soon established themselves on the air.'

In future years successive party leaders would exploit television's concentration on them and British general elections would come increasingly to resemble American presidential campaigns. But in 1959 television remained respectfully distanced from the Prime Minister and the Leader of the Opposition. Throughout the campaign there was not a single TV interview with either Macmillan or Gaitskell. In contrast, the 1987 general election was to be dominated by interviews with Margaret Thatcher and Neil Kinnock in news and current affairs programmes as well as at their daily televised press conferences. In 1959, the parties' own election broadcasts remained the prime means of seeking to influence the viewers. Three quarters of the electorate now had sets and there were to be more election broadcasts than ever before. 'This general election can be lost quite easily in one of two television practice studios in Smith Square, Westminster [where both parties had their headquarters],' proclaimed the *Observer*.

The Conservatives began the campaign convinced that they would win the battle of the election broadcasts; over the years they had shown far more professional skills in their use of television than Labour. With the advantage of knowing in advance the date of the election, a team of senior Conservatives prepared their series of broadcasts in great detail. 'We decided that we must do everything right; we thought ahead, we put everything in the can and we had the whole series ready when the election was finally declared,' says Edward Heath, the Government Chief Whip, who was one of the team: 'And when I sat down to watch the first programme, it was absolutely catastrophic – awful. It was meant to be a report on our term in office and there was Mr Macmillan sitting very comfortably in an armchair with his senior Cabinet colleagues around him. And Harold said: "Well now, Rab, I think we've done very well, don't you?" And Rab said, "Oh yes, I think we've done awfully well, particularly the things I've been doing." And Iain Macleod then said, "Yes, well, I've done awfully well and we've all done very well indeed." After we'd had quarter of an hour of this we were driven absolutely up the wall. And the next programme was just as bad.'

The Conservatives' first election broadcast had been filmed seven weeks earlier – well before the Prime Minister had announced the date of the election – at Macmillan's country home, Birch Grove in Sussex. 'It was meant to be an intimate and useful discussion revealing to the public the thoughts of ministers about affairs,' said Macmillan. 'But in spite of all our efforts, it was a failure and seemed stilted and ineffective. Much would therefore depend on later appearances.' And the Prime Minister noted in his diary on 22 September, at the start of the second week of the campaign, 'The Socialists had a very successful TV last night – much better than ours. Gaitskell is becoming very expert.' The Labour party's election broadcasts were masterminded by Tony Wedgwood Benn. A year earlier he had produced a secret blueprint, which was a highly sophisticated document for its time. It showed that Benn had thought long and hard about the techniques of persuasion and manipulation that he was later bitterly to attack television reporters and producers for using.

Benn's central aim was to build up the television image of Hugh Gaitskell as an alternative Prime Minister. To do this, he said, Labour would have to create a linked series of election programmes that would be both credible and attract 'viewer loyalty'. The announcement: 'there now follows an election broadcast . . .' was an 'audience killer', wrote Benn. Labour's programmes had immediately to grab the viewers' attention with strong music and pictures. He gave an example, to which time has lent ironic enchantment: 'Suppose we decide our theme is to be the "Land and the People". Then the opening film sequence should be an atomic power station under construction, seen across fields of waving corn. And our music should be "Jerusalem", sung by a Welsh choir.'

In Benn's view two men were crucial to the success of the election broadcasts. One was the Prime Minister-in-waiting, Hugh Gaitskell. The other was the programmes' chairman, who would fill the same role for the viewer as Richard Dimbleby, the presenter of *Panorama*, or Cliff Michelmore, the presenter of *Tonight*. In his private briefing paper, Benn described the qualities the chairman would need. 'He is the man we shall soon get to know very well – the link between the Party and public – the impresario. He is in a curious way non-political. He is the man who builds up the viewers' confidence throughout the campaign. It is no exaggeration to say that the success or failure of this whole idea will very largely depend upon the person of the television chairman.' And Benn knew exactly the right man for the job – himself. 'The chairman must be friendly, not smarmy. He must set a cracking pace without appearing to rush the important people with whom he will be dealing. He must be the friendly, warm symbol of the Labour party today.'

Benn then went on to describe how the image of Mr Gaitskell would be built up in each programme. 'Whenever the Leader appears – which should be often – he will be seen in a set especially created for him. The construction of this set is of great importance. The desk, the table lamp, the crystal ashtray, the globe, the bust of Keir Hardie, the wallpaper and so on will all create the image of a Prime Minister waiting to take office. Only the Leader himself must ever appear on the Leader's set. This VIP treatment does not mean the Leader must take himself on the same level. He must move with easy informality through his own set.' Gaitskell accepted Benn's proposals but was unhappy when he first saw the Leader's desk. He insisted on a larger one and the whole studio set had to be rebuilt to accommodate it.

Benn had many difficulties in translating his ideas on to the screen. To help him, the Labour party requested that the BBC provide one of its brightest young men, Alasdair Milne, as technical producer of the broadcasts. Milne came from the popular *Tonight* programme and together with Benn ensured that Labour's election broadcasts appeared as similar as possible in style, format and content to *Tonight*. There were short films, animated cartoons, interviews and two regular studio reporters who had become familiar television figures – Christopher Mayhew and Woodrow Wyatt. Benn introduced each programme from what he called 'Labour's operations room', which was, in fact, the regular *Tonight* studio in Lime Grove.

Twenty-eight years later the attacks on Neil Kinnock's election broadcasts echoed those made against Labour in 1959. According to Ludovic Kennedy in a Liberal broadcast, Benn's programmes were 'smooth, glossy and slick – all those bright young Public School Labour boys directing non-existent operations from a non-existent operations room'. Kennedy, again fighting Rochdale, was one of a number of prominent broadcasters who had crossed the studio floor to stand for Parliament in 1959. Robin Day also stood for the Liberals and lost. His fellow ITN newscaster, Christopher Chataway, won for the Conservatives as did Geoffrey Johnson-Smith, the *Tonight* interviewer. But the Tories made little use of their professional broadcasters until the general election was well advanced. 'Many Conservative leaders are openly contemptuous of television,' said Ludovic Kennedy in his broadcast, 'and because they have never learned to use it, we have seen lumbering across our screens in these past ten days, a succession of old party cart-horses, earnest, amiable, smug – and looking, let's face it, as though they've never had it better.'

Kennedy's assessment of the Conservatives' broadcasts was privately shared by Macmillan's campaign managers. The gloom that Ted Heath felt about the favourable press and public reaction to Labour's television campaign turned to black depression when he was shown a preview of the Tories' planned penultimate broadcast. It began with a shot of Lord Home, the Commonwealth Secretary, and Alan Lennox-Boyd, the Colonial Secretary, walking out of 10 Downing Street together. 'One of them said: "Perhaps we had better talk about these foreign people and the colonies," ' remembers Ted Heath. ' "Where shall we go?" And the other said, "I think we'll go to the Club, old boy, don't you?" And in the next picture they were seated in deep leather chairs with their drinks. And I was absolutely horrified at this and I said: "look this can't go on" – by this time we were losing the election, it was going right down.' The Conservatives decided to scrap the whole broadcast, even though they had already advertised it. They called in Christopher Chataway, who presented a much sharper programme, while mocking Labour's style of presentation. There was still a final broadcast to make and it became the subject of anguished discussion among Macmillan's advisers. What form would it take, should it be made by the Prime Minister alone, who should produce it? In an atmosphere of panic, Lord Poole, Deputy Chairman of the Conservative party, decided he had to replace the team who had produced all the other broadcasts and find someone completely new.

'I knew that much would depend on the success or failure of my last broadcast,' said Macmillan. 'I decided to put myself in the hands of a consummate expert in the field – Norman Collins.' Collins was Lord Poole's choice. Since his resignation from the BBC in protest against its restrictive coverage of politics in 1950, Collins had become one of the most powerful figures in commercial television. By 1959, he was both Chairman of ATV and a successful novelist. Never having met Macmillan, Collins insisted that he had to watch the Prime Minister in action and making a campaign speech before he could attempt to produce him. 'The first thing Collins saw was the soldier in him,' said John Wyndham, Macmillan's private secretary, 'because the Prime Minister was bolt upright and had his shoulders squared. Collins realized that he was dealing with a man who understood his own value in public and how to make use of it. He straightaway decided that the Prime Minister, to be shown at his true worth, should do his television broadcast standing up.' Collins put this to Macmillan. 'Oh, I see,' said the Prime Minister, 'but am I allowed to?'

Collins assured the Prime Minister he could do exactly as he wished and was to teach him a great deal more about television before the final broadcast was transmitted. He arranged for Macmillan to come to rehearse in ATV's London studios. 'The plan was to keep on my feet,' said Macmillan, 'and to use as accessories only a globe, a map of Britain and some letters on a table to pick up and read at random. I hoped by this plan to bring a certain life and ease into the performance. But at lunchtime I was depressed. It was an ambitious idea. But could I make it successful? If it did not come off, it would be a crashing failure and the stakes were high.' Collins felt that Macmillan looked stiff and inhibited; a couple of strong drinks and a little subterfuge were needed to enliven the Prime Minister's performance. Collins told Macmillan that his voice was sounding hoarse and the best medicine he knew was port. A bottle was produced and Collins then said it was absolutely essential in the rehearsal for the timing of the broadcast to be exactly right. Macmillan tried again, fortified by the port. 'I hope I shall be better when I do it live, tonight,' said Macmillan. Collins responded: 'Prime Minister you have already done it and you have been recorded.' 'You are a remarkable fellow,' exclaimed Macmillan, 'this is like going to the dentist to have a tooth out and being told it has already been drawn.'

Macmillan's surprised gratitude was understandable. At that time recording was very rare and had never happened for a broadcast from the studio by a party leader. Collins had used the new videotape system and proposed to send the recording to the BBC, which was responsible for transmitting election broadcasts. When they learned of the plan, the BBC's senior officials were affronted. First, they suggested that ATV's technical standards might not be up to their own; second, they feared the Labour party would complain that it had not been offered the chance of recording, and third they wanted the kudos of the Prime Minister coming to their studios to make the broadcast: the Corporation was not just a transmission agency for a tape made on commercial premises. Macmillan asked his private secretary to settle the matter with the BBC. John Wyndham enjoyed affecting an air of aristocratic other-worldliness in his dealings with the Corporation's senior mandarins: 'The Director-General's principal assistant, Mr Harman Grisewood, telephoned to say that the DG wished to speak to me. I – no doubt as the result of a bad line – thought that DG were the initials of someone whom I did not personally know. When this misunderstanding was sorted out it was made plain that the can and not Mr Macmillan would be coming round.'

In the end the Prime Minister decided to go to the BBC studio, 'for fear of a breakdown or even sabotage', as he put it. The BBC had laid on a cold buffet and Macmillan was able to watch his own recording being transmitted. 'It really was a most remarkable broadcast,' says Ted Heath. 'Harold Macmillan was completely relaxed. The most dramatic part was when he walked over to a vast globe and he just turned it round and the whole world revolved as people watched him. And he said, "let me tell you what I want to do about the rest of the world." Dramatic. It changed everything.'

Macmillan's final broadcast drew the highest television audience of the campaign and was generally acclaimed a great success. 'Even the *Daily Mirror* joined the Conservative press in praising it as a real corker and quite the best that had been delivered by a politician of any party,' said John Wyndham. The Prime Minister had made up for the Conservatives' disastrous early campaign broadcasts. In Downing Street on election night, he watched Hugh Gaitskell become the first British party leader to concede defeat on television.

Macmillan was back in office with a majority of over a hundred. In less than three years he had succeeded in lifting his party up from the morass of Suez and taking it to an unprecedented third election victory in a row. The country's booming prosperity was the decisive factor in the election result. Alongside it was the skilled creation of the Prime Minister's image as a political miracle-worker. His 'meet the people' tours in Britain, his role as a globe-trotting seeker after peace, his insouciant dismissal of 'little local difficulties' and his confident assertions that people had never had it so good had all been extensively covered by television. By October 1959, he was better known and better liked than any previous prime minister in history. But Macmillan was soon to discover that those who live by the box, can perish by the box.

CHAPTER 6

The Twentieth-century Torture Chamber

'I have never dared to look at one of my own television performances: not that I am spared anything, because my family are numerous and candid.'

Harold Macmillan, November 1961

'That all went off rather well,' remarked Harold Macmillan on television when the scale of the Conservative victory in the 1959 general election became clear. At first he believed, like Margaret Thatcher a quarter of a century later, that a Tory majority of over a hundred was an unmixed blessing. The Prime Minister was at the height of his political power and reputation. He had learned the skills of projecting himself favourably on television. But he was now to discover the extreme fragility of a TV image. Like a delicate adjustment of focus on a camera, the public perception of a prime minister can subtly alter. Macmillan's unflappability, showmanship and Edwardian *élan* would come to appear complacent, contrived and out of touch. Through television, he had ensured that the public gaze had been more concentrated on him than on any other prime minister in history. He was the major political beneficiary when people felt they had never had it so good, but when things began to fall apart Macmillan was to become public scapegoat number one.

For his first year back in Downing Street, Macmillan enjoyed an extended political honeymoon; there were few signs of the convulsions to come. The Prime Minister saw no need to work on the image that he had been so assiduous in polishing before the election. Harold Evans, his press secretary, wrote in his diary at the end of March 1960, almost six months after the election: 'The tension has gone out of politics and government at the moment, with the large Conservative majority. The Prime Minister no longer feels any compulsions in his public relations and has largely lost interest.' And Evans went on to record a conversation with the Cabinet Secretary: 'Is the PM becoming too godlike? The last PM was ruined by failure, it would be ironical if this one was ruined by success.' Macmillan's political dominance was due, in part, to the internecine warfare in the

Labour party. The new Conservative Party Chairman, Iain Macleod, was moved to announce a year after the election that the Labour party was finished and the Tories would have to provide their own opposition. The highlight of the 1960 Labour conference was Gaitskell's pledge to 'fight, fight and fight again to save the party I love'. It made a compelling piece of television and the viewers noted that the Labour leader's bitterest enemies were on his own side.

At exactly the same time, the Prime Minister was able to demonstrate on television that he was more than a match for Britain's main enemy in the world. In September 1960, he went to address the United Nations' General Assembly in New York. From early on in Macmillan's speech, Nikita Khrushchev fervently demonstrated his disagreement. The Soviet leader took off his shoe and banged it noisily on his desk, then he stood up and roared in Russian at Macmillan. The Prime Minister waited patiently at the rostrum for a pause in the tirade, then remarked nonchalantly: 'I'd like it translated if you would, sir.' It brought the Assembly down. A bemused Khrushchev was forced to take his seat as the laughter echoed around him. Television coverage of the incident enhanced the image of the unflappable Supermac, the world statesman who could tame the Russian bear.

Harold Evans was determined that the Prime Minister should exploit his UN success. He suggested a big airport news conference for the press and television on Macmillan's return to London. Evans noted in his diary: 'The Prime Minister agreed, provided he could see the questions to be asked by the television interviewers. This I duly arranged. I had prepared briefs, particularly on defence and on points arising from the Labour Party Conference. It went more smoothly and with less irritation than most airport occasions, and his opening statement dominated the television evening bulletins.' Evans' was a frank account of how easily prime ministers could manage the television news; Macmillan set the precedent that his successors were to follow. But in the months to come he would find the real world less amenable than airport TV interviewers.

The Prime Minister was failing to fulfil the buoyant promises of his election campaign. Abroad, the summit meeting had collapsed in fiasco after the Soviet shooting down of the American U2 spy plane. At home, he was paying the price for the pre-election boom. In place of his optimistic expansionism came the shocks of the sterling crisis, the pay pause and the sharp restrictions on hire purchase. The Shadow Chancellor Harold Wilson mocked Macmillan as the creator of the 'candy-floss society'. The Prime Minister decided he had to try to rally the public through television. In August 1961, he noted in his diary: 'For several weeks there has been a press campaign against me carried on in almost every paper as being tired, failing, losing grip etc., culminating in a report that I had had a heart attack.' He now accepted a BBC invitation to make a television 'report to the people'. He had declined previous invitations, but prime ministerial appearances tend to rise in direct ratio to the decline in the popularity graphs.

Preparations for the broadcast completely disrupted the normal smooth running of the Prime Minister's office. There was a fracas with independent television, which protested against the BBC having a Macmillan exclusive. The Prime Minister lamented to his press secretary that he was no longer able to learn scripts by heart. Conservative Central Office objected strongly to its exclusion by the Prime Minister's official entourage from drafting his script, as did Rab Butler, Macmillan's deputy. Finally, to the chagrin of the Prime Minister's publicity advisers at Number 10, Macmillan insisted on calling in Norman Collins, the ATV Chairman, who had devised the highly successful final broadcast in the 1959 election campaign. Harold Evans noted in his diary that the actual drafting of the script 'could hardly have been a more tiresome, frustrating and worrying process. Everyone was trying to get in on the act.'

Evans and Charles Hill, Macmillan's minister in charge of the information services, prepared one draft. 'Norman Collins, ostensibly advising on the form of presentation, infiltrated into the drafting process and in particular wanted to reverse the sequence of subjects in the script,' said Evans. Then one of Macmillan's private secretaries, Freddie Bishop, prepared a completely different draft which he submitted independently to the Prime Minister. This was followed by a meeting in the Cabinet room which Evans describes as 'a shambles'. Subsequently another of Macmillan's private secretaries stayed up all night to write a final draft of the broadcast. At the same time Macmillan was dictating to his secretary at midnight his own final draft.

The broadcast was to be recorded at Admiralty House, the Prime Minister's temporary residence while Number 10 was being modernized. Evans decided that it would be inappropriate for Norman Collins from commercial television to be present on a BBC occasion: 'So I had his black Bentley organized at the Horse Guards door and saw him off with protestations about how jolly nice it had been to meet each other.' Macmillan had a first attempt at the broadcast. But neither his advisers nor the BBC producer, John Grist, were happy with the result. They felt it was too long and sagged in the middle. Together they hurriedly cut and rewrote parts of the script. There was a delay as the new draft was typed on to the teleprompter. The Prime Minister tried again, unsuccessfully. He gave the wrong figure for Britain's invisible earnings: the Treasury had provided the figure two days earlier but had since drastically revised it. Macmillan made a further attempt, without using the teleprompter. 'It went sweetly enough, despite some initial hesitations, which on the whole we thought more effective than not,' said Evans.

Macmillan noted in his diary: 'I found the broadcast a troublesome task. I had learned to do interviews or discussions adequately. But the "solo" which is thought suitable when one speaks as Prime Minister to the nation is much more difficult. Fortunately the broadcast was well received.' Harold Evans, in his diary, was ecstatic: 'Just how it turned out to be such an effective piece of broadcasting, goodness only knows. But in the end it proved to be exactly right, it served to wrap up the parliamentary session neatly, logically and triumphantly. The BBC were able to get the text out in good time and this contributed to the excellent press. We have seen a transformation in the Prime Minister's standing. Even Peregrine Worsthorne hails him as a statesman.'

Encouraged by the success of his broadcast, the Prime Minister accepted an invitation to be the guest of honour at a glittering banquet given by the BBC to mark the twenty-fifth anniversary of the start of television. He was to propose the health of the Corporation in a televised after-dinner speech at the Grocers' Hall in the City. The occasion marked a high point in the self-confidence both of the Prime Minister and of the BBC. The guest list for the banquet collected together the Great and the Good from Lord Reith to the Archbishop of Canterbury. Before the event, Macmillan was very concerned about his speech; much of it had been drafted by Harold Evans and typed out in the familiar psalm form. The Prime Minister was gloomy in the car on the way to the banquet, thinking it was not his kind of occasion and not understanding some of the allusions to popular television programmes that Evans had put in the speech. But when he spoke, Macmillan was on top form and produced a scintillating performance.

He began with a mock apology: he was not the right person to make the speech. 'For one thing I hardly ever see a television programme. Now, that is not just the stock boast of those who like to feel intellectually superior. On the contrary, I say it with a feeling of resentment and deprivation. Not for me the joys of Half Hours with Hancock. No Dixon. No Maigret. No Chislebury. No Lone Ranger. No Lennie the Lion. It isn't actually that we can't afford a set at Number 10, but the trouble is my employers never give me an evening off.' The Prime Minister delivered the list of popular programmes with an expression of infinite sadness and a comedian's sense of timing, pausing after each title to allow the laughter to build.

Macmillan then talked about his own experiences in front of the cameras. 'Television has introduced a new dimension into politics and some of us don't know quite what to make of it. I've never dared to look at one of my own performances. Not that I'm spared anything, because my family are numerous and candid.' Nearly a quarter of a century later, when Margaret Thatcher became the first prime minister to appear on a TV chat show, she expressed the same feelings to Michael Aspel: 'I never watch myself and the family know it. I know that I'm on quite often, in the news or doing some kind of talk or interview. And usually I've recorded it and the family want to watch. I just cannot stay in the room. But I do turn to my family for advice. I will say to them when they have watched this show, "How was it?" And, my dear, they will tell me.'

'Why then do we do it?' asked Macmillan in his speech. 'Partly because television is so vivid, personal and instantaneous a means of communication. People often write to me and say, "Why don't you explain things on the television?" But it is not as easy as they think. Television will never, I hope, become a propaganda instrument of the government. Happily neither the Prime Minister nor any other minister can appear on television at will. These services are not under government control and that is to my mind fundamental to a free society. It also means that these fireside talks are not so easily arranged – quite apart from the difficulty of doing them effectively. I've never quite mastered the art of looking into the lens and treating it as one of the family. Of course some people can do just that. The exuberant personality, agile of tongue, gifted at saying extravagant things colourfully. Politicians in office certainly do not come up to that description. Out of office they are more colourful.'

This, said Macmillan, was the hub of the matter: was television primarily for entertainment or for enlightenment? Somehow a balance had to be struck. 'I see no objection to making enlightenment as entertaining as possible. But it is not always easy in programmes on current affairs, for example. The entertainment formula in these programmes usually lies in what I believe are called "confrontations" – clashes of personality combined with aggressive interviewing, which means that everybody should be as rude as possible within a short time to everybody else. Well, this may be right. You cannot expect to hold your audience with a routine plod through your lines – however worthy they may be. The comedian has to work for his laughs. The politician has to work even harder, for his material is basically serious, not to say boring. I don't think he should complain of that for he is, broadly speaking, a hardy creature.'

Macmillan's speech was carried live on television. It had a huge audience and was very favourably reviewed in the press the next day. The anniversary banquet had provided an ideal stage for his histrionic abilities: the gestures, the timing, the cadences were all managed to perfection. But as he entered his sixth year as Prime Minister, in January 1962, Macmillan's theatricality was becoming more pronounced. In the Commons, Michael Foot claimed that he resembled nothing so much as an old ham actor playing the part of Macmillan. It seemed as if the Prime Minister was consciously starting to mimic his own caricatures. 'As he grew older and into the part, his gestures became more eccentric,' his biographer, Anthony Sampson, noted, 'the shake of the head, the dropping of the mouth, the baring of the teeth, the pulling in of the cheeks, the wobbling of the hand, the comedian's sense of timing – the whole bag of tricks seemed in danger of taking over.'

The problem with a prime ministerial act on television is that so many people see it. Stand-up comedians complain that in the old days the same jokes would last them for months on tours of variety palaces throughout Britain, but now they use them all up in one night on television. So it was with Macmillan: the viewers were beginning to feel that they had seen it all before. The old Edwardian had always seemed an unlikely figure to lead Britain into the sixties, now he was beginning to appear dated and out of touch. In part this was due to the contrast with the image of boyish vigour radiating from John Kennedy, the new American President, who had succeeded Macmillan's old wartime contemporary, General Eisenhower. The Prime Minister was distantly related by marriage to Kennedy and returned from a visit to the US at the end of 1961, greatly impressed by the new President's use of television. The British newspapers were mounting a series of bitter attacks on Macmillan with *The Times* calling on him to resign as inflation and unemployment rose. The Prime Minister noted in his diary on 23 December 1961: 'Happily I think the press with its gossip and sneering and pomposity and pettiness – as well as downright lies – is losing influence every day. BBC television, ITV and radio – these are the instruments. Kennedy told me he was using the television to appeal to the people over the heads of a broadly hostile press. I wonder whether a monthly televised press conference on American lines would be a good thing for me to try?'

The notion of regular televised talks to the people is one which has attracted successive prime ministers from Eden onwards. But, as Macmillan had put it in his speech at the BBC's anniversary dinner, 'these fireside chats are not so easily arranged'. At the start of 1962, he sought to emulate Kennedy by means of a party political broadcast. This gave Macmillan the putative advantage of a captive audience, as party politicals went out simultaneously on BBC and ITV, even though they met with strong consumer resistance.

Macmillan's press secretary, Harold Evans, decided the Prime Minister needed a gimmick to grab the attention of his audience. As a neutral civil servant, Evans should have had nothing to do with the broadcast, which was a party political occasion. But he was not the last prime minister's press secretary to ignore the rules. On Evans' suggestion, the broadcast opened with Macmillan sitting in front of the fireplace at Number 10; also in the picture were a television camera crew, the lights and the microphone, as well as the floor manager. The mechanics of production, normally so carefully concealed, were deliberately on display. As the programme began, the viewers saw the floor manager giving the Prime Minister his cue. Macmillan began: 'Well, there you are, you can see what it is like. The camera's hot, probing eye – these monstrous machines and their attendants – a kind of twentieth-century torture chamber – that's what it is. Well, I must try and forget all this paraphernalia and imagine that you are sitting here in the room with me.' Macmillan went on to deliver a pep talk. The country had done 'jolly well, but not quite well enough'; what was needed now was 'just that little extra effort from everybody'.

The press next morning was divided. *The Times* thought Macmillan had done well. The *Mirror* headline was 'Waffle'. The *Daily Telegraph* felt the opening introduction was 'too mannered', but claimed that the Prime Minister looked twenty years younger: 'his neatly brushed hair shone and his moustache, contrasting with a practically unlined face, seemed darker and heavier than usual. Sitting at his desk in a soft-collared shirt worn under an open double-breasted jacket, the effect was one of complete relaxation.' In the *Sunday Telegraph*, however, Peregrine Worsthorne claimed the Prime Minister's fireside chat was almost wilfully misleading: what Britain's body politic needed was drastic surgery. Macmillan believed in not frightening the patient by telling him the truth – 'he still sees himself as the great anaesthetist and not the great surgeon'. Macmillan himself said: 'Although the broadcast was said to be acceptable to the public as a whole, I did not feel satisfied. There was a mood of disappointment throughout the country.' The Prime Minister was right. At the Orpington by-election two months later, the Conservatives lost what was normally regarded as a very safe seat to the Liberals. It seemed that among the privet hedges and neat semis of suburbia, there was a twin-sided revolt against Macmillan's brand of materialism: some felt he was failing to deliver the goods, others wanted more idealism. On Friday, 13 July 1962, the Prime Minister who had so assiduously built up the image of unflappability – panicked. In a single day he sacked seven of his Cabinet – some of them his oldest political friends – including the Chancellor, Selwyn Lloyd. In the House of Commons, a young television reporter who had become a Liberal MP, Jeremy Thorpe, delivered a scathing judgement: 'Greater love hath no man than this, that he lay down his friends for his life.'

The aim of the purge, like many that would follow over the years, was to give a younger, fresher look to the Cabinet and promote effective television performers. The Prime Minister had noted in his diary: 'the public really are tired of us – of our faces, our caricatured faces, our appearance.' One of Macmillan's new Cabinet ministers was William Deedes, who had appeared with him in the first ever party political broadcast, nearly ten years earlier. Deedes, given the title of Minister without Portfolio, was in reality the Minister of Propaganda, charged with improving the image of the Prime Minister and his government. The new minister produced a secret paper on how the Government should make best use of the cameras. It was a sophisticated and perceptive description of the state of the relationship between broadcasters and politicians after twenty-five years of television. 'No field of communications', wrote Deedes, 'offers greater possibilities in the time at our disposal before an election to improve the public mood towards Government than that of broadcasting and television. Their impact on the public mind is immense. Though we have come a long way, there is still a tendency in many places to view the resources available with suspicion and to use them half-heartedly. The Government always has a monopoly of news value and to this extent a natural lead over other parties. The reconstructed Government improves our chances of making a good impression.'

Deedes then went on to identify what he saw as the primary weakness in the Government's public relations: 'that while all ministers are associated with politics, not all ministers are associated with subjects of more general and social interest, which make good television. Hitherto, we have tended to favour ministerial participation in suitable political programmes, but to be cautious as to their appearance in what we regard as "entertainment" programmes. Carefully increased ministerial participation in such programmes, thus identifying government with problems people feel and understand, would have advantages. No such opportunities can be exploited without risk. Practice helps. We never have had a team of ministers better equipped to exploit the openings with a minimum of risk. The BBC have been made aware than we are not going to have ministers "bounced": called up at short notice and trick questioned. The leaders of television, certainly the BBC's, show an eagerness to get better arrangements and working relations with us. This gives us some bargaining power. We ourselves should not in this field always be looking for "Pinkies under the bed". There is scope for horse trading. Given ministerial willingness to appear on occasions which we might have thought dubious hitherto, we may on occasions be able to secure appearances on particular subjects which suit us without a lot of fuss about balance.'

The first of these occasions came for Macmillan in September 1962. He had launched Britain's application to join the European Common Market. It had become an explosive political issue. With the greatest difficulty, Macmillan had managed to prevent his fellow Commonwealth Prime Ministers from coming out against him. He wanted to use television to try to soften the bitter divisions among the people at home over the Common Market. He felt that neither a party political, nor a ministerial broadcast – to which the Opposition could have the right to reply – was appropriate. Instead, he wanted to initiate a new form of broadcast, where he would appear as the unchallenged national leader, like General de Gaulle in France or President Kennedy in America. 'Macmillan found it inconceivable that anyone should be in a position to question the right of the Prime Minister to use television, or any other mechanism, to address the nation at moments of national significance,' said Grace Wyndham Goldie, who had become the BBC's Head of TV Current Affairs.

Hugh Carleton Greene, the BBC's Director-General, came up with a new formula: from time to time, the Corporation would invite the Prime Minister to address the nation. There would be no automatic right of reply by the Opposition. Instead the BBC itself would decide whether the broadcast was national in character, or whether it had been a disguised party political in which case the Opposition would be invited to reply. It was an idea which put considerable political power in the hands of the BBC and was intended to pre-empt the Prime Minister from seeking the legislative power to broadcast to the people when he liked. On 20 September, Macmillan was invited to address the nation about the Common Market.

In the Prime Minister's office, there followed the now familiar battle of the draft scripts between Number 10 and Conservative Central Office. Macmillan favoured his own staff's work and on the day before the broadcast, he practised with a tape recorder in the Cabinet Room. He went to bed that afternoon and had second thoughts; a new script was prepared. But the next day the BBC producer, Huw Wheldon, preferred the earlier draft. Macmillan was eventually persuaded. While his script was being redrafted, he mused with Wheldon and Harold Evans about television. 'How absurd it was, said the Prime Minister,' Evans noted in his diary, 'to expect television to produce a constant succession of outstanding programmes, when they had to be turned out so quickly and in such profusion; it was not expected that outstanding books or plays should be produced with greater frequency than perhaps once a year – why then should it be thought that television could do any better?'

With a large entourage gathered to watch in the drawing room of Admiralty House, Macmillan went through three takes of the broadcast (one of his young grandsons fell asleep on the sofa during the first take). He became more fluent and confident each time and the third version was transmitted. His script showed that Macmillan and his advisers had taken on board what Huw Wheldon had told them at the time of his first broadcast as Prime Minister nearly six years earlier: he was seeking to avoid terms that no one single human being would use to address another. 'A lot of people look backward but the real test you must bring to this question is – are we going to look forward?' said Macmillan in his broadcast. To compete with Russia and America, Europe had to come together, and if Britain stood outside: 'we shan't find the true strength that we have or ought to have. We shan't be able to exercise it in a world of giants.' And he concluded, 'Many of us, especially those who are young in heart or in years, are impatient of the old disputes; intolerant of obsolete conceptions; anxious that our country should take its part, and if possible a leading part, in all these new and hopeful movements.' Harold Evans felt it was the Prime Minister's best ever broadcast because Macmillan was saying the things he wanted to say and did not depart from what had eventually been a good script. The press shared Evans' view.

Immediately the broadcast was transmitted there was a row between Number 10 and the BBC. Hugh Gaitskell at once demanded the right to reply. And Hugh Carleton Greene, feeling that Macmillan had put his case with such force on what was clearly a controversial and divisive issue, conceded. The Labour leader would broadcast the next night. But Harold Evans felt he had been let down by the BBC and sought to prevent the reply. On the telephone to the BBC, he put Macmillan's view that 'as a matter of principle, the Prime Minister should have the right to broadcast to the nation without having the Leader of the Opposition put up the following night to make a counter-statement, with the last word'. Macmillan shared his press secretary's resentment at the BBC but felt it would be politically unwise to make a formal protest. Instead he proposed to use his televised speech to the Tory Party Conference a fortnight later to exacerbate Hugh Gaitskell's party difficulties over Europe. Labour was deeply split. Gaitskell had seemed to make his own attitude clear when he questioned whether Britain should throw aside a thousand years of history for the sake of a marginal advantage on the price of a washing machine in Düsseldorf. But in his broadcast reply to Macmillan he hedged and said he would wait to see the terms of entry before he committed himself.

At the Conservative Party Conference in Llandudno the following month, Macmillan made mock of Gaitskell's dithering. The older members of the audience would recall the popular song:

> She didn't say 'yes', she didn't say 'no'.
> She didn't say 'stay', she didn't say 'go'.
> She wanted to climb, but dreaded to fall.
> So she bided her time and clung to the wall.

It was delivered with impeccable timing to delighted applause and laughter. The extract dominated the television news and conference reports. The Prime Minister felt immensely bucked. 'My speech was enthusiastically received, we had surmounted triumphantly any hostile opinion in the Conservative Party,' he noted in his diary. The Llandudno conference was Macmillan's last great triumph. The Common Market issue would soon rebound on him. In the meantime there was a novel development in television's coverage of politics.

1962 was the year of the satire boom. A new television programme started which took a sharply irreverent look at all politicians – with the Prime Minister as its particular target. Two years earlier the undergraduate review, *Beyond the Fringe*, had become a huge hit in the West End of London. One of its sketches featured Peter Cook lampooning Macmillan's final election broadcast in the 1959 campaign, where he had used the globe as his prop: 'I explained to the American President Britain's role in the world as an honest broker. He agreed with me that no nation could be more honest; I agreed with him no nation could be broker.' The following year *Private Eye* began, along with The Establishment, 'the world's first satirical night club'. Suddenly it had become fashionable to ridicule Britain's ruling class. In November 1962, BBC television followed the trend with *That Was The Week That Was – TW3*, as it became known. 'The programme has bite and pungency and spares neither institutions, nor persons, neither Prime Minister, nor bishop nor courtier,' enthused Hugh Carleton Greene.

Greene was a subversive at the top of the Corporation, which had been regarded until then as a central pillar of the Establishment. As a *Daily Telegraph* reporter, he had enjoyed satire in the night clubs of Berlin in the thirties and supported the aim of *TW3*, 'to prick the pomposity of public figures'. And while many Conservatives hated the programme, Greene found an ally in the Prime Minister. After the first edition, which mocked Macmillan and his government, political journalists rang up the Postmaster-General, Reginald Bevins. 'The reporters asked Bevins', said Greene, 'whether the Government could stand for this sort of thing and whether he would be doing something about it? And Reg Bevins was foolish enough to say: "Yes, I will." The next morning he found on his desk a very short memo from the Prime Minister saying, "Oh, no, you won't".'

Macmillan was displaying his customary insouciance and tolerance: partly because he had not seen the programme. He did not realize that *TW3* would soon become extraordinarily popular – required Saturday-night viewing both in pubs and at dinner parties – and it would contribute to weakening his own government. The programme's creators believed it would at best attract two million viewers; soon five times that number were watching. The Prime Minister, who so often appeared to caricature himself, presented an ideal butt. William Rushton regularly played Macmillan as an aristocratic, political fixer who had peopled the Cabinet with his own relations. One of the early programmes featured a scene from a filmed profile of Macmillan that had been shown on television earlier in the week. 'At one point in the profile', leered the *TW3* compère, David Frost, 'Mr Macmillan opened his dispatch box and revealed a copy of Roget's *Thesaurus*. What word could he have been going to look up – politics? Section 702 gives the following alternatives, "cunning, craftiness, sharp practice, manoeuvring, chicanery, knavery, jugglery, concealment, foul play". And the section goes on: "artful dodge, white lie, tricks of the trade, imposture, deception, sly boots, gerrymander" and finally "intriguing, time-serving, artificial, deceitful, too clever by half, double-tongued, foxy, underhand, shifty, crooked", and, of course, "*spargare voces in vulgam ambiguas* – to sprinkle the people with half-truths".'

Ian Trethowan, who had become the presenter of the BBC's new serious weekly political programme, *Gallery*, says that *TW3* had a profound effect on television's coverage of politics. 'Although at times anarchic, and on occasion contemptibly unfair, *TW3* swept through British broadcasting as a cleansing agent, scouring away the last of the bland and the banal.' He is also convinced that, in the longer term, the programme contributed to a strong feeling among politicians that the BBC was not so much hostile to any one party as contemptuous of the whole parliamentary process. But in 1963, the Conservative party had more immediate concerns. *TW3* was regularly depicting Macmillan's ministers, notably the Home Secretary, Henry Brooke, as upper-class figures of fun or hard-hearted bunglers. Many Tories, including members of the Cabinet, feared that the programme was undermining the credibility of the whole government and unfairly influencing the voters. Then, just as *TW3* reached the height of its popularity, a series of political events took place that went way beyond the realms of television satire.

At the start of 1963, Macmillan told Harold Evans: 'It will be a year of destiny.' He was soon proved right. On 18 January, Hugh Gaitskell suddenly died. Macmillan paid a moving tribute to his long-time opponent on television and the Labour party began the lengthy process of electing a new Leader. The result of the election was to be affected by a row with the television authorities. A fortnight after Gaitskell's death, President de Gaulle of France announced that he was vetoing Britain's entry into the Common Market. Macmillan was desolate. 'What happened at Brussels yesterday was bad, bad for us, bad for Europe and bad for the whole free world,' he said in a ministerial broadcast, but claimed that all was not lost. The BBC decided that Macmillan had spoken as Prime Minister, not as a party politician and refused to give the Opposition the right of reply. When Sir Robert Fraser, Director-General of the ITA, threatened to follow suit, he received the full flow of emotional spleen from Labour's acting Leader, George Brown. Lurid accounts of Brown's behaviour were leaked to the press on the eve of the leadership election; they helped convince some Labour MPs that Brown was too unstable to lead the Party. Two months earlier he had easily beaten Harold Wilson for the deputy leadership, now the positions were reversed. In his diary, Macmillan wrote of the new Labour leader: 'Harold Wilson is an able man – far more able than George Brown. He is good in the House and in the country and – I am told – on TV.' In the next few months, as the Prime Minister's problems multiplied, he was regularly to see for himself the Opposition leader's small-screen talents.

From the moment he won the leadership, Wilson regarded television as the essential vehicle to take him to Number 10. 'TV had one great advantage for the Labour party,' says Wilson, 'most of the press were against us. And if the right-wing press were tempted to say about me – "this is a terrible man, looks like an ogre, his voice is terrible", then you go on television and the people say – "oh look, he is an ordinary chap like the rest of us." ' To play up his ordinariness, the former Oxford don and ex-President of the Board of Trade co-operated fully with a *Panorama* profile of him. Wilson presented the image of a down-to-earth and practical family man by mending his son's bicycle for the cameras in his living room. While most other leading politicians had concentrated their attention on newspaper proprietors and senior broadcasting executives, Wilson had over the years built up good relations with working journalists and television producers. Now he made himself readily available to them.

Convinced that Macmillan might hold an early general election, Wilson felt he had only a few months to build himself up as a credible, alternative prime minister. He wanted to project an energetic, youthful image to contrast both with Macmillan and with his own predecessor as Labour leader. 'Harold has a grammar schoolboy's curious classlessness which makes him belong to a younger generation than Gaitskell,' Richard Crossman noted in his diary after Wilson's first television appearance as party leader. An erratic Wykehamist and wartime expert in propaganda and psychological warfare, Crossman had helped manage Wilson's leadership election campaign; he now found himself for the first time part of Labour's inner circle. 'It is fun to take part in creating a political image and building up a leader,' wrote Crossman on 5 March 1963, and added, 'whenever I go to see Harold, I look into those grey eyes and see nothing.'

In his first broadcast as Party leader, Wilson turned out to be effective at speaking directly to the camera. He had learned the technique of scarcely moving his eyeballs as he read the teleprompter (or autocue, as it now became known). 'I was worried in those early days whether I would be able to read it properly,' says Wilson, 'because my eyesight is not all that good. I had to be taught and rehearsed. The big difference is that I felt the camera was my friend not my enemy.' His first broadcast was specifically designed to create the impression of a vigorous leader, who could scarcely wait to release the latent energies and talents of the British people. The whole nation, he said, had to be called into action in a new partnership of hope and adventure. 'Harold Wilson made a very clever broadcast last night,' Macmillan noted in his diary. Richard Crossman believed it had been 'confidence-building because it was so solid and unclever'. In fact the broadcast, which achieved a record 21 million viewers, had been fraught with problems.

Wilson's closest confidante was his political secretary, Marcia Williams (later Lady Falkender). She was to become his image-maker-in-chief throughout his time as Party leader. 'When he gave his first broadcast, he kept raising his fist to emphasize his point,' says Lady Falkender. 'It appeared in a very threatening manner on the small screen – this enormous fist in front of his head. And we just looked at it in total horror and said: "God, we must stop him doing this." So when we had finished the broadcast we sat down to work out how we could make it better. And we decided the best way to deal with the fist, was to give him his pipe – which was one of the reasons he would always appear with his pipe after that. He also used to rest his left hand on his face during interviews – which had the bonus of showing his wedding ring. So you had this comfortable picture of the dependable young family man – it gave the image of reassurance. It wasn't immediate; it took a number of broadcasts and interviews before he was comfortable using these props as part of the tricks of the trade.'

Wilson took as his television role model President Kennedy. His textbook was Theodore White's insider account of the 1960 presidential campaign, *The Making of the President*. Wilson was able to study the American's media techniques at first hand. He managed an invitation to see the President within two months of taking over the Labour leadership. At the White House, he posed happily for the cameras at Kennedy's side. And he stressed to the waiting TV interviewers that he and the President were two of a kind – representatives of the new generation in politics. 'I think there is a worldwide feeling, not so much for young men as such but for young ideas: a general desire to get into the 1960s and start thinking in terms of the 1970s as quickly as we can. Some of the older gentlemen are perhaps not so well fitted to do that.'

On their return to Britain, Harold Wilson and Marcia Williams pored over each of Kennedy's major political speeches. They knew that the President's speech-writers produced specific paragraphs and phrases that were solely designed to be picked up and used by the television news shows. Together they worked on the techniques of producing short, self-contained, punchy passages that no TV producer could resist. It would take many months before they succeeded; but their instincts were far in advance of anything that had been seen in British politics up to that time. 'We also realized that Kennedy had lots of messages that were relevant to the British scene,' says Lady Falkender. 'He talked about the need to get the country moving again after a period of stagnation – we adopted it as our central theme. And we adopted some of the techniques he used on television to communicate directly with the people. We realized that as you were broadcasting direct into people's homes, you could not be some stiff, remote figure. You had to be a relaxed figure that people could identify with.' The man in the Gannex raincoat had arrived – with a pipe in place of the cigars he smoked in private, a well-publicized love of HP sauce and a Yorkshire accent still carefully preserved.

Wilson and Marcia Williams were not alone in seeking to draw from Kennedy's example. The Tory Party Chairman, Lord Poole, was continuing to cajole Macmillan to hold regular televised press conferences. Harold Evans noted in his diary at the end of April 1963: 'Poole proposes to get a film of a Kennedy press conference through ATV (*that* won't stay secret).' But while Macmillan's publicity advisers waited for the film to arrive, Wilson was already following Kennedy's electronic example. The contrast between Macmillan's aristocratic langour and Wilson's classless *bravura* was beginning to make an impact. Macmillan noted in his diary that the number of critics within his own party was 'reaching formidable dimensions. "Macmillan must go" is the cry. Faced with Wilson, we must have a young man (Maudling or Heath). This line of approach leaves out poor Butler as well as me.' Macmillan's greatest political problem was that his government, which had once seemed so competent and self-assured, was now becoming accident-prone. One Labour Shadow Cabinet minister told the press – exactly twenty years before the phrase was recycled for Mrs Thatcher – 'If there were only one piece of banana skin in the whole of Britain, Mac would step on it.'

Macmillan's troubles came to a climax in the summer of 1963. John Profumo, who had been the Conservative party's first television officer and chief backbench lobbyist for ITV, was Macmillan's Secretary of State for War. In June he finally confirmed persistent rumours of his role at the centre of a sensational sex scandal. The saga of the call-girl who reportedly shared a bed with the Tory War Minister as well as the Soviet Defence Attaché and the associated revelations of the aristocracy's adventures in the underworld were beyond the wildest imaginings of the television satirists. John Profumo, Christine Keeler, Colonel Ivanov, Lord Astor, Mandy Rice-Davies and Stephen Ward were given full nightly coverage by television in its uninhibited new role. The Editor of ITN, Geoffrey Cox, said: 'The Profumo affair posed a peculiarly difficult problem. It involved television, essentially a family medium, in handling material which told of sex orgies and of two-way mirrors, of perversions and practices which until then were to be found only in the pages of Krafft-Ebing or Havelock Ellis, or in pornography smuggled in from the Continent.'

The affair threatened to bring down Macmillan. With Downing Street still being rebuilt, the Prime Minister was at Admiralty House, which had a large open courtyard. Each day throngs of TV cameramen and reporters would gather to waylay ministers as they came and went. 'There were mornings when it looked like a bear-pit,' said John Whale of ITN, 'in the end the cameras were asked to stay away.' The crisis reached its height with demands from the press and some Conservative backbenchers for Macmillan's resignation. In a vitriolic leader, *The Times* claimed that Macmillan had brought the country to a low ebb in every respect and must go. The time was ripe for a sacrifice to the gods, Macmillan remarked later: 'Who could be a more convenient victim for this purpose than an elderly but respectable Conservative Prime Minister?' And the authorized version of his life claims that without the satire of *That Was The Week That Was* and *Private Eye*, the 'temptation to focus the whole scandal on the instantly recognizable Edwardian at the head of the Government would have been less strong'. The Prime Minister's future seemed to depend on the outcome of a parliamentary debate on the Profumo affair. Macmillan decided he had to use television to try to influence the public mood in his favour before the debate. He felt the most effective way was not by appearing himself, nor by allowing any of his other ministers to appear – save one.

Lord Hailsham, with his combination of Christian fervour, intellectual agility and legal training, was the man to salvage in the studios whatever there was of Macmillan's case. In response to all the requests from TV companies for interviews with ministers, the Leader of the House of Lords made a single appearance. Interviewed by Robert McKenzie on the BBC's *Gallery* four days before the debate, Lord Hailsham put on a remarkable performance. He argued that the Profumo affair in no way reflected on the Government or the Conservative party – it solely concerned the morals of one man and his 'dingy companions'. 'A great party is not to be brought down because of a squalid affair between a proven liar and a woman of easy virtue. He lied and lied and lied. Lied to his friends, lied to his family, lied to his colleagues, lied to the House of Commons.' Lord Hailsham, his face suffused with moral indignation, turned on his interviewer, whom he referred to throughout as 'young McKenzie'. It was beyond belief contempt-ible to try to turn the Profumo affair into a party issue; it was a scandal that could as easily have occurred in the Labour party. 'So you think that those who have spoken out', asked McKenzie, 'like *The Times* and the bishops and so on have been trying to turn it into a party issue?' Hailsham rocked forward in his chair and shouted: 'I think *you* have.'

The whole interview looked like a spontaneous outpouring of righteous rage by Hailsham. In fact he had not come to the studio unprepared to produce it. Grace Wyndham Goldie wrote at the time, in a report to senior BBC officials: 'Whereas Hailsham's general moral indignation about being caught up in so sordid a set of circumstances was genuine, nevertheless as part of the tactics of handling the interview he had been determined not to be on the defensive but to go out and attack. After the broadcast he was extremely friendly with us all, including Bob McKenzie and everything went off in an aura of amiability.' The Labour party complained to the BBC that the interview had effectively been a party political broadcast for the Tories. The Prime Minister's press secretary noted in his diary that Hailsham's television performance had helped create a more favourable mood towards Macmillan in the press, on the eve of the parliamentary debate.

In the debate Macmillan came under scathing attack from one of his own backbenchers, Nigel Birch – a member of the Treasury team which had resigned in the 'little local difficulties' five years earlier. Birch quoted from Browning's *The Lost Leader:*

> Let him never come back to us!
> There would be doubt, hesitation and pain,
> Forced praise on our part – the glimmer of twilight,
> Never glad, confident morning again!

Macmillan succeeded in disarming some of his critics with a speech that laced candour with humility. He admitted that he had been astounded by the revelations of the Profumo affair and added plaintively: 'I don't live among young people.' It was an admission which exactly suited Harold Wilson's television campaign of presenting himself as a young and in-touch leader in contrast to the elderly Macmillan. The Prime Minister managed to survive the vote, but twenty-seven of his own backbenchers abstained. 'I was astonished on the Monday of the debate by the absolute rage of fire which worked through the Conservative party in favour of a younger man,' remarked Rab Butler.

To provide his backbench Tory critics with a televised demonstration of the strength of his support in the constituencies, Macmillan made a visit to Wolverhampton at the start of July. Central Office had trundled out the traditional secret weapon of loyalty to the Leader: three thousand people from sixty Midlands constituencies had been organized to attend a mass rally. 'It was the most extraordinary demonstration of loyalty and affection,' remarked Macmillan. In Wolverhampton he gave an interview to ITN, in which he effectively challenged his Conservative opponents. 'All being well, if I keep my health and strength, I hope to lead the Party into the election. Of course I must have the support of the Party and I think I have it.' He noted in his diary that night that 'the MPs who were working against me were rather knocked off their guard' by the broadcast and the rally. At the same time Macmillan sought to counter Harold Wilson's attempt to take on the image of President Kennedy.

The Prime Minister knew he could not match the Labour leader for youth and vigour. Instead he decided to play up his close personal relationship with the President – which he had strengthened by appointing David Harlech, a member of his extended family, as ambassador to Washington. For American electoral reasons, Kennedy had planned a sentimental journey to Ireland – 'home of the Kennedys' – at the start of July. The Prime Minister prevailed on the President to fly over to England for a working weekend at his country home, Birch Grove. Macmillan greeted Kennedy at the airport in front of a battery of television cameras. The whole presidential apparatus was in tow: the secret service men, the communications experts, the military, the diplomats and the White House press corps. They commandeered the nearby Sussex houses of the Prime Minister's family and the local hotels.

Harold Wilson, who had recently returned from seeing the Soviet leader, Nikita Khrushchev, asked if he could come to Birch Grove to brief the President on his meeting. Macmillan turned him down flat. He was not having his limelight stolen. The TV cameras filmed the Prime Minister and the President together at Birch Grove. 'The visit was a *great* success from our point of view,' Macmillan noted in his diary, 'we got all that we wanted – notably the President's commitment to go "full steam ahead" for a nuclear test ban treaty with the Russians.' Kennedy came and left by helicopter. Television coverage of the weekend provided the indelible impression of a powerful young knight come to pay court to the wise old king: the youthful President relying on the elder statesman for advice and guidance. It was exactly the impression that Macmillan had sought to create.

A month later, the Test Ban Treaty was signed and Macmillan gave a television interview to ITV's *This Week*. Earlier in the year the programme had requested an interview 'on the basis of a beleaguered Prime Minister being given the chance to explain himself,' said Harold Evans. 'I told them this would not do at all.' Now, with the ink still wet on the Treaty and with the economy improving, was the chance for Macmillan to demonstrate that Profumo was just another 'little local difficulty'. The recording of the interview did not start well. Asked how long he intended to stay Prime Minister, Macmillan replied: 'Can *you* tell me when there is going to be a general election?' Evans persuaded Macmillan and the senior executives of the ITV company to record the whole interview again. And he noted in his diary afterwards: 'The interview went as well as we could have hoped and its timing was precisely right: "confident", "buoyant", "relaxed" – these were the adjectives used by the press. And that the right effect was achieved can be seen from Maurice Wiggin's comment in today's *Sunday Times:* "Macmillan didn't actually say much but he presented an attractive picture of a man rooted in family loyalties and the immemorial decencies of life as most of us like to live it." ' It was the image not the words which were important to Macmillan and Evans.

The following week, as a signal to the world that he was back to his unflappable, Edwardian self, Macmillan took a decision that would be unthinkable in today's Tory party. He went off for ten days' grouse-shooting on the Yorkshire moors and the television cameras filmed him there. The Prime Minister intended the TV pictures of men with guns in shooting-breeches, women in head-scarves, the labradors and Land-Rovers to signify that everything was back to normal: what else should he be doing on the Glorious Twelfth of August but enjoying a good shoot? To his critics it was further evidence that he was dangerously out of touch with the modern world – a representative of a privileged élite whose colourful excesses had become public knowledge. The following month Lord Denning's official report on the Profumo affair became an overnight bestseller and Harold Wilson launched a bitter personal attack on Macmillan for 'debauching and corrupting public life'.

Macmillan was under the fiercest pressure to step down – both from his opponents and from within his own party. As a result of his ministerial purge the previous year, he was by some way the oldest member of his Cabinet, with its average age of fifty-one. Macmillan was now sixty-eight and looking his age. But, after a period of dithering, he determined he would do his utmost to hold on to power: 'I was not going to have the British Government pulled down by the antics of a whore,' he told a newspaper interviewer. Operation Limpet was the code name for his survival campaign. It came unstuck almost immediately. What in modern terms would be called a 'photo-opportunity' on the grouse moors turned out to be Macmillan's last special television appearance as Prime Minister. At the start of October he announced his resignation in the most dramatic circumstances. He sent a message from his bed in the King Edward VII Hospital for Officers to the Conservative Party Conference, which had just opened in Blackpool. A prostate operation had suddenly brought the curtain down on the political career of the theatrical Prime Minister. The news threw the Conference into turmoil. It meant that what Macmillan called 'the customary processes of consultation' to find his successor would be carried out beneath the full glare of the TV lights at the Blackpool conference. He had emerged as Prime Minister from the soundings taken in the most discreet possible way by Lord Salisbury. Now, his final act as Prime Minister provided television with a unique opportunity to intrude into a political process normally kept completely shut off from the public gaze. It was an appropriate epilogue to what had been the first television premiership.

In nearly seven years since Macmillan had come to Downing Street, television's role in politics had been transformed. Many of the restrictions on reporting had been lifted; scepticism and sometimes ridicule had replaced the old deference. The country's political leaders had come to give television first priority, as almost the whole population now had sets. Macmillan himself had altered his appearance for the TV cameras early in his term of office. He had become Prime Minister with trousers that disgraced his tailor, an unkempt moustache and teeth in disarray. Some eighteen months later, according to his official biographer, Alastair Horne, 'a new self-confident Macmillan appeared on the scene. The schoolmasterly glasses have disappeared, the disorderly moustache has been rigorously pruned, the smile is no longer toothy and half apologetic, and he is wearing a spruce new suit. The first incumbent of Number 10 to emerge as a TV personality has arrived and the success is almost immediate.'

In his years at Number 10 the old dog had tried to learn many new TV tricks. He never mastered the teleprompter or the art of speaking direct to a camera like a friend. But he had worked out how to give a successful interview and how to stage pseudo-political events and to provide good pictures for the TV cameras. He had discovered that a prime ministerial act – like a long-running TV series – can run as a great hit and then appear threadbare and dated. He was the first prime minister to see television as an impressionistic medium and to acquire some of the skills needed to create a favourable impression. He was also the first to find out the difficulty of using television to reverse a political trend; a single successful appearance will rarely turn the sour into the sweet. His successor at Number 10, the unlikeliest figure to emerge as Prime Minister this century until Margaret Thatcher, was soon to discover another fact of small-screen life for himself: that television is the cruellest medium.

CHAPTER 7

Dull Alec versus Smart-Alec

'I never thought I was going to be Prime Minister, so I had never practised television. I hated it, it was a burden all the time.'
Sir Alec Douglas-Home

No modern politician seemed less well-equipped to deal with television than the man who emerged, to general astonishment, as Prime Minister in October 1963. Lord Home (or plain Sir Alec Douglas-Home as he soon became) had almost no experience of the cameras and a distinctly untelegenic appearance. A wartime illness had left a part of his face paralysed. When he was nervous in an interview, his tongue would dart out like a lizard's and lick his dry lips. He looked and sounded as if he had spent most of his life on the grouse moors – a representative of the class that had been born to rule but was now going out of fashion. He appeared an amateur politician up against a most skilled and ambitious media professional: Harold Wilson, said the commentators, would walk all over Lord Home. But even though the new Prime Minister came to hate and fear television, he made surprisingly effective use of it and almost succeeded in pulling off a remarkable election victory.

Lord Home was fighting a rearguard action from his first moment at Number 10. The party he now led had been racked by dissension and scandal. He was also up against the most powerful electoral sentiment: that after twelve years it was time for a change. As Harold Wilson talked of the urgent need to revolutionize Britain in the white heat of technology, the fourteenth Earl of Home – the first Prime Minister from the House of Lords since the start of the century – appeared on television as the most unlikely agent of change. He confessed to using match-sticks to work out economic problems, while the Labour leader boasted his use of a slide rule. Even the way Home had come to power seemed the antithesis of modern democratic politics. The new Prime Minister had emerged from what Iain Macleod, Conservative Party Chairman at the time, later denounced as the manoeuvrings of 'the magic circle of Old Etonians'. Macmillan's sudden retirement at the start of the Conservative Party Conference in Blackpool had bathed the normally secret process of selecting a new Tory leader in the lights of television.

King-makers met behind locked doors in Blackpool hotel suites. Tory grandees took soundings and campaign managers of the real or self-appointed variety emerged. Lord Hailsham threw his coronet into the ring at a televised fringe meeting. To the frenzied adulation of his supporters, he announced he was giving up his peerage to make himself available for the premiership. His chief supporter, Randolph Churchill, produced campaign badges marked QH (Quintin Hogg, Hailsham's family name). The four other obvious contenders were Rab Butler, Reginald Maudling, Ted Heath and Iain Macleod. Lord Home did not even seem to be a candidate: Churchill said on the BBC's conference report it was 'tommy rot' to suggest he had a chance. Home's appearance on the same programme wearing a dinner jacket, anxiously licking his lips and countering questions with a high-pitched laugh appeared to strengthen Churchill's case. Robin Day asked Home if he was doing anything to discourage people from advocating his name: 'I am neither encouraging nor discouraging people. I am taking no part in this at all because I don't believe that people should go round canvassing for themselves or canvassing for other people.' But he refused to rule himself out as a candidate. 'I am not going to be trapped or induced to answer any questions on the leadership, except to say that it will be done by the customary processes of consultation.'

Five days later those processes had produced Lord Home. The new Prime Minister immediately made a brief television broadcast, in which he could scarcely have presented a stronger contrast to the Leader of the Labour party. 'I never dreamed of holding the position of Prime Minister,' says Lord Home. 'Had I done so, much as I would have detested the exercise, I would have taken trouble to master the techniques of television.' His first broadcast on the day he was appointed Prime Minister lasted just two minutes. He had learned his script by heart and his brief message to the country included a dig at Harold Wilson: 'No one need expect any stunts from me, just plain straight talking.' In a speech that evening, Wilson launched into a bitter attack on the new Prime Minister as an elegant anachronism and the symbol of the counter-revolution. 'After half a century of democratic advance, of social revolution, the whole process has ground to a halt with a fourteenth Earl.'

But in his first major television interviews as Prime Minister three days later, Home was to demonstrate an unexpected deftness of touch. He had worked out a response to Wilson, but it would need prompting by the interviewer. He had agreed to give interviews on the same night to the BBC and ITV. Macmillan's press secretary, Harold Evans, who stayed on for a time to help the transition, candidly remarked in his diary: 'I made sure that Kenneth Harris [of ITV] asked the right question: astonishingly the television networks had not intended to tackle him about the fourteenth Earl criticisms.' When the arranged question came, Home replied: 'I don't see why criticism should centre on this. Are we to say that all men are equal except peers? I suppose Mr Wilson, when you come to think of it, is the fourteenth Mr Wilson.' It was a riposte that drew the sting of Wilson's attack, much to the Labour leader's private annoyance. Lord Home's interviews were regarded as a great success. The press stressed their soothing qualities: after the turmoil of the Profumo affair and the leadership battle, the new Prime Minister seemed in control and at home in Downing Street. He spoke reasonably and – in marked contrast with Wilson's style – was prepared to give straight and simple answers.

But the new man at Number 10 might have been made to order for the television satirists. They showed him no mercy. David Frost appeared on *That Was The Week That Was* in a Victorian frock-coat and a pointed black beard to deliver Disraeli's message to Lord Home: 'Your acceptance of the Queens's commission to form an administration has proved and will prove an unmitigated catastrophe for the Conservative party, the Constitution, for the nation and for yourself. The art of statesmanship consists as much in foreseeing as in doing. You, my Lord, in your sixty years have foreseen nothing. As you yourself have confessed in the past – you lack many of the basic qualifications for political leadership at this time. You know little of economics, little of all the manifold, complex needs of a country that has become tired in a technological age, and nothing of the lives of the ordinary people who must now, without consent, submit as your subjects. You have foreseen nothing; you are qualified to do only – nothing.' The programme ended with a final crack from Frost back in his normal garb as presenter: 'And so there is the choice for the electorate – on the one hand Lord Home and on the other Mr Harold Wilson: Dull Alec versus Smart-Alec.'

The BBC switchboard lit up with complaints about the programme – over five hundred people telephoned and a further three hundred wrote letters of protest at the attack on the Prime Minister. Home himself believes that *TW3* harmed him politically. When asked about it twenty-five years on, an expression of pain comes over his face. 'It was called satire and it did get under my skin. I don't mind criticism, after all you ask for it when you go into politics. But I think it was a bit cruel. And these personalized attacks place the exposed politician in a dilemma. If he reveals he is affected he is an even more tempting target, so the only alternative is to present the hide of a rhinoceros, which is singularly unattractive. I must say I did not like that series at all. It was aimed at the Establishment and the Prime Minister was an irresistible target. I think the constant knocking from that programme probably *did* have an effect on people's minds – and it was nasty.'

The Prime Minister did not have to endure *TW3* long after his return to the House of Commons as Sir Alec Douglas-Home. At the end of 1963 the BBC Director-General, Hugh Greene, suddenly announced that he was taking the programme off the air. It was not the result of direct Government pressure. Although a number of Cabinet ministers and their Labour shadows were deeply unhappy with the programme, none had protested publicly for fear of appearing unBritish and lacking a sense of humour. But Greene knew that many of the BBC's Governors and senior managers shared the politicians' concern; they were also worried about what they called *TW3*'s 'smutty jokes'. He decided to pre-empt any Government pressure by killing off the programme. 'I knew that 1964 was bound to be an election year and the BBC has to be especially impartial during an election. It is very difficult to be fair with laughter. When I took the programme off the air, the political parties hastened to issue statements saying, quite rightly, they had brought no pressure to have the programme removed. They knew it would be politically damaging to be in any way associated with my decision.'

Ironically within three days of Greene's announcement, one of the last ever editions of *TW3* won universal praise. It was a tribute in words and music to President Kennedy on the night after the assassination. The death of the President deprived Harold Wilson of his television role model and he feared it would have a damaging effect on his electoral chances. In the uncertainty, Wilson told his colleagues, people would cling for comfort to the government in office. Sir Alec Douglas-Home's newly appointed speech-writer, Eldon Griffiths, attempted to build up this sentiment. On the night of the assassination he claimed on ITV that the Prime Minister was now the dominant figure in the Western Alliance. The BBC hurriedly mounted a special tribute programme and sought frantically to contact the Prime Minister and the Leader of the Opposition. In the pre-election atmosphere, the two party leaders were to be given absolute parity of treatment. But the tragedy at Dallas was almost matched by farce in the London TV studios. Sir Alec, who had just arrived to spend the weekend with the Duke of Norfolk, had to turn round from Arundel Castle and drive straight back to the BBC. 'We reached Broadcasting House with a margin of three minutes to spare,' says Sir Alec, 'and I got into a lift, which then proceeded to stick. Luckily it would move down, but then I had to run up three flights of stairs. My lungs were bursting and my heart was doing treble overtime, and I cannot imagine to this day how my plight was not detected by viewers.' Unsurprisingly, Sir Alec's tribute came over as somewhat hesitant and formal compared to Harold Wilson's.

Those people who saw the Labour leader at the studios that night were struck by how personally he seemed to be taking the news of the assassination.

At one stage, after a telephone call from Downing Street, he pressed his head silently and helplessly against the wall. As Anthony Howard and Richard West put it in *The Making of the Prime Minister:* 'subconsciously Wilson must have been aware that the death of the forty-six-year-old President kicked one of the main props from under Labour's appeal. From the moment of his election in 1960, Kennedy represented, if obliquely, a challenge to everything that was stuffy, traditional and out of date in Britain.' But Wilson was determined to play up in the public mind his association with Kennedy. He lobbied ferociously to ensure that he was invited to attend the heavily televised funeral as one of Britain's official mourners, along with Prince Philip and Sir Alec. The three flew off together on a plane of the Queen's Flight, 'Harold's going was almost entirely due to a good friend in the press who constantly asked in the White House whether there was a place for Wilson, forcing a reply,' Crossman noted in his diary.

In the election year of 1964, Wilson did his utmost to wrap himself in the dead President's mantle. In his speeches and television interviews he continued to adapt Kennedy's phrases and ideas to a British context. In his inaugural address the President had talked of creating 'the New Frontier'. In Birmingham at the start of the year, Wilson proclaimed: 'We want the youth of Britain to storm the new frontiers of knowledge.' In a party political broadcast which featured Anthony Wedgwood Benn as his would-be thrusting interviewer, Wilson said: 'What I think we are going to need is something like President Kennedy had when he came in after years of stagnation. He had a programme of a hundred days of dynamic action.' Before the broadcast Wilson had told Benn, 'I want some of your youth to rub off on me.' The press mocked Wilson's pretensions, and Sir Alec felt there was more to be gained by associating himself with Kennedy's successor, Lyndon Johnson.

The Prime Minister went to America in February 1964 for a meeting with a less than enthusiastic President. 'I can see what's in it for him, but what's in it for me?' Johnson remarked to a crony. On his return home, Sir Alec agreed to appear on *Panorama* to talk about both his American trip and domestic politics. It was his first television interview in four months; but he had now had hours of training in the TV studios at Conservative Central Office. 'They put me through various practice sessions,' says Home. 'I had to make a mock speech to the camera and that was considerable torture. I wasn't prepared for television: I had been thrown in at the deep end as Prime Minister.' He rehearsed for *Panorama* with a series of mock interviews by two experienced television performers: Christopher Chataway, the former ITN newscaster who had become a Conservative MP, and Nigel Lawson, then a financial journalist and broadcaster, who was one of Sir

Alec's speechwriters. Together they ran through the range of subjects that it seemed likely *Panorama* would raise. Sir Alec was the first of many prime ministers to go through this routine. Chataway remembers that when he asked a question about the 11-plus examination, Sir Alec said plaintively: 'They don't really expect a prime minister to know about things like that, do they?' Chataway wrote out the answer for him to learn but during the next run-through, Sir Alec unfortunately reproduced it in response to a question about social security. The Prime Minister's advisers looked forward with considerable trepidation to his appearance on *Panorama*; but they felt he had to be seen on television by the electorate.

Sir Alec had agreed that the interview should be not at Number 10 but at the BBC's studios in Lime Grove. The Corporation's commissionaires were all instructed to wear their full ceremonial kit, including white gloves. The Head of Current Affairs, Grace Wyndham Goldie, was delighted at Sir Alec's decision. She felt that prime ministers had an unfair advantage if they were interviewed in Number 10. 'The historic setting clothes a prime minister with an authority which does not exist visually in a drawing room or a studio. And this affects the interviewer. In Downing Street he is seen to be asking questions of a person who has been entrusted by the nation with power and the surroundings proclaim it. A greater courtesy of manner by the interviewer becomes appropriate. In the television studio the interviewer is more at home than the politician and so their roles are changed in small, subtle ways.' From the first, *Panorama* made it plain who was the host and who was the guest. To portentous music, the Prime Minister was shown walking on to the set and shaking hands with Richard Dimbleby: 'Good evening, sir, welcome to *Panorama*.' 'Nice to see you, how are you?' Dimbleby then prodded Sir Alec gently and unsuccessfully to reveal the date of the general election before handing him over to Robin Day: 'Your chair for your serious interview is over here.'

The Prime Minister's hours of rehearsal had not been wasted. The political correspondent of *The Times* wrote: 'Sir Alec parried and returned every thrust with ease – not least when Mr Day raised the question of amateurish and indecisive leadership, a description that with every passing minute seemed more absurdly inappropriate to his intended victim.' Despite the supposed disadvantage of coming to enemy territory, the Prime Minister had succeeded in the interview. 'His sense of assurance through a maze of thorny questions surprised most political observers and raised his stock substantially throughout the nation,' enthused Sir Alec's biographer, John Dickie. In the early months of 1964, the opinion polls showed the Tories' fortunes rising and the political commentators chorused a single question – when? Would there be an early general election? In his speeches, the

Prime Minister seemed to give the game away: 'When the election comes in June,' then a long pause, 'or in October.'

With the aim of attracting favourable television coverage in the months before the election, both Sir Alec and Harold Wilson had embarked on meet-the-people speaking tours across the country and would trade long-distance insults. Sir Alec described the Labour leader, in the phrase provided for him by his speech-writer, Eldon Griffiths, as 'the slick salesman of synthetic science'. In turn, Wilson mocked reliance on speech-writers (although he used them himself) and attacked 'the grouse moor conception of Tory leadership'; Labour would create a society in which brains would take precedence over blue blood. Sir Alec responded: 'The Socialists are as stuffy and dated as a Victorian front room.' It was a charge that worried Wilson. His aim was to attach himself to everything that was modern and successful in Britain in the hope that some of the sheen would rub off on him. And in the spring of 1964, there was nothing to compare with the Beatles.

Wilson readily agreed to present the group with awards from the Variety Club of Great Britain. He was seen on television joking with the four young millionaire Liverpudlians and looking like their favourite uncle. 'Thank you very much', said Paul McCartney, 'for giving us this silver heart, but I still think you should have given one to good old Mr Wilson.' It was a publicity coup that the Prime Minister's advisers attempted to match. But Sir Alec was less adept at blending politics with show business. In one speech, he mangled the title of a Beatles' song into unrecognizability. In another, he sought to link the group's success with Conservative free enterprise policies. A TV interviewer asked George Harrison what he thought about being praised by the Prime Minister. 'Oh, it was all right. But what was all that stuff about us earning dollars for Britain. Does he think we're going to share them all out?'

In April, Sir Alec finally ended his teasing about the date of the general election. He announced it would be in the autumn. The BBC wanted the party leaders to agree in advance that the election campaign on television would have a new feature. It proposed to follow the example of the Kennedy–Nixon debates and stage a confrontation between Home and Wilson. In public, Wilson favoured the idea, but the Conservatives stalled. They suggested instead that there should be confrontations not just between the Prime Minister and the Opposition leader – but between a number of ministers and their shadows. With doubts about the televisual abilities of their captain, the Tories wanted to stress the merits of their whole team: 'We bat all the way down to number eleven,' claimed one of Home's staff.

In a speech which infuriated the Labour party, Home said that he was willing to face Wilson on television, 'but when I want it, I shall send for him and not the other way round.' In private both leaders' fears were greater than their desire for confrontation. As Wilson admitted: 'I was none too keen on the broadcasts. Some small thing might have gone wrong. I might have got hiccups from smoking a dusty pipe.' In the end there were no confrontations, although Wilson chose for tactical reasons to raise the issue again during the election campaign. Sir Alec declined, claiming he had no wish to turn the election into an American presidential campaign: 'I saw the Kennedy–Nixon confrontation, that cured me for ever.'

Harold Wilson had begun his election campaign at the Empire Pool, Wembley, with a rally that mixed traditional Labour politics and show business. The Grimethorpe Colliery Brass Band, the Welsh Male Voice Choir and parades of manual workers were interspersed with Pakistani dancers, African drummers and Humphrey Lyttelton's jazz band, as well as with performances by Harry Corbett, of the hugely popular TV programme *Steptoe and Son*, and Vanessa Redgrave. The aim of it all was both to enthuse the party workers and help persuade the television audience that Labour was a modern, swinging party. The Wembley rally ended with Harold Wilson delivering a Kennedy-style message: 'The choice we offer, starting today, is between standing still, clinging to the tired philosophy of a day that is gone, or moving forward in partnership and unity to a just society, to a dynamic, expanding, confident, and above all purposive new Britain.'

Wilson was determined that Labour's whole election campaign would be based around himself – only he would appear on the election posters and he would take charge of all the party political broadcasts. He paid infinite attention to detail, deciding on exactly the length of the signature tune and on the studio backing for his own appearances. 'He could not yet broadcast from Number 10,' said Grace Wyndham Goldie, 'but he made certain that he should be seen seated in front of an executive-type desk in front of a Georgian window which created the atmosphere of an office in Whitehall.' Wilson was, however, aware of the force of the Tories' charge that under him Labour had become a one-man band; he decided he would appear only briefly in the first party election broadcast and reserve himself for the final one. But he had no intention of keeping himself off other programmes.

In 1964, there was to be more news and current affairs coverage of the campaign than ever before. ITN planned special extra programmes each night as did the BBC, which now had two channels. During the campaign Wilson was to show more sophistication in his use of the airwaves than any previous Labour or Tory leader. The Conservative party's Vice-Chairman, Lord Poole, enviously described Wilson as the only really competent political

TV performer this country had produced. And with both political parties convinced that television provided the key to electoral success, many raw nerve ends were on display in the run-up to the campaign. In Harold Wilson's case, it led to a blazing row with the BBC. He arrived for an interview in the studio with Robert McKenzie, although he was convinced that the LSE professor was ineradicably anti-Labour. Wilson discovered that he was to be interviewed sitting in front of a desk, with McKenzie behind it. Labour's Broadcasting Officer, Clive Bradley, complained that the set-up would make McKenzie look like a headmaster dealing with a naughty schoolboy. After furious arguments, Grace Wyndham Goldie eventually decreed that the desk should go. It was an opening skirmish in what was to become over the years a sulphurous feud between Wilson and the BBC.

Sir Alec, too, had his troubles with the broadcasters. On the day he announced that the election would be on 15 October, he agreed to give interviews to both television networks. While the Prime Minister was being made up, George Ffitch of ITV explained that he planned to ask what were the real issues in the campaign. Sir Alec grimaced. He refused to do an interview on that basis: he was only prepared to talk about the constitutional significance of the date of the election – a matter of interest to virtually no one. The Prime Minister was deaf to the entreaties of the producers from ITV and the BBC. 'I don't know what the issues of the election are,' he protested and, like a petulant schoolgirl saying 'shan't', the Prime Minister folded his arms and sat tight in his make-up chair: 'No, I'm not doing it. I'm on strike.' Eventually the TV people agreed to leave him to consult his advisers. A few minutes later the Prime Minister emerged. He had changed his mind – of course he would talk about the issues in the campaign. The ITV producer, Jeremy Isaacs, who later went on to become head of Channel 4, was convinced at the time it had all been an act: 'He knew he was going to do the broadcast all the time. It's just that he's a player who wants to be thought a gentleman, a player who wants to be considered an amateur. The man's a professional in-fighter. He knew what the whole thing was about at the start.'

There was no doubt that Sir Alec was considerably tougher than his lairdly exterior led people to believe but, equally, he had by the time of the election become totally traumatized by the prospect of appearing on television. In part this was due to his advisers continually stressing how important it was for him to learn the techniques. It also stemmed from an incident in a BBC make-up room. 'I was being made up for some prime ministerial performance and my conversation with the young lady who was applying the powder and tan went like this:

"Can you not make me look better than I do on television? I look rather scraggy, like a ghost."

"No."

"Why not?"

"Because you have a head like a skull."

"Does not everyone have a head like a skull?"

"No."

'So that was that. Somehow I haven't got the looks of a natural.' A former *Panorama* studio director, Andrew Quicke, remembers: 'There was a standard BBC lighting instruction, issued to all studio lighting directors, laying down a procedure so complicated that it took forty minutes of valuable studio rehearsal time, while lighting and studio make-up staff struggled to give the unfortunate Prime Minister the appearance of a chin.'

Although there were to be no confrontations in 1964, the two party leaders had, for the first time in any election campaign, agreed to appear on a programme which was not one of their own political broadcasts. The BBC had come up with the idea of *Election Forum*. Viewers were invited to send in the questions they wanted asked. A representative selection would be put to the party leaders by a team of television interviewers who could ask their own supplementary questions. The BBC received 18,000 postcards with questions. Almost all were concerned with the domestic economy: prices, pensions, health and housing, with less than a thousand on foreign policy and defence. Wilson was to appear first on *Election Forum*, followed by Home the next night. The two men's attitudes to the programme were in marked contrast. Grace Wyndham Goldie said: 'Wilson arrived early: polite, wary and prepared, with a posse of advisers. He ate cold ham and salad with the production staff and went to the studio with the air of a serious politician dealing with an important situation. Home arrived shortly before the programme started, accompanied only by the Director of the Conservative Research Department. He looked so exhausted that his skin appeared to be drawn tightly over his skull. His answers to the questions fired at him seemed totally unprepared.'

Neither man was at his best in the programmes. Wilson came out with ponderous answers, which he would often unconvincingly preface by 'Quite frankly', or 'Let me be absolutely honest about this'. In talking to the studio technicians after the programme, Wilson admitted that his greatest concern had been to avoid losing votes by a rash slip. The biggest contrast on the programmes was in the appearance of the two men: Wilson looked relaxed and Sir Alec tortured. The Labour leader watched the Prime Minister's performance at his home in Hampstead Garden Suburb. On the telephone to friends afterwards he said: 'He was much better than I expected, but he left himself open on pensions.' In answer to one question, Sir Alec had talked about giving hard-up pensioners 'donations' – for Wilson, the word revealed the Prime Minister's patrician attitudes. He never let go of it throughout the campaign. He built up a highly effective passage in his campaign speech. 'I saw the Prime Minister on television the other night.' Pause for laughter. 'It's a fact. I did. I'm just as much entitled to watch television as any of you. I have my favourite programmes as you have.' Long pause. 'This wasn't one of them.' Howls of laughter.

In his campaign speeches, Wilson made full use of his knowledge of television techniques. He knew that BBC news and ITN would regularly carry a live extract from his speech. The moment he saw the red light on top of the camera glow – which meant he was on air – he would stop in mid-sentence and pick up a piece of paper which contained a crisp, sharp paragraph for the benefit of the viewers. One minute into ITN's broadcast, at 9.16, Labour's Broadcasting Officer, Clive Bradley, would confide: 'He'll be doing the bit about people, tonight.' On the platform Wilson would suddenly produce his sub-Churchillian piece for the cameras: 'We care for people, they care for profit; we care about opportunity; they are preoccupied with inheritance. They are concerned with the retention of power, we are concerned to exercise power democratically for the benefit of our people as individuals and our people as families.'

For his part, Sir Alec wanted to pretend that television did not exist. He embarked on an exhausting series of cross-country tours; sometimes he would have eight open air meetings in a day. He would begin his speech: 'I like to come and see you in person to show you that I'm not exactly what they make me look like on a TV screen.' The aim of Sir Alec's campaign managers was to counter the Labour charge that he was a remote figure, who never met ordinary people. But one senior minister believed the tactics were profoundly mistaken: 'They allowed Alec to exhaust himself talking to hundreds at farm gates, instead of making effective use of television where he could talk to millions.'

Unlike Wilson, the Prime Minister had no idea when the camera was covering him. He had no prepared passages that could be picked up and used easily by the TV news bulletins. In his campaign speeches, he stumbled and rambled; the reporters covering his election tour joked they would club together to buy him the other half moon for his half moon spectacles. In the TV cutting rooms, both BBC and ITN tried to edit him kindly and take out his fluffs. Cameramen went to great lengths to avoid unflattering shots. They were spurred on by an incident early in the campaign. At the Market Square in Norwich an ITN crew, trapped by the crowd one side of the speaker's platform, could only film an extreme profile shot. This drew anguished complaints from Conservative Central Office. But worse was to follow for the Prime Minister.

Wherever he went on his speaking tour, Sir Alec was accompanied by hecklers. At one stage he claimed that the Labour party had hired them. The demonstrators attracted the cameras and the cameras attracted the demonstrators: 'Who Exhumed You?' asked one much-filmed banner. Television, for so long dumb and blind at election time, now thrived on the sound and fury of Sir Alec's meetings. The Prime Minister's technique for dealing with barrackers was disastrous compared with Harold Wilson's. The Labour leader was well aware that the television microphones, which were pointed at him, normally did not pick up interruptions by the audience. So he would repeat the heckle for the benefit of the TV viewers, which gave him a chance to think up a sharp way of knocking it down. Sir Alec felt that he had to try to drown out the hecklers by shouting at the top of his voice. His worst experience was in the Bull Ring at Birmingham, where he was met by chanting from as many as fifteen hundred people in the crowd of five thousand. He was unaware that the viewers at home would see him bellowing and hear only distant noises off. He now believes the election began to turn at that point. 'It produced an appearance of strain which inevitably conveyed itself to the television onlookers – I looked rather hunted and that had a bad effect. I blame myself for not studying the techniques of television more than I did.' If he had known about the way directional microphones work he would have looked more confident to the audience.

Harold Wilson's own concern with the minutiae of television even extended to poring over the proposed transmission times for non-political programmes. With the opinion polls showing both parties neck and neck, the Labour leader was convinced that his chance of winning depended on a high turn-out. He was greatly concerned when he saw the BBC's plans for polling day. Its most popular programme, *Steptoe and Son*, was scheduled for eight o'clock, just an hour before the polls closed. The BBC schedulers' intention was to beat ITV by grabbing a large audience early in the evening and holding on to it throughout election night. Wilson immediately protested to the Director-General, Sir Hugh Greene: the majority of *Steptoe* viewers were Labour voters and they would stay in and watch rather than go to vote. 'Harold argued that the BBC was being very undemocratic,' says Lady Falkender, 'and he asked Greene to take *Steptoe* off altogether that night. Greene asked: "What do you propose I should put in its place?" And Harold replied: "I suggest you put on *Oedipus Rex* – Greek tragedy." ' Eventually Greene agreed to postpone *Steptoe* until after the polls had closed at nine and Wilson rang to say: 'Thank you very much, Hugh, that will be worth a dozen or more seats to me.' 'I think that was an exaggeration,' said Greene, 'but I've often wondered in view of the closeness of the eventual outcome whether I should have a bad conscience.'

In the last days of the campaign, both Sir Alec and Harold Wilson had become convinced that all would depend on their final party political broadcasts. Each believed that Macmillan's last programme in the 1959 election had been decisive. Academic research suggested that party political broadcasts, if they had any effect at all, tended to reinforce existing impressions and voting intentions, rather than win converts. But by October 1964, Macmillan's appeal to the viewers five years earlier – with the help of a globe and Norman Collins – had taken on the status of golden myth in the eyes of both party leaders and their television advisers. Wilson determined he would leave nothing to chance with his final election broadcast.

He had five different advisers to help him write it. Ted (later Lord) Willis, the television scriptwriter and creator of the hugely popular police series, *Dixon of Dock Green*, helped produce one version and Marcia Williams another. Wilson worked long after midnight marrying the two drafts. The next morning, while Wilson was on his campaign tour, the advisers rewrote his draft – each attempting to reinsert favourite passages. Once again Wilson was reshaping the text in the small hours. He was to record the broadcast later that day at the BBC's studios in Manchester. According to Anthony Howard and Richard West in *The Making of the Prime Minister*, Wilson's arrival made a curious scene. Every BBC person in the city turned out to line the walls of the studio; even a couple of policemen from the beat came in as well. Wilson was surrounded by his five advisers; suddenly in the middle of it all, he looked a little man lost. The producer assigned to help Wilson was Stanley Hyland, a fellow Yorkshireman who was to become known as 'Harold Wilson's gold microphone-in-waiting'. He taught Wilson that he had to use direct and simple language without appearing to talk down to people – and that the impression he made was more important than the actual words he used.

'I want you at the start of the broadcast to smile and look friendly,' Hyland told Wilson. This was no easy task. Wilson was still demanding further changes in the script. And he was having difficulty reading the autocue. But to put on his glasses would detract fatally from his youthful Kennedy image. Three times Wilson had to stop the recording: 'Stanley, I'm sorry I can't read it, you'll have to bring the camera in nearer.' As the deadline for sending the broadcast by land line to London approached, Wilson and his advisers grew increasingly nervous and irritable with each other. They broke off for tea. Wilson had a glass of brandy and scraped minestrone off his suit with a pair of scissors. Time was running out: the GPO could not guarantee the land line for much longer. It seemed as if only a stumbling version of the broadcast would be available. Then, with no chance for a retake, Wilson finally managed a word- and expression-perfect recording. Everyone sighed with relief and those who a few minutes earlier had been at each other's throats were now exchanging compliments as they watched the recording being sent down to London. Wilson offered a running commentary on his own appearance: 'Who's that chap? He looks like the pig we've just seen on the children's programme. No, I don't like the look of him. I wouldn't vote for him myself.'

Wilson and his advisers had devised the final broadcast to counter Sir Alec's two strongest campaign themes – that Labour was not fit to govern and that it would render Britain defenceless by unilateral nuclear disarmament. The first two and a half minutes of the programme were taken by the symbol of Labour respectability – Clement Attlee. The former Prime Minister, looking very old and frail in his armchair, claimed that the idea of an independent British deterrent was nonsense and that ownership of the bomb was unnecessary to our foreign policy. Wilson then mixed compassion with patriotism and talked of the need to modernize Britain by taking government out of the hands of the old boy network. 'If the past belongs to the Tories, the future belongs to us – all of us.'

His problems in recording the broadcast had been minor compared to the Prime Minister's. Unlike Wilson, Sir Alec felt he was an electronic victim. 'Don't misunderstand me,' he says, 'I am a fan of television as far as sport and ceremonial are concerned. I think it is less suited to politics than to anything else. You are dealing with the most complicated issues in a very short time and it is bound to be superficial.' Sir Alec liked least of all what he was expected to do in his final election broadcast – to speak straight to the camera. 'The set piece bored me stiff. I disliked all the fuss of it. All the advancing of the cameras and the constant repetition. They were always saying: "It's not quite right, let's do it again." And by then you would have forgotten what you had said the first time. I didn't like the whole paraphernalia of it. And no doubt it showed on my face. It just had a physical effect on me. I felt worse after I had done it.' To help him overcome his camera phobia, the Prime Minister turned for his final election broadcast to Norman Collins, the Managing Director of ATV. The Tories regarded him as their own TV miracle-worker.

In strict secrecy, Sir Alec and Collins went to rehearse at ATV's studios in Elstree for the whole of the Sunday before the final broadcast, which was to be transmitted two days later. Collins knew the Prime Minister, who was neither a showman nor an actor, represented much less promising material than Macmillan five years earlier. Although Sir Alec could come over reasonably naturally in an interview, he froze when he talked direct to the camera and looked like a ventriloquist's dummy. And there was another problem. In all his years, he had never used a teleprompter or autocue. Collins might have decided to stage an interview. But the Conservatives' own private research into the effectiveness of their TV broadcasts had reached two main conclusions: 'First, that *any* questioner is suspect in a party political broadcast: the impression is that the whole thing is rehearsed – a put-up job. Second, speaking direct *to* the viewer is much more successful – though some of the effect is lost if the script is read from notes.' And since Eden's successful final broadcast in the 1955 election, it had become accepted that the Prime Minister would end the campaign with an appeal to the people direct to camera.

Collins felt he had no choice but to follow the TV convention. He decided it was too late to try to teach Sir Alec how to use an autocue; it seemed the only alternative was for the Prime Minister to learn the whole of his fifteen-minute script by heart. But even had that been possible, it would not have been desirable. 'He would have come over like someone reciting a lesson,' Lord Poole, who was also at the Elstree studios, said later. Instead Norman Collins decided that the Prime Minister should learn his script two minutes at a time. Collins would record him in seven separate takes and film shots of him looking down at his notes to cover the joins.

For Sir Alec the recording of the broadcast was a nightmare. Collins devoted the whole of the Sunday session to trying to defrost the Prime Minister in front of the camera. Although Collins secretly recorded him, as he had done with Macmillan, by the end of a long day he did not have a transmittable version. Much to Sir Alec's chagrin, he had to go through the whole process again on transmission day. He planned to complete the recording in the morning; but it took all day. Again and again, Collins made the Prime Minister re-do his two-minute sections. 'I sweated blood,' says Home, 'eventually I had finished the thing and I thought it had been rather good. And then a fellow came down from the roof and said there had been an electrical fault. And I had to do the whole thing all over again. So you can see why I so disliked television.' At last, Collins was satisfied that he had enough good takes to edit together the complete broadcast. But this time the ATV Managing Director had failed to work the magic.

In his broadcast, Sir Alec exactly echoed Macmillan five years earlier. Never had our people been more confident, buoyant and self-reliant. There was full employment and living standards were rising year by year. Not only did the Socialists threaten all this but, he added, they were prepared to surrender all Britain's authority in the world by renouncing the Bomb. *The Times* judged Sir Alec's broadcast harshly. 'It proved to be a symphony in black and white delivered by a tone-deaf pianist. For though the notes were all there and in the right order, the performance was so totally lacking in style and emotion that its impact was lost on the ear.' It was an uninspired end to what had been a surprisingly successful year as Prime Minister.

Sir Alec had come to Downing Street with his party, racked by sexual scandal, at its lowest ebb for twenty years. The TV satirists had depicted him as an effete aristocrat, totally unsuited for modern political leadership. He remained fearful of television throughout his time in office. But he appealed strongly to traditionally deferential voters and came over on the screen as decent and unclever.

The Conservatives contrasted the Prime Minister's straight style with the Labour leader's. 'Would you buy a used car from Harold Wilson?' asked Anthony Barber, one of Sir Alec's Cabinet ministers, during the election campaign. It was a question designed to counter Wilson's carefully burnished Kennedy image and to associate him instead with the loser of the 1960 Presidential race – 'Tricky Dickie' Nixon. And when they went to the polls on 15 October, Britain's voters were split down the middle in answer to Barber's question.

It turned out to be a very long election night. Wilson yo-yoed between hopes of a landslide and fears of humiliating defeat. Early on he held his own Merseyside consituency of Huyton with a greatly increased majority. George Ffitch of ITN asked Wilson whether he now felt like a prime minister. 'Quite frankly I feel like a drink,' replied the Labour leader. It was a rare moment of humour in what became an increasingly edgy night. When he arrived by train at Euston the following morning Wilson uncharacteristically refused to talk to the waiting TV crews. 'It's getting more like Kennedy's election all the time,' he confided, remembering how his hero had won by the smallest majority of the vote in American history: 'All we are waiting for now is the result from Cook County.' The respectable British equivalent of the Illinois district where Mayor Daley had stuffed the ballot boxes full of Democrat votes turned out to be Brecon and Radnor. Nearly eighteen hours after the polls had closed the Welsh seat gave Wilson his majority. After thirteen years of Conservative government a Labour Prime Minister was back in Downing Street.

With an overall majority of only four, Harold Wilson determined to embark on his Kennedy-style hundred days of dynamic action. He would also follow the President's example in his use of television. The new Prime Minister planned to appear regularly on the air to explain what he was doing and to enlist the public to his side. In his first eighteen months at Number 10, the highly accomplished political broadcaster would succeed brilliantly. But even in his moment of greatest triumph, Wilson was to demonstrate his suspicion and distrust of the TV authorities. And after that, his feelings that he was the victim of persecution by television – shared to some extent by all prime ministers – would reach unprecedented levels.

CHAPTER 8

The Cheque that Bounced

'Harold Wilson thought he had money in the bank with the BBC;
but when he came to cash his cheque, it bounced.'

Sir Hugh Carleton Greene

Harold Wilson arrived at Downing Street determined that he would have a totally different relationship with television from any of his predecessors. And he did. But not at all in the way he foresaw on the heady day he came to power in October 1964. He planned to use the airwaves as a major instrument of government. He would make regular broadcasts to explain his policies direct to the people. He felt he had two great advantages over every other recent occupant of Number 10. One was his youth – at forty-eight, he was the youngest prime minister this century. He also rather enjoyed appearing on television and thought he was pretty good at it. The studio was not for him a twentieth-century torture chamber; rather it was a political pleasure-dome. Straight into the homes of over ninety per cent of the population went the medium with built-in rules for impartiality and fairness. It was the essential counter to what he saw as the overwhelming pro-Tory bias in the press.

Harold Wilson had put a great deal of faith, hope and hard work into his relationship with television: in his early days as Prime Minister he had a kind of love affair with the small screen. He had turned himself into a TV professional. 'If a cameraman asked him to walk down the garden steps from the Cabinet room, across the lawn and stop on a certain leaf facing in a certain direction, he did it, without any sense of condescension, and got it right the first time,' said John Wale of ITN: 'If it fell to him to begin some brief filming session by reading aloud the communiqué he was to answer questions about, he realized that he had to wait while the cameras were run p to speed before he spoke.' Television and the Prime Minister needed each other. But things were to go wrong in the relationship; suspicion and recrimination were followed by the bitterest acrimony. Yet Harold Wilson had begun his premiership with as close a relationship to the small screen as the Black Queen in *Snow White* had to her mirror on the wall.

As he purred into Downing Street on 16 October, the new Prime Minister faced the most perplexing economic and political problems. He had inherited a record balance of payments deficit; many investors in the City and abroad, traditionally distrustful of a Labour government, were convinced that Wilson would soon have to devalue the pound. Speculation against sterling began immediately and was to continue for the next three years, however loudly Wilson proclaimed his determination not to devalue. 'The Gnomes of Zurich' – as George Brown, the new Secretary of State for Economic Affairs, dubbed foreign speculators – now entered Labour's demonology. Politically, Harold Wilson had his back to the wall of Number 10 from the start. With a parliamentary majority that was to shrink within months from four to only one, his government could fall at any time. But it was a situation that was made for him. He was the master of the short term. He had produced his maxim 'a week is a long time in politics' in one of the first Lobby briefings he gave as Prime Minister to political journalists. Twenty years later he took as the motto for his peerage '*Tempus Rerum Imperator*', which he translates as 'timing is everything'.

Throughout his first eighteen months in office, Harold Wilson turned up regularly on television to announce a new plan, initiative or mission. To the White rebellion in Rhodesia, the war in Vietnam, the latest sterling crisis and the wildcat strikers in industry, the Prime Minister had an instant response. As Richard Crossman, the Housing Secretary and a leading member of Wilson's 'Kitchen Cabinet', noted in his diary, 'Harold is just moving from emergency to emergency, picking up bright ideas as he goes along. . . . He jumps from position to position always brilliantly energetic and opportunist, always moving in zig-zags.' It was government by gimmick. Wilson's aim was to stay in office long enough to convince the voters that a Labour government worked. Then he would call an election at a time of his own choosing and not be forced into one. He regarded television as essential for the success of his tactics.

The new Prime Minister took two American presidents as his role models. He wanted to use television for his own blend of Franklin Roosevelt's radio 'fireside chats' and John Kennedy's press conferences. He planned to adapt the existing arrangements for ministerial broadcasts to his purposes. But his plan led to the first of many clashes with the BBC. Sir Hugh Greene, the BBC Director-General, had devised a scheme to replace the old system of ministerial broadcasts, with its complex and contentious rules over the Opposition's right of reply. Now the BBC issued 'invitations' to the Prime Minister to speak direct to the people on matters the Corporation itself considered were of national importance. And the BBC alone decided whether the Opposition leader should have the right of reply. The system had worked effectively under Macmillan and had not been used for Sir Alec

Douglas-Home, who hated talking solo to camera. But Harold Wilson was different.

He believed that he achieved the greatest impact by talking direct to the camera; was convinced he had mastered the technique and wanted to appear regularly to create a bond between himself and the people. He did not want his chosen message diluted or deflected by the intervention of producers or interviewers. Initially, it seemed the system of invitations would work for Wilson. He accepted the first on 16 October, the day he became Prime Minister, and announced that his tiny majority would not affect his determination to govern. Ten days later he was on the air again to explain why his government was imposing a 15 per cent surcharge on imports. But it soon became clear that there was a crucial shortcoming in the informal arrangements: the Prime Minister wanted to come to the studio far more often than the BBC wanted to invite him. He felt ministerial broadcasts provided a unique opportunity to present himself as a national leader, who was above party. But the Corporation's top officials feared that, with the parliamentary balance so precarious, any such appearance was bound to be partisan; they had to take special care to be fair and impartial and prevent the Government abusing the delicately constructed machinery for ministerial broadcasts.

After his first two invitations, the Prime Minister had to wait three months before he had another. In January 1965, the BBC invited him to talk to the viewers about his government's economic emergency measures. Wilson expressed his wish to make a further broadcast the following month, but instead he was invited for an interview on *Panorama*. Wilson declined and said that he would do a broadcast direct to camera into the programme – 'it will be an appeal to the nation to tighten their belts' – but he would not answer any questions. To the Prime Minister's fury, the BBC turned him down. It argued that Wilson was offering a ministerial broadcast in disguise and to accept would fatally blur the distinction between those programmes that were under the editorial control of the Corporation and those controlled by the politicians. According to Grace Wyndham Goldie, to have accepted the Prime Minister's offer would have been 'disastrous' and would have made 'the assurance of independence of broadcasting from government interference in regard to its programmes and day-to-day administration worthless'. But the BBC had rather spoiled its case because it *had* at first agreed to Wilson's proposal. Its subsequent refusal to allow him to broadcast direct on *Panorama* marked the opening of hostilities between the Prime Minister and the Corporation.

Wilson was becoming convinced that the BBC's attitude towards him had changed since he reached Number 10. 'After thirteen years in opposition,

Labour leaders had become very close to people in the BBC,' Sir Hugh Greene told the author. 'Harold Wilson thought he had money in the bank with the BBC. But when he came to cash his cheque, it bounced. Labour had no particular credit with the BBC.' Wilson was discovering for himself that friction was built into the relationship between any prime minister and the BBC – with three main areas of potential conflict. The first concerned the belief of successive prime ministers that they should have the right to address the nation on television without the Opposition having the right to reply. The BBC interpreted the rules on ministerial broadcasts differently. 'The right of reply is a national safeguard against a kind of dictatorship and a hogging of the microphone by the leader of the party in power,' said Grace Wyndham Goldie. The second regular battleground was over the licence fee. The BBC boasts proudly of independence from government control while depending on the government to increase its income. Every prime minister, especially in the run up to a general election, regards putting up the licence fee as highly unpopular and feels even less inclined to do so when the BBC produces anti-government programmes.

Programmes were the third and most frequent source of conflict. The natural stance of most current affairs programmes was to be agin' the government – any government. Producers felt that ministers and their policies should be subject to searching and critical examination. The BBC produced so many news and current affairs programmes that some were bound to offend a government which had so obsessive a student of the media as Harold Wilson at its head. As political events turn against them, prime ministers become ever more assiduous in seeking to use television to their political advantage and to project a favourable image. Often they do not succeed. They begin instead to believe in a campaign by the BBC solely to report the negative and deliberately to ignore the good news in the government's message.

The attacks Mrs Thatcher would make against television in the mid-eighties for biased and selective reporting matched Harold Wilson's twenty years earlier – just as the bias-monitoring unit the Tory Party Chairman, Norman Tebbit, would set up at Central Office paralleled the group that Wilson put to work to find examples of BBC bias against his Government. Ironically the first offender identified by the Wilson group was on Independent Television. In the summer of 1965, Number 10 made strong protests to the ITA about a current affairs programme called *Division*, claiming that it put on too many left-wing Labour MPs, who were unsympathetic to the Government. The ITA Chairman was Lord Hill, formerly the 'Radio Doctor' and a member of Macmillan's Cabinet. He decided that the Prime Minister had a case and instructed that left-wingers be excluded from the programme. Wilson was impressed by Hill's speedy and decisive action; he wished the heads of the BBC would be as amenable.

Wilson believed his Government's survival depended on his use of television. To build up his image, he believed he had to appear as often as possible. In his first eighteen months in office Wilson established a new prime ministerial record. He averaged a major appearance a month – which included five long interviews on *Panorama* and six ministerial broadcasts (his successors were to average three major appearances a year). The gentle satire on the successor programme to *That Was The Week That Was* had John Bird appearing as Harold Wilson: 'Good evening, it is more than a day since I last talked to you. I am sure you have been wondering what I have been doing since tea-time yesterday. Well, Mary and I . . .' It was an accurate rendering of the colloquial style that the Prime Minister adopted for television. Gerald Kaufman, who became his parliamentary press officer in 1965, says: 'Harold took great care to use language that was clear, direct and uncomplicated. He was the first prime minister to realize that on television you didn't have to speak in complete sentences – with a subject, verb and object. He really worked at his television appearances: he is the only man I know who deliberately acquired a sense of humour. I remember when I first knew him – I was Chairman of the Oxford University Labour Club – and I have to say it, he was an extraordinarily boring speaker. And then suddenly he decided to have a sense of humour – he turned himself into a politician who could make very amusing, sharp, witty cracks. He had just worked at it and he did the same with television.'

Harold Wilson often used his 'cheeky chappie' style on television to put across a serious message. When he arrived at Lagos airport in Nigeria for the first Commonwealth Prime Minister's Conference to be held outside Britain, he was greeted by a scene of chaos. In an atmosphere like the hothouse at Kew Gardens, hundreds of journalists were packed together for an impromptu press conference in the VIP lounge. John Whale of ITN put a question and as Wilson attempted to make himself heard, an official from the Nigerian Ministry of Information began loudly issuing orders to the journalists. Wilson turned to him and said pleasantly but firmly: 'Belt up, do you mind? I'm trying to answer a question from Mr Whale here.' 'It was a political utterance of some skill,' claims Whale, 'it showed he knew the vernacular, that his liberalism was of the unforced kind that allowed him to speak to a black man with the kind of friendly rebuke only used among equals; that at the same time it did not extend to the point of allowing him to be publicly interrupted by a black man and that with all this his real attention was reserved for his countrymen, his own, whom he knew by name.' The Prime Minister had demonstrated similar colloquial skills on television for a serious purpose a few months earlier.

In April 1965, he flew to Paris to negotiate a loan from the French in an effort to shore up the pound. He arranged a press conference, mainly for French journalists, in the gilt splendour of the Elysée Palace. But it became clear that while the Prime Minister wanted to talk about sterling, the French reporters did not. As the conference meandered on, John Whale realized he was in danger of missing the ITN deadline for his film to catch the plane to London. 'I jumped up and made some question about sterling heard. The Prime Minister seized on it with evident gratitude and delivered a trenchant answer in which he said that people who speculated against the pound in the belief that it might be devalued were "nutcases". It had its effect on the exchanges. The next time he saw me he said: "You know you put five points on sterling with that question of yours." '

The Prime Minister's easy familiarity with television and its practitioners presented a sharp contrast to the inhibitions of the Leader of the Conservative Party. Sir Alec Douglas-Home was even unhappier about appearing on television in opposition than he had been in government. He felt temperamentally unsuited to providing what he called the 'slick knock-about and indiscriminate bludgeoning' that now seemed necessary from the Opposition leader. In July 1965, he suddenly announced his resignation with a sense of intense relief. 'I have no regrets or, if I am to be true to my image, if I must be – no grouse,' he told the Party Conference that October. He waved his half-moon glasses at the audience and added: 'But what a total nonsense this business about an image is. Now I can even put on my spectacles without being told I am going to lose the next election on television.' The Conference cheered him to the echo. Sir Alec himself had created the new machinery to elect his successor. He still had complete faith in the old system: 'the magic circle of selectors had almost everything to be said for it', he wrote a decade later. But he realized that the televised shambles of the Blackpool conference from which he had emerged as Leader in 1963 and the subsequent accusations that the whole process had been rigged meant that, as he put it, 'with all its disadvantages, it was necessary to adopt a system of election of a leader where from start to finish the whole thing was seen to be above board'.

For the first time every Conservative MP would vote for the Leader. What they wanted above all was someone who would be a match for Harold Wilson. The two main candidates were Reginald Maudling, the former Chancellor, and Edward Heath, the ex-President of the Board of Trade; the outsider was Enoch Powell. The election campaign was conducted away from the public view, in the House of Commons: Maudling's was a rather haphazard affair, while Heath's campaign manager, Peter Walker, left nothing to chance and canvassed every Tory MP. All the TV cameras saw of the contest was a picnic Heath staged in a seaside car park and a family game of football laid on by Maudling. Heath had one major advantage over the other two candidates. For the past few months he had been by far the most prominent Conservative in Parliament. As Shadow Chancellor, he had been leading the opposition to Labour's Finance Bill with sharp and well-co-ordinated attacks. Heath had impressed his fellow Tory MPs at the crucial moment: they chose him as their leader. (In the Conservative leadership election ten years later, the Shadow Chancellor who was to benefit in exactly the same way was Margaret Thatcher.) At the age of forty-nine, Edward Heath was the youngest Conservative leader in over a century.

It was ironic, in view of the many problems Heath was subsequently to have with television, that in July 1965 most Tory MPs had taken his TV skills for granted. While he was at Oxford before the war he had considered working for the BBC. He had been offered a job by Lord Reith, but turned it down: 'I couldn't work for God Almighty,' says Heath. He took lowlier employment after the war as a sub-editor on the *Church Times*. For almost the whole of his first decade in Parliament from 1950, Heath had never appeared on television. He had been confined to the Trappist silence of the Whips' Office. But in the early sixties he was scarcely off the screen, as he led Britain's abortive negotiations to join the Common Market. His authoritative manner had so impressed the Party managers that they chose him as presenter of the Conservative election broadcasts in 1964. A year later most of his fellow Tory MPs had forgotten how stilted and ill at ease he had appeared in the programmes. Their central concern was for Heath to match Harold Wilson's apparently classless TV image.

The new Tory leader was the grammar schoolboy son of a carpenter and a lady's maid – the exemplary product of the meritocratic age and far removed from Eton and the grouse moors. Yet despite the similarities of social background, it soon became clear that the two leaders could scarcely be more different in style, character and belief. Heath publicly professed cold contempt for what he described as Wilson's gimmickry, slipperiness and media manipulation. He claimed he would never stoop to such devices; he was not always to live up to his own expectations.

In August, just after the Conservative leadership election, Harold Wilson invited the TV cameras and press photographers to film him on holiday on the Scilly Isles. It was a carefully contrived performance – designed to give the electorate and foreign bankers the impression that the Government was totally relaxed about the state of sterling. Wilson had arranged that the Chancellor, James Callaghan, the Governor of the Bank of England, Lord

Cromer, and he should all leave for their holidays on the same day. On the Scillies, the Prime Minister chartered a boat for the cameramen and reporters. Reclining on the beach in his shorts and sandals, he gave an informal press conference. 'It happened this was the day that the very good set of trade figures was published, though, as ever, I insisted that extravagant deductions should not be made from a single month's figure,' says Wilson. Not to be outdone, Heath invited the television cameras to film him swimming and sailing his dinghy at Villefranche in the South of France.

The Tory leader had only recently started sailing, after his doctor advised him to slow down and take up a relaxing weekend recreation. Although his dinghy looked more like a toy boat than the ocean-going series of *Morning Clouds* he was subsequently to own, Heath had problems in controlling it. But the TV men edited out Heath's difficulties. (They were kinder to him than *Panorama* was to Dr David Owen twenty years later, when it gleefully featured the Social Democratic leader sailing his dinghy straight on to the rocks.) Heath was also filmed romping with his host's children in Villefranche, where he had been joined by his Party Chairman, Edward du Cann. Conservative Central Office was anxious to demonstrate that the bachelor Heath could be a family man. Later that month the television cameras showed him at the seaside in Broadstairs with his father and stepmother. It was the start of a major campaign of image-building by the Conservatives. Harold Wilson's parliamentary majority had fallen to only one; an election could come at any time. Heath knew he had precious little time to impress himself on his party and the electors.

But from the first, the Prime Minister was determined to prevent the new Tory leader from finding his feet. The opinion polls showed that Heath lagged far behind Wilson in terms of public recognition and personal popularity. 'Harold decided that the best way to stop Heath getting a good run at his job was never to mention him by name at all,' says Lady Falkender. 'He felt that it would build up Heath's position if he used his name. So the guy remained nameless for many years.' In his television interviews and speeches, the Prime Minister referred to Heath only as 'the Leader of the Conservative Party'. But Wilson was not only seeking to keep the identity of his main political opponent obscure in the minds of the voters; he was also attempting to lay down the terms for television coverage of himself and his Government. In October 1965, his efforts were to bring him into open conflict with the BBC at the Labour Party Conference in Blackpool.

In the ten years since the parties had first admitted the cameras, the television companies had been steadily building up their conference coverage. Both ITV and BBC now transmitted all the proceedings live and produced lengthy reports each night. This suited the political parties.

According to *The Times* in October 1965, 'television has become the principal electoral shop window for the politicians and the main display with which to dress it is the party conference'. But what did not suit the politicians – and Harold Wilson in particular – was the way the BBC had been developing its conference reports. Producers from Lime Grove, wanting to escape from the dullness of much current affairs coverage, were translating on to television the methods of the newspapers. Instead of confining themselves to showing extracts from speeches, they were introducing comment, analysis and criticism into their conference programmes. This put them on a collision course with the Prime Minister when Labour's 1965 conference opened in Blackpool.

Following the Conservatives' example, Wilson planned for a succession of ministers to deliver glowing reports to the conference of their achievements in office. He felt the BBC should faithfully reproduce extracts at peak evening viewing time. But to his fury, the BBC included in its first nightly report an interview with Clive Jenkins, the left-wing leader of ASSET, the white-collar trade union. The feline Jenkins was sharply critical of the Government's incomes policy. After the programme, Wilson summoned the BBC conference producer, John Grist, to his suite at the Imperial Hotel and bitterly reproached him. The Prime Minister claimed the BBC's only interest was in stirring things up, as Clive Jenkins had not even addressed the conference that day. Grist argued that Jenkins had appeared in *24 Hours*, which had been designed to cover current affairs and not specifically the conference, and it was therefore fair to bring in those who deviated from the Government line. Wilson was far from satisfied. He threatened that if the BBC did not mend its ways then the Government would have to think of methods of bringing it under tighter discipline.

Three days later there was another major row. It centred on an interview between George Brown, Wilson's deputy, and Robin Day. At the end of the interview, Day had put a question which Brown had clearly not been expecting – about his attitude to immigration. In the BBC's hospitality room, where he had come to watch the interview, Wilson told Grist that it was an outrage to try to trap a minister in that way and claimed that Day had quoted Brown out of context on the programme. He also complained that Brown had been unfairly roasted under the television lights in an unventilated room. Grist denied all the Prime Minister's charges, but Wilson then launched into a general attack on the BBC's conference coverage. There had been far too much concentration on the Government's critics – particularly those from the Transport Workers' Union. Would the BBC turn on the Tories in the same way and spotlight, say, Mr Enoch Powell's differences with Mr Heath? Grist replied that it was up to the BBC not the Government to decide on its form of political coverage. With raised voices, the two men argued toe to toe and the Prime Minister eventually left quivering with rage. He offered an ominous parting shot: 'We shall be watching throughout the Tory conference to see if you treat them in the same way as you treated us.' But in the event, it was the Prime Minister himself who ensured a lack of balance.

That weekend Wilson told the press that he was setting up a special unit of Transport House officials and senior ministers to monitor the BBC's coverage of the Conservative Conference – Ted Heath's first as Leader. Heath had resolved to exploit the annual gathering of the faithful in a new way. The Conservatives had adorned the hall with the words, 'RIGHT AHEAD WITH HEATH' – the first time they had ever put their Leader's name in a Conference slogan. The Tory tradition was that the Leader would only descend on the conference to deliver his address on the final day – a god sprung from the Party machine. But Heath, the first democratically elected Leader, had decided that he would be there for the whole week: he would be on display, listening to every debate and mixing with the faithful. He calculated that this would greatly increase his TV exposure. But Harold Wilson had determined to steal the headlines and the television spotlight from the Tories and their new leader. As the Party representatives gathered in Brighton on the eve of the Conservative Conference, Wilson demanded, and was given, a ministerial broadcast.

The subject was Rhodesia, where it was becoming clear that the White minority government in the Crown Colony was planning a unilateral declaration of independence (UDI). In his broadcast on the eve of the Conservative Conference, Wilson extracted the maximum drama from the prospect. He warned the Rhodesian Prime Minister, Ian Smith, in the strongest terms against reckless action and ended: 'I know I speak for everyone in these islands, all parties, all our people, when I say to Mr Smith, "Prime Minister, think again".' Harold Wilson says he had 'observers' at the Conservative Conference who told him, 'your broadcast was heard in silence and with very deep feeling.' One of his observers was Gerald Kaufman. He was at the Conference as a reporter for the *New Statesman* and was to become Wilson's parliamentary press officer later that year. 'I was with a large number of very important people from the Conservative party when Harold made that broadcast and they were seething with anger because what he had done – and he had done it quite deliberately – was to try to wreck their conference.' The Prime Minister was to go one better in upstaging the Conservatives the following day.

As the Tory representatives arrived for the opening session, they received a dramatic piece of news. The Prime Minister had taken off from Heathrow to fly to Balmoral for a sudden audience with the Queen. 'I was seen off by a number of journalists and photographers,' says Wilson, 'subsequent reports indicated that this news had a somewhat disturbing effect on the Conservative Party Conference that morning.' Wilson had thrown the Conference into panic. Journalists rushed from the press tables and were followed by senior Tories – all ringing their London offices and demanding of each other what was happening. Top of the rumour parade was that Wilson was seeking a dissolution of Parliament and an immediate general election. 'Faced with this possibility, not every delegate was able to concentrate as fully as they would have wished on the words of wisdom from the Tory platform,' says Wilson archly, 'some delegates were heard to say bitterly – as though realizing for the first time that the Conservatives were no longer in office – "we've just sung the Queen, he is seeing her".' Wilson allowed the Conservatives to sweat. Eventually he revealed to the throngs of reporters waiting for him at Aberdeen airport that his audience had nothing to do with a general election. It had been about Rhodesia.

The Prime Minister had achieved his purpose. 'Nobody was interested in what the Conservatives were going to say that week,' says Gerald Kaufman, 'they were interested in what Harold said. And since Harold knew that he was going to hold a general election the following spring what he had deliberately done was to wreck the last Tory conference before the general election. And it had even more significance because it was Ted Heath's first as Party leader.' The Prime Minister's publicity coup had begun with his melodramatic ministerial broadcast on the eve of the Tory Conference. The timing and content of the broadcast had further strained his relations with the BBC. Under the guise of speaking as the national leader, Wilson had used the broadcast primarily to achieve a party propaganda victory. To the BBC, it again revealed the Prime Minister's consistent desire to control the coverage of politics on television.

A fortnight earlier, as well as the fracas at the Labour Party Conference, Wilson had applied direct pressure on the Corporation. The Rhodesian Prime Minister, Ian Smith, had come to Britain for talks with Wilson and had made a successful appearance on ITV's *This Week*. The former wartime RAF fighter pilot had drawn a sympathetic response from many viewers. The BBC then invited Smith for an interview on *24 Hours*. But Wilson made clear to the BBC Chairman, Lord Normanbrook, that it would be in the interest of neither the Government nor the Corporation for the Rhodesian leader to appear. The Director-General, Sir Hugh Greene, was abroad. As a former Secretary to the Cabinet, Normanbrook had been trained to respect a prime minister's wishes. He cancelled the invitation. The decision enraged the Current Affairs staff at Lime Grove. And it made the Director-General, on his return, all the more determined to stand up to the Prime Minister. He felt that in keeping Smith off the air because his views were too extreme, Wilson was paradoxically taking his cue from the Salisbury Premier, who had turned the Rhodesian Broadcasting Corporation into a government mouthpiece. Greene's determination that the BBC should not suffer the same fate intensified the continuing wrangle with the Prime Minister over ministerial broadcasts.

The BBC's independent role in arbitrating on whether a ministerial broadcast had been controversial and so merited an Opposition reply was at the heart of the dispute. Wilson's re-election strategy was based on presenting himself and his ministers as national figures; he felt that allowing a Tory response reduced ministerial broadcasters to partisan politicians. An early skirmish came in the autumn of 1965. Wilson wanted his deputy and Secretary of State for Economic Affairs, George Brown, to make a ministerial broadcast about Labour's economic blueprint for the next ten years – the so-called National Plan. The Prime Minister argued that Brown's would by definition be a broadcast on a national matter and so there should be no question of an Opposition right of reply. The BBC responded that in the pre-election period the Brown broadcast was likely to be regarded as highly controversial and contentious by the Conservatives, who in any case opposed the whole idea of the planned economy. The BBC stuck to the agreed rules and – after Brown had made his broadcast – granted the Conservatives the right of reply. The Shadow Chancellor, Iain Macleod produced a particularly savage piece of invective, which enraged the Prime Minister. He felt that the BBC had been 'bloody-minded' over the Brown broadcast and he was developing a fixation that the Corporation was treating him far worse than it had treated Conservative prime ministers.

His most loyal acolytes – in particular the Paymaster-General, George Wigg – fed his beliefs. Wigg, a bloodhound-faced Labour MP and former colonel in Intelligence, was Wilson's chief trouble-shooter and media monitor. He convinced the Prime Minister that the Labour Government was not being allowed to make anything like the number of ministerial broadcasts for its own political purposes that the Conservatives had made. In essence, Wigg's charge was that with Labour now in office, the BBC had moved the goalposts. Armed with Wigg's findings, in November Wilson launched his attack in Parliament. He claimed that while in office the Conservatives had made about ninety ministerial broadcasts with hardly any right of reply by the Labour party. In Opposition they were now being granted replies to almost every broadcast the Government made. 'It is clear,' said the Prime Minister ominously, 'that there has been a change of practice.' At that stage, Edward Heath intervened. Deadpan he pointed out that most of the Conservative broadcasts had been on the radio and many had been exhortations to post early for Christmas. The House laughed and a discomfited Prime Minister snapped back that his figures included two broadcasts on the Tory Rent Act of 1957, to which no reply had been allowed. It was a pretty inglorious parliamentary performance by the Prime Minister; but he continued to listen to Wigg and the more he heard, the greater grew his resentment at the BBC.

The Prime Minister was constantly drawing the contrast between the BBC's attitude to him and what he called 'the absolutely scrupulous impartiality' of the ITA, under Lord Hill. Although the Labour party had opposed the creation of independent television, its links with the commercial companies and in particular with Independent Television News were becoming much closer than they were with the BBC. Says Lady Falkender: 'The Editor of ITN, Geoffrey Cox, was a friend of George Wigg and came to know Harold very well through Wigg. Their relationship became a close one.' Cox, who received a knighthood in the 1966 New Year's Honours, says: 'Of course we had our share of rows, but I think that because ITN was a smaller organization problems, protests and complaints were brought very quickly to the top and many of them I dealt with myself. The trouble with the BBC is that being such a big organization, by the time it had gone through the various layers, the politician was getting more and more angry and the problem tended to fester.'

Harold Wilson's quarrels with the BBC were to flare into open conflict during the general election of March 1966. He had decided he wanted to conduct a quiet campaign. The image would be of a Prime Minister and his Government resolutely tackling the problems they had been bequeathed – with calm confidence and efficiency. In two of Labour's five election broadcasts, the Prime Minister spoke reassuringly to the camera from behind an imposing desk. 'Harold Wilson expressed to me the opinion that a political leader should try to look, particularly on television, like a family doctor,' said Sean Lemass, the Irish Prime Minister, who met Wilson immediately after the election campaign. 'The family doctor image Mr Wilson wanted to project was of the kind of man who inspires trust by his appearance as well as by his soothing words and whose advice is welcome.' But while the Prime Minister wanted a quiet campaign, Ted Heath believed his only chance lay in raising the temperature. Wilson became convinced that the BBC was aiding and abetting the Opposition leader in his efforts.

The Prime Minister's plan was to say little that was new or newsworthy at his daily press conferences, while Heath's was constantly to raise fresh issues. Wilson complained that the BBC's nightly *Campaign Report* either followed the Tories' lead or attempted itself to set the agenda for the election. When Labour's campaign was concentrating on housing or prescription charges, the BBC mounted discussions about two of the issues that Wilson specifically wanted to avoid – the Common Market and the trade unions. The Prime Minister angrily rejected a BBC invitation to be interviewed on the so-called 'noose trial'. Some car workers in Cowley had revealed that they had been 'tried' by their Union for not joining an unofficial strike; in the mock courtroom a hangman's noose had swung down from the rafters. 'No noose is good noose', was the private slogan of Wilson's campaign committee, which wanted the story buried. During the election, Wilson turned down frequent requests for interviews from *Campaign Report* – while he accepted all three from the ITN equivalent, *Election '66*. He claimed that the BBC only wanted him to discuss issues raised by Heath; in fact, three of the BBC invitations had come with no strings attached.

The root of the problem was that – as with its coverage of party conferences – the BBC was developing its political journalism in a way which did not suit the Prime Minister. While only eleven years earlier the Corporation had been too timid even to carry a single word about the general election, now it wanted to cover the campaign fully – like a newspaper. But sharp reporting and studio 'punch-ups' on topical issues clashed with the Prime Minister's desire to conduct a low-key campaign. In his diary, Richard Crossman, who was Wilson's chief campaign adviser, noted that Labour had decided on a 'deliberately boring approach' and he objected to television's treatment of the election, which he claimed 'concentrates so on personalities and leadership and gimmicks that the viewer gets a picture of bickering politicians and no real understanding of the issues involved'. The BBC now replaced the capitalist press as Wilson's whipping boy in his election speeches. Privately he complained about two other matters. One was that the BBC often referred to him in its election reports as the 'Leader of the Labour Party' rather than the Prime Minister. The BBC replied that it was following precisely the same procedure as in the previous election with Sir Alec Douglas-Home.

Wilson's other major complaint was over the BBC's handling of a possible televised confrontation between himself and Heath. The Prime Minister had publicly come out in favour of a confrontation, though privately he was totally opposed to the idea. 'We felt that a confrontation would have given Heath an advantage,' says Lady Falkender, 'he was trying to make his leadership stick, while Harold was by then a very well-known figure and by definition lots of people would have tuned into him. It would have given Heath a lot of exposure in a setting that he wanted and needed – exposure as a potential Prime Minister. Harold's office would have rubbed off on Heath. He decided that Heath was not going to appear on equal terms with him.' Wilson's complaint was that the BBC had gone on pushing proposals for a confrontation, against his will, whereas in 1964 it had immediately accepted Sir Alec's refusal. The problem was that tactically Wilson wanted neither to appear with Heath, nor for it to look publicly as if he was refusing to do so. As Nigel Lawson remarked sardonically in the *Spectator:* 'Wilson had already declared himself – on BBC television no less – in favour of a confrontation with Heath. The BBC naturally took this up. Wilson is in effect accusing the BBC of taking him at his own word. This is admittedly somewhat eccentric, but hardly evidence of Tory bias.'

Throughout the campaign Wilson's resentment at the BBC mounted and he determined to take retributive action once the polls had closed. To journalists following his campaign, it had all the makings of a Sicilian vendetta. The irony was that despite the BBC's attempts at independent coverage, Wilson had largely succeeded in running the low-key campaign he planned. 'The Tories can't find a way to break through the complacent acceptance by the electorate of Super Harold,' Richard Crossman noted. Ted Heath was having the greatest difficulty in projecting himself to the electorate. In speeches and on television he had come up with the slogan '9—5—1' to prove how disastrous the Labour Government's record was. Wages were rising by 9 per cent a year, prices by 5 and production by only 1 per cent, he claimed. It may have been bad for the economy, but it was an ideal formula for winning an election. Heath's best joke of the campaign also backfired. A fortnight before polling day, he made a speech deriding the way the Prime Minister latched on to successful show business personalities. Referring to the news that London Zoo had just sent a panda over to mate in Moscow, Heath said: 'No doubt in a month's time we shall see Mr Wilson having tea at Number 10 with a pregnant panda.' It seemed the Leader of the Opposition was publicly conceding that he did not expect to find himself in Downing Street after the election. As the campaign reached its end, Heath looked an increasingly forlorn figure on television, while Wilson appeared ever more confident.

The TV highlight of the campaign for the Prime Minister was his meeting at the Bull Ring in Birmingham. In the previous election eighteen months earlier, Sir Alec Douglas-Home had so suffered from the hecklers there that he felt the election slipping away from him. This time local Tories planned to avenge their fallen leader. Wilson had timed his speech so that it would coincide with ITN's main bulletin of the night, then at nine o'clock. Geoffrey Cox, the Editor of ITN, decided to take a live extract into the bulletin. Wilson had arranged that he would be given a cue when ITN was on the air by his new press secretary, Gerald Kaufman. 'Harold felt that this appearance on the news was very important because we knew that

Labour voters watch ITV and he needed to know exactly when ITN was piping him in live. He had prepared a passage – he knew precisely how many words he spoke to the minute – 140 – and he needed a signal when he was going on the air.'

Geoffrey Cox was in ITN's London control room watching Wilson's speech coming down the line from Birmingham for the twenty minutes before the news bulletin began. The audience was packed with Conservative barrackers – many of them students. 'Wilson began slowly, lingering over the sentences of his written speech and this leisurely approach stimulated the hecklers,' says Cox. 'For the next twenty minutes we in the control room were treated to a virtuoso performance by a remarkable television performer, as Harold Wilson varied his replies from scorn to wisecracks, from derision to apparent indignation, seeming deliberately to tease the audience. He was certainly in no hurry to get on to the main parts of his speech. The reason was not hard to guess. He was playing the audience along, warming them up as the compère of an entertainment show warms up his audience until he was ready to come in.'

Gerald Kaufman remembers that he stood waiting in the hall, just below the Prime Minister's lectern. 'Harold obviously couldn't get the signal direct that he was on the air, as he was speaking in this enormous barn-like auditorium. What happened was that ITN gave the signal to another member of Harold's staff, who then passed it down the hall to me. I was in Harold's eyeline and I gave it to him. He immediately stopped what he was saying and turned to his prepared passage.' According to Geoffrey Cox there was a dramatic transformation: 'Harold Wilson dropped the attitude of the jesting debater. And, almost as if he had changed his very garb, became in a flash the serious statesman. Gravity now marked his features as he set out the core of his argument swiftly and vigorously. The crowd which had by then passed from heckling to uproar, were taken by surprise and for a moment silenced. But within a minute or so they were back on the attack. At home the audience saw the Prime Minister seeking to expound his policy to the country, being shouted and yelled at, but battling on in the face of uproar – steadily putting his message across and pausing only to deliver an occasional riposte. It provided some of the most remarkable television seen in a news programme. I let it run for four and half minutes.'

The BBC did not carry live coverage of the Birmingham meeting or of any other speech in the 1966 campaign. It felt Harold Wilson had been so skilled at exploiting his live coverage in 1964 that he effectively took over editorial control of the news bulletin. The Corporation wanted itself – and not the Prime Minister – to decide what to transmit from his speeches. Harold Wilson saw this reversal of policy as a further instance of how he received better treatment at the hands of ITV than he did from the BBC. He also found that Sir Hugh Greene was less amenable to changing TV schedules on polling day than he had been eighteen months earlier. The Prime Minister pressed him to postpone showing its popular spy series, *The Man from UNCLE*, until the polls had closed: but Auntie said *UNCLE* must stay. For Wilson this was yet another slight in what he saw as a consistent campaign against him. When he arrived at Lime Grove to make his final election broadcast he was in a state of fury with the Corporation.

To the viewers he projected his family doctor image. His appeal for stability and patriotism made an ironic contrast to Ted Heath's final broadcast the previous night calling for radical change. In the Lime Grove hospitality room after the broadcast, Wilson vehemently attacked Paul Fox – the Head of Current Affairs, who had taken over from Grace Wyndham Goldie on her retirement – and other senior BBC officials. The Prime Minister claimed he had been fighting the election against two enemies – the Conservatives and the BBC. He wanted the Corporation to pay dearly and publicly: he had devised an exemplary punishment. It would take the form of robbing the BBC of the expensive scoop it had planned for the day after the election. On that morning, Wilson was due to travel back to London by train from Liverpool. The BBC had equipped a whole carriage with electronic gear and proposed to transmit the first ever live interview from a train. Wilson would by then be either the victorious Prime Minister or the shock loser of the election. The BBC equipment could only transmit on a certain stretch of line in Buckinghamshire, where a receiving dish had been set up on a hill overlooking the track: the interview was planned to take place as the train came out of the tunnel near Bletchley. But Wilson now declared that he would refuse to do the interview.

He stormed out of Lime Grove and set off for his Merseyside constituency. The next day Paul Fox sent Wilson's favourite producer, Stanley Hyland, to try to change the Prime Minister's mind. Although Hyland had a friendly dinner with Wilson in the Adelphi Hotel in Liverpool on election night, he failed. 'It's nothing personal against you, Stanley,' said Wilson, 'but I'm going to teach your masters a lesson they won't forget in a hurry.' The next morning, Labour had won by a landslide. Hyland and his reporter, John Morgan, joined the train hoping that in the euphoria of victory the Prime Minister would relent. He did not. They found themselves locked out of Wilson's carriage, with men guarding the door. Hyland and Morgan sat disconsolately together in their specially equipped electronic studio, alternately stamping their feet with rage and sucking their teeth in depression. As the equipment trundled unused to London, the Prime Minister twisted the knife in the BBC's wounds. He agreed to give an exclusive interview to John Whale, the ITN reporter on the train. Whale did not have the advantage of an electronic studio, but arranged to put his recording off the train at Crewe and half an hour later it was on the air. Whale ended the interview pointedly: 'So from what I believe is the first electronically recorded interview in a train, back to the studio in London.'

It was a very public snub for the BBC, which had heavily trailed its railway scoop in advance. Wilson subsequently claimed he had refused the interview because the BBC had taken him for granted: that he had only learned of the proposed interview from reading about it in the press two days before the election. 'They announced they were going to the interview before they invited me to do it,' says Wilson. In fact his office had accepted the BBC's invitation three weeks earlier, on the dissolution of Parliament. Morgan was reduced to interviewing three other political journalists in his expensively equipped carriage. The BBC managed to salvage something from the mess when Wilson arrived at Euston. Waiting to meet him at the station was Desmond Wilcox, who had just joined the BBC after five years with ITV's main current affairs programme, *This Week*. Paul Fox, in overall charge of the BBC's election coverage, correctly calculated that the Prime Minister would not realize that Wilcox had changed sides. Fox instructed Wilcox to take off his BBC identity badge and stand as far from the BBC cameras as he could. Wilcox succeeded in buttonholing the Prime Minister for a five-minute interview on the platform. It had been an ingenious comeback, but did not further endear the BBC to Harold Wilson.

He was back at Number 10 in seemingly unchallenged control. But like Margaret Thatcher nearly twenty years later, Wilson was to learn that a large majority spelt trouble. As his Government stumbled from one crisis to another, the Prime Minister was to become convinced that the BBC was part of a conspiracy to remove him from Number 10.

CHAPTER 9

Harold and the Hatchet Men

'Broadcasting is really too important to be left to the broadcasters.'
Anthony Wedgwood Benn, 1968

Harold Wilson had succeeded in transforming his majority from one into nearly a hundred – partly through his skilful use of television. Seats that had been Conservative for a century had fallen to Labour. But from the Prime Minister – who sometimes adopted Churchillian poses – there was to be no magnanimity in victory towards the BBC. 'Harold Wilson became ever more suspicious of the BBC,' claimed Sir Hugh Greene, 'he developed an almost paranoiac belief in plots – in which he believed some of his own colleagues and the BBC were involved to do him down or even replace him.'

From the moment of his return to Number 10 things began to go wrong for Harold Wilson. Almost immediately the seamen went on strike, there was a major sterling crisis, followed by a panic wage and price freeze and slashing public expenditure cuts. Richard Crossman claimed in July 1966 that less than four months after his famous election victory Wilson had gone 'from catastrophe to catastrophe and suffered the most dramatic decline of any modern Prime Minister'. The worse the political and economic situation became, the worse Wilson's relations with the BBC grew. He felt his large majority entitled him to more sympathetic treatment. TV producers believed it was time to examine whether the Government was dealing with the deep-seated economic problems it had ignored during its previous eighteen months of hand-to-mouth existence. Says Lady Falkender: 'The big majority was one of the main causes of the rows with the BBC. You have the support of the electorate and you think: "Why the hell are these people being like this to me?" Also governments get complacent with a big majority: they tend to issue orders and directives rather than to consult, as they did when they were working their passage. And you become – not arrogant, but over-confident in your handling of the media.'

Harold Wilson had been ideally suited to draw the maximum political benefits from his small majority. He was a master of tactics and the art of survival. Leading the Labour party was like driving an old stagecoach, he said: 'If it is rattling along at a rare old speed most of the passengers are so exhilarated – perhaps sea-sick – they don't start arguing or quarrelling. As soon as it stops, they start arguing about which way to go. The whole thing is to keep it at an exhilarating speed.' But short-term tactics, publicity gimmicks and media manipulation provided no answer to the problems of managing a country in long-term decline. Even those closest to him now began privately to admit that Harold Wilson seemed psychologically incapable of adjusting to the powers a large majority gave him. George Wigg, who remained in Number 10 as Paymaster-General and Wilson's chief trouble-shooter until the end of 1967, said that aspects of life in Downing Street assumed a total unreality; uncomfortable facts were pushed aside in favour of rose-tinted assumptions. 'The Prime Minister spoke often about purposeful decisions and the smack of firm government: this was Harold Wilson in the role of Walter Mitty.' And Richard Crossman claimed that Wilson had one overriding aim: to remain in office. He would use 'almost every trick or gimmick' to achieve it.

BBC programmes which stated publicly what some of the Prime Minister's advisers said privately were far from popular with Wilson. 'For them just to come out with blatant anti-Government programmes which they did during this period,' says Wilson, 'and the plain bias they showed at various times, I thought was very unfair – because we had done a lot to help the BBC. We had almost all the newspapers against us, and the BBC interviewers took their inspiration from the newspapers. They would base their questions on what they had read in the *Daily Mail* or the *Daily Express*. They would concentrate on some tiddly little problems which had been in the news, whereas I thought that what the Government was doing or trying to do was more important.' The Prime Minister and those closest to him now developed the belief that the central phalanx of the BBC's current affairs staff – Paul Fox, his deputy, John Grist, Robin Day, Ian Trethowan and Robert McKenzie – all had a conscious or unconscious predilection against the Labour Government.

Wilson had complained to the BBC in 1965 about its use of Nigel Lawson, Sir Alec Douglas-Home's former speech-writer, as an interviewer. Now Wilson's discovery that Ian Trethowan was the anonymous political correspondent of the strongly pro-Heath *Economist* strengthened his suspicions about supposedly neutral BBC commentators. And he reserved his special dislike for Professor Robert McKenzie, whom he referred to scornfully as merely an academic with an academic's grasp of politics. 'McKenzie can never interview me without bringing up why I stood against Hugh Gaitskell for the Party leadership. He would even find a reason to ask me that, if we were having a discussion on differential calculus,' claimed Wilson.

The Prime Minister's belief that the BBC was a nest of Tories caused hollow laughter among the Conservatives themselves. They retained and were regularly to repeat over the years the conviction that the Corporation was a hot-bed of left-wingers. In 1966, Nigel Lawson offered to supply a list to Harold Wilson of what he claimed was 'the preponderance of Labour sympathizers' working in Lime Grove although he added that their common desire was 'to do a first-class journalistic job in a thoroughly fair-minded way'. Almost all governments come to believe that the BBC, and sometimes ITV, are seeking to do them down. And most prime ministers from Harold Wilson to Margaret Thatcher have drawn up their own 'enemies list' of interviewers and producers: a number have had the distinction of appearing in the black books of both Labour and the Conservatives. These recidivists are normally seeking to use television to reveal the gap between a government's rhetoric and what is going on behind the scenes. Prime ministers are often given a harder time than Opposition leaders because governments do things and make decisions which affect people's lives; Oppositions merely talk.

But in 1966 Sir Hugh Greene did accept that Harold Wilson had some genuine cause for complaint. 'We had treated him too casually,' Greene told the author, 'we didn't treat him with quite the respect due to a Prime Minister; we forgot that he was no longer "dear old Harold". To try to put matters right the Chairman, Lord Normanbrook, and I went to see him at Number 10 after the 1966 election. He asked us to go in through the side door in Whitehall and not through the front door in case the press should see us. And the Prime Minister proceeded to go through a long list of complaints of things where he thought the BBC had been unfair to him over the years. Sometimes Normanbrook and I contradicted him; sometimes we admitted the BBC had been at fault. But I don't think it any way helped to restore the old relationship.'

The Prime Minister worked on a variety of methods to try to discipline the BBC and bring its political coverage into line. One was to use his powers over the licence fee. Tony Benn, who as Anthony Wedgwood Benn was Postmaster-General from 1964 to 1966, told a meeting of BBC journalists in 1981: 'Harold Wilson's view was quite clear. If there was anything he did not like on the BBC he would threaten them with not putting up the licence fee – it was as crude as that.' In 1966, the Prime Minister acted on his threats at a time calculated to have maximum impact. The Corporation was in dire financial straits. It put in a request to the Government for an increase in the licence fee which at £5, had scarcely risen in ten years and had not kept pace with inflation. Wilson refused the request.

Licence fee negotiations were normally conducted discreetly away from the public gaze. But Greene and Normanbrook decided to go public. They gave an unprecedented news conference listing economy cuts the BBC had

'Tired of getting Government complaints, Sir Hugh?' (Franklin, *Daily Mirror*)

been forced to make as a result of the Government's decision and pointing out that the British licence fee was the lowest in Europe. Wilson was enraged. He gave his backing to a Wedgwood Benn plan to reform the BBC by introducing some commercials and hiving off parts of radio. The plan sent shock waves through Broadcasting House: 'One BBC' and 'No Ads' were twin articles of faith. The Corporation mounted a skilled lobbying campaign to resist the proposals. At the end of 1966, Richard Crossman told the BBC's Board of Mangement annual dinner that the defeat of the plan would go down in history as the first time an 'all-powerful Corporation' had successfully overturned a decision of the British Cabinet. In fact, although a Cabinet Committee had endorsed it, the Cabinet had never formally adopted the proposal; it was the Musicians' Union's refusal to allow extra needletime for more pop records on the air which finally scuppered the plan.

Harold Wilson was becoming obsessive about the BBC. In the first half of 1967, he regularly treated his colleagues in Cabinet to a diatribe against what he called 'the prejudice and bias of the BBC, compared to the meticulous impartiality of ITV'. On 8 June, the Cabinet instructed the Chief Whip, John Silkin, to write a formal letter complaining to the Corporation in the strongest terms. And a week later the Prime Minister had an unexpected opportunity to transform the BBC from the top. Its Chairman, Lord Normanbrook, died suddenly. The Chairmanship is in theory and sometimes in practice the most powerful position in the BBC. The Prime Minister alone appoints the Chairman – a powerful piece of patronage in the hands of a Premier who had become convinced of the uniquely sinful ways of the Corporation. The man Wilson chose to deliver his revenge on the BBC was the former Tory Cabinet minister and Chairman of the Independent Television Authority, Lord Hill.

Wilson summoned Hill to see him in his room at the Commons. The Prime Minister was sitting smoking a large cigar after lunch – a sight he always carefully kept from the screen, preferring a classless pipe. 'You've done very well at Independent Television,' said Wilson to Hill, 'I want you to go to the BBC.' 'There will be an almighty row if I do that,' replied Hill. 'You and I are used to almighty rows,' said Wilson. The appointment caused a sensation. The Prime Minister regarded it with malign glee. At an *Economist* party just before the appointment was publicly announced, Wilson told Robert McKenzie that news later that night would 'leave the BBC on its beam ends'. Wilson's motives seemed to be threefold. He expected Hill, as a former Cabinet minister, albeit a Tory, to act as a member of the 'politicians' union' and curb the independent spirits of the BBC. He sought to humiliate the BBC's senior executives – with their highly developed sense of corporate loyalty – by foisting on them the Chairman of their hated commercial rival. Third, the Prime Minister wanted to force Hugh Greene to resign.

The first man at the BBC to learn of Hill's appointment was the Deputy Chairman, Sir Robert Lusty. 'When I told Hugh, I might just as well have shot the DG.' On hearing the news, Greene leapt out of his seat, exclaiming: 'How can I work with a man for whom I have the utmost contempt?' Greene said later that he had never experienced such rage about any other event in his life and decided to resign on the spot. Persuaded to sleep on the decision, Greene eventually resolved to stay on as he became convinced that the aim of the appointment was to force him out. Wilson denies this was his main motivation. 'I would have done something far more torturing than appointing a Conservative politician. The fact was that Hill had distinguished himself by the scrupulous fairness with which as Chairman of the ITA he had administered the Television Act in respect of comment in public affairs.' Richard Crossman noted in his diary that Hill had run ITV to suit the convenience of the politicians and had carefully avoided all the irritating things the BBC do: 'So Harold has coolly switched Hill to the BBC to bring it to book and above all to deal with Hugh Greene.'

Wilson and his Kitchen Cabinet referred to ITV as 'our channel': it stuck to the rules while the BBC operated as an arrogant and unaccountable empire. Whichever Corporation satrap Number 10 rang to complain, the responsibility always seemed to belong to someone else. Now the Prime Minister would have his own man at the top – to whom he could go direct. Wilson had also decided to extend the Board of Governors, which he also appointed, from nine to twelve members. As the Governors, headed by the Chairman, have the power to hire and fire the executive management, including the Director-General, Wilson would now have a greater influence on the choice of Greene's successor.

Joe Haines, who became Wilson's press secretary in the late sixties and served for the next eight years, has no doubts about what the Prime Minister expected of the new Chairman. 'Harold appointed Hill to bring the BBC into line. He thought the BBC needed someone from the world of politics to tell them what the real world was about – to bring in some discipline, some curbs. But it did not work. Hill went native. He ceased to be a politician; he became a television chairman. He became just as bad as everyone else at the BBC.' Twenty years on Mrs Thatcher would feel rather the same about Stuart Young. But in Hill's case the process took a little time. He remembers the Corporation greeted his arrival with acute suspicion. One of his early bridge-building dinners was with the youthful, animal-loving Controller of BBC2. David Attenborough told Hill: 'It is as if Rommel had been suddenly appointed to command the Eighth Army.' Hill fidgeted a bit and said: 'Well, Rommel wasn't a bad general, was he?' 'Agreed,' replied Attenborough, 'but we don't know which side you are on.'

As it turned out, Hill was mainly on the side of the broadcasters. He soon became the regular recipient of the Prime Minister's angry complaints – the first in September 1967, just two months after his appointment. Wilson had agreed to appear on *Panorama* at the start of the Labour Party Conference. The programme began with a powerful film about unemployment in Cumberland. It was interspersed with shots of the Prime Minister sitting in the studio watching the filmed reproaches of disillusioned Labour supporters: 'People are being hurt and they don't deserve to be, particularly in communities like this that are staunch and loyal.' 'Wilson is not as good a man as he's supposed to be. There's going to be a lot of people out of work here.' And one miner put it succinctly: 'If he closes this bloody pit, his bloody Labour party is buggered.' Following the film, the Prime Minister faced a panel of three *Panorama* interviewers, James Mossman, Robert McNeil and Robin Day. The programme was enlivened by a squabble between the interviewers, with Mossman protesting that Day was not allowing him follow-up questions. Wilson commented in amusement, 'I thought I wouldn't try and mediate between you.' The Prime Minister had worked out in advance with his advisers the line he wanted to put across: that he was now in personal charge of the economy, there would be a hard winter, but British industry had now shed its dead wood and was lean and fit enough to expand.

'The major thing Harold did and a thing which in my own small way I learned from him is this,' says Gerald Kaufman, Harold Wilson's parliamentary press officer from 1965 to 1970: 'He didn't go to the TV studio to answer the questions. The questions were an irrelevance which had to be listened to. He went there to say something. He decided what he wanted to say – the message he wanted to communicate to the people who were watching and then, regardless of the questions that were put to him, he said what he meant to say.' Even though Wilson believed he had succeeded in putting his chosen message across on *Panorama*, immediately he was off the air he rounded on Lord Hill and complained bitterly that the programme had been 'scandalously organized': to interview him after a gloomy twenty minute film on unemployment must have lost him a large part of his audience. The Prime Minister then stormed out of the BBC saying that he would never come into the studio again to have to answer questions on a film that preceded him.

Panorama used the same film-and-interview technique with even greater effect on Ted Heath three weeks later. Ever since the Tories' crushing defeat in the 1966 election, doubts had been growing among his own supporters about Heath as a leader. They centred on his coldness and inability to put himself across on television. *Panorama* picked up the theme for its film. Like Wilson, Heath was shown sitting in the studio watching the film, which made very uncomfortable viewing for him. It began with Heath opening a new Conservative Club. He appeared awkward and embarrassed as he had to greet the faithful, then pull and drink the first pint. 'He tried very hard like a sensitive man in a butcher's shop to conceal a faint nausea, still pasting on a grin, laughing a little too determinedly at all the fleshy cordiality,' ran the commentary from Robert McNeil, who then interviewed some of Heath's own supporters. 'In politics today,' said one Tory woman in a hat, 'the television image appears to be far more important than a man's ability. And I think Mr Wilson's homely attitude comes across on television, but Mr Heath doesn't have the same appeal.' A bespectacled young Conservative added: 'When we got rid of Sir Alec we said, "God knows we can't have anyone worse than Home." Well, we've got someone worse than Home.'

Straight out of the film, Robin Day went for the kill. 'Mr Heath, how low does your personal rating from your own supporters have to go before you consider yourself a liability to the Party you lead?' Heath had little choice but to stonewall. 'Well, popularity isn't everything. What matters is doing what you believe to be right.' Such 'when did you stop beating your wife?' questions were in vogue for the Tory leader (not that he had a wife). On ITN the following night, George Ffitch asked: 'Mr Heath, are you at all worried by your total failure to make a breakthrough as Tory leader?' 'No,' responded the hapless Heath. The Conservative leader was having real problems with his television appearances. But at first he had no time for those who sought to try to improve his image. 'I am sick to death of people who talk about political life in terms of image and imagery,' he told a TV interviewer in 1966. In part this was a conscious reaction against Harold Wilson. 'I was against gimmicks,' says Heath. 'I was against all the cosy pipe-smoking and evading every issue. Mr Wilson always seemed to be concerned with some improvisory gadget to tide him over and in that he was supreme at getting the press on his side.'

Heath scorned the early suggestions from aspiring TV image makers at Conservative Central Office. 'The first advice I got,' says Heath, 'was that I ought to buy a racehorse, because Churchill had had great success with a racehorse. I said that I hadn't got the money but they said I could buy part of a racehorse. But if I bought part of a racehorse and it was not successful, the situation would be far worse than it was without one. Did you ever hear such nonsense? There was this general idea that they had to change my image; I don't believe in changing images. An image is trying to create something which isn't there.' But despite this initial scorn for their efforts, over the next few years a colourful variety of professional image makers would be employed to sell the Conservative leader on television to the voters. It was to prove no easy task. But they were given a great boost in the month following the two *Panorama* programmes by a TV event that dramatically transformed the relative standing of Heath and Wilson.

On his *Panorama* interview, the Prime Minister had insisted that he would not devalue the pound. Although a number of his closest advisers and Cabinet colleagues were in favour of devaluation, Wilson had turned the defence of sterling into an ark of the Labour covenant. But on 18 November 1967, the Cabinet suddenly concluded that it could no longer resist the speculators: it devalued the pound by nearly 15 per cent. Wilson planned a ministerial broadcast. But to steal a tactical advantage over Heath, he decided to make it not on the Saturday that devaluation was announced but the next day. 'If Harold had done his broadcast on the Saturday,' says Lady Falkender, 'then Heath would have had peak viewing time on Sunday, which would have given him a marvellous opportunity for putting across his criticisms.' The Prime Minister and his political secretary calculated that the immediate shock of devaluation would have worn off a little by the

Monday evening of Heath's reply, when television audiences were in any case smaller. But for once the tactical wrong-footing of Heath rebounded on Wilson. His own peak time devaluation broadcast was to do the Prime Minister more political damage than any of his other television appearances.

The first draft of the broadcast was written by Harold Wilson on a train from Liverpool to London and he showed it to his closest adviser, Richard Crossman. The two men subsequently blamed each other for injecting the buoyant optimism which was to alienate so many viewers. Crossman noted in his diary that he found the first draft of the broadcast 'ghastly', and that he told the Prime Minister 'to admit the defeat and cut out the excuses. But Harold was in a mood of real euphoria.' Wilson says the opposite: 'I was pressed above all by Dick Crossman to drop the references to setback and defeat and exult in our decision. I believe I was wrong to accept his advice.' Lady Falkender, who was present at all the drafting sessions, supports Crossman's view that Wilson himself proposed the upbeat message, which she supported: 'It would have been unnerving for a nation to see their Prime Minister appearing full of woe and foreboding, rather than reassuring them and giving them good reason to hope. The leader had to rally the troops.'

But Wilson went too far. In the most notorious passage of the broadcast, for which he does not blame Crossman, the Prime Minister said: 'From now on the pound abroad is worth 14 per cent less in terms of other currencies. This does not mean that the pound here in Britain in your pocket or purse or bank has been devalued.' He went on to say that prices of some imports would rise. Wilson claims that 'nothing said by any political leader has been more dishonestly misrepresented or twisted for political purposes. The process began the following evening in a shrill broadcast by Mr Heath.' The fact was that devaluation represented a crushing defeat for Wilson and he had succeeded in making it worse by the 'pound in your pocket' rationalization.

Crossman himself watched the broadcast in the company of the Queen at Windsor Castle, where he had gone for a Privy Council meeting. As they sat together on a sofa, he realized they were in some difficulty. 'What on earth were we to say to each other when the broadcast finished? I saw her wrapping her fingers around each other and sure enough when it stopped there was a long, long silence and then she said *sotto voce*, "of course it's extraordinarily difficult to make that kind of speech." ' On that same Sunday, Sir Hugh Greene, the BBC Director-General, had been under siege at his house in Suffolk – not this time from Wilson but from Heath. Once again the subject was the right of reply to the ministerial broadcast. Heath wanted to appear after Wilson that evening, but Greene offered him the following night. The Tory leader lost his temper.

'Heath was kind enough to call me a liar among other things,' remembered Greene, 'and he said that one of his aims would be to break the tyranny of the BBC – as if that were the most important thing in the world.' Twenty years later Heath retains a marked antagonism to Greene and the whole BBC: 'That frightful man Hugh Greene was responsible for *That Was The Week That Was* and for the fashion to knock things down and doubt a man's integrity. In addition to that the BBC is extraordinarily arrogant – and that comes from Reith.' Under protest, Heath eventually agreed to make his reply to Wilson's devaluation broadcast the following evening. He vehemently attacked the Government for failing in its prime duty to protect the value of people's money. Twenty times in thirty-seven months it had denied it would devalue; now it had gone against its own policy. The Prime Minister had broken faith with those who had trusted Britain's word and had brought the country to the depths of disappointment and frustration.

Wilson was well aware that his own broadcast had broken his private axiom: that Canute would have had better results at high tide. By attempting to present devaluation as a panacea and implying he had really favoured it all along, the Prime Minister had shot a large hole through his own foot. All oppositions seek to prove that governments cannot be trusted and the Conservatives had spent nearly five years seeking to demolish Harold Wilson's homespun credibility on television. His own broadcast had done it for them. The Prime Minister was never really to recover from 'the pound in your pocket', which even Wedgwood Benn privately described as 'an absurd broadcast'. Four days after it, Wilson appeared on the ITV *This Week* programme. 'He has at last talked about a defeat, setbacks and mistakes. But the bloody fool should have done this on Sunday,' Crossman fumed. It was to be Wilson's last TV broadcast for nearly a year. He decided it was now counter-productive for him to appear on the air. 'Wilson observed an unprecedented broadcast silence. His understanding of television extended to the realization that television alone could not restore his damaged credit,' said John Whale of ITN.

Although the Prime Minister did not appear, he now took to monitoring obsessively all BBC television and radio broadcasts. He did not like what he saw and heard. What worried him most was any reference to his 'credibility gap' which had yawned wide open since devaluation. To Wilson's fury, one topical comedy programme came up with a bitter joke in April 1968: 'You know how you can always tell when someone is lying – there are always unconscious bits of body language which give him away every time he tells a whopper. It might be a nervous tic near his eye, or his hand may go up to touch his face, or a vein in his neck might stand out. But what's the tell-tale sign with Harold Wilson? What's the piece of body language to look for to tell if he's lying?' (Pause.) 'When you see his lips move.' The BBC sent a letter of apology to Wilson. But a few days later the joke was repeated on another programme. The Chief Whip, John Silkin, wrote to the BBC Chairman, Charles Hill, saying the Prime Minister was taking legal advice about suing for libel and wanted a public apology.

'This seemed to me absurd,' said Hill. 'Politicians including prime ministers have to take a great deal of abuse. To broadcast an apology for such admittedly insulting remarks would give the insults a circulation they would not otherwise have had. We would be accused of kow-towing to the Prime Minister and he would be dubbed thin-skinned.' Hill arranged to see Wilson in the Commons. The Chairman said it would be ludicrous for the Prime Minister to issue a libel writ – as he would be suing Hill himself, who was Wilson's appointee. Said Hill: 'It became clear at the meeting that the Prime Minister was intensely suspicious of the BBC, even regarding it as a conspiracy against him and his government.' Wilson illustrated this with a long catalogue of the BBC's wickedness going back over many years. The former Radio Doctor persuaded the Prime Minister to drop his legal action but was unable to treat his Beebophobia.

At a Cabinet meeting the following month the Prime Minister revealed his conviction that the BBC's vendetta against him extended to employing anti-Government disc jockeys. In a discussion about a possible increase in the licence fee, 'the Prime Minister chose to indulge in one of his anti-BBC tirades,' noted Crossman. 'He had been listening to Radio One and noticed how some disc jockeys bring in news items with an anti-Labour slant. He insisted that a special study be made; he supported this decision with an extraordinary outburst about the wicked political bias of the BBC compared with the honesty of commercial television.' To his chagrin, the Prime Minister was finding that Lord Hill, the man he had brought in from ITV to discipline the BBC, was not living up to his expectations. The BBC Chairman was demonstrating a robust independence of spirit in response to the Prime Minister's calls to curb the Corporation's anti-Government bias. 'The point about politicians, and I was one for a number of years,' says Hill, 'is that they regard something that is impartial as biased against them and something that is biased in their favour as beautifully impartial.' It was not a line which recommended itself to Harold Wilson.

At the Labour Party Conference in Blackpool that October, the Prime Minister made his distrust of the BBC and his preference for ITV abundantly clear. When he stood up to deliver his speech, the Party faithful greeted their leader with rapture – the applause and cheering were unbroken for two minutes. Wilson began: 'Thank you for what the BBC, if they are true to their normal form, will tonight describe as a hostile reception.' He added insult to insult at the Conference by giving his first television interview for a year to ITV. He had been deliberately keeping himself off the screen. 'I had decided to adopt what the Americans call a "low profile posture",' said Wilson, 'it was useless, I felt, to answer on television the hostile questions I must expect with a mere reiteration of our hopes and expectations of economic recovery. I preferred to wait until there was something to show.'

Wilson chose to make his comeback on ITV's *This Week*, where three newspaper journalists he deemed 'acceptable' questioned him. He refused to give the customary Conference interview to the BBC and was to continue his boycott for a further four months. Meanwhile two of his closest acolytes developed the Government's anti-BBC campaign with powerful and well-publicized speeches delivered within three days of one another. The first came from the Minister of Technology, Anthony Wedgwood Benn; the second from the Social Services Secretary, Richard Crossman.

With the exception of the Government, claimed Benn on 18 October, scarcely any other body in the country could match the Corporation's 'enormous accumulation of power'. A few hundred privileged executive producers and broadcasters were shaping public opinion. This sinister cabal was devoted to political calumny. Their biased personal opinions were given the authority of the BBC. There was a rough and ready mixture of fact, comment and interpretation which, in news and current affairs programmes, often led instant communicators into instant error. The BBC had also appointed itself chief investigator into ineptitude and inefficiency in politics and industry and into 'the wilful ways of foreigners'. Where the government once sent a gun boat, 'the BBC now sends the *Panorama* team with instructions to bring back the head of the offender, to be shown on the box'. Nobody was ever allowed to say all he wanted to say in the way he wanted to say it. All were subject to the editorial control of the BBC.

Benn concluded there should be 'a new framework of public service control and operation over the constitutional monarchs who reside in the palatial Broadcasting House. Broadcasting is really too important to be left to the broadcasters.' By implication it should be left to the Government. Woodrow Wyatt – later himself to become a scourge of the BBC and a Tory peer, but at that time one of Benn's fellow Labour MPs – said: 'Mr Wedgwood Benn is one of the most admirable ministers we have, but he has over-excited himself in attacking the BBC. He is not de Gaulle and this is not France. The BBC runs the best radio and television service in the world.' Harold Wilson, who shared Benn's views, did not think so.

Three days after the Benn speech, Richard Crossman delivered a longer and more thoughtful condemnation of the effects of television on politics in the annual Granada lecture. He claimed that television trivialized great events by snippety treatment and personalized politics into a vulgar gladiatorial contest. Competition between the BBC and ITV meant that politics were 'gimmicked up' to attract a mass audience. Crossman admitted that politicians had aggravated the 'trivialization effect' because the notion of the personal image had seized hold of them all and most of them could not resist an invitation to even the most fleeting or unsuitable appearance. Although he accepted that there should always be some tough confrontations and interrogation, the danger was 'the viewer will conclude that politicians who constantly have to be cross-examined like criminals in the box really must be criminals in the box. The men who are always challenged as liars must really be liars and the party leaders who are always squabbling violently in public, while in Parliament they seem to collaborate on many issues quite well, really are the hypocrites they are constantly called.'

Crossman's remedy was for there to be more coverage of politicians at work, more uncut political speeches and lengthy illustrated talks by ministers and their shadows. Politics should be given the same time and treatment in the schedules as football, cricket, racing or all-in wrestling. His fellow Labour MP and former ministerial colleague, Christopher Mayhew, did not agree. In a speech three days after Crossman's lecture, Mayhew said: 'The greatest enemies of free, serious political broadcasting are not the broadcasters but the political leaders themselves. If political programmes or interviews deviate a hair's breadth from what they themselves consider fair, they rise up in wrath.'

The speeches by Benn and Crossman led to a fierce political row. Ted Heath attacked 'the sinister plans by Harold Wilson and his ministers' to run the BBC and to intimidate producers and commentators: the speeches were a calculated and concerted effort to bring the BBC to heel and to dictate how the nation should be informed. Wilson denied this. Yet he had approved the texts in advance. His colleagues were voicing his views, although the Prime Minister felt it tactically wiser not to mount the broad frontal assault on the Corporation himself.

By the start of 1969, Wilson had been off the BBC's screens for fourteen months. He decided the time had come once again to use television to launch his latest political initiative. His Government was in deep political trouble. The polls showed that Wilson was the most unpopular Prime Minister since Neville Chamberlain. Devaluation had not produced economic recovery. The Prime Minister was now persuaded by his Employment Secretary, Barbara Castle, that the Government had to curb the powers of its strongest supporters – the trades unions. Unofficial or 'wildcat' strikers had become Public Enemy Number One. The Law would tame them. Mrs Castle prepared her White Paper – 'In Place of Strife' – for publication on

17 January. The Prime Minister arranged to have himself invited on to that night's *Panorama*.

In the interview Wilson said he was 100 per cent behind Mrs Castle's proposals. His new line was to rejoice in the Government's alienation of its own supporters. 'I have never tried to get a compromise policy out of the Cabinet, I have always said we must get the answer right, however unpopular, and I have lost colleagues in the course of it.' Wilson was delighted afterwards with his *Panorama* appearance. He felt that he had come over as the strong Prime Minister: he seemed to be using his Government's unpopularity as proof of his own statesmanship. The new Bill to reform the trades unions now became an absolute commitment on which he claimed the whole future of the Government depended. He wanted the BBC to give the Bill favourable treatment.

The Prime Minister agreed to have lunch with the BBC Governors a week after his *Panorama* appearance. Lord Hill noted in his diary: 'Harold Wilson was friendly, confident and chatty. Clearly he wanted to bury the hatchet (leaving himself free to dig it up). As a senior colleague put it afterwards: "He has buried the hatchet, but marked the spot".' The ceasefire was short-lived. Within a month of the Governors' lunch the Prime Minister was back on the attack. With the parties entering a pre-election period, Wilson wanted to play up his role as an international statesman by emphasizing his close relationship with the American President. (Every Prime Minister from Harold Macmillan to Margaret Thatcher has used the same ploy.) When the newly elected President Nixon arrived on 24 February for a two-day visit to Britain, Harold Wilson allowed the TV cameras for the first time into the Great Hall and the Long Gallery at Chequers to film the two of them together. 'There was the most daunting display of lights and cables that the "ancient home of rest and recreation" – to quote its donor Lord Lee – had ever seen,' says Wilson. But in the Prime Minister's view the BBC had spoiled the party.

The BBC's commentator for the presidential visit was David Dimbleby, best known then for being the son of his father. The memory of Richard's reverential tones made the commentary of Dimbleby *fils* appear all the more waspish. Richard Nixon had arrived 'wearing his face for all seasons'. Both the President and the Prime Minister had 'expensively hired press secretaries, whose job is to disguise the truth'. Wilson made a formal complaint to the BBC and demanded a transcript of the commentary. Hugh Greene and Lord Hill decided to put out a pre-emptive public apology to Wilson and to the American Ambassador. Wilson admitted privately that his protest backfired in publicity terms. It so dominated press coverage that it eclipsed the story that he did want covered. He had arranged for the

President to attend a late night meeting of the Cabinet. But it went largely unreported.

At the same time, Wilson's plan to reform the unions was running into the sand. Although he claimed the Bill was absolutely essential, most of his Cabinet, his Party and the TUC did not agree. On 18 June, Wilson and Castle accepted defeat. He told the Cabinet that he was scrapping the Bill and was accepting the TUC's pledge to put its own house in order. Mrs Castle and Wilson left their Cabinet colleagues, 'oozing contempt for the cowards from every pore', as she put it, to explain their *volte-face* to the press and on television. In a ministerial broadcast the Prime Minister said that the TUC had made more progress in a single month than in the past forty years. This was why he was prepared to accept 'a solemn and binding' declaration from the TUC that it would reform itself. 'Solomon Binding' sounded like a character from a Victorian novel and now joined 'the pound in your pocket' in the prime ministerial TV glossary. The broadcast had marked another humiliating climb-down. The Wilson credibility gap which the trade union reform plans were intended to bridge yawned wider. In his reply the following night, Heath used the Prime Minister's earlier promises to condemn him. Wilson had said the proposals were absolutely essential but 'now they have all been abandoned. Everyone knows the Government has surrendered. However long his administration drags on, he knows, you know, the world knows that although they may still wear the trappings of office, the power resides elsewhere.'

Wilson considered the BBC was partly to blame for his defeat. Although the only major row had come over Mrs Castle's appearance on what she called a 'wickedly biased' edition of Thames Television's *This Week*, the Prime Minister felt that the BBC's overall coverage of the reform proposals had been too critical and it had provided too ready a platform for the Bill's Labour and TUC opponents. With the approaching general election in mind, the Prime Minister looked for a new way of polishing his tarnished image, while continuing to punish the BBC. He decided to grant commercial television the plum that current affairs people most prize – access. The lucky recipient was David Frost, a co-founder of London Weekend Television. Three years earlier the Prime Minister had gone to a lavish breakfast party given by Frost at the Connaught Hotel in Mayfair. Frost knew intuitively that Wilson would attend because of 'television's power to reduce everyone from prime ministers to pop stars into bit players in a universal dream world', claimed the former satirist, Christopher Booker. Now Wilson gave Frost for the first time the full television run of Number 10.

'Hello, good evening and welcome to 10 Downing Street,' began Frost, in *The Prime Minister and Mrs Wilson at Home* on 25 July 1969. Frost was then shown round the house by the Prime Minister's wife, Mary. Jacqueline Kennedy had acted as the camera's guide to the White House seven years earlier, but Mary Wilson was no *grande dame*. The Wilsons talked about how they first met in the tennis club, how he could still recite the Boy Scout laws by heart, why they always went to the Isles of Scilly on holiday, how her ambition was to have a book of her poems published and how – despite the *Private Eye* caricature of her – she had never drunk a glass of Wincarnis in her life.

The Prime Minister and his publicity advisers felt the programme offered the ideal opportunity to counter the charge that he lacked credibility. When Frost asked about the quality she cherished most in her husband, Mrs Wilson responded, without hesitation, 'courage'. And Wilson himself, invited to sit down in his own study by Frost, said that when his obituary came to be written: 'I'd like them to say that in the hardest times, we kept our nerve, showed that we'd got guts, didn't get pushed from one side to the other and went right on to the end of building up Britain's economic strength.'

The programme was a revealing exposure of the Prime Minister's private life: sometimes banal, occasionally hilarious, punctuated by laughter and cries of 'absolutely fascinating' from Frost, reported Philip Howard in *The Times:* 'It is doubtful whether any previous inhabitants of Downing Street (Gladstone for instance?) would have coped so well with the intrusive eye of television or indeed put up with it.' The *Daily Telegraph* agreed. 'WILSONS AT HOME – A HIT ON TELEVISION' ran the headline. Its political editor, Harry Boyne, felt the programme could prove a substantial plus for Labour in the electioneering balance sheet: 'This is because it marked the contrast between Mr Wilson the happy family man and Mr Heath the lonely bachelor.' Wilson had spoken of his wife and family as 'an essential release, relief and inspiration in trying to do the job one has got to do'. The key word was essential: viewers were invited to suppose that Mr Heath's yacht and piano might not provide the same qualities.

This was something that greatly concerned Heath's senior publicity advisers. Conservative Central Office had arranged for the Leader to be filmed in various 'family settings'. In the spring of 1969, Mrs Heath launched her stepson's new thirty-four-foot yacht *Morning Cloud*, in front of a battery of cameras. Heath told a TV interviewer that he did not think that the strains on him were increased because he was not married nor did his bachelorhood prevent him understanding the ordinary problems of life: 'I come from a very happy family myself, which is constantly together.' But Geoffrey Tucker, the Conservatives' Head of Publicity since the spring of 1968, was having great difficulties with 'the Heath problem' – as it was known in

Central Office. Tucker, who was on secondment from the American-owned Young and Rubicam advertising agency and had worked for the Tories' traditional advertisers, Colman, Prentis and Varley, was a resourceful marketing man. He commissioned regular private opinion polls about the Tory leader and was discovering considerable consumer resistance.

Heath lagged far behind Wilson in terms of personal popularity and voters thought that the way he came over on television was positively off-putting. Compared to Harold Wilson with his pipe, his labrador dog Paddy, and his homely style, Heath appeared aloof and 'incredibly uncosy', as one senior Tory lamented. 'It was my fault if you like that I wasn't able to project myself through the television screen,' says Heath. 'But that is something which some people are good at and others aren't.' He was brusquely dismissive of Geoffrey Tucker's initial attempts to improve him on television. Tucker realized he had to use a softly, softly approach. 'No way was he going to be dolled up or be seen cuddling babies. He was against anything schmaltzy. I had to work with the grain.'

Tucker felt his main problem was to project the leader to the television audience in more human terms: 'I wanted the viewers to think of him as Ted Heath rather than Mr Edward Heath.' Tucker's extensive market research into party political broadcasts showed that the public were turned off by politicians talking straight to camera and had become more receptive to faster-moving programmes – in the style of ITN's *News at Ten*, which had started in 1967. Tucker recruited a top advertising copy-writer, Barry Day, the creative director of McCann-Erickson, to help handle 'the Heath problem'. Says Day: 'At that time the party political broadcasts had sunk into utter disregard. With rare exceptions, the parties had reduced them to the viewing level of a Boris Karloff B-picture – *The Curse of the Talking Head*.'

Tucker and Day devised a party political broadcast aimed at making Heath come over as a more attractive and accessible figure. The plan was to film the Tory leader on a trip round his south-east London constituency of Bexley, using the latest developments in television technology to achieve a natural effect. The old, bulky 35mm film cameras fixed to a tripod and the blazing lights had become obsolete. Now hand-held 16mm cameras and eavesdropping sound recordists could work relatively unobtrusively in natural light to produce 'fly on the wall' or *cinéma vérité* programmes. These entailed filming up to twenty times more than would be eventually used and lengthy editing sessions. Television current affairs programmes were starting regularly to use – and politicians regularly to complain of – the new techniques, which the Tory admen now sought to deploy in the service of their leader.

They filmed Heath talking to local people in the shops, at school playing fields, in private houses and at the Conservative Club. Over a pint of beer, the Tory leader had an exchange with a cloth-capped drinker, who began:

'Are you going to reduce the income tax?'
'We'll reduce it for you.'
'What about reducing mine, because I'm a family man?'
'Well, you will get it reduced more.'
'You see, I am a home-loving man.'
'Well, you had better go home now, I think.' The Leader's shoulders heaved with laughter.

'I remember after the programme Geoffrey Tucker asked Heath what he thought about it,' says Day. 'And Heath said, "I feel pretty good, how do you feel?" And Geoffrey replied, "Well, the product is fine, but I am not sure about the star." And Ted looked at him and those blue eyes were very, very baleful indeed – and then he laughed. And after that I think he trusted us.' 'The New Heath' received a good press. 'He came across more warmly and likeably than he has done in countless productions carefully mounted in the studio,' said the *Daily Telegraph*: 'Corny it may have been, but the popularity of many a long-running TV show suggests that Britain still has a pretty extensive cornbelt.' And the *Guardian* reported: 'The policy was tossed off between the jokes and his constituents seemed just as pleased by it as he did.'

Tucker and Day saw the problem of selling Heath to the electorate like a long-term advertising campaign aimed at establishing a product in a market. 'The campaign was controlled by a tightly-knit group of professional communicators,' says Day. Among the Thursday Team, as it became known, was a young television director called Gordon Reece – subsequently to achieve celebrity and a knighthood as Mrs Thatcher's media guru. And it was Heath himself who added the name of the feature film director, Bryan Forbes.

Says Forbes: 'I had watched him on television making a broadcast to camera and just bled for him. I thought it was nothing but him staring into the teleprompter with the reflection of the firing squad in his eyes. All they were photographing were varying degrees of fear.' Forbes wrote in the spring of 1968 offering his services to the Tory leader and was at once invited for a drink at Heath's Albany flat. But it was a further nine months before the Conservatives took up Forbes' offer. He agreed to make a film about Heath on three conditions: that he was given a larger budget, but no personal publicity or payment. Heath suggested that Forbes should film him on his Leader's tour of the North-East in February 1969. As the two men drove together through the slums of Newcastle, Heath said to Forbes: 'If I lived here I wouldn't vote for Harold Wilson. And I wouldn't vote for myself, either.' 'Who would you vote for?' asked Forbes. 'Robespierre.'

'In Newcastle I tried to relax him in front of the camera,' says Forbes. 'I followed wherever he went with a hand-held camera. My only suggestion was when we went to watch Newcastle United playing football that he go down to the changing room afterwards. A man talking to footballers is likely to come across as more human than talking to another politician or a captain of industry.' But the sequence appeared too contrived and ended up on the cutting room floor. The final film was a mixture of Heath talking sympathetically to people in a variety of locations and heavily edited 'vox pops' with men and women in the street. 'The programme presented Mr Heath as a friendly approachable person interested in people and at ease in any company,' said the *Telegraph*: 'It should encourage the Party to go on personalizing its leader in this way.' Sometimes the efforts of Heath's image-makers went over the top. The journalist Patrick Cosgrave, who worked in the Conservatives' research department, says: 'I spent some days with Forbes working on a broadcast the centrepiece of which was Mr Heath reclining on a meadow with the strains of classical music wafting around him.'

Although Heath could come over well in carefully selected pieces of location filming, he was still having great problems with his appearances in the television studios – when he had to talk to the camera or give interviews. Douglas Hurd, who was the Tory leader's political secretary for six years from 1968, says that the experts correctly observed that Mr Heath had two voices – a public voice used for speeches and a private voice used in conversation. 'The two voices sounded quite different and the private voice more attractive. Moreover, the private voice used shorter, simpler words whereas the public voice often strayed into jargon.' The whole thrust of the expert advice given to Mr Heath was that he should use his own private voice and vocabulary; in short, he should be himself.

Geoffrey Tucker and Barry Day would arrange for private video recording sessions with Heath. The three men would sit together watching the playbacks in the studio. Day gave Heath tips on TV techniques: 'I would try to find words that had quotability, which would give his broadcasts a bit of life. Then he would rehearse and record and we would give a critique of his performances. And he would do it again until we all felt we were happy with it.' They prepared for long studio interviews on *Panorama* and *This Week* by trying to work out the questions in advance. Tucker says that for one *Panorama* interview they managed to get all the questions right and in the right order. One of the Thursday Team, the commercials director Terry

Donovan, played the role of aggressive interviewer in the closed-circuit studio. Says Heath: 'I found the mock interviews very effective. The thing to do before a big programme is to be clear in your mind about what you want to say, because the interviewer will always try to deal with something else.'

Heath's opponents in the Conservative party noticed only a marginal improvement in his TV technique as a result of his intensive coaching. 'His replies were always fluent and unhesitating, but usually banal,' wrote Andrew Alexander of the *Daily Telegraph*, 'and Heath's taut, sometimes hectoring manner in the TV studio suggested constantly that he was on the defensive.' But Robert Carvel, the *Evening Standard*'s Political Editor, wrote after a *Panorama* interview at the start of 1970: 'It was probably the most impressive of his whole broadcasting career. His vitality and crispness in replying to questions is bound to be contrasted to Mr Wilson's recent appearances, which have seemed greyer and a bit boring.'

Wilson himself was becoming convinced that the BBC was collaborating with Heath's image makers to further the Conservative cause. He was particularly enraged by an incident on the night of the Queen's Speech at the end of October 1969, when Parliament began its final full session before a general election. Wilson had let the BBC know two weeks earlier that he was willing to appear on *Panorama* to mark the fifth anniversary of his Government. But no invitation had come. Instead, to his fury, Ted Heath appeared on the late evening *24 Hours* programme. Wilson summoned Lord Hill to see him and argued that the BBC was being very unfair. Heath had attacked him in the House that day and was given the opportunity to say it all again on television that night, without a balancing appearance by the Government. What made it all the worse was that five by-elections in Labour seats were coming later that week. Hill wrote in his diary of 30 October. 'He is right in his criticism and I said so.' 'The Prime Minister could have papered his study with the private apologies we received from the BBC,' claims Joe Haines, who was Wilson's press secretary.

Since the spring Number 10 had been dealing with a new Director-General. Wilson's appointment of Lord Hill had largely contributed to Hugh Greene's premature retirement. The safe figure of Charles Curran, previously the Secretary to the BBC, had taken his place. On Sunday, 7 December, the Prime Minister invited Curran for dinner at Chequers. On the menu was a formidable list of complaints about the BBC. Wilson and his staff at Number 10, particularly Haines and Marcia Williams, had become assiduous monitors of TV and radio programmes. They claimed to have discovered bias everywhere – from the choice of newspaper extracts on morning radio to what they perceived as the consistently anti-Government stance of the presenter of the motoring programme on BBC2. But Wilson's main concern was that he appeared less regularly on the BBC than Heath. At his dinner with the Director-General, the Prime Minister wanted to extract a firm assurance that he would be interviewed on *Panorama* the following evening. Curran made encouraging noises and left Chequers pleased with the way the dinner had gone. Wilson felt sure he would receive his invitation from *Panorama*. It never came.

Using the precedent that the Prime Minister himself had laid down in October, Lord Hill decided that as Wilson was making a speech in the House that day he should not be allowed to broadcast that night. The BBC suggested an alternative date, but the Prime Minister was far from happy at finding his own argument used against him. He rang Curran at home immediately *Panorama* was over. 'Wilson was hopping mad,' said Curran. Lord Hill was then summoned to see Wilson at Downing Street the following day. The Prime Minister's office made a full record of the meeting, which has never been published before. It graphically illustrates the state of relations between Harold Wilson and the BBC on 9 December 1969:

The meeting began at 12.15 p.m. The Prime Minister said he was utterly disheartened with his present relationship with the BBC and saw no way out of it. For the second time in six weeks the BBC had declined to invite him to appear. The Prime Minister had to ask whether it was an aberration – another one – or whether what had happened was endemic to the Corporation, not at the Hill–Curran level, but at Brigade level, though it was obvious that Lord Hill and Mr Curran had no control over those lower down the line. What had happened did not fit his conception of the BBC Charter . . . The Prime Minister said there should be equality of appearance. Apart from news broadcasts and the Party Conference, he had not been on BBC TV since the spring. He had waited to be invited, waited until it was almost too late. A broadcast last night would have been of enormous public interest. It was now no good for the BBC to throw him a sop with the suggestion of a *24 Hours* broadcast on the coming Thursday. The incident was part of an endemic situation which was sheer political bias.

Lord Hill asked the Prime Minister if he really thought that and the Prime Minister replied that he did. He said he had been one of the most fervent supporters of public service broadcasting. He had opposed the introduction of independent television at first but had come round to it because of the utter fairness with which it had been handled. He had come to doubt his philosophy, not because of what had happened the previous evening but because, for example, of the ban on his wife appearing on the BBC. He had told Charles Curran that this was monstrous. [According to Lord Hill, Wilson believed the BBC had deliberately kept his wife off the screen because Heath was a bachelor.] If Mrs Wilson could be blacklisted what was to stop the BBC blacklisting an actor, a comedian or a commentator?

Lord Hill said that he found it difficult to believe there was any common attitude of hostility towards the Prime Minister or to Mrs Wilson – or that there was steady and consistent bias. The Prime Minister said he did not think there was such a bias from Hill or Curran. But there appeared to be a vassal state, with a Duke of Burgundy somewhere. There was a lack of control at Lime Grove which allowed this to happen. Lord Hill said the generality of the Prime Minister's remarks filled him with despair. The Prime Minister said the effects filled him with despair. Lord Hill said that if what the Prime Minister said was true the current affairs and news divisions of the BBC would be politically corrupt. He did not accept that. There was no conspiracy against the Prime Minister or the Government. The Prime Minister agreed: conspiracies were organized, he said, and this was disorganized. Lord Hill said the Prime Minister was describing a Corporation which he [Lord Hill] did not recognize. The Prime Minister said he was describing the facts. Lord Hill said he was disturbed and disheartened. The meeting ended shortly before 1p.m.

Joe Haines, Wilson's press secretary at the time, says: 'I think the Prime Minister's basic message to Lord Hill was that the BBC was like a dinosaur – a large body with a small head. And the unspoken implication was – "remember what happened to the dinosaur".' Hill returned from Number 10 with the message for Curran that the BBC had to be scrupulously careful to maintain impartiality in the run-up to the general election. But the Chairman had little confidence that the Director-General could himself act as editor of *Panorama* and *24 Hours*. Hill noted in his diary at the start of 1970: 'I suspect that whenever an instruction or request or guidance goes down from Broadcasting House the instinctive reaction of Lime Grove is to do as little as possible to carry it out.'

In the next six months leading to the general election of June 1970 relations between the BBC and both political parties worsened. Iain Macleod, the Shadow Chancellor, launched into a blistering attack on the BBC after a by-election in March which the Tories won. 'I have decided that it is not in the interests of the Party that I should appear on the political programmes of the BBC. These programmes are of such sustained hostility to the Conservative party that it is a net loss to appear.' Joe Haines believes that this was just a pre-emptive strike by Macleod in the run up to the general election. 'Macleod knew that a kick in the teeth paid off faster than a nod or a wink. He was taking out the kind of insurance policy to appeal to a political Scot born in Yorkshire. It cost nothing, would mature quickly and could be quoted against the Labour party when *they* complained as evidence of the BBC's impartiality – i.e. they must be impartial because both sides were against them.'

For his part, the Prime Minister was becoming greatly concerned at what he saw as the BBC's build-up of Heath. The extensive TV coverage of Heath skippering his yacht *Morning Cloud* to victory in the Sydney to Hobart race was bad enough. But on the Tory leader's return to England in January

1970, the BBC made him the star of a special *Sportsnight with Coleman*. 'It was one of the best and certainly most enjoyable broadcasts I had ever taken part in,' says Heath. But Wilson was the specialist at appearing on popular programmes that appealed to the great non-political audience. Only a few months earlier he had sung a duet with Ena Sharples of *Coronation Street*. Now he objected to the BBC putting on Heath looking like a winner. And he grew even angrier with the BBC when Heath held a weekend meeting of his Shadow Cabinet at the end of January.

Heath had arranged the meeting at Selsdon Park in Croydon to finalize Tory policies for the election campaign. Wilson was subsequently to deride the policies as the product of 'Selsdon man' – a throwback to right-wing atavism. But immediately after the conference he complained bitterly that the BBC had helped Heath to achieve an unfair publicity coup. 'I have seldom heard Harold admit a success to the other side, but he said this had depressed him,' noted Crossman. The Prime Minister protested to Curran that the Selsdon Park conference had not only received full TV news coverage over the weekend, including numerous appearances by Heath, but the Tory leader also went unanswered on *Panorama* the following night. Wilson conveniently ignored the fact that he had been on the programme the previous week for a whole fifty minutes while Heath only had a quarter of an hour.

The Prime Minister began a meeting of the Inner Cabinet on 11 February with a half-hour account of his battle with the BBC. He had had his successes in bringing in Hill as Chairman and in replacing Hugh Greene with Charles Curran. But he felt that down below in the Current Affairs department under John Grist there was 'implacable enmity to the Government'. He was anxious about the build-up of Heath and asked his colleagues how they could counter it. Crossman suggested that ministers should concentrate on appearances in news bulletins. If they worked hard there were always two interviews available during a ministerial visit – one on the BBC and one on ITN. Often these interviews went out both on the regional programmes and the national bulletin. 'This is the way ministers can get a two-minute appearance and it may be of more help to the Government than a forty-five-minute *Panorama* programme of the sort Harold loves,' Crossman noted that evening. 'But he is as self-centred as he has ever been and as much concerned with the personal struggle between him and Ted Heath which will decide the next election.'

The opinion polls continued to show that Wilson was more popular than his own party. Having deliberately kept off television for a year after devaluation, he was determined to appear regularly in the run up to the election. He went on ITV's *This Week* on 16 April and then sought to undermine Heath's balancing appearance on the programme a fortnight later. On that night the Prime Minister arranged to have himself invited on to *Sportsnight with Coleman* – purportedly to talk about his love of football and England's prospects in the World Cup. But the Prime Minister had another purpose. He wanted to build up public opposition to the forthcoming cricket tour of Britain by the South Africans, which would give the Government a pretext for cancelling it.

'Harold told me privately that there was no way he was going to have a massive anti-Apartheid demonstration outside Lords on the day the country went to the polls. He decided one way of arousing opposition would be to appear on *Sportsnight*,' says Joe Haines. On the programme, Wilson effectively called for demonstrations against the South African visit. A few days later James Callaghan, the Home Secretary, announced that he had decided to cancel the tour because of the threat to public order. Wilson says that when Quintin Hogg for the Conservatives denounced the decision 'he was clearly expressing a sense of deprivation, not at the opportunity of seeing some lively cricket, but of the prospect of Britain's television screens portraying anti-Apartheid demonstrations.'

Two days after *Sportsnight*, the Prime Minister was on television yet again. He had given another exclusive facility to ITV: this time Alastair Burnet was treated to a tour of Chequers, the Prime Minister's country house. The programme began with Wilson, the genial host, conducting Burnet through the gardens and into the house. The Prime Minister pointed out a secret staircase leading to the prison room where Lady Jane Grey had been held. In the Long Gallery he talked of Oliver Cromwell and showed Napoleon's table from St Helena. 'Mrs Wilson, a television natural, made a charming impression as she dispensed coffee in the flower-gay drawing room, her son Giles seated beside her,' reported the *Daily Telegraph*. And Lady Falkender said: 'This programme, like the Downing Street tour with David Frost, was a success. The general public saw not only the house but the Wilson family and Paddy the dog all relaxing at a weekend.' Burnet asked Wilson when the election would be held and the Prime Minister gave the answer that was to become standard over the years: he had not yet made up his mind. But a fortnight later he had.

Polling day was to be 18 June. Four years earlier Wilson had made the decision in principle to hold the election in the summer of 1970. He had asked Gerald Kaufman to draw up a list of possible dates immediately after his return to Downing Street in 1966. But the Prime Minister only felt able to stick with his decision because the opinion polls had at last turned in Labour's favour and Roy Jenkins' Chancellorship had created signs of an economic recovery. Wilson calculated two other factors would help the

Government: the England football team would be in the semi-final of the World Cup by polling day and the long-term weather forecast promised a flaming June.

The broadcasters faced the prospect of the election with considerable apprehension. The events of the past four years had exposed the raw nerve ends of the politicians and the television authorities. One of Wilson's last acts before the dissolution was to announce the creation of the Annan commission to look into the future of broadcasting. The election campaign began with the Prime Minister's threats still ringing in the Corporation's ears. And from the opposite flank came charges of left-wing bias by Iain Macleod and other leading Tories: the normally moderate Sir Ian Gilmour even suggested that Wilson's anger was really a smokescreen to hide the Corporation's Marxist leanings. While Heath himself had declined publicly to join the attack, he and his Thursday Team of media professionals were convinced that only by the most skilled use of the cameras in the election campaign would he manage to become Prime Minister. The scene was set for one of the most remarkable election campaigns of modern times – with television playing a central role.

CHAPTER 10

The Acceptable Face of Ted

'Mr Heath believed that people deserved the evidence and, by God, they were were going to get it.'
Douglas Hurd, Ted Heath's political secretary, 1968–74

Ted Heath was to become Prime Minister with the help of the most sophisticated television election campaign ever seen until that time in Britain. But once in office he would turn his back on his media advisers. He seemed to think they had no further part to play in the business of government: election campaigns were one thing, running the country was something completely different. Heath promised a new style of government as different as possible from Harold Wilson's. Television was to be the medium for detailed exposition to the viewer, of the facts and figures behind government policy; there was to be no more image projection or publicity stunts for the cameras. 'Mr Heath believed the people deserved the evidence and, by God, they were going to get it,' says Douglas Hurd, who was Heath's political secretary throughout his time in Downing Street.

But in May 1970, when Harold Wilson called the general election, there seemed little likelihood that Heath would come to power: the Tory leader looked no match for Wilson on the small screen. Even the way the Prime Minister announced the election date demonstrated his skills as a media manager and appeared to wrong-foot his opponent. Wilson agreed to give an interview in the garden of Number 10 but insisted that it could only be done by an accredited political correspondent. This ruled out Robin Day and any of the other aggressive current affairs interviewers. The BBC's political editor, Peter Hardiman Scott, a gentle soul, asked the Prime Minister some gentle questions. Wilson smiled, relaxed, puffed on his pipe and talked of the British people's preference for quiet government. Why had the polls turned his way? 'Because many people are proud that Britain is strong and paying its own way.' In contrast Heath came to the studio, where Robin Day put him under searching cross-examination. It was, as it turned out, a paradigm for the whole election campaign.

'Mr Wilson insisted on being filmed in the garden of Number 10,' says Heath, 'and he sat down in a very comfortable chair with the sun shining and artificial geraniums all the way round him – put there for the event –

'I thought they weren't allowing no more political satire until after the election.' (Trog, *Observer*)

and it was the old stuff all over again. But I was against gimmicks.' In general that was true, but in 1970 the Tory campaign was not short of publicity stunts. To match Wilson's televisual attractions, during the first weekend of the campaign Heath's media advisers arranged for him to go sailing in the company of a young woman he had never met before. Camera crews from the BBC and ITV were invited to film the couple setting sail on *Morning Cloud*. The aim was to counter the Tory leader's remote bachelor image. But he rather spoiled it all when the press asked who the young woman was and whether there was romance in the air. 'Of course not,' replied Heath, 'she is only the cook.'

The publicity advisers to the two leaders had worked out very different styles of election campaigns. Both were geared totally to television. Wilson was to be informal and relaxed; Heath was to concentrate on set pieces. The Prime Minister was taking his campaigning example from Lyndon Johnson's landslide victory in the 1964 American presidential election. 'One of the things we did,' says Joe Haines, 'was to run through LBJ's commercials and Harold thought we should have a fairly quiet campaign. It would be the old seasoned Prime Minister, the man you know and love so well, against the rather nasty Tory party.'

The inspiration behind Wilson's campaign was Marcia Williams (later Lady Falkender), his political secretary. 'We had had three years of public meetings where he had been heckled badly, eggs had been thrown, as well as tomato ketchup and flour,' says Lady Falkender. 'He used to come home looking absolutely awful and his clothes had to be cleaned. So we had had these bad images on television and we were determined to counter them.' The Prime Minister and his political secretary came up with an idea new to British electioneering – the televised walkabout. American presidential candidates had first used the device of inviting TV cameras to film them descending on innocent passers-by in shopping malls. By 1969 it had spread to the British Royal Family: on a tour of Australia the Queen had shed her normal formality and staged the first royal walkabout for television.

Wilson's campaign tour was to take him by rail to a string of marginal Labour constituencies where local supporters would be lined up to cheer him. He would walk among the faithful and wave down at them from first-floor windows – a picture of popularity for the TV cameras. Wilson would also visit Labour committee rooms to put heart into local activists who had been alienated by the Government's decisions over the previous four years. The Prime Minister planned to make no great speeches about policy – the election was to be effectively a referendum about himself.

In contrast, Heath was to fly round the country in a fifty-seat chartered jet. His meetings would be for ticket-holders only, to avoid hecklers. Tory officials were convinced that television had concentrated on the hecklers to Heath's considerable disadvantage in the 1966 campaign. And it had become an article of faith at Conservative Central Office that TV cameramen conspired to film Heath from unflattering angles, just as they had done with Sir Alec Douglas-Home. Geoffrey Tucker and the Thursday Team were determined to avoid this happening in 1970. Tucker had arranged for the construction of a sophisticated travelling backdrop to be set up behind the Tory leader wherever he spoke. It featured a series of concentric circles against a royal blue background, which the Tory publicity men believed would come over well on television – particularly on the new colour sets.

Three 'advance men' travelled with the backdrop to each of Heath's speaking locations – the set designer, a specialist in presentation on loan from the J. Arthur Rank film company and a professional lighting cameraman. Their task was to set up camera positions for BBC and ITN which would produce the most flattering pictures of the Tory leader. His speeches were carefully timed to begin in the early evening for the convenience of the TV news bulletins. 'The extracts taken for television from these rally speeches were regarded as their most important feature,' says Douglas Hurd, Heath's political secretary from 1968 to 1974. 'Geoffrey Tucker had dinned into all of us his conviction that the election would be won or lost on television.'

By 1970 the Tories had learned a great deal about the use of television in election campaigns. They had closely studied Richard Nixon's highly successful TV commercials in the 1968 presidential race. Ironically Wilson, who had studied the television techniques of both Presidents Kennedy and Johnson – and had set the pace in his two previous election campaigns – was now much more casual about deadlines. He often spoke too late for the main BBC evening bulletin at 8.50. His aides would then complain that he was not properly covered while Heath's speech was.

Geoffrey Tucker's Thursday Team set great store by the Tories' own election broadcasts. They planned to make them the slickest and hardest-hitting ever seen in a British campaign. Barry Day felt the party broadcasts had been a greatly undervalued asset in previous elections. He knew he had a captive audience as the Tories, like Labour, insisted that their five ten-minute broadcasts during the campaign should be transmitted simultaneously on all three channels. 'There you were with fifty minutes of prime-time TV and nothing else for the viewer to watch while you were on – something which would cost you hundreds of thousands of pounds commercially, *if* you could buy it. We felt we shouldn't regard the time as five ten-minute slots but as fifty cumulative minutes of the Tory Story.'

At the start of the election campaign, the major political parties reached agreement with the BBC and ITV that all their election broadcasts would start at ten o'clock. This could not have suited the Conservatives better. They had long planned to model their programmes on ITN's highly successful and popular *News at Ten*, which had been running for three years. The Tories had a portentous theme tune specially composed and their broadcasts opened with two familiar figures side by side behind newscasters' desks. In place of Reginald Bosanquet and Alastair Burnet sat Geoffrey Johnson-Smith and Christopher Chataway, who had both worked as television reporters before becoming Conservative MPs. 'We used them because they were amongst our best people at television: they knew to how handle a broadcast and they did it extremely well,' says Ted Heath. Any confusion the public may have felt as to exactly what and whom it was watching was purely intentional.

'Factual programmes like *News at Ten* were the touchstone of opinion for the people we had to reach,' says Barry Day. 'So why not have our own programme? In that way we could blend in with the media background. Our anchormen had established their familiarity with the public in factual programmes in the first place.' The Conservatives' first broadcast of the campaign set the pattern for those that followed. They had planned to cut together a montage of film clips of Wilson making promises in previous campaigns which he had failed to keep. But the excerpts were the copyright of BBC and ITV and the broadcasters were nervous about putting them in the hands of one party for use against another. Instead Chataway and Johnson-Smith read alternately what sounded like short news items but were in fact a series of political attacks on Wilson as a man whose word you could not trust.

To keep up the impression of a normal ITV programme, the Tories had built an *ersatz* commercial break in the middle of their broadcast. 'We'll be back in a moment,' said Chataway and there followed three brief 'Tory commercials' produced in the style of television advertisements. Says Barry Day: 'We couldn't buy commercials, but there was nothing that said we couldn't put them into our own programmes. A fact of modern life is that a TV commercial is one of the key ways in which people expect to get their information. Its essence is its single-minded simplicity. One of our commercials showed a pound note – shades of Wilson's pound in your pocket – being brutally attacked by a pair of scissors. As each segment was snipped away, a voice-over stated the date and depleted value of the pound, ending with the inescapable fact that the continuation of Labour policies would lead to "the ten-bob pound".' That commercial was repeated many times in the Tories' broadcasts, as was another which featured a wastepaper basket steadily filling up with crumpled pieces of paper containing 'Wilson's broken promises'. The Tories' message permeated the television companies' own coverage of the election.

The BBC invited viewers to send questions that its interviewers would put to the party leaders on *Election Forum*. Many of the postcards for Wilson uncannily echoed the Tories' party political broadcasts over the previous year. Robin Day began the programme: 'This question represents an angry theme running through many of these cards. In view of your past record of lies and broken promises do you really expect the electorate to place any reliance on your word?' Wilson calmly turned the question round to say that he hoped to have the opportunity of nailing the lies that had been put out about him in the previous five years. Michael Barratt, another of the interviewing panel, asked: 'Can you give a reason, other than there is a sucker born every minute, why anybody should trust you and vote for you again?' 'What a charming letter,' replied Wilson. He dealt effectively, though somewhat wordily, with the questions. But while he sounded cool, he looked hot and bothered.

The *Daily Telegraph* the next day headlined the Prime Minister's perspiration. His press secretary, Joe Haines, suspected BBC dirty tricks. 'The studio was intolerably hot that day and almost as soon as Harold went on the sweat was running down his face. It looked on television as if he was wriggling under the intensely hostile questioning. And it was made much worse when the floor manager at the BBC apologized and said that when

Mr Heath had been in the previous day it had been so cold that she had had to send out for a cardigan. Hence conspiracy theory.' Transport House logged the incident in the dossier of complaints about the BBC's election coverage that it told the Corporation it was preparing.

At the start of the election Wilson again ruled out the idea of a televised confrontation between himself and Heath – he neither wanted to give the Opposition Leader prime ministerial status nor risk losing his lead in the polls by an unforeseen slip. The Prime Minister also vetoed face-to-face discussions in the studio between his ministers and their 'shadows'. To circumvent the ban, the new Editor of *Panorama*, Brian Wenham – an astutely dead-pan recruit from ITN – decided on a surrogate confrontation. Lord Cromer, Governor of the Bank of England until 1966 and a high Tory, was matched in a discussion on the economy with the industrialist Lord Kearton, thought to be a Labour sympathizer. To the Prime Minister's chagrin, their encounter provided the Conservatives with more campaign ammunition than would have been likely in any studio clash between front-benchers. Cromer derided Wilson's main economic claim – that Britain was strong again. 'There is no question that any government that comes to power is going to find a much more difficult financial situation than the new [Labour] Government found in 1964.' Kearton seemed to agree.

The Conservatives seized on the warning from the former Governor, who had become a public figure in Labour's battles to prevent devaluation, and recycled his words in their election broadcasts. In his campaign speeches Heath also drew gratefully on Lord Cromer (and would later make him Britain's Ambassador to Washington). Wilson attacked what he called 'the curious intervention in the campaign of the belted Earl'. But Cromer's gloomy prognosis was to be first of a number of public contradictions of the Prime Minister's sunny claims. Yet in the first fortnight of Labour's campaign everything seemed to be going to plan.

Wilson's tour was coming over on television as an unqualified success. He went by train and then motorcade from constituency to constituency, often late and always cheerful. The presence of Mrs Wilson at his side reminded viewers of Heath's bachelorhood. At each stop the Prime Minister would banter with a happy crowd in the sunshine. 'You don't want a speech from me,' he would begin and his supporters would cheer in contradiction like children at a pantomime. 'It's great to have a summer election. I'll allow you ten minutes off your canvassing so you can see me on TV tonight.' Then he would contrast his informal outdoor gatherings with Heath's 'dreary indoor meetings – that lonely figure with the *Dr Who* apparatus behind him'. The Prime Minister dealt so effectively with the odd heckler that some journalists on the campaign tour suspected that Wilson's publicity advisers were deliberately planting feedmen in the crowd. 'You are better than Morecambe and Wise,' shouted one heckler. 'Thank you,' responded Wilson, 'but it's no use thinking you're Robin Day. I bet you are one of those who sent postcards to the BBC. Or perhaps yours was the one they had to leave out. Next time put a stamp on it.' The Prime Minister would end his stand-up routine with a regal farewell: 'Mary and I will now go on our way, thank you for coming. God bless you.'

For the crowds and the viewers this was Wilson in his role as the cheeky chappie – the little man who, whatever his troubles, always got up, dusted himself down and came back smiling. His campaign trips were one long laugh-in with Harold. 'The audience loved it,' wrote Hugh Noyes in *The Times*. 'If this is the thing that wins elections – and it certainly seems to be – then Mr Heath should go into training with Arthur Askey.' Heath's campaign advisers were becoming desperately concerned at the way their man was coming over to the viewers. 'The press and television quickly began to paint a damaging contrast between Wilson's folksy campaign and Mr Heath's aeroplane and solitary set speeches,' says Douglas Hurd. The Tory leader's travelling backdrop made it seem on television that he was always speaking in the same place, while Wilson was clearly talking to the voters in different parts of the country. Ironically, the presentational devices aimed at ensuring a perfect picture of Heath for television were making him appear even more aloof and out of touch with ordinary people – exactly the image his publicity advisers wanted to dispel. Half way through the election the Tories decided they had to change the campaign plan.

Heath would start to do walkabouts as well. His first was in Edinburgh. He did not prove a natural. The would-be Prime Minister accosted shoppers in the manner of an orderly officer asking his men if there were any complaints. After half an hour, he turned to his aides and said: 'I think that is enough for them, don't you?' The following day's effort was worse. It began at Norwich airport, where Jim Prior had arranged for a friend to push his two children forward to seek Heath's autograph. As the TV cameras whirred and the press looked on cynically, Heath signed. The children ran back to their father and asked: 'What do we do with these, Daddy?' 'It was going to be one of those days,' says Prior in his memoirs. 'How wrong we were constantly to think up these gimmicks for Ted. They always turned sour. But how were we to get across his real human qualities to the public?' Prior remembers driving into Norwich for Heath's second walkabout. 'But the streets were almost deserted. It was early closing day. In all the planning of Ted's campaign a simple, silly oversight had let him down.'

Paradoxically, while the Tories were reacting to what they saw as the success of Wilson's campaign, Lady Falkender's nerve ends were beginning to twitch. She felt the repeated message of the Tories' election broadcasts and the television coverage of Heath's speeches were beginning to make an impact. His promises to reduce the rise in prices at a stroke, to bring down unemployment and cut taxes were seductive. 'Suddenly we panicked,' says Lady Falkender. 'I said to Harold, "God, we have to get you into situations where you actually make speeches that deliver the Party's policies". The first attempt was a disaster. When he went to Nottingham they had him speaking from a sash window. It was a rickety old thing and he had to hold it up with his shoulders and television showed pictures of him trying to address a rather bewildered crowd below. It gave the worst possible image of him.'

She determined that Wilson would look better when he came to speak in the West Country later that week. She rang the Labour party's regional organizer to ensure there would be a proper platform in the hall for good TV coverage of the Prime Minister's speech. 'I remember the reply to this day: "Don't worry, we have got it all arranged, the BBC are here and they are erecting a scaffold for him outside." And when I put the phone down I collapsed in hysterics. It seemed to symbolize both our relationship with the BBC and our suspicions about the way the campaign was going.'

Despite Lady Falkender's forebodings, the press was united in depicting Wilson as leading a brilliantly successful campaign while Heath stumbled woodenly towards defeat. But far from relaxing over television's coverage of the campaign, the Prime Minister became involved in a public row with the BBC. For its last election programme *Panorama* wanted to stage a confrontation between the Foreign Secretary, Michael Stewart, and his Tory Shadow, Sir Alec Douglas-Home. Both men agreed to appear. But Wilson had reached a separate agreement with Charles Curran, the BBC Director-General, that Denis Healey, the Defence Secretary, would be Labour's spokesman on the programme and there would be no confrontation. The Prime Minister claimed that during the election the parties had the right to nominate the spokesmen and the subject they wanted. The producers of *Panorama* said this made a nonsense of editorial freedom and they intended to stick to Stewart.

It seemed like deadlock. But Wilson put heavy pressure on the BBC's top management and at the same time persuaded Stewart to withdraw. Under protest, *Panorama* accepted Healey. A senior BBC official told *The Times'* Political Editor, David Wood, that 'the Corporation had to live with Wilson and the Labour Government for the next five years and the objective must be to get through the election without trouble.' 'Diplomacy is all or nearly all when you rise above the production floor,' added Wood. The assumption that Labour was on the brink of another election victory was shared by almost every pundit and politician.

Heath's campaign managers were deeply gloomy. 'The only ray of light for us was that repressed minority – the working-class housewife,' says Barry Day. In the year up to the election and throughout the campaign, Tucker and Day had used sophisticated marketing techniques to track the opinions of specific groups of voters. They had identified a potentially richly rewarding group of 'target voters'. 'We found that many young working-class housewives voted Labour because their husbands did and – even though the ballot was secret – many of them believed that somehow their husbands would find out how they voted.' The Tories decided, at the last moment, to scrap their planned programme and put together an election broadcast targeted solely at working-class housewives.

The broadcast opened with wedding bells and featured Sylvia, a young Wandsworth housewife who was married to a Labour-voting lorry driver. Sylvia was a natural with a South London accent. Day had picked her from a 'vox pop' in an earlier Tory broadcast. Housewives were none too subtly invited to identify with Sylvia as she went to the supermarket, played with her child and talked unaffectedly about her difficulties in making ends meet. Although her husband always voted Labour, Sylvia felt the Government did not understand women's problems. The Conservatives must make the country better 'because they couldn't make it worse'. She was going to give them a chance. 'It had never been put to working-class housewives like that – in their own terms before,' says Day.

The broadcast was a return to the long-standing Tory belief that women were more likely 'changers' than men if they could be encouraged to think for themselves. 'In some respects Sylvia resembled television's familiar slightly feckless housewife whose life is transformed by discovering some new detergent,' wrote Martin Harrison in *The British General Election of 1970*. But Barry Day is unrepentant about the use of the techniques of TV commercials. 'The Sylvia broadcast caused havoc. The Labour party cried "foul, foul". People said that we were selling the Conservatives like a packet of detergent – as if that were a very bad thing. Frankly, the quality of advice that goes into selling detergents the Tories couldn't afford to pay for and would be very lucky to get.' Subsequent research showed that a substantial number of working-class women did vote Conservative for the first time.

But as the campaign reached its climax, the result of the election seemed a foregone conclusion. The opinion polls were united in showing Labour well ahead. In a speech at the last weekend before polling day, Heath sounded in despair: 'I have to say to the British people: "for Heaven's sake, wake up." I want them to recognize what the real issues are because Labour has pursued a policy of diversion with a bogus story of sham sunshine.' Yet even as the Tory leader spoke, clouds were forming over the Prime Minister's campaign. First the sun disappeared as June briefly stopped flaming. Then twenty-five million viewers – many more than watched the parties' election broadcasts – saw England's footballers knocked out of the World Cup in the quarter finals, after leading 2-0 at half time: the West Germans had upset the Prime Minister's calculation that England would be set for the finals by polling day. Finally the trade figures published on 15 June showed a deficit for May of over £30 million. This was a disaster for Wilson.

He had devoted many of his prime ministerial television appearances over the previous six years to giving the British people an extended tutorial in simple economics. He had taught about the trade gap, the balance of payments and the difference between visible and invisible exports. The £800 million deficit inherited from the Tories in 1964 had become the most familiar of the skeletons that Labour had found on opening the Treasury's cupboard. The public had learned to wait expectantly for each month's trade figures and to treat each improvement as a cause for great national rejoicing. Now with a large deficit in May, the achievement Wilson trumpeted most loudly – the annual surplus of £600 million – suddenly appeared illusory. Here was a last-gasp vindication of Heath's campaign theme as well as a sharp reminder of the Prime Minister's long-term credibility gap. And the implications of the poor trade figures gave a special edge to the two parties' final election broadcasts.

The Tories' programme was designed as a showcase for Ted Heath – the man of integrity and vision, who was human after all. It was a highly professional piece of political promotion. Hand-held cameras had been following Heath on his campaign tour. Bryan Forbes put together a rapid montage of the shirt-sleeved leader endlessly shaking hands and grinning hugely. Ecstatic crowds of backslappers greeted him wherever he went. 'Cold, aloof, distant,' ran Christopher Chataway's commentary, 'these were the kind of words the press were always ready to trot out about Ted Heath. But as the election got into its stride, they began to use them less. Heath was a man come to life and clearly enjoying himself.' Chataway told how Heath had risen from humble origins to become Tory leader. 'The public Heath has rarely managed to convey the convictions he can so easily express in private. He does not believe that a leader need necessarily be an entertainer as well. But as the months have gone by audiences have seen more of the private man – the real man.'

The film flashed to Heath in *Morning Cloud* winning the Sydney to Hobart yacht race. 'I see no point in competing', said Heath, 'unless you are determined to win.' The film cut back to Heath with cheering election crowds: 'And then as the days shortened,' ran Chataway's voice-over, 'his message began to get through – or perhaps it was just the quality of the man that began to get through. People had begun to realize this isn't just another politician talking. And he's felt the change, too. Hardened newspapermen have been heard to remark that this is a new Ted Heath. It is not a new Ted Heath – it is the one who has been there all the time. Perhaps he's not an easy man to know but when they know him, people feel he is a man worth knowing. A man to trust.' A caption of the last words was frozen over a picture of the laughing leader, while on the soundtrack the cheering reached a crescendo.

A serious Heath then delivered his final message to the electorate from behind an ornate desk. 'I well remember being driven to the boat for the start of the Sydney–Hobart race. There was a bright blue sky with the sun beating down over the glorious harbour. And I said to the young Australian driver: "What confidence there is here, what's it all about?" And without batting an eyelid, he said, "Well, you see, everyone here knows that tomorrow will be better than today." Nobody in this country would say that. And yet why not? . . . Do you think we should settle for second rate? I think you should enter a race to win . . . Do you want a better tomorrow? That's what I want and that's what I will work for with all my strength and with all my heart. I give you my word and I will keep my word.'

Wilson's final election broadcast the following night began in exactly the same way as Heath's: shots of the leader making triumphal progress through cheering crowds. 'This is the way the Prime Minister and Mary Wilson have been greeted in every part of Britain,' ran the voice-over from the actor Stanley Baker (later knighted on Wilson's recommendation). 'You have seen it on television every day – the enthusiasm and the warmth.' Since both Labour and the Conservatives presented their Leader as universally popular with not a dissenter in sight, viewers must have felt the election broadcasts were even further removed than usual from their own feelings and experience. For over five years, rhapsodized Baker, the strong personal bond had been building up between the Prime Minister and the people – together they had shared work, problems and in the end, success. The film then cut to Wilson apparently speaking from behind his desk at Number 10. In fact he was sitting in a specially designed prime ministerial set in Lime Grove, known as 'the Churchill'.

The Prime Minister picked up from the happy crowd scenes: 'It has been like this all over the country, because people everywhere are feeling a new confidence.' He was echoing Harold Macmillan's final election broadcast of 1959: 'Wherever I have gone around the country, what has struck me is how buoyant everybody is.' Wilson went on to claim that no prime minister this century had fought an election against such a background of economic strength and he derided 'the so-called economic crisis which Mr Heath has invented'. Under the Labour Government Britain was once again a great country, admired and respected throughout the world because it was tolerant and compassionate; it combined stability with change and had 'broken the bonds of poverty, privilege and class'.

Some of Wilson's advisers felt that Stanley Baker's build-up was too fulsome and the Prime Minister came over as tired and complacent, with nothing fresh to say. The Labour party complained to the BBC that when the broadcast was transmitted there was an echo on Wilson's voice. Joe Haines accepted that this was a technical accident but he felt that the Prime Minister had been unfairly treated by the Corporation throughout the campaign. The final entry in Labour's dossier of complaints instanced the eve-of-poll news interviews with the two leaders. Heath was given a series of soft questions, claimed Transport House, while the questions to Wilson were trivial except for the final one. It enabled the Prime Minister to hit back at Heath's suggestion that a Labour victory would inevitably mean another devaluation. 'Wilson's attack had only one defect,' said Haines, 'it was not carried by the BBC.' It was yet another unhappy incident in election coverage which Haines saw as 'a series of insults to Mr Wilson and grovelling adulation to Mr Heath'.

The Prime Minister planned to make public his fury with the BBC by excluding its cameras from the count at his Huyton constituency on polling night. But the Corporation gently pointed out that this would take Wilson off the air altogether. Granada television was on strike and the BBC had agreed to share its pictures from Huyton with ITN. The Prime Minister relented. But as the polls closed, Joe Haines remarked ominously: 'It will be a long time before the Corporation and the Labour Party are friends again.'

On polling day, it was almost universally taken for granted that Wilson would be back for another term. The bookmakers had stopped taking bets with Labour 33–1 on. *The Times* reported that in the years ahead 'Wilson's confidence in his own undeniable skills as a worker of miracles and his ever-growing cockiness are going to make him unbearable at times.' As the television companies launched into their marathon results programmes on the night of 18 June, virtually none of Ted Heath's Shadow Cabinet colleagues believed he would be Prime Minister the next day. Many Tories were now saying openly that he was a born loser. Plans were being made to ditch him.

At opposite sides of the country both Party leaders appeared calm as they sat watching TV screens waiting for the results. Guildford came first: a 5 per cent swing to the Conservatives. In his Bexley constituency, Heath smiled slightly and murmured to himself, 'Well, well'. Wilson was sitting alone on a sofa in the Prime Minister's suite at the Adelphi hotel in Liverpool when the Guildford result came. 'He caught my eye and made a slight grimace,' remembers Lady Falkender, 'we knew it was all over.' It was soon evident that Guildford was no flash in the pan. 'There was cheerful pandemonium at the tiny Bexley constituency office at Crook Log,' says Douglas Hurd. 'We were winning handsomely. Extraordinary news to me but to Mr Heath it was simply the logical result of long years of preparation and of the fact that the people in Britain, like the people of Bexley, were a sensible lot.' Heath came back to London in triumph. Outside Central Office only one man in the crowd seemed less than delighted and managed to stub a lighted cigarette out on the Tory leader's neck. Wilson returned by car to London with what Phillip Whitehead described as the look of a man who had just suffered a stroke.

Heath had become Prime Minister with the help of the most professional media campaign up to that time in British history. His advisers naturally felt that they had put him into Downing Street. But it was not as simple as that. Hard evidence of the effect of television on voting patterns scarcely exists. Some academics claim that election campaigns make no difference at all: that the voters have made up their minds in advance and the campaign is merely shadow boxing staged for the benefit of the TV cameras – a ritual the electorate has come to expect. Against that, detailed research by Leeds University shows that in an election campaign television is the prime source of information for voters and there is a clear, although not overwhelming, link between changes of voting intention and watching election programmes.

It seems most likely that television works on viewers during elections as it does between campaigns. TV's strength is as a medium of impressions – rather than analysis. And in the heightened atmosphere of an election campaign it tends not to make miraculous new converts but to confirm prejudices and impressions that have themselves been built up by the small screen in the preceding years. Where the Conservative campaign seemed to have succeeded in 1970 was not in convincing voters of an economic crisis or of the existence of a brand-new Ted Heath, but in graphically reminding them of Harold Wilson's failures and of the broken pledges of the previous four years. As Geoffrey Johnson-Smith put it in the first Conservative election broadcast, 'That is life under Labour: four years' freeze and four months sunshine.' And the packaging of Ted Heath as 'a man to trust' for his final appeal seemed particularly effective. Both the BBC's audience research and the Conservatives' private opinion polls showed that his broadcast was far better received than Harold Wilson's the following night. Heath received the best rating for honesty – the quality most highly valued by the electorate in the surveys – and Wilson the worst for any politicians in any of the two parties' ten election broadcasts.

Although party political broadcasts induce apathy and groans in most households, in the 1970 election each was watched by more than ten million people. For the first time the Tories attempted to use the techniques and the idiom of television with which viewers – particularly of ITV – were most familiar. They also employed all the most sophisticated modern means of persuasion and marketing that the advertising industry had devised. If these had no effect at all then commercial advertisers who had for years been using the same techniques had been completely wasting their money: an unlikely possibility for some of the most hard-headed businessmen in Britain. It seems more likely that the Tories succeeded in increasing the marginal propensity to buy among the voters, while many Labour supporters were reduced to complacency or indifference. Certainly Ted Heath himself felt he owed a considerable debt of gratitude to his team of professional persuaders.

'I remember on the day he won the election his secretary rang with obvious glee in his voice and said "I have the Prime Minister on the line",' says Bryan Forbes. 'And Heath came on and said "I want to give a party on Monday at Downing Street for all your television camera crews and their wives." This was when he still had to form a Cabinet. I just thought to myself – for him to remember to do that: full marks, ten out of ten.' Forbes recollects that as well as working on the Conservatives' election broadcasts he provided Heath with his first five public words as Prime Minister. 'To govern is to serve,' Heath announced to the massed ranks of TV cameras at the door of Number 10 on 19 June. His government would be at the service of all the people; his purpose was to create one nation. To help achieve his aims it seemed initially that Heath would stick to the talented media team that had helped bring him to power.

On his first Sunday evening at Chequers he invited the Thursday Team for a celebration dinner of steak and claret. 'We sat late with the Prime Minister discussing the ways in which during the next five years he should try to keep in touch with the nation,' says Douglas Hurd. 'I cannot remember what was decided. I do remember accepting a lift back to London in Geoffrey Tucker's Giulia Sprint. We got lost in the first two minutes and ended up in a haystack on the Chequers estate. It was an omen.' However good the Prime Minister's initial intentions were about communicating with the public, they were to disappear under the cares of office. According to Hurd, once in Number 10 Heath began to put aside what he had learned about television in the painful years of opposition: he was better in front of the cameras during the election than at any time as Prime Minister.

Heath had accepted the painful necessity of deploying the latest television techniques of marketing and persuasion in the election campaign. He had bowed to his professional advisers. 'He was the first modern British political leader to use media technology to its fullest in the projection of an image,' says Patrick Cosgrave. But once behind the door of Number 10, he reverted to type and rejected the advances of the media men. 'It was a return to the idea that advertisers were somehow practising an ill-concealed version of the black arts – that we were the manipulators, the hidden persuaders, the Madison Avenue hucksters,' says Barry Day. 'If any conventional advertiser stopped advertising when he had a brand leader on the market, his competitors would think he was mad. And they would have a point.'

To handle his relations with television, radio and the newspapers, Heath appointed as his press secretary a man who could scarcely have been more different from the flamboyant advertising men and film directors of the Thursday Team. Donald Maitland (later knighted on Heath's recommendation) was a low-key Scot and a career diplomat. He had worked with Heath during the abortive negotiations to join the Common Market in the early sixties. As with many a Whitehall public servant, discretion was for Maitland like the calcium in his bones. Both he and Heath rejected Harold Wilson's style of prime ministerial image projection. 'Sometimes in a discussion at Number 10,' says Maitland, 'a suggestion would be made as to what Mr Heath should do. And the comment would come "but that would look like image building". This was something that faces had been set against.'

Ted Heath wanted his premiership to be as different as possible from his predecessor's. Wilson believed in instant government; he would take the long view. Wilson temporized and papered over the cracks; he planned the most far-reaching reforms. Wilson's stop-go economic policies had allowed the country's decline to continue; he favoured go-go policies – continuous economic expansion was to provide the remedy for the British disease. The shackles would be removed from industry and the trades unions fundamentally reformed. People would learn to stand on their own two feet. And Britain would at last find her new role in the world as a part of the great, new European Community. It was to be, Heath told his party conference in October 1970, 'a change so radical, a revolution so quiet and yet so total that it will go far beyond the programme to which we are committed'. He had set up a Number 10 Think Tank under the multi-faceted Lord Rothschild to provide an alternative to Whitehall orthodoxy and to identify and analyse the problems government would be facing in the next generation. A week was no longer a long time in politics. Heath was thinking in decades.

The Prime Minister's dealings with the media were also to be a complete contrast to Wilson's. Heath said he planned to throw open the musty windows of Whitehall. He would not have a coterie of sycophantic Lobby correspondents. There was to be no feverish scanning of the first editions, no angling for invitations from *Panorama*. Publicity stunts for the TV cameras were out. He was not going to pop up on the screen all the time on the most trivial subjects. Instead he planned to make his television appearances major national events where he would provide lengthy and detailed expositions of facts and figures to support Government policy. 'I felt the people deserved all the information on which they should base decisions,' says Heath. Rational arguments would persuade rational people. But as Prime Minister he was rarely to come over effectively on television.

'He ignored the lessons from advertising that we had tried to teach him,' says Barry Day: 'how to compress a lot of information into a small space, keeping a message simple and relevant to as many people as possible – and then giving it immediacy and impact. All the things a politician needs his utterances to achieve.' His advisers sought increasingly desperately during his years at Number 10 to soften the Prime Minister's public *persona*. 'They gave up in despair,' says Heath resignedly. 'There were people who talked about "the natural Heath" as against "the Heath who appears on television". They discovered there was nothing they could do about that.'

Part of the reason for Heath's lack of success on television as Prime Minister was that he deliberately allowed himself so little experience of it. He had decided from the first strictly to ration his appearances. Unlike Wilson, he had no intention of suffering from what was known in Downing Street as 'over-exposure'. The expression was music to the ears of the Tory leader who regarded television with a mixture of contempt and fear. He gave just three big interviews in his first year in office. During his first hundred days he did not appear at all. Press cartoons showed inquirers at the door of Number 10 asking if anyone lived there. Conservatives in the constituencies and in Parliament demanded with increasing urgency to know when they were going to hear from the Prime Minister. He broke silence with Alastair Burnet (later knighted on Mrs Thatcher's recommendation) on Thames Television's *This Week* at the end of September.

It was a confident and unequivocal performance. Heath claimed that the economic situation he had inherited was in some ways worse and more inflationary than he had feared. He was determined to cut back public spending and was prepared to face a general strike if that was necessary to ensure the radical reform of the trade unions. 'What we are going to do is withdraw government from those areas where we think it has no need or right to be,' concluded Heath in a peroration delivered against the clock. 'I know there are going to be a great number of howls going up. But when people have responsibility they will find freedom.' The *Daily Telegraph* reported: 'Skipper Ted succeeded in finding a place of lonely eminence for himself on the bridge, with coxswain Alastair Burnet tottering amidships and almost drowned by the smack of firm government.'

Six weeks later the Prime Minister had a much rougher ride on *Panorama*. His Chancellor, Anthony (later Lord) Barber had introduced a controversial mini-budget – ending free school milk, raising prescription and dental charges and cutting income tax. Labour accused the Government of making the poor poorer and the rich richer. At the same time a commission of inquiry into the wages of lower paid local council workers, like dustmen, had recommended an inflationary settlement of 18 per cent. *The Times* warned that the Government was in danger of losing its economic grip. There was increasing press and parliamentary speculation that Heath would he be forced to make a U-turn, as the newly fashionable phrase had it. But Heath had committed himself categorically against the imposition of an incomes policy or wage freeze. He had agreed to appear on *Panorama* to ram the message home.

He had rehearsed thoroughly what he planned to say. His key point was that people had to face up to their responsibilities: the Government would neither bail them out nor introduce a compulsory wages policy. In the interview, with Robin Day and Nicholas Harman, he constantly repeated his message. And, as Harman in particular attempted to draw him out, the Prime Minister kept turning the question back on his interviewer. 'Are you really trying to tell me the British people are not capable of facing up to their responsibilities and solving their problems in a free society? . . . To compel people, is that what you are asking me to do? . . . What you are asking for – although you will never admit it – is a compulsory policy for wages.'

It was an abrasive performance by the Prime Minister. He seemed at times to resemble the *Private Eye* parody of himself as the peremptory Managing Director of Heathco – forever issuing directives to staff against the lax use of the company's disposable plastic beakers. The interview contained little in the way of detailed argument or exposition of the facts and figures behind Government policy, which Heath claimed was his preferred method of communication with viewers. It seemed as if the Prime Minister was seeking to browbeat his questioners into submission; the interview would show the country that he was not a man who was going to be pushed around – and the trades union leaders should take note.

Although the Prime Minister had chosen to employ a vigorously disputatious style on *Panorama*, he put the blame for the resulting confrontation squarely on his interviewers. Heath injected his own asperity into the long-running debate about whether political broadcasters were abusing their power. 'What I find infinitely boring is when a questioner keeps on and on and on about the same subject, when you have already told him "no",' says Heath, 'and that is incompetence by the interviewer – not by the person who is answering.' Television interviewers tend to respond that most politicians are so slippery that they have to put the same question in three or four different ways in an attempt to elicit a straight answer.

For his part, Heath compared the British style of political interviewing unfavourably to his experience in the United States. He felt that American interviewers 'acted as impresarios' trying to bring out the different qualities of the person they were interviewing. 'We have such a different system from theirs,' says Heath. 'Ours is inquisitorial with the interviewer there to make clear to everybody that he is much cleverer than the politician he is interviewing. So you have to be quite clear in advance as to what you want to say and what you want the audience to hear. I remember once saying to Robin Day: "why don't we just have a civilized discussion, you are one of the best informed people in the country". We started off, and we had got about eight minutes into a half-hour interview at my flat and I saw his hand reach down and out came the board and we were back with his written questions.' 'I am just a humble seeker after truth,' claims Day and rejects the idea that his interviews are like court-room inquisitions: they are much shorter, the interviewee is not under oath and he does not *have* to answer the questions.

Heath had come to believe that television interviews were specifically designed to degenerate into rough-houses. While Harold Wilson had relished coming to the studios, Heath's first two prime ministerial appearances on *This Week* and *Panorama* had strengthened his growing distaste for interviews on television. 'Mr Heath did feel that television had one great advantage over the other media: on television you cannot disguise insincerity or incompetence,' says his then press secretary, Donald Maitland, 'but he felt the great snag was that you cannot televise an idea. So the tendency was for ideas to be televised in the form of an argument, therefore you had these endless confrontations.' After the *Panorama* interview, Heath and his advisers began looking for a new way of reaching viewers direct.

Like all his recent predecessors at Number 10 the Prime Minister envied the apparent ease with which his fellow leaders in democratic countries – particularly France and America – exploited the power of the small screen for their own political ends. 'The divine right of interviewers to govern a discussion is not absolute,' wrote Heath's political secretary in his memoir, *An End to Promises*. 'A new device was needed if the Prime Minister was to dispense with interviewers and journalists and speak simultaneously through the media to the people.'

Heath came up with the idea of staging a grand televised address to the press. He had been struck by the way President de Gaulle of France had made a major production of his encounters with the Fourth Estate. In the summer of 1971, the Prime Minister planned to follow the General's example. The subject would be the one closest to his heart – Europe. Britain was making her third application to join the European Common Market. In the early sixties, as Macmillan's chief negotiator, Heath had led the first attempt. It had ended with General de Gaulle sitting in the solitary splendour of the Elysée Palace and announcing his peremptory 'Non' to the world's press and television. Heath relished the prospect a decade later of emulating the General with the opposite message.

De Gaulle's resignation in 1969 had removed the biggest obstacle to British entry. In place of the messianic General with his lofty concept of an *Europe des patries*, stretching from the Atlantic to the Urals, was a chain-smoking pragmatist, Georges Pompidou. But the new French President both wanted to convince himself about Britain's intentions and to exact a high price for entry. In the spring of 1971, negotiations were deadlocked and Heath decided to take direct charge. He flew to Paris and on arrival at Orly made a valiant attempt to prove his European credentials by speaking French to the waiting TV cameras. 'Je suis convaincu que nous vivons un moment historique comparable à celui d'il y a vingt ans,' Heath read haltingly from his notes. The satirists had long mocked his English vowel sounds; now his televised Francophone attempt gave them a field day. 'To broadcast successfully is almost as difficult for a minister as to speak in a foreign language,' says Douglas Hurd. Heath was trying to do both at once, but was guilty of cruelty to the language. The television cameras showed the French Premier, Jacques Chaban-Delmas, scarce concealing a grin and members of his entourage had to turn their faces away.

But the British Prime Minister impressed Pompidou with his determination and belief in the European ideal. Heath managed largely to dispel the traditional Gaullist fear that Britain would be America's Trojan Horse within the Community. After twenty-four hours of intensive talks, ten of them involving just Heath and Pompidou with their interpreters, the two men emerged to face the press and TV cameras. In the *Salon des Fêtes*, the room where de Gaulle had first announced the veto, a new *entente cordiale* was on display: the two leaders expressed their belief that this time Britain's application would be successful. But Heath knew that at home he faced many sceptics, as well as outright opponents of entry – both in his own party and among the Opposition. He determined to lead what Douglas Hurd called 'a powerful effort to take public opinion by storm'. A television spectacular *à la* de Gaulle was to launch the campaign.

On 12 July, Heath and his advisers staged what they described as 'the first world press conference by a British Prime Minister'. In the gold and white grandeur of the Music Room at Lancaster House, rows of television cameras and hundreds of journalists waited for the Tory leader. The huge chandeliers glistened brighter in the TV lights. Exactly on cue, a smiling Heath strode in unaccompanied. He talked for ninety minutes without a note – starting with a lengthy statement and then taking questions. His central message was that the Common Market negotiations had been a great success story for Britain. 'I do not think that public opinion has yet quite appreciated that all the members of the Community now welcome us. The reason for this is the meeting I had with President Pompidou in Paris.'

It came over as a highly effective piece of television. Across the political spectrum the press hailed his performance. 'There was confidence all the way,' wrote Hella Pick in the *Guardian:* 'The suntan was there reinforced by a sailing weekend, there was a light blue shirt and a darker blue tie to accentuate the blue eyes. Only a Tory blue cornflower was missing.' 'He stood like a soldier. Half a ton of gold paint gleamed on the walls around him and whichever way you looked at Ted Heath's performance – he came out a winner,' enthused the *Daily Mail.* 'It was the picture that told the story,' commented *The Times.* On the Prime Minister's final words, 'thank you, ladies and gentlemen', the twenty-foot high gilt doors behind him swung open – and he departed with a smile.

The press reporters, long resentful of the growing influence of television, protested to Heath's press secretary, Donald Maitland, about the Lancaster House event. They felt they had been used as extras, with occasional tiny speaking parts, in a TV spectacular. They wanted Heath to revert to the normal prime ministerial practice of briefing Lobby journalists in off-the-record sessions that supposedly never took place. But Heath and Maitland believed they had hit upon an effective device for conveying information directly to the public at home without need of the TV interviewer with his airs and graces and tiresome questions. Heath had been so encouraged by his Lancaster House experience that he urged his advisers to plan a series of fireside chat shows to be broadcast simultaneously on both TV channels. This would enable him, said the then Political Editor of *The Sunday Times*, James Margach, 'to reach the carpet-slippered nation, while bypassing Parliament, Fleet Street and the Lobby'. *Sunday Night at Number 10* was seen as a rival to *Sunday Night at the London Palladium.* In the event the idea foundered when it was pointed out that the Opposition would inevitably demand equal air time in which to reply.

1971 was the high point of Heath's premiership. He won a parliamentary majority of over a hundred in favour of Britain's entry into the Common Market. In August he skippered *Morning Cloud* to victory in the Admiral's Cup, the foremost ocean-racing trophy in the world, and allowed a young Granada producer, John Birt, to make a special television documentary about his sailing. The programme depicted Heath as the great helmsman steering the nation to victory. 'If you are going to helm effectively, you can never let your attention waver for a moment,' Heath told Granada, 'what is important is sailing to win.' Heath was using television to cultivate the image of the strong leader.

He was to hold further grand press conferences in the coming years at Lancaster House. They served Heath's purpose of providing a television platform for expatiating to the nation in true Gaullist fashion. But they had a disadvantage which he was only to consider too late: they made the Prime Minister appear an aloof figure, out of touch with the concerns of ordinary people. In Opposition, the Thursday Team had worked long and hard to counter his image of remoteness. But Heath had his own clear idea of what a prime minister should look and sound like: it was to appear as different as possible from Harold Wilson. And in the summer of 1971, the alternative Prime Minister was refighting his old battles against the BBC with fresh ferocity.

On 17 June 1971, the nightly BBC current affairs programme 24 *Hours* transmitted *Yesterday's Men*. Anthony Smith, the 24 *Hours'* Editor, claimed the following year that the documentary caused 'the biggest and most furious row that a television programme in the English language has ever provoked'. He was right at the time, although TV's Richter scale would register even more violent convulsions in the years ahead. The idea for the documentary had come to its reporter, David Dimbleby, in Downing Street when he was interviewing a shell-shocked Harold Wilson on the day of Labour's 1970 general election defeat.

The aim of *Yesterday's Men* – the ill-fated slogan the Labour party had itself devised to describe the Conservatives in the election campaign – was to look at the traumatic effects of suddenly losing power on Wilson and six of his leading Cabinet colleagues.

At first the programme seemed to be going well. The producer, Angela Pope, whose innocent air masked a sharp film-making talent, turned her cameras on the Wilson family's Christmas holiday on the Scilly Isles. The former Prime Minister was filmed playing golf, leading the sing-song with 'Ilkley Moor ba't tat' at the local pub, and reading the Lesson in church –

'there is a time to reap, a time to sow . . .' Pope had failed the persuade the vicar that the book of Samuel, 'How are the mighty fallen', would provide a more appropriate text. Wilson was delighted with the programme's progress and remarked to the author at the time: 'Your Angela Pope has taken the best film there has ever been of me.' It appeared a perfect relationship, but it was to end in tears.

Yesterday's Men was due to be transmitted in mid-June, the first anniversary of the election defeat. Pope and Dimbleby arranged to film their final interview with Wilson in his Commons room on 11 May 1971. Half-way through filming Dimbleby put what he described as a bantering question, to which he expected a bantering response: 'Many of your colleagues have told us that they are suffering financially from being in Opposition, but you are said to have earned between £100,000 and £250,000 from writing your book. Has that been a consolation to you over this time?' It was a clever and cheeky question. But it broke the taboo of polite English society – by asking a man about his money – and it suggested the former Labour Prime Minister was coining it. Wilson told Dimbleby he should not believe press rumours, but Dimbleby rephrased the question, with a smile. Wilson ignored the smile: 'I don't think it is a matter of interest to the BBC or anyone else. If you are interested in these kind of things you had better find out how people [i.e. Mr Heath] buy yachts. Have you asked him that question?' 'I have not interviewed him,' replied Dimbleby and Wilson exploded: 'If people can afford to buy £25,000 yachts does the BBC not regard that as a matter for public interest? Why do you come snooping with these questions . . . You are just repeating press gossip. You have not put the question to Mr Heath. When you have got an answer from him, come and put that question to me. This last question and answer are not to be recorded . . . I think it is disgraceful. I have never heard such a question. If this film is used or this is leaked then there is going to be a hell of a row.' 'Well I certainly would not leak it,' responded Dimbleby. 'You may not leak it, but these things do leak out. I've never been to Lime Grove without it leaking.'

Within minutes, Wilson's press secretary, Joe Haines, was telephoning Charles Curran, the BBC Director-General, to complain about Dimbleby's questions. The following day Haines believed that he had secured an assurance from John Crawley, the Director-General's Chief Assistant, that the whole exchange about payment for the memoirs and the subsequent argument would be cut from the finished film. Under pressure, Pope and Dimbleby agreed to cut out all but the first two questions and answers about the memoirs. The story of Wilson's demand for cuts in the interview leaked to the press on 10 June, just a week before the programme was to be broadcast. The Opposition leader and the BBC then became engaged in the most bitter public row, which mingled the direst threats with the purest farce.

Wilson threatened libel writs and an injunction to stop the film being shown if the BBC would not agree to changes. His solicitor was the redoubtable Lord Goodman. 'Harold asked Arnold Goodman if he would take some legal action, and Arnold replied that he would sooner someone else did it as he was a guest in the BBC's box at Ascot the next day,' says Joe Haines. Wilson's political secretary, Marcia Williams, tried to summon the BBC's top men to a midnight meeting with Lord Goodman at his London flat. But Lord Hill, the BBC Chairman, made himself unavailable and told his wife not to answer the telephone at home. 'My purpose was to avoid being put in the position of having pressure applied to me,' Hill noted in his diary. Charles Curran and Huw Wheldon, the Managing Director of Television, could not evade the call: they drove from an official BBC dinner to Goodman's flat in Portland Place. Unfortunately they did not have the exact address and were reduced to trying to read bell-plates with a cigarette lighter in the middle of the night. According to Haines, the two BBC men arrived 'very merry, but they were not very helpful'. The meeting went on until two in the morning with Curran promising nothing more than to consult the BBC Governors.

Eight hours later, Lord Hill arranged for fellow Governors to look at *Yesterday's Men*, in advance of transmission. It had taken Hill some time to locate the programme. Angela Pope had slept with the transmission copy under her pillow for fear cuts would be made in the film if it were out of her possession. The Governors agreed to meet the first of Wilson's demands – that what remained of the questions about payment for his memoirs should be cut. But they rejected Wilson's other two demands: the photos of his country house and the title were to stay. The decision to view the programme in advance was effectively unprecedented (although the same thing would happen in the *Real Lives* affair fourteen years later, with similarly momentous consequences) – and it left the Governors very exposed. They were meant to be the guardians of the public interest and would normally make their independent judgement on a programme *after* it had been transmitted. But their prior approval committed them to defending the programme, if there were subsequent complaints. And there were.

The programme itself was a fast-moving and gossipy picture of six fallen men and one woman: Messrs Wilson, Callaghan, Crossman, Jenkins, Healey, Crosland and Mrs Castle. Much of it was revealing and entertaining. Extracts from interviews were kept short and sharp while specially commissioned Scarfe cartoons and satirical songs by the Scaffold pop group reinforced the editorial message – that money and ambition were prime

1. Peace in our time: Neville Chamberlain's return from Munich in 1938 formed television's first political outside broadcast. (*Syndication International*)

2. John Profumo (with his wife Valerie Hobson) was the Conservatives' first broadcasting officer and sought to convince Winston Churchill of television's political potential. (*Popperfoto*)

3. Winston Churchill, convinced that the BBC was 'honeycombed with Communists', at first rejected television.

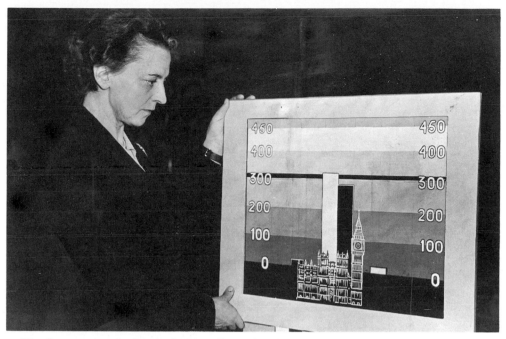

4. The first woman of political television: Grace Wyndham Goldie with graphics for the programme BBC mandarins wanted to ban – the general election results of 1950. (*BBC Hulton Picture Library*)

5. 'Now you see me': Churchill's secret TV screen test filmed at Number 10 in 1955. (*Humphry Crum Ewing*)

6. 'I'm glad you asked me that': Anthony Eden (left) and Leslie Mitchell spent days rehearsing for the Conservatives' supposedly spontaneous first ever election broadcast in 1951.

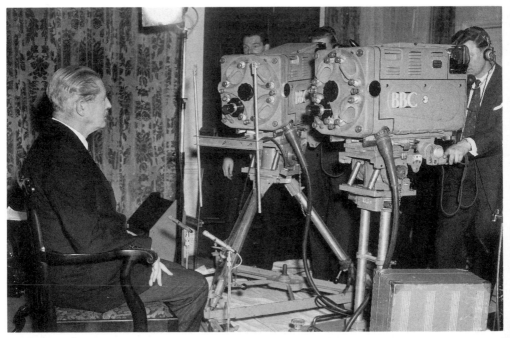

7. 'A twentieth-century torture chamber' was how Harold Macmillan described a television studio with its 'monstrous machines and their attendants'. In January 1957 he makes his first broadcast as Prime Minister. (*Photo Source*)

8. The Mac 'n' Ike show. Harold Macmillan invites the TV cameras and President Eisenhower to Number 10 before calling the 1959 election. (*Associated Press*)

9. Norman Collins, Harold Macmillan's television miracle-worker. (*Topham Picture Library*)

10. Stand-ins: testing for lighting and cameras. (*Michael Peto Collection*)

11. The real thing: Reggie Maudling, Jo Grimond and Harold Wilson. (*Michael Peto Collection*)

12. Watching his image: Sir Alec Douglas-Home was given a crash course in television techniques on unexpectedly becoming Prime Minister in 1963. (*BBC Hulton Picture Library*)

13. Three's company: Harold and Mary Wilson with his political secretary, Marcia Williams (later Lady Falkender), who brushed up his television appearances. (*BBC Hulton Picture Library*)

14. The man to trust: Harold Wilson and his press secretary, Gerald Kaufman, at Granada Television studios in 1966. (*Topham Picture Library*)

15. In and Out: After Harold Wilson's appointment of Lord Hill (right) as Chairman of the BBC Governors in 1967, Sir Hugh Carleton-Greene resigned as Director-General. (*BBC Hulton Picture Library*)

16. Leave it to me: Anthony Wedgwood Benn, a key member of Harold Wilson's 'kitchen cabinet', said in 1968 that broadcasting was too important to be left to the broadcasters. (*Popperfoto*)

17. Election Forum: Ted Heath with the BBC floor-manager Joan Marsden, known as 'Mother', during the 1970 general election campaign. (*Topham Picture Library*)

18. Three-day week: Ted Heath tells viewers in December 1973 that Britain faces its worst winter since the war. (*BBC Hulton Picture Library*)

19. Crisis, what crisis? Jim Callaghan's airport conference on his return from Guadeloupe during the 1979 winter of discontent. 'As I watched, my heart sank,' recalls his adviser Tom McNally (right).

20. Leading lady: Margaret Thatcher on the eve of her 1979 election victory. (*Express Newspapers*)

21. Image-maker Sir Gordon Reece: 'When this job is over I will have produced the product I set out to produce.' (*Neil Libbert/Observer*)

22. 'Just let me finish, Mr Day.' Mrs Thatcher's first *Panorama* interview as Prime Minister in 1980. (*BBC Hulton Picture Library*)

23. 'Take that!' Mrs Thatcher instructs the cameramen during her sudden visit to the Falklands in January 1983. (*Press Association*)

24. Three times a lady: Mrs Thatcher during the 1983 general election campaign. (*Press Association*)

25. Aspel and Company: Margaret Thatcher, the first serving Prime Minister to appear on a chat show, with singer Barry Manilow (left) and Michael Aspel. (*London Weekend Television*)

26. Hot-line to the mighty. Harvey Thomas, organizer of campaign rallies for Billy Graham and Margaret Thatcher, during the 1987 general election. (*Times Newspapers*)

27. Conference report: all the annual party conferences are now designed and staged for television. (*Mike Abrahams/Network*)

28. Cameraderie: Mrs Thatcher takes over during the 1987 election campaign. (*Press Association*)

29. Repeat performance: Harold Macmillan followed his 1959 visit to Moscow with a 100-seat general election victory. (*Topham Picture Library*)

30. Margaret Thatcher followed her 1987 visit to Moscow with a 100-seat general election victory. (*Topham Picture Library*)

motivations of Labour's leading lights. But *Yesterday's Men*'s greatest sin was that it did not take the politicians seriously or at their own estimation: it sent them up. As the Editor of *The Times*, William Rees Mogg (himself to be a Governor of the BBC during the *Real Lives* row) put it: 'It is much more dangerous to trivialize than ever it is to criticize politicians.'

Following transmission, there was a stream of ferocious complaints from the Labour party. Joe Haines claimed the programme had been 'a deliberate, continuous and calculated deceit', while Richard Crossman alleged that his and other interviews had been 'fraudulently' edited.

The Labour party's rage was not softened by the edition of 24 *Hours*, made by the author and Tom Mangold, that went out the following night. Called *Mr Heath's Quiet Revolution*, it was seen as the companion programme to *Yesterday's Men*. In fact the two programmes had been made quite separately, the editorial decision to run them on successive nights was only taken at the last moment, and neither production team saw the other's programme until transmission. On the day the Heath programme was due to go out, a flustered Head of Current Affairs, John Grist, told the author: 'I do hope your film is really tough on Ted.' James Callaghan, who was due to appear in a studio discussion after the Heath film, rang to demand reassurances: 'I'm not going to be taken for a ride two nights in a row.' The fact that the press described *Mr Heath's Quiet Revolution* as conventional and even pro-Tory confirmed Wilson's belief that the BBC was engaged in a conspiracy against him.

The BBC Governors set up an internal inquiry into the making of *Yesterday's Men*. The findings cleared Pope and Dimbleby of the main charges of deceit and unfairly cutting interviews, but it was ruled that the music and the title had been mistakes. 'It's like making a film about family doctors, with their co-operation, and then calling it *Quack, Quack*,' said Huw Wheldon. In the furore that had surrounded the programme, Anthony Smith, the Editor of 24 *Hours*, claimed there was one consistent underlying impulse: 'It is the desire to dethrone television, to depose it from its dominating position in the hierarchy of media. Print journalists and politicians, pressure-groupers and miscellaneous public figures all combined to see in the *Yesterday's Men* affair above all else a sign that television had become too big for its breeches – that the new breed of television reporters were unreasonable in their use of the power and authority conferred upon them.'

The programme established David Dimbleby as a television figure in his own right although in the short term Dimbleby's new-found notoriety had disadvantages. Says Joe Haines: 'Harold said he would never be interviewed by David Dimbleby again. The BBC would telephone and ask for an interview with Harold – and the interviewer was to be David Dimbleby. I would say I would consult. I would put the phone down and then ring back ten minutes later – not having consulted – and simply say "No".'

Seventeen years after *Yesterday's Men*, the scars have still not healed for Harold Wilson. He says: 'It was a completely biased programme, with very provocative questions. The BBC in all its history has never put that kind of question [about his earnings] to a Conservative leader. I never had that kind of thing from independent television. It was also a very offensive title, implying that we were all flat on our backs, has-been MPs. It did have a lasting effect on the trust between politicians and television.'

According to David Dimbleby, one result of the programme was 'a rather hideous softening' in the approach of television to politicians. It was a verdict the Annan Commission on broadcasting was to endorse in 1977: 'At all levels in the BBC, the row over this unfortunate episode was blamed for the caution, lack of direction, touchiness and unsteadiness in current affairs output.' As Angela Pope put it: 'I have had my fingers burnt. I wouldn't try it and no one else would try it for a very long time. Nobody must do *Yesterday's Men* again. You mustn't. Better be safe than imaginative.' Irreverence towards leading politicians on television now became a rarity. It was not until the 1980s and the moulded foam lampoons of *Spitting Image* on ITV that a form of political satire returned to the screen.

Yesterday's Men had one other lasting effect. On 4 October, 1971, the BBC announced the creation of an independent Complaints Commission, consisting of three wise men – the ex-Speaker of the Commons, the ex-Lord Chief Justice and the ex-Ombudsman. They were to be a court of appeal for people who felt they had been wronged or unfairly treated by the BBC. The Governors would no longer have to act as the final judge and jury in their own case. The announcement of the Complaints Commission was seen as an astute pre-emptive move. The Heath Government was itself considering setting up a powerful Broadcasting Council, which according to Lord Hill, would have had three main aims: 'Control, censorship and suppression'. Heath had apparently intended to announce his plan at the Conservative Party Conference later that October and had asked Bryan Forbes to draw up terms of reference for the Broadcasting Council. But as Hill put it: 'They regard us as having killed or at least injured their fox.'

Unlike Harold Wilson, Heath deliberately kept himself from direct involvement in rows with the television companies. He had gone to lunch with the BBC Governors at the end of September. Lord Hill noted in his diary that the Prime Minister was 'pleasant and uncommunicative: his letter of thanks dealt mainly on the theme that the food and drink were excellent (which they weren't)'. 'Lord Hill wanted to be told all the confidences of

'Thank you, Mr. Prime Minister, and now in conclusion, and to balance the programme
Yesterday's Men . . .' (Mahood, *Punch*)

Government,' says Heath, 'and he expected me to spill the whole lot of
beans on the table. Well, I wasn't prepared to do that: certainly not.' Lord
Hill noted of the Governors' lunch that while Wilson wielded his anti-BBC
hatchet in public, 'with Heath we just did not see the hatchet – but had a
feeling it was there.' Within three months the former Radio Doctor's
diagnosis proved correct. The Heath Government became involved in a
battle with the BBC which caused what Lord Hill described as 'a storm of
a severity unprecedented in my experience'.

The BBC planned to put on a three-hour programme at the start of 1972
called *The Question of Ulster – an Inquiry into the Future*. It was to feature
eight leading Protestant and Catholic political figures; the IRA and Loyalist
gunmen were excluded. A distinguished three-man panel, led by Lord
Devlin, would question each of the eight, who in turn could call their own
expert witnesses. The programme was to begin with the views of the British
Government and Opposition. 'A long cool programme of talk, not action,
would do something to complement the day-to-day newsfilm of violence
and disorder,' claimed the producer, Dick Francis. The Northern Ireland

Prime Minister, Brian Faulkner led the Stormont Government's opposition to the programme on the ground that it would contain only one Official Ulster Unionist. On 13 December, Reginald Maudling, who as Home Secretary had responsibility for Northern Ireland, summoned Lord Hill and Charles Curran to see him. With his taste for good living, Maudling was normally the most relaxed of Heath's ministers. But the two BBC men had never before encountered the Home Secretary in such a vehement mood. 'Maudling blew his top,' the *Daily Telegraph* reported after an unattributable Home Office briefing about the meeting. The Home Secretary said he was seriously disquieted by the project which he regarded as potentially dangerous. 'It is scarcely surprising that some ministers and Conservative MPs believe there are no limits to the irresponsibility of the Corporation,' added the *Telegraph*.

Dick Francis had described the programme as 'a tribunal'. In Maudling's view the implication was that the Corporation would produce its own solution to the Irish Question and was thus directly interfering in Government affairs. Charles Curran said, 'We were faced with a decision as to whether to abandon a programme which the BBC had judged to be entirely responsible, because of representation from Government quarters that it would be a hindrance to possible negotiations in Northern Ireland which had not then been initiated.' There then followed what the BBC's Editor of News and Current Affairs, Desmond Taylor, called 'the most sustained attempt to keep a programme off the air that any of us had ever experienced'. Separate Cabinet ministers put pressure on separate BBC executives. Maudling and Faulkner attempted censorship by abstention: they both refused to take part and sought to keep all other Conservative and Unionist MPs off the programme. It seemed they had succeeded until at the last moment a BBC producer discovered an independent-minded Unionist MP. 'Maudling came to the brink of using his power as Home Secretary to ban the programme altogether. But he shrank back,' wrote Michael Leapman in *The Last Days of the Beeb*. On the day before transmission Maudling made public a letter to Lord Hill attacking the Corporation's obstinacy and claiming that 'the programme can do no good and could do serious harm'. But the BBC Governors resisted the Government's pressure.

The programme was transmitted on 5 January with Ludovic Kennedy as Chairman, in place of Robin Day who had withdrawn a few days earlier. Harold Wilson put the Opposition's view and to represent the Government's position the BBC included interviews with Maudling and Faulkner which had been recorded for other programmes the previous year; this further enraged the two men. Seven-and-a-half million people tuned into the programme, including two-thirds of the population of Ulster, which enjoyed its quietest night on the streets for months. Half the audience stayed with the programme until midnight. Despite the Home Secretary's fearful predictions, the programme was thoughtful and unprovocative. As one of Lord Devlin's panel put it: 'We may have been dull but we have not been dangerous.' Curran described the programme as an example of how 'the BBC's independence had to be defended even in circumstances of the hottest controversy'.

The Prime Minister had carefully kept himself from direct involvement in the row over *The Question of Ulster*. But a number of his Cabinet ministers made Heath's private displeasure clear to the BBC. Lord Hill noted in his diary on 6 January: 'One cannot help reflecting that when I was appointed the accusation was that I was a Government stooge put in to quell the BBC and keep it under control. In the event we have had a bloody row with the Labour party over *Yesterday's Men* and now a bloodier row with the Conservative Government over this programme.' Later that month, after a lunch with one of Heath's ministers, who had complained about the decision to transmit *The Question of Ulster*, Hill wrote: 'I am pretty sure Heath would like to get rid of me, but that is not easy when the issue is the BBC's independence . . . It is pretty clear that the Prime Minister has got a deepseated dislike of the BBC. He makes scornful references rather than detailed criticisms.'

At the time, Heath summed up his own view of the Corporation tersely to one of his colleagues: 'The BBC's in a mess.' Today he says: 'The BBC has always been extremely arrogant in the way it handles its programmes and the way in which it handles people who take part. As a government, we were concerned about whether the BBC was being efficiently run. This enormous bureaucracy, growing and growing and growing, that was bound to concern everybody.' Asked why, unlike other prime ministers, he never seemed to become involved in public rows with television companies, Heath gives a large grin: 'I was much too sensible. It is very undignified to have a prime minister having a row with the BBC or ITN or any of those people.' Heath was also unusual among prime ministers in that he did not make his private annoyance with the BBC felt by boycotting programmes – unlike Harold Wilson, James Callaghan and Margaret Thatcher. But by the start of 1972 the problems he faced in coming over effectively on the screen were growing – and they would have a critical effect on his final two years as Prime Minister.

CHAPTER 11

The Lights Go Out

'I don't think a miners' strike is the time to come on television and ooze charm.'

Edward Heath

Ted Heath believed that 1972 would be a year of destiny for Britain and for himself. He turned out to be right – although not in the way he had envisaged. At the start of the year he decided to ignore the bitter row with the BBC over *The Question of Ulster* and gave *Panorama* special access. He had arrived in Brussels on 22 January, to sign the Treaty of Accession that would make Britain a full member of the Common Market. His European dream was coming true. 'The BBC had the absolutely splendid idea of filming the signing and then interviewing him in the bar of the Metropole Hotel in Brussels, where he used to go and talk to journalists during the very first round of negotiations in the early sixties,' says Sir Donald Maitland, then Heath's press secretary. The two interviewers for *Panorama* were Michael Charlton and the German newspaper editor, Theo Sommer. 'Now in that environment with two people with whom he was on very good terms, talking about something which was actually a great success for him, he was buoyed up,' says Maitland, 'the adrenalin was flowing, as the sports commentators would say. And there was Mr Heath talking lucidly exactly as we knew him to do in private: so it was possible for the public and private person to come together. But on other occasions maybe the adrenalin got stuck somewhere.' Heath had gone to the Metropole from a champagne party hosted by the BBC's representative in Brussels. His *Panorama* interview was to be his last successful television appearance as Prime Minister.

Back in Britain, his economic policies were running into deep trouble. Unemployment passed the psychologically significant figure of one million and Harold Wilson called Heath on his return from Brussels 'the first dole queue millionaire to cross the Channel since Neville Chamberlain'. As strikes and industrial troubles mounted in 1972, the Prime Minister and his advisers felt that television was loading the odds against the Government.

'When we had strikes in a nationalized industry or even a private industry, you could never get the chairman to go and put his point of view,' says

Heath. 'Every time the trades union leaders were there, telling their story, they were taking full advantage of the media – I am not blaming them, they were entitled to do it.' Douglas Hurd claimed that the union movement was highly skilled at producing for the television cameras during an industrial dispute someone with a hard-luck story, 'whose take-home pay is miserable, whose wife hardly knows where to turn, whose children will have no Christmas stocking. Then the camera switches to a plump-looking person from the employers' side with an unsympathetic voice who conducts the argument in terms of abstract percentages. Or even worse, does not switch at all.' Hurd's was not the view of the Glasgow University Media Group. It was to argue that all television coverage tended to be biased against strikers – even in its routine vocabulary: trade unions always 'demand', whereas employers 'offer'. But the Group's analysis ignored, among other things, the manipulative skills of a number of young union leaders who first became national figures during the industrial confrontations with the Heath Government.

For nine months from the summer of 1971 a charismatic Communist shop steward, Jimmy Reid, led a 'work-in' at Upper Clyde Shipbuilders and invited the TV cameras to film its daily progress. The Government had decreed that companies like UCS which could not pay their way were 'lame ducks' – to be killed off, not artificially respirated with taxpayers' money. But television film of the volunteer workers and Reid's constant articulation of their case helped force the Heath Government into one of its first economic U-turns. For fear of adding to the unemployed, it decided to put £47 million into UCS. This was a humiliating reversal of the non-intervention policy. And the spring of 1972 saw the emergence of another young Marxist union leader, who had a seductive way with the TV cameras and curious red hair. He was to inflict an even greater defeat on the Government.

In January, the coal miners had gone into their first national strike since the General Strike of 1926. Busloads of miners went as 'flying pickets' to blockade key depots. The unknown young leader of the Yorkshire NUM led fifteen thousand miners to a symbolic victory by closing the gates of the Saltley Coke depot. 'Here is living proof that the working class had only to flex its muscles and it could bring governments, employers, society to a complete standstill,' Arthur Scargill told the waiting cameras in the hand-chopping, hyperbolic style that was to become his trademark. But on that occasion the Cabinet believed him. Douglas Hurd noted in his diary on 11 February: 'The Government are now wandering vainly over the battlefield looking for someone to surrender to and being massacred all the time.'

'The Government left the projection of the case against the miners to the Coal Board,' says Ian Trethowan, then Managing Director of BBC Radio and a friend of Heath's, 'but the Board in turn made little public effort to state the case on the grounds that it was really a matter for the Government. As a result for days on end the miners had virtually a clear run throughout the media.' Heath says, 'I could never persuade the Chairman of the Coal Board to go on and put his point of view. And ministers themselves were cautious. They were in an impossible position if they tried on television to intervene in a dispute that was being handled by the industry and the unions.' On 18 February, the Government submitted to the miners in a manner which Heath took as a personal humiliation. A hastily convened inquiry had recommended a 20 per cent wage increase for the miners, but the NUM Executive refused to accept. Much against his inclinations, the Prime Minister invited the Executive to Number 10. Until that moment, he had been determined never to follow Wilson's habit of calling union leaders for crisis talks over beer and sandwiches at Downing Street. Now Heath felt there was no alternative.

In his own Cabinet Room, the NUM wrung a further £8 million from the Prime Minister. Remembering how Harold Wilson used to emerge from his Number 10 talks and take the credit in front of the TV cameras for ending a strike – indeed on one occasion delaying his final announcement until the end of *News at Ten*, so that the progress of the talks ran like a cliff-hanger through the bulletin – Heath remained closeted inside Number 10. He left the cámeras to the NUM and the Opposition. Wilson himself appeared that night on an ITV *This Week* interview. The occasion had a certain piquancy as it marked the emergence of another Dimbleby – David's younger brother, Jonathan. The Wilson boycott over *Yesterday's Men* clearly did not extend to the whole family. But the Opposition leader had developed a fresh ploy for his television appearances.

To discountenance his young interviewer, Wilson produced a new gaslighter for his pipe. A jet of flame, then a cloud of smoke faced the perspiring Dimbleby as he sought to frame his questions. 'Harold used it as a device for thinking,' says Joe Haines, 'if you have just been asked a tricky question, it's a good idea to distract the attention of everybody and give yourself a few moments to formulate the answer. So out would come this enormous flame-thrower and Harold would take a few puffs while deciding what he was going to say.' 'I realized I was in the presence of a Master,' said Dimbleby. 'I did find it hard asking questions through inches of flame.' In the interview, Wilson claimed that the miners' strike was the most costly disaster Britain had ever seen. He blamed what he called 'Mr Heath's crisis' on the Government's determination to have a showdown: 'they have set their stern, hard-hearted faces against any prices and incomes policy and gone in for this annual virility contest.'

It was another week before Heath emerged from his Downing Street redoubt to make a ministerial broadcast on television. 'Nobody has really won, everybody has lost,' claimed the Prime Minister. He sought to identify the national interest with the Government's policies, promised to protect 'people with no big sticks to wave around' from violence and he ended: 'We have to find a more sensible way of settling our differences.' It was a grim-faced performance, with no hint of informality – not even a 'good night'. The more relaxed style that had been in evidence in the *Panorama* from Brussels had disappeared. As Douglas Hurd put it, instead of trying to talk to viewers he reverted in his broadcasts to speaking at them: 'the voice once again became heavy and unattractive, the vocabulary grew stilted and the tone defensive.'

Everything was going wrong for the Government. Inflation was rising fast, the much-vaunted Industrial Relations Act was proving unworkable as five dockers were jailed and then suddenly released on Government orders in farcical circumstances. In July Heath initiated talks to seek agreement on wage rises between the unions, the employers and the Government. The tripartite talks failed. By the autumn of 1972, Heath had reluctantly decided to embark on his biggest U-turn of all. He had spent most of his first *Panorama* interview as Prime Minister two years earlier vehemently denying he would ever introduce statutory controls on prices and incomes and senior ministers were still privately describing a compulsory policy as 'madness'. But on 6 November, Heath was back in the *Panorama* studio to explain how his Government proposed to control wages and prices more tightly than any in history. The first stage would be a total freeze for at least three months, although annual increments for salary earners were not affected. Robin Day asked the Prime Minister whether his new policy did not mean, as a leading trades unionist had put it, 'a freeze for the little man and an absolute bonanza for the big boys'. 'This really is absolute nonsense,' Heath expostulated, 'can't we keep this on a reasonable level? There is no bonanza here for anybody: it applies right across the board.'

The Prime Minister was on the defensive throughout the interview. In the 1970 election campaign, his party's broadcasts had produced a telling image of pound notes encased in ice, which had been described derisively as 'a frozen wage packet from Mr Wilson'. Now Day reminded Heath that his election manifesto had said: 'we resolutely reject the policy of compulsory wage control.' Heath sought to maintain that this was still his aim: he was imposing not 'a freeze' but 'a standstill' to enable the standard of living to rise steadily and avoid a return to stop-go economic policies. Day ended the interview by asking if the Prime Minister should not call a general election to see if he had the support of the people – otherwise should he not 'get out and let someone else take over?' The Prime Minister claimed he had the whole-hearted support of the people. It was a less than convincing performance.

The tripartite talks aimed at reaching a voluntary incomes policy had broken down three days earlier, on 6 November. By chance Heath was to make a televised speech that night in the Guildhall, where he was guest of honour at a banquet to celebrate the Fiftieth Anniversary of the BBC. (Graffiti in Broadcasting House claimed: 'The BBC has always been fifty years old.') The Prime Minister used the occasion to show how the Corporation could help restart the dialogue between the employers, unions and the Government. 'Was it not Lord Reith's vision that the BBC had an educational function and could help people to understand and think wisely about the issues of the day? No doubt conflict and tension make better television, but the BBC and the other media could now render a great service to the country if they could bring out that our shared interests are greater than our differences; that immense opportunities will be open to the country if we can deal with the problems of a complex, sophisticated, industrial society in co-operation and partnership.'

This was not to suggest, the Prime Minister quickly added, that the BBC should be overawed by the point of view of the Government, or the TUC or the CBI. Lord Reith had rightly wanted to make the BBC independent of government and private interests but had never believed that independence should be 'used as a cover for irresponsibility, an excuse for breaches of decency or a device for propagating particular views'. Reith's legacy was that people expected the highest standards from the BBC: 'I do beg of you not to resent the criticism that comes from these expectations,' said Heath. He then attempted a few jokes, although he was unable quite to match the *bravura* performance of Macmillan at the BBC's anniversary dinner ten years earlier. 'I gladly acknowledge my personal debt to the BBC – in the field of music, if not in politics,' said Heath. 'In the years since Reith, television has become a necessity of life and colour is taken for granted. Instant replays – one of the BBC's most brilliant and devilish developments – are already taking the place of football referees. And the political possibilities, were they ever to enter the House of Commons, are horrific. But that eventuality is long to be frustrated by the reactionaries among us.'

The Prime Minister proposed the health of the Corporation. 'I would like to say what immense pleasure it gives your guests to find so many old friends from the BBC here. And how happy I am to say that relations between Number 10 and the BBC should be so good. I cannot help noticing on every occasion on which members of the BBC come to Number 10, how much they enjoy themselves.' Turning to Lord Hill, the Prime Minister paid tribute to the BBC Chairman as a man of remarkable character and added: 'I well recall what you used to say about relations between the government and the media when, as a colleague, you were responsible for government information services.' Pause. 'But I promise not to reveal it tonight. I am told that a new Chairman is to be appointed shortly,' said Heath – relishing the in-joke that he alone would make the appointment – 'Whoever it is will inherit an organization that can look with pride to its past and with immense confidence to its future.' It was a graceful speech. None of Heath's successors was to pay such public tribute to the Corporation at its not infrequent anniversary celebrations in the years to come.

The Golden Jubilee dinner was Lord Hill's last public appearance as Chairman; he was to retire at the end of 1972. In his speech, Hill recalled that over the past fifty years there had been attempts by governments to contest the independence of the BBC. The attempts had been resisted in the past and he trusted they would be in the future. But he did not believe that in its next half century governments of whatever parties would find the BBC much easier to live with than it was now. He said that an essential part of a democracy was a free broadcasting system, but acknowledged this entailed risks: 'experiments may misfire, judgements may err, bricks or even clangers may drop. But the gains in such a system of intellectual freedom far outweigh the losses.' Over the past fifty years there had been 'some humour, some errors, some scars'. He summed up the congratulatory messages the BBC had received from broadcasting organizations throughout the world: 'We envy your independence and admire your achievements. Hang on to that independence, for our sakes as well as your own.'

The following month Heath appointed a new BBC Chairman. The Prime Minister had been presented with what Ian Trethowan described as the 'longest short list for the post in living memory'. Heath had rejected every one of them. In the end he settled on a suggestion from his Education Secretary, Margaret Thatcher. Sir Michael (later Lord) Swann, the Principal of Edinburgh University, was a distinguished scientist with no political track record. Heath told Swann that he had come to the conclusion that the BBC was most like a university: it had the same kind of anarchic creativity and a large number of potentially wayward and contrary people. Virtually unknown outside the academic world, Swann was initially seen as a creature of the Prime Minister by Opposition politicians and many in the BBC. He offered a complete contrast to Lord Hill's high public profile and rumbustious style. 'The Prime Minister felt that the time had come for a somewhat quieter exercise of the authority of the Chairman,' Charles Curran wrote later. Swann's way was to seek agreement by persuasion and to show that he was his own man. He was to prove a discreetly effective advocate of the BBC's cause at Downing Street. Yet 1973, his first year as Chairman, was to end in circumstances which are always the most difficult of all for the BBC: the country was split down the middle and both sides in the dispute wanted to use television for their own political ends.

The Prime Minister began 1973 with another grandiose televised 'world press conference' at Lancaster House. This time the subject was more down to earth than the historic opportunities offered by Britain's entry into the European Community. The aim was to sell the second stage of the compulsory prices and incomes policy to the unions and the public. To appease the newspaper reporters, Heath's press secretary had agreed that only the Prime Minister's opening statement would be televised. The cameras would be switched off for the subsequent question and answer session. Heath's advisers felt this made his opening statement all important: it should be in a language and style that was accessible and attractive to viewers. But the Prime Minister was determined to talk in Gaullist terms of his grand design for the British economy. Douglas Hurd remembers he was rebuked for trying to guide Heath's opening statement 'on to crude politics'.

'At the press conference, the Prime Minister gilded his proposals as effectively as the craftsmen who embellished the gilt and marble setting of the Long Gallery at Lancaster House,' reported the *Financial Times*. Heath claimed that stage two of the incomes policy was 'designed to take advantage of the progress we have made through the standstill. These are fair proposals and they should continue to have the whole-hearted support of the whole nation in the battle against inflation, and that is a battle on which the future of the whole nation depends.' Asked whether he was not following the style of a president in presenting his policies, Heath replied: 'This is the fourth presidential, er, fourth press conference I have given,' his shoulders shaking in sympathy with his smile. But whatever techniques a prime minister uses, claims Douglas Hurd, he will not communicate well unless he has a reasonable relationship with communicators. Heath did not.

The Prime Minister's critics – both from outside and inside the Conservative party – claimed that he seemed to be cutting himself off from political reality by his remote presidential style and his decision effectively to ostracize journalists at Westminster. 'It was as though he blamed the machinations of the media for the failure of his policies,' wrote James Margach, the Political Editor of the *Sunday Times*. Heath was reaching what Hurd called the 'phase of weary disillusionment' in his relations with press and television: 'since interviewers were mere butterflies of the moment, trivial or malevolent beyond cure, it was not worth bothering with them.' Two months after his

Lancaster House press conference Heath's advisers persuaded him to revert to the system of the totally rehearsed political interview used by Anthony Eden in the first Conservative election broadcast of all, twenty-two years earlier.

On 21 March, the Chairman of the Young Conservatives, Clive Landa, presented a party political broadcast which began with a vox pop of pensioners and housewives and shopkeepers saying how much they liked the Government's policies. Landa then put some 'I'm glad you asked me that' questions to the Prime Minister: what would happen under the policy to those who did not receive a pay packet? Heath answered woodenly, 'You're thinking particularly, I expect, of the pensioners . . . the Christmas bonus, I've had so many letters from pensioners telling me how much they appreciate that.' The Prime Minister ended with a carefully rehearsed peroration. The people of Landa's generation would be 'the great beneficiaries of the Government's policies – with more and more wealth, better social services, better roads, better schools, better hospitals, above all a better environment in which we can all live and work'. Not for the first time the Government's message, carried simultaneously on all three channels, was out of sync with the real world.

While wage rises were limited by law to 5 per cent, the property boom had pushed house prices in London up by 70 per cent in two years. New fringe banks were making money faster than they could count it and even the Prime Minister himself condemned tax-avoidance arrangements in the Cayman Islands as 'the unpleasant and unacceptable face of capitalism'. But by the summer of 1973, the bubble was bursting. World commodity prices were rising fast and the Government was forced to raise the rate of interest from 7 to 11 per cent over the course of six weeks. Heath was persuaded to undertake a series of political tours round the country in an attempt to increase his supporters' morale and to achieve favourable publicity on television. He agreed to give his first major political interview in nearly a year to *Panorama* on 9 October – the day he planned to launch Phase Three of the prices and incomes policy.

Phase Three was a highly complex package and Douglas Hurd attempted to coax Heath into using 'the language of the living room, and the saloon bar' on *Panorama*. In a memo to the Prime Minister, Hurd wrote: 'Words to avoid because meaningless to the audience – regressive, relativities, anomalies, unified tax system, productivity, threshold agreements, deflation, realignment. Also avoid percentages where possible.' Hurd says he cannot pretend he was brilliantly successful with this advice. 'We would have fared better with a man who had more time to think his way back into everyday language. He allowed himself to become too technical. Much of his matter was incomprehensible to the television audience.'

On *Panorama* Heath sounded exasperated with the failure of the British people to comprehend the economic realities his Government was facing. 'You may say this is a failure on our part to explain clearly enough the impact of external events – of a world increase in prices during these last nine months – but surely the British must recognize the importance of this factor. After all, we are the nation that went across the world and sank mines; we planted right across the world, cocoa, coffee, rubber – and we must recognize if there is a sudden demand for it, up goes the price. I really think the British ought to realize what happens when you get tremendous increases in world prices like this.' Heath's baleful humour was momentarily on display when his interviewer, Alastair Burnet, suggested that the Prime Minister's own persuasive powers had failed; 'Yes,' responded Heath, 'I am not having any influence with you.'

Despite the problems the Government faced, Heath said he felt sure the unions would accept Phase Three of the incomes policy, even though the NUM was making threatening noises. 'I do not think that the miners want to see industrial unrest during the winter.' The Prime Minister believed he had reached a secret agreement with Joe Gormley, the NUM leader: in return for treating the miners as a special case there would be no strike. But the outbreak of the Yom Kippur war three days earlier meant that all bets were off.

The Arab cutback on oil supplies to the West greatly increased the miners' bargaining power. In November the NUM announced an overtime ban and work to rule in support of its wage claim. 'A further engagement with the miners was what most of us dreaded beyond anything else,' says Douglas Hurd, who feared the Government was once again being outgunned in the propaganda battle. He wrote to Heath: 'On television the NUM have it mostly their own way. Last Thursday [8 November] Gormley appeared ten times and was only matched once. Despite assurances, the National Coal Board are almost silent. Ministerial appearances have been fitful and not good. Ministers ought to appear each day on one aspect or another if we are not to lose ground.' Margaret Thatcher would feel much the same about the Coal Board's failure to match the voluble Arthur Scargill at the start of the 1984 miners' strike.

Heath's Government sought desperately to keep the initiative in the coal crisis. The Prime Minister declared a State of Emergency; there were restrictions on the use of electricity and petrol coupons were distributed in preparation for rationing. Television news showed film of panic-buying with long queues at the petrol pumps. In the Commons the Government's announcement that all TV programmes were to end at 10.30 each night was greeted by loud cheers from Conservative MPs. Although most MPs are rare viewers, many Tories shared Heath's view that television was hostile to the Government and the less there was of it the better. At the end of November Heath invited the NUM Executive for talks at Number 10. These only made matters worse. The Communist Mick McGahey told the Prime Minister that the union's aim was to bring down his Government. Heath's resolve to stand firm hardened. To save energy, the Government cut the working week in factories and shops to three days. Street lighting was switched off and the public were instructed to use minimum electricity and heating: the junior Energy Minister, Patrick Jenkin, suggested people clean their teeth in the dark.

Throughout the crisis the Prime Minister had kept off television. 'He appeared to believe that virtue would be its own reward and the correctness of his policies would come to be understood,' says Ian Trethowan. The pressure was now mounting from Conservatives in Westminster and the constituencies for Heath to carry his message more positively to the public at large in a TV broadcast. 'There was no very clear notion as to what he should say. But that he should say something was evident to all,' remarks Hurd wryly. Heath decided to make a ministerial broadcast on 13 December. It was the most important TV appearance of his time at Number 10. For three years he had sought to project himself as an Olympian figure above the vulgar party political brawl: he had made no attempt to build up any rapport with viewers. Now he wanted to use television to rally the nation behind him. But as he sought to draw on the bank of public opinion, he found he had no reserves.

When the Prime Minister arrived to make his broadcast he was so tired he could scarcely speak. He had gone virtually without sleep for the previous four days. As well as an endless series of meetings with ministers and civil servants over the miners' crisis, he had kept to a full schedule of other business. Formal banquets with visiting statesmen were followed by helicopter flights to the secret, all-night Sunningdale talks aimed at creating a power-sharing executive in Northern Ireland. In between was the Cabinet and briefings for the European summit meeting that was about to start. The Prime Minister had been left with no time to go through the script his advisers had prepared for his broadcast.

In calculated contrast to Harold Wilson, Heath believed that bad news needed to be presented bleakly. His advisers had not let him down. The carefully rehearsed optimism of his party political broadcast with the helpful Young Conservative nine months earlier was gone. Now Heath looked straight into the camera and attempted to summon up the Dunkirk spirit via his autocue. 'As Prime Minister, I want to speak to you simply and plainly about the grave emergency facing our country.' As a result of the miners' action life would be very much harder for those at work as well as at home. Jobs would be in danger and take-home pay less. 'In terms of comfort we shall have a harder Christmas than we have known since the war ... At times like these there is deep in all of us an instinct which tells us we must abandon disputes amongst ourselves, we must close our ranks so that we can deal with the difficulties which come to us whether from within or from beyond our own shores. That has been our way in the past and it is a good way. Today again the need for national unity is overwhelmingly clear ... As Prime Minister I ask the nation to weigh these matters carefully, to carry out the measures we have put forward in the national interest and to give us your support.' His face grey with fatigue and his eyes like slits, the Prime Minister had never looked worse on television. Ted Heath seemed to match his anagram: the death.

The broadcast sounded like an election appeal, but it was not – yet. Heath and his advisers were split on whether he should use the crisis to call a snap general election on the theme: 'Who rules the country – the miners or the Government?' Two of Heath's closest Cabinet colleagues, Lord Carrington, the Party Chairman, and Jim Prior, the Leader of the House, were in favour of going early but the two ex-Chief Whips, Willie Whitelaw, the new Employment Secretary, and Francis Pym, the new Northern Ireland Secretary, favoured delay. The next seven weeks were spent in agonized debate. At the same time the Prime Minister made desperate last-minute attempts to woo the public and the media. He issued urgent invitations for talks at Number 10 to journalists and editors he had virtually ignored for the previous three and a half years. Downing Street sought to suggest to the television companies how they should cover the crisis. 'We began to hear the argument that the BBC should concern itself with the national interest,' says Ian Trethowan. 'At least some of the union leaders were clearly bent on undermining our democracy, it was said, and the BBC should not give them too much access to the air.'

By the middle of January it seemed there would be no early election. Lord Carrington, who was also Energy Secretary, had announced that coal stocks would see the country through to the spring and it might be possible to move to a four-day week. The NUM thought differently. At the start of February, 81 per cent of the miners voted for a strike. Heath reacted by calling a general election. He was going to the polls sixteen months before he had to – on 28 February. The first crisis appeal to the country since the Second World War was to be the most curious general election of modern times. By a double irony both Heath and Wilson were to adopt each other's television techniques from the previous election campaign.

Heath did not help his campaign by the first two decisions he made on the day he called the election. He announced he was lifting the 10.30 television curfew. While this was necessary if the election was to have full coverage without driving all entertainment off the evening airwaves, the psephologist David Butler argued that it contributed to dispelling the crisis atmosphere that the Conservative strategy demanded. And on television that evening Heath revealed that he had decided to send the miners' wage claim to the Pay Board and agreed to be bound by the results. As this offered a way out of the miners' strike and had previously been resisted by Heath, it raised the question why there was any need for an election at all. In his broadcast the following night, Harold Wilson said scornfully: 'For the first time in history, we have a general leading his troops into battle with the deliberate aim of giving in if they win.'

The Conservatives' first election broadcast on 11 February made their campaign plan clear. The theme was Edward Heath – man of destiny, the strong leader who would protect the weak. The programme began with what purported to be a vox pop of ordinary people – no plummy or tweedy Tories included. 'He has done all that is expected of a Prime Minister.' 'I think he'll get England back on its feet.' 'I would say "good luck to Mr Heath and get on with it and finish what you have started".' Heath then appeared and dismissed the notion that he was engaged in a 'confrontation' with the NUM. 'This isn't a pitched battle between a stubborn government and obstinate miners. Our quarrel is with a small group of extremists . . . It is time to take a firm line because only by being firm can we hope to be fair . . . We must stand up for all those who cannot stand up for themselves, in particular the low paid and the pensioner. Only a strong government can protect the weak . . . We have a hard road ahead. Let's make sure we travel it together.'

Heath's campaign was aimed at creating a strong personal bond between the Prime Minister and the public. He had decided to follow Wilson's 1970 example and go on walkabouts and visit many local constituency parties to enthuse his own supporters. The intention was to present Heath on television as in touch with ordinary people – the embodiment of Conservatism with a human face. But there is all the difference in the world between an individual politician walking up to people and talking to them in a shopping centre, with a single camera crew discreetly nearby to record the conversation, and what happened on Ted Heath's campaign walkabouts.

He would stride down the street surrounded by camera teams, aides and detectives. Shoppers he managed to accost felt hopelessly intimidated and

Heath's lack of small talk did not help. The walkabouts helped further defuse any crisis atmosphere surrounding the election. Heath himself now admits they failed. 'I never quite know what good walkabouts do. All the television crews fall over each other and finally land on the children. You try to press through the throng, but you don't meet many people because you have got television crews all around you. And if the British aren't interested any more then you have French, German and American television crews.'

The Tories had decided to centre their whole election campaign on the Prime Minister. He dominated the televised daily press conferences, in effect chairing them himself and answering nearly all the questions. 'At press conferences seasoned journalists agree they've never come across anyone with such a complete grasp of the whole range of government,' claimed one of his election broadcasts. But the decision to focus the whole campaign on the Prime Minister was a high-stakes gamble. In his nine years as Tory leader, Heath had never caught the public imagination or become a popular figure. Ironically, the Labour party did recognize that Harold Wilson's popularity, which had been the main selling point of the 1970 campaign, had fallen sharply. This time teamwork was the campaign theme.

'The next Labour Government will be a team,' began one of the Party's election broadcasts. It featured contributions from Roy Jenkins, James Callaghan, Michael Foot, Shirley Williams, Denis Healey, Tony Benn and Tony Crosland. 'Between them they share over forty years' experience as government ministers,' said Harold Wilson, 'they were among the men and women who got Britain out of the mess last time and whatever the difficulties we will do it again.' At the televised daily press conferences, Wilson regularly deferred to his Shadow Cabinet colleagues. James Callaghan – with his air of blunt commonsense – handled questions on the trades unions. 'He had the unions' trust and was also the most effective television speaker,' says Joe Haines. In Labour's first election broadcast Callaghan blamed Heath for turning moderates into militants. Labour would get Britain back to work.

For his campaign tour Wilson had decided to eschew the glad-handing presidential style of 1970. Although he claimed to have invented walkabouts, he felt no need to prove he was in touch with ordinary people: 'Mary and I are people.' Instead he followed Heath's example from the 1970 election and addressed large set-piece campaign rallies, using a master speech with topical passages added each night to catch the television news programmes. And Wilson's closest advisers sought to give him a less tired image on the screen.

'Our aim was to improve and restyle the public presentation of the Leader of the Opposition,' comments Lady Falkender, who had been greatly impressed by the Tories' skilful use of the tricks of the TV and film trade in 1970. She worked with Wilson's old friend, the actor Stanley Baker and David Wickes, a young television and film producer, who subsequently made *The Sweeney*. They brought in George Blackler, a skilled make-up man from Hammer horror films, who travelled on the campaign tour with Wilson. 'Blackler's job was to keep Harold spick and span,' says Lady Falkender. 'He was to remove the shine from Harold's face and the great bags from under his eyes which develop during the campaign and make a bad picture.' Wickes adds: 'We also made sure the Leader's hair was freshly washed and he was properly coiffed.' He arranged for Wilson to buy six new suits – three blue and three grey. As the Labour leader arrived for a campaign meeting, Wickes would whisk him into a freshly cleaned jacket and send the creased one to an instant dry cleaners or hand it to Blackler, who travelled with an ironing board.

'We wanted to present a very competent, clear-cut, well-groomed image, which is what people expect of their leaders – frankly,' says Lady Falkender. 'And Harold himself was always conscious of the need for an image that was, above all, reassuring.' No detail was too small for Lady Falkender's attention. She was particularly concerned to protect Wilson's throat. At meetings, he would drink regular quantities of warm water with honey and lemon, or glasses of Lucozade for energy. 'But on colour television either of these could look like brandy or whisky, if he drank them from a clear glass,' says Lady Falkender, 'and to avoid everybody saying "he's becoming an alcoholic, swigging in the middle of his speeches", I bought green glasses and a carafe from Habitat. It was these tiny details which make the image.'

Wickes used professional lighting and sound men to ensure that the BBC and ITV took the pictures that Labour wanted at Wilson's rallies. He prevented the television companies from taking shots of any empty seats. 'We also put the cameras at the angles we wanted them, which made a tremendous difference,' says Lady Falkender. 'We didn't have the terrible shadows on Harold's face of earlier campaigns, which had made what he was saying seem either gloomy or sinister.' Wickes worked with the Labour party's youth officer, Neil Vann, to turn Wilson's entrances at meetings into a television event. Traditionally a Labour leader would slip unobtrusively on to the stage by a side entrance during one of the candidate's speeches. Wickes stationed people with walkie-talkies outside the hall to alert him to Wilson's arrival. 'I would have a microphone so I could cut off whoever was speaking and I would announce at full blast: "Ladies and gentlemen, the next Prime Minister: the Right Honourable Harold Wilson." ' The idea was for the Labour leader to make a triumphal entrance through the centre of the hall with two spotlights on him.

It was all a direct crib from American presidential campaigns and met with fierce resistance from local Labour officials. 'They were highly suspicious of this show-biz way of doing things: they didn't want Harold to be packaged like soap powder,' says Lady Falkender. The early results of Wickes' work alternated between chaos and bathos. The brash build-up for Wilson's entrances sometimes served to emphasize what an insignificant figure he could cut. In the first week of the campaign the Labour leader appeared lacklustre and defeatist. Wilson had been recovering from what was described at the time as a heavy cold, although there was speculation that he had suffered a stroke. 'It was abysmal,' admits Joe Haines, 'I watched his speeches fall from tired lips on to a leaden audience.'

As usual, Labour blamed the media, which it sought so elaborately to manage, for its campaign failures in the first week. 'Most of the press and the BBC were on the side of the Government,' claims Haines. Wilson believed that by concentrating campaign coverage on the miners' strike, the television companies were harming Labour and taking their cues from the Conservatives. He turned on Robin Day when asked if the miners were justified in continuing their strike now the Pay Board was considering their claim. 'I think the nation is getting a little tired of these questions from Mr Heath for clearly political purposes now peddled by you, inspired by the old principle of have you stopped beating your wife. . . . Let's get this thing settled and let the country get back to work. That's my answer to all these trick questions.' Day, determined to defend his own reputation, protested that Wilson was accusing him of bias. 'Don't get so sensitive,' said Wilson. 'Good Heavens, you ought to be in politics. You mustn't behave like a child about it.' 'You said I was peddling trick questions,' complained Day. 'Don't get touchy, Robin, keep calm,' responded Wilson.

Labour had taken as its election slogan: 'One Nation: Working Together'. David Wickes and Neil Vann had designed a travelling backdrop for Wilson's speeches which featured a map of Britain made from a Union flag. They were determined not to be outdone in what they called 'the patriotism stakes'. The Conservatives incorporated four Union flags in Heath's platform set. The Prime Minister travelled to his election meetings in a chartered jet called 'Halcyon Days'. This was an inappropriate description of his campaign.

Heath had hastily reassembled the advertising men, Geoffrey Tucker, Barry Day and James Garrett, along with other members of the Thursday Team who had helped him win the 1970 election. But, according to Day, 'the Conservatives had forgotten many of the lessons we had all learned the hard way in the last campaign. We didn't get the team together with the simple construction and decision-making power we had in 1970. It was all over the place – a diffuse rabble.' Heath had deliberately kept the Thursday Team out of Downing Street for three and a half years, believing that the business of government had nothing to do with the business of elections. Now they were called 'the outside help' and there was not the same total dedication there had been in 1970. When Day and Garrett came to prepare the Conservatives' election broadcasts they found themselves very short of film material. 'We had told the Conservatives "record, record, record," you are going to need it,' says Day. 'But when we looked through the Central Office archives for the achievements of individual ministers over the past four years, we found one shot: of Sir Keith Joseph entering a synagogue in the rain. This is not the stuff of political communication.'

The Tories' election broadcasts were technically less polished and politically cruder than in 1970. One programme aroused furious resentment. It claimed that beneath Labour's moderate exterior lurked the extremists and that the Party effectively took its orders from the Communists. Photographs of the reassuring Wilson and Callaghan dissolved to show the faces of the extremist bogey-men behind them – Tony Benn and Michael Foot. A Labour government would take away 'your bank account, your mortgage and your wage packet' – all were stamped with an echoing thud 'State-owned'. 'It wouldn't take much more of a move to the Left and you could find yourself not even owning your own home': on cue a young couple's house disappeared from the screen. Quotes from leading British Communists then purported to show how they controlled Labour policy. Wilson attacked the programme as a 'squalid piece of television' and claimed it showed how rattled the Tories were becoming. Like the Conservatives, Labour was now systematically monitoring and recording every television election programme. Journalists at Labour's press conference the next morning were treated to a playback of the broadcast, together with a list of its misrepresentations. 'It was a sorry broadcast in its ethical blindness, its clumsy cascade of visual gimmicks and its abysmal view of the electorate's intelligence,' wrote Martin Harrison in *The British General Election of February*, 1974. 'It confirmed the fears of what can happen when admen are given their head without adequate political control.' One disdainful Central Office official remarked: 'It was not clear whether Garret and Day were working for the Conservative Party or the Party for Garrett and Day.'

The Tories had calculated they would be helped in the campaign by television coverage of the miners' strike. But the NUM failed to oblige. Unlike 1972, there was no mass picketing and no nightly scenes of violent confrontations with the police on the TV screens. The NUM Executive had reduced pickets to six at any depot and had instructed them to be on their best behaviour. For his part Heath made little direct use of his prime ministerial position in the campaign. He refused to offer the television companies shots of himself working in Number 10 and spurned the idea of calling a crisis Cabinet meeting as a gimmick – 'the sort of thing Harold Wilson would do'. But his campaign, like Wilson's, obstinately failed to catch the public imagination. The undoubted star of the election was the Liberal leader, Jeremy Thorpe.

While television depicted the two major party leaders spending much of their time slugging it out from the opposite sides of Smith Square, Thorpe came over as an attractive and sympathetic figure who was above the party fray in his North Devon constituency. It was a virtue dictated by necessity. Thorpe's majority had been reduced from five thousand to three hundred in the previous election and he had decided that he could scarcely afford to leave his constituency throughout the campaign. But the Liberals arranged for an expensive closed circuit television link from London. Thorpe took his daily press conferences 'down the line' with journalists at the National Liberal Club in Westminster asking him questions. This gave Thorpe's campaign a distinctive look on television. And reporters found it harder to put tough questions to a man who was not physically present. With wit and charm, he presented himself as the moderate alternative.

Heath attributes the dramatic increase in the Liberal vote in the election to the television advantage Thorpe drew from his press conference arrangements. 'I thought it was wrong of the broadcasting companies to accept this – because there were the rest of us being filmed the whole time at every press conference. The press cross-examined us with questions, no matter how penetrating, and there was the Liberal leader just quietly having a cosy time down in Devonshire and he wasn't subject to this cross-examination at all. And it was the Liberals who took votes from us – they went up to over six million instead of their usual two million. I think it did have an impact, simply because the proper procedures weren't followed.' Evidence to support Heath's view came from Gallup after the election. In a survey, 55 per cent of viewers felt that Thorpe's TV appearances improved his Party's prospects, compared to 32 per cent for Wilson and 23 per cent for Heath.

Heath did not prove himself a lucky campaign general. Almost all the unexpected incidents went against him – from the CBI Director-General's denunciation of the Industrial Relations Act to the news of a record trade deficit. The most damaging of all was the revelation that the Government appeared to have overestimated miners' earnings. After a Pay Board briefing, the Press Association reported in the late afternoon of 21 February 'a sensational slip in calculations over miners' pay' – instead of being above the national average for manufacturing industry as the government maintained, it was 8 per cent below. It seemed that Heath and his ministers were either incompetents or double-dealers and that the crisis election had not been necessary. Within minutes, Joe Haines had telephoned the report to Wilson, who immediately inserted a scathing denunciation of the Government in his campaign speech. Wilson's remarks led all that evening's news and campaign report programmes. 'There was no response from ministers on television that night,' says Joe Haines. 'I discovered later that Heath only learned of the briefing five hours after we did, as his Number 10 staff were unable to reach him.' Douglas Hurd admits it was the worst moment of the campaign and he noted in his diary that night, 'Edward Heath retires to bed in a cloud of stubborn and unconvincing negatives.'

In the final week of the campaign, the Tories' other man of destiny and Heath's old enemy, Enoch Powell, returned to taunt him. Powell managed to secure more television coverage than anyone other than the party leaders – and he was not even a candidate. At the start of the campaign, he had denounced the snap election as an 'act of total immorality' and stood down in his Wolverhampton constituency. In the following two weeks, Powell had skilfully built up the expectation of the press, radio and television for a speech he was to make in Birmingham on the weekend before polling day. He stoked speculation as to whether he would call on his fellow anti-Common Market Conservatives to vote Labour. But the Birmingham speech, which led all the evening election programmes, did not make Powell's message explicit; he promised a further instalment at Shipley two days later. The Tory renegade's skill at keeping himself in the TV limelight infuriated Heath and his campaign managers. They feared that Powell could have a decisive influence over wavering Tories in marginal seats – particularly in the Midlands. And they learned with dismay that *Panorama* planned to devote its final edition before the election to the Common Market and include an extract from Powell's Shipley speech that night.

The Conservative Chairman, Lord Carrington, rang the BBC protesting against the choice of subject and the prominence likely to be given to Powell. The BBC agreed that *Panorama* would not go over 'live' to Powell's speech and would not include any abuse of Heath in recorded extracts: this failed to satisfy the Conservatives. The Prime Minister decided to break with his normal practice and apply direct pressure himself at the top of the BBC. This had its effect. *Panorama* went ahead with its Common Market programme, but took no extract at all from Powell's Shipley speech, using a clip from an old speech instead. And the BBC cancelled an exclusive interview with the Wolverhampton wanderer arranged for the following night. Says Powell: 'The producer, Miss Anne Faber, telephoned in great embarrassment to tell me that the interview had been cancelled on "higher authority" and she personally was annoyed and distressed by this. I suggested that "higher authority" was higher than the BBC, but she did not accept this. I subsequently had confirmation from an internal party source that Lord Carrington and finally the Prime Minister in person had telephoned the BBC to countermand the interview.' The BBC denied it had given in to Government pressure. It had taken an editorial decision that Powell, who had refused to give interviews on the actual days of his speeches, was deliberately seeking to extend his coverage for as long as possible. The Corporation had decided to stop playing Enoch's game. As did ITN, which cancelled its planned interview with him.

Powell was only able to arrange one interview: on a Thames Television programme that was seen in the South-East, but more widely reported. He announced that he had already voted by post in the election – Labour. Harold Wilson had been kept in close touch with Powell's intentions after a chance meeting at the start of the election campaign. According to Lady Falkender, the two men had met in the gentlemen's lavatory at the House of Commons – and Powell had confided that his only likely contribution to the election would be two speeches about Europe. Wilson recognized that the Tory renegade's news management skills would ensure him maximum coverage. 'So Labour could not afford to ignore Europe – the problem was that Harold did not want to appear to follow Powell,' says Lady Falkender. An Enoch loyalist, Andrew Alexander of the *Daily Mail*, agreed to provide Joe Haines with advance details of Powell's plans. 'It was thanks to these arrangements that Harold Wilson was forewarned about each of Powell's major speeches,' says Lady Falkender.

Labour picked up the theme of the Common Market in its final election broadcast on 26 February, the day that Powell revealed that he had voted Labour. The broadcast featured contributions from Labour's 'united team – men and women who understand down-to-earth problems: together they can put us back on the road to recovery'. Almost half the team then talked about the Common Market. Michael Foot claimed British housewives were paying high prices in the shops to subsidize French farmers; Shirley Williams said Labour would renegotiate the terms of Britain's entry and Denis Healey added 'we can get out altogether if we don't get what we want'. Harold Wilson ended the programme with an uninspired call for national unity: 'Trades unionists are people. Employers are people. We can't go on setting one against the other except at the cost of damage to the nation itself.'

The Conservatives' final election broadcast concentrated solely on Ted Heath. A lengthy film build-up to his final studio appearance continued the man of destiny theme. 'Ted Heath knows his country and he has come to know it the way he knows best – the hard way. And that way he knows more about what is going on in people's hearts and minds than anybody stuck behind a desk in Whitehall . . . It takes an extraordinary man to be Prime Minister. But this is an extraordinary man – a private man, a solitary man . . . This is a man the world respects. A man who has done so much and yet a man who has so much left to do.' Heath then appeared as the champion of the poor and the disadvantaged: the strong man helping the weak. The Government had helped millions of people like the pensioners and the lower paid, who had no strong trade union. 'They haven't needed one, because this Government has had the strength to look after their interests. We are their trade union.' He ended his final television appearance as Prime Minister with a direct personal appeal. 'I love this country. I'll do all that I can for this country. And isn't that what you want, too? We've started a job together. With your will, we shall go on and finish the job.' It had a certain wooden poignancy, but was not among the rare occasions when Heath came over sympathetically on television.

As the results came in on polling night, it was soon clear that Heath's gamble had failed. The Tories' share of the poll had fallen even more sharply than Labour's, while the Liberal vote trebled. Results in the West Midlands showed a higher than average swing against the Conservatives, apparently confirming Wilson's judgement of Enoch Powell's importance. It seemed at first that Labour would win a small overall majority. Michael Charlton of *Panorama* advanced on Wilson for an interview at his hotel in Liverpool with the words, 'Prime Minister'. 'We had waited four years for that,' says Lady Falkender. But Labour had to wait a further four days. No party won an overall majority but Labour with fewer votes had four more seats than the Conservatives – 301 out of 635. Jeremy Thorpe, whose party had won 14 seats, toured North Devon in triumph claiming 'we are all minorities now'. Heath stayed put in Downing Street desperately attempting to reach a deal with Liberals, Ulster Unionists or Nationalists to sustain him in office. There were no takers. The television cameras showed Heath's grand piano carried out of the famous front door and driven off in the Steinway removal van. Heath's political symphony was unfinished. The musical Prime Minister who had consistently failed to hit the right notes for the television audience was gone – never to return to Number 10.

It had been a bizarre election campaign; neither Wilson nor Heath had sparkled. The Labour leader had often looked like an old actor struggling to remember his lines, the attempted slickness of Labour's campaign only serving to emphasize this jaded appearance. And Heath, who had presented himself as an aloof presidential figure over three and a half years, had suddenly sought to show his common touch and make a direct personal appeal to the voters. He had failed. As his friend Ian Trethowan puts it: 'Heath's curious inability to project his private charm had a decisive effect at a moment critical not only for him, but for the country.' Asked today what he feels about that judgement, Heath says: 'But I don't think a miners' strike is the time to come on television and ooze charm – do you?' When no reply comes, he breaks into the familiar shoulder-shaking laugh and adds: 'Ah, the unanswered question.'

CHAPTER 12

Enter Tomorrow's Woman

*'It's not really me you are seeing, because so far I don't feel natural
on television.'*

Margaret Thatcher, 1975

Those who watched the news on 4 March 1974, could be forgiven a sense
of *déjà* view. Harold Wilson's return to Number 10 looked like a repeat
programme. But the familiar prime ministerial figure was determined to
use television in a completely different way from his first spell in office ten
years earlier. He paused briefly on the steps of Downing Street with a
message for the TV cameras: 'We've got a job to do. We can only do that
job as one people. I'm going in to start that job now.' The immediate job
was of winning Labour an overall majority in the election that seemed bound
to come before the end of the year. Labour's position as a minority
government was ideally suited for Wilson's tactical skills. It appeared that
1974 would be a re-run of 1964, when he had an overall majority of only
three. But then Wilson wanted maximum television exposure for himself.
Now he wanted the minimum.

'We thought the thing Harold needed to do was not to appear on the
screen,' says Joe Haines, who was back in Downing Street as the Prime
Minister's press secretary. 'Television exhausts a politician's appeal and
encourages cynicism. We felt the country needed a period of quiet. There
had been intensive politics going on for some months because of the miners'
strike. I wanted to reach the stage where whenever the Prime Minister came
on, instead of everybody rushing to switch off, they would say, "hold on, it's
Harold Wilson, let's keep him on". And so we kept him off the screen.' At
the start of April, the Prime Minister was literally hidden from the cameras
when he went to Paris to attend a 'working funeral' for President Pompidou.
Since Macmillan, British prime ministers had gone to great lengths to
appear on television with American presidents. But Richard Nixon, also at
the funeral, was drowning in Watergate. Wilson concealed himself behind
the rose bushes in the garden of the British Embassy to avoid being filmed
with the President.

During his first five months back in office, Wilson turned down all
requests for TV interviews from the BBC. His sole appearance was on

Granada's *World in Action*. 'We deliberately gave the interview to ITV. It was part of getting our own back on the BBC, who seemed suddenly to have rediscovered his value,' says Haines. *World in Action* followed *Coronation Street* in the ITV schedules and inherited a large part of the soap opera's audience. For non-political viewers, Wilson produced a football analogy that he was to polish in the months ahead to describe his new style of government. In his first administration, so few of his colleagues had ministerial experience he had to occupy almost every position on the field himself: 'I had to take corner kicks and penalties, administer to the wounded and bring on the lemons at half-time and score all the goals myself. Now I will be the deep-lying centre half, concentrating on defence, initiating attacks, distributing the ball for my star forwards. They'll score the goals and, by Heavens, they are scoring goals.'

World in Action had begun with film of the whole Cabinet coming down the steps together into the garden of Number 10. 'The idea is to show that we are a team,' Wilson had told his colleagues. They strolled round the garden together casually forming and reforming groups. It set the style for a homely programme. The founder of Granada was Sydney Bernstein, a Labour supporter whom Wilson had made a life peer. In his interview, Wilson referred repeatedly to Granada, even to 'Granadaland', the company's advertising invention. 'Mr Wilson was jokey, beamy, cosy and chatty,' reported Nancy Banks-Smith in the *Guardian*. 'He was evidently far more at home than I have seen him on, say, *Panorama*. I am not altogether persuaded that a politician has any right to feel at home on television. I'm the one who is at home.'

For all his soccer analogies, Wilson's strategy for survival was more that of the professional poker player. Despite his poor cards, he was determined to bluff the voters into believing he had a strong hand. His Government would act resolutely, as if it had a solid majority. Within days of returning to Number 10, he had settled the miners' strike on the terms the Pay Board recommended, plus a little extra. 'The three-day week was ended in a blaze of extravagant publicity, television for insomniacs restarted, and everything done to convince the electorate that things were better for them,' says Haines. Government subsidies held down food prices and mortgage repayments, while pensioners received a record rise. Wilson's plan for re-election was to close his own credibility gap by showing that he now led a Government which kept its promises.

For the first few weeks it all seemed to be going well. 'We *could* turn out to be the most successful government in history,' the Social Services Secretary, Barbara Castle, noted in her diary. But the Prime Minister suddenly found himself embroiled in a political scandal which he sought obsessively to defuse. Central to the story was the Prime Minister's political secretary, Marcia Williams, and her brother, Tony Field, who had been Wilson's office manager for two years in Opposition until 1973. The *Daily Mail* alleged that Field and his sister had made profits from a speculative purchase of slag-heaps near Wigan – 'the Wigan Alps', as they became known. As 'land speculators' featured high in Labour's demonology, the story caused acute political embarrassment at Number 10. And a letter – allegedly signed by Wilson – written to a colourful middleman, the bouffant-haired Ronald Milhench, made it appear that the Prime Minister himself had been a party to the deals.

In the Commons Wilson drew ribald laughter when he claimed that Field had been involved not in land 'speculation' but 'reclamation'. He also defended his political secretary and her brother on *World in Action*. 'I have the fullest confidence in everyone concerned in this story. The whole thing is a pretty seamy, squalid press story. This doesn't happen to Conservative prime ministers: the aim is to destroy the Labour Government.' Wilson claimed that Field never expected to make a profit from the land itself, but only by selling off the slag. Field had done a public service by removing an eyesore, nearly driven himself to bankruptcy, and had in fact broken his leg when he had slipped on the site. 'May I say that land speculators don't break their legs sitting in office chairs in Mayfair,' added the Prime Minister. As the *Guardian* wryly commented, the answer to the question 'how do you stand on slag-heaps?' is indeed 'with difficulty'.

Wilson's *World in Action* interview and Commons statement failed to defuse the scandal. 'His performances were sad, vindictive and utterly predictable,' editorialized the *Daily Mail*. For weeks the land deals dominated the life of Number 10 to the exclusion of almost everything else. The Prime Minister issued writs for libel against the *Mail* and the *Express*, as journalists laid siege to Marcia Williams' Marylebone mews house. 'It was impossible even to watch television, such was the noise coming through our sitting room windows,' she says. When the story eventually died down with the arrest of Milhench for forging Wilson's signature, the Prime Minister suddenly gave it a new lease of life by nominating his political secretary for the peerage. The announcement caused a sensation. According to the new Lady Falkender, Wilson's aim was 'to do a Harvey Smith [put up two fingers] at the press'.

So zealous was the Prime Minister to protect his political secretary's reputation that he went to the length of complaining directly to the BBC about an episode of *Steptoe and Son* which featured the younger Steptoe falling in love with a girl and bringing her home for his father's approval. On Wilson's instructions, Joe Haines pointed out to the Director-General,

Charles Curran, that the younger Steptoe's name was Harold and his girl-friend was given the name Marcia Wigley. The Corporation was making a clear imputation about the Prime Minister's relationship with his political secretary which was totally false.

Haines minuted the Prime Minister: 'Charles Curran phoned to say that when the episode was first shown, Bill Cotton [Head of Light Entertainment] said the scriptwriters were being mischievous. Cotton remembered saying to them that the BBC had enough trouble without that.' Haines asked Curran why the programme had been shown again. The Director-General replied that dropping the episode would have have drawn attention to it. Haines's minute to the Prime Minister ended with an authentic whiff of Downing Street paranoia: Steptoe's father was called Albert – near enough to Herbert, the name of Wilson's own father. Wilson took his complaint to the BBC Chairman, Sir Michael Swann. It was one of a steady stream during the summer of 1974 designed to keep the Corporation under intense private pressure in the run-up to the election. Allegations of bias in interviews and in reporting the Government's economic achievements came from Haines, Transport House and individual ministers. But the Prime Minister did not himself, as he had before, publicly attack the Corporation.

As with the 'pound in your pocket', Wilson aroused the most controversy on television in his new term in office with a broadcast he controlled himself. His subject was Northern Ireland. Within two months of regaining power, the Labour Government was up against a general strike by hardline Ulster Protestants; their aim was to destroy the power-sharing Executive of moderate Unionists and Catholics that had been set up by the Heath Government at Sunningdale. As the Province neared paralysis, Wilson flew back from a holiday in the Scilly Isles to make a ministerial broadcast. Advised that the Army could not break the strike, he decided to substitute television rhetoric for action.

'The people on this side of the water,' Wilson declaimed, had seen their sons in the Army spat upon, vilified and murdered and their taxes poured into Northern Ireland almost without regard to cost. 'Yet people who benefit from this now viciously defy Westminster, purporting to act as though they were an elected government. They spend their lives *sponging* on Westminster and British democracy and then systematically assault democratic methods. Who do these people think they are?' With hindsight, Wilson admits that his reference to 'sponging' was 'open to criticism and was picked up by the extremists'. A mass demonstration led by Ian Paisley swept up to Stormont, many of them wearing small pieces of sponge in their buttonholes. Paisley bellowed to the TV cameras: 'We resent his vile insinuation that we are spongers: the greatest sponger in the country is Mrs Marcia Williams.'

According to Joe Haines, Wilson's broadcast was largely dictated by electoral considerations at home. Haines claims that the Prime Minister had made up his mind to hold the general election in October and felt his line about 'sponging' reflected voters' attitudes. 'It was done, I fear, for the reason that we needed to win the election and it was a popular attitude to take,' says Haines, 'but it closed up any hope of making progress in Northern Ireland and was the biggest mistake I thought he made in his second term of office.'

Although the Prime Minister hoped to repeat 1966 history with another landslide election victory, Lady Falkender is convinced that unnamed enemies were seeking to undermine the Government. 'The summer months between the two elections were filled with story after lurid story: talk of close liaisons with KGB Colonels, orgies and drug-taking parties in mansion flats in the West End, mystery East European benefactors supposedly bankrolling Harold Wilson's election campaigns. It was all bunkum, but it hurt,' she says. Inside Number 10, the Prime Minister was having the greatest difficulty in holding his team together. A bitter personal feud had developed between Haines and Falkender, who vied for the Prime Minister's ear. And the fissiparous strains within his Cabinet were showing publicly.

Tony Benn, the Industry Minister, was promising sweeping new national-ization measures. But Roy Jenkins, the Home Secretary, warned publicly that by 'telling everybody who doesn't agree with you to go to hell', Labour would alienate moderate opinion. There was growing talk of the need for a coalition government of like-minded moderates. Wilson would have none of it. At the start of August he finally accepted a BBC invitation for a TV interview. He chose not *Panorama* but *Nationwide* – a new, early evening current affairs magazine with over ten million viewers, largely housewives, manual workers and children. It was the first, but was not to be the last time a prime minister agreed to appear on such a popular programme. On *Nationwide*, Wilson ruled out Labour taking part in a coalition government and rehearsed his election appeals. 'I think we have in the past few months carried through more of our election pledges than any Government since the war. This is a thing people haven't got used to over the past three years – political honesty.'

He claimed Mr Heath's team 'was not very good at the last election and most of them have now left him or been sacked.' In contrast, the Prime Minister boasted he had 'a very brilliant Cabinet – the most experienced we have had in this country since the war and the most talented. I believe a Cabinet which has people like Michael Foot [the Employment Secretary] and Roy Jenkins working together is the only hope for Britain – that is in the best sense of the word a coalition.' His own job was to keep together his Cabinet 'team of pretty headstrong horses. I am enabling both the Government and the country to have the benefit of all their points of view, and then see they speak as one Cabinet on our decisions.' The following month he announced the date of the election after the shortest Parliament this century.

It was to be largely a re-run of the February campaign, although this time both sides attempted to avoid the asperities which had so alienated voters. Cosmetic treatment for television had been applied to both Wilson and Heath – literally. The Prime Minister's tobacco-stained front teeth had been capped, while a gap in the Opposition leader's lower set, which sometimes gave him a snarling appearance on the screen, had been plugged with a false tooth. Heath's media advisers were determined to erase memories of confrontation and present a more conciliatory, even cuddly, image of the Tory leader. He had appeared the previous month on the André Previn programme wearing a powder-blue, chunky sweater. It was, Heath told the trendy American conductor, the first time he had been interviewed on television without a tie. 'Edward Heath was presented as a rather jovial, overweight and always tanned, grocer with thirty-two tomb-stone teeth and a big laugh. He might be suspect for wearing rope-soled sandals and perhaps even blue rinsing his hair, but it was a very clever image,' says David Wickes, the film director who helped organize Harold Wilson's election tour.

Labour's campaign managers had produced a special recording to herald the Prime Minister's appearances at rallies. To the tune of 'Hello Dolly', the loudspeakers blared out: 'Hello Harold, it's so good to have you there where you belong.' David Wickes says that one night he saw Wilson run the last two steps from the hall on to the platform. 'He just skipped up the steps and it looked very attractive as if he were very capable and physically robust. I got him to do it at every meeting after that.' The actor Stanley Baker again worked on Labour's election broadcasts and brought in the playwright John Mortimer. 'John was of great help with Harold's broadcasts and he suggested many passages and themes we used,' says Lady Falkender. Again the main theme was the team. Specially shot glossy film showed Wilson's ministers involved in high affairs of state and meeting ordinary people: this was a Cabinet of all the talents – 'Labour's government of national unity'.

At his televised press conferences, Wilson would arrive with a different minister and a fresh policy proposal each day. It did not always work out as planned. The Chancellor, Denis Healey, produced press guffaws with a graph purporting to show that inflation was only rising at 8.4 per cent a year. Healey was being decidedly economical with the truth – the annual figure was nearer 20 per cent. When Labour's private polls showed that most voters did not believe the Chancellor, the Party's campaign managers paraded the Cabinet minister with the highest 'credibility rating': the Prices Secretary, Shirley Williams, was to try to undo the damage. But to the Prime Minister's annoyance, the BBC's Parliamentary Correspondent, Christopher Jones, insisted on putting a question to Mrs Williams not about inflation but about the Common Market. In view of her passionate commitment to Europe, would she stay in the Cabinet if the public voted against Britain's continued membership in the referendum Labour was pledged to hold? Wilson sought to prevent her from answering: 'Press conferences are to ask the Labour party and the Government what their policy is, not to try to put individual questions to individual members.' He then launched into a lengthy discourse on how united his Cabinet was. But Mrs Williams refused to take direction. She replied bluntly: 'I would not remain in politics if the referendum went wrong from my point of view.'

Her response led the TV news bulletins. It was a large stone through the glasshouse of Labour unity that Wilson had so painstakingly sought to construct. The next day reporters gleefully produced a similar projectile from Roy Jenkins. 'This was a diversion which drew blood,' says Wilson, 'those replies undoubtedly drove a number of committed Marketeers into abstention or into voting for the Conservatives or Liberals.' The event fed suspicions in Number 10 that the BBC was conspiring with the pro-Europeans to do down the Prime Minister. Wilson himself had adopted so low-key an approach in his speeches that press and television men on his tour labelled him 'the Labour Club bore'. But he was following the findings of the Party's private opinion polls which showed the voters were turned off by the politics of confrontation and abuse. 'What the people want, what every family needs is a bit of peace and quiet,' Wilson repeated in his speeches and television interviews.

Wilson's main selling point was the grandly styled Social Contract. The unions would agree to restrain wage demands so long as the Government produced legislation they liked – although there was no contract enforceable by law. The BBC drew a complaint from the Labour party at the start of the campaign by referring to the 'so-called Social Contract'. Heath claimed on television that the original author of the phrase, Jean-Jacques Rousseau, must have been turning in his grave at the use the Labour party was making of it. But in an effective piece of campaign knockabout, Wilson parodied the discussion of the Tory High Command: 'Labour's got a Social Contract – we want a Social Contract. All God's chillun should have Social Contracts.' While the faithful laughed, the polls showed that almost half the electorate had no faith in the Social Contract. Most voters distrusted the unions and felt they had no business in government.

Like Labour, the Tories had identified a strong mood in favour of consensus policies. This translated into Heath's promise to create 'a government of national unity', which would include political outsiders. He knew his days as leader were numbered if he lost his third election in four. The Central Office post mortem into the February result had revealed that Heath was 'a serious electoral liability': his television manner was off-putting and he seemed to stand for confrontation. 'The need to present a softened, unabrasive appeal was increasingly recognized,' wrote David Butler and Dennis Kavanagh in their book on the October election. For the campaign Heath admitted a woman into the hitherto exclusively masculine ranks of his entourage.

Sara Morrison, a Party Vice-Chairman and wife of a Conservative MP, travelled by Heath's side throughout his campaign tour on the calculation that he would benefit from being shown in female company. But she denied that she was cast as a substitute wife: 'I think Ted would be shattered if that's the sort of role I've been given. I'm a sort of cock-eyed Mary Poppins, perhaps. I think he looks on me as a somewhat turbulent watchdog, who wants the campaign to go in a way which relates to people.' Sara Morrison advised Heath that he would come over better on television if he started to say 'we' rather than 'I' and showed he was prepared to listen.

'We should stop calling each other liars, and put an end to this party political bickering,' became a standard passage in Heath's campaign disser-tations. He had agreed not to take the majority of the press conferences himself and to make few speeches at formal rallies. His campaign managers arranged instead for him to appear in shirt-sleeves meeting small, informal groups in question and answer sessions in local halls. 'You can take your jackets off too – it doesn't matter if you're wearing braces,' the new, informal Leader told his audience with a grin. The hope was that somehow the private Heath, over whom his friends enthused, would emerge for the cameras. It did not work. He still came over as stiff and stilted. And the sessions themselves produced little that the television companies used, partly because the meetings were papered with Tory supporters asking banal questions.

So marked was the change in Heath at his election press conferences, that journalists questioned him about the new style. 'I am adopting the technique you have so often urged on me of quiet, reasonable conversation,' he replied. And in his first election broadcast, the Conservative leader said: 'I think perhaps sometimes too much is asked of politicians, too much is asked of governments. It might also be the fault of politicians that they lead people to expect too much of them. Perhaps there ought to be a little more modesty and humility all round.' It was a startlingly different Heath from the assured, infallible presidential image he had sought to project only a few months earlier. 'We had relied too much on the cult of a single personality,' said one of Heath's publicity advisers. In the October campaign, the Conservatives – like Labour – had decided to concentrate on the team. This new tactic produced its own irony: the chief beneficiary was the only woman in his Shadow Cabinet, Mrs Margaret Thatcher.

She was given a bigger role in the party's election broadcasts than Heath himself. As Shadow Environment Secretary, Mrs Thatcher had the task of introducing the Conservatives' only two hard pledges of the campaign: the commitment to reduce mortgages to 9.5 per cent by public subsidy and to abolish domestic rates. Although the mortgage promise conflicted with her free market views, she accepted it as an electoral necessity and defended it robustly both in current affairs programmes and in a Tory election broadcast. On the strength of her performance, she was promoted to introducing the next broadcast herself.

Mrs Thatcher was tutored for her television appearances by the flamboyant independent producer, Gordon Reece. His varied career had taken him from ITN through religious programmes to the light entertainment shows of Bruce Forsyth and Eamonn Andrews. Reece had become a member of Heath's Thursday Team of media consultants in 1970. In that year's election the Conservatives had hoped to use Mrs Thatcher, then Shadow Education Secretary, in one of the party's election broadcasts. But her contribution had ended up on the cutting-room floor. 'In 1970, she was filmed in a park, where she was surrounded by kids going up and down slides screaming,' remembers the Thursday Team leading light, Barry Day: 'Margaret looked extremely out of touch. She was saying "I believe you should have a choice for your children" and gave the impression she hoped they wouldn't be sick all over her dress. She was very ill at ease with the camera and the children: it was amateur night. But she was clever enough to ask for help. Margaret wanted to learn while most of the rest of the senior Tories wished television would just go away.'

Reece took on the role of unpaid, personal television adviser to Mrs Thatcher. The two formed a professional relationship that was to become central to her political success. By 1974, her four years as Education Secretary in the Heath Government had greatly increased Mrs Thatcher's television experience, although she still hated appearing. She had come to rely on Reece's calming presence in the studios to help her relax. For the first of her two party broadcasts in the October election, he went through lengthy rehearsal sessions with her on closed circuit to prepare for a purportedly spontaneous interview. The next programme saw her talking direct to camera on a street corner, affrontedly denying Wilson's charges that her mortgage proposals were ' a blatant electoral bribe'. 'We got a very high response from viewers to her broadcasts in 1974; they gave her the public visibility that was very helpful to her a little time later,' says Barry Day.

The second election campaign within nine months failed to stir the viewers. Most people felt there was far too much of it on television, although coverage had been cut back sharply from the February levels. Even the Liberal campaign, which had been so successful earlier in the year, lacked lustre. It was symbolized by the sight of the Liberal leader assailing holiday beaches from a hovercraft which kept breaking down. Clad in oilskins, he would emerge and declare: 'I'm Jeremy Thorpe.' 'That's your problem, not mine,' retorted one holidaymaker. For the first time, Thorpe and the other two party leaders agreed to answer questions direct from voters in the studio. Granada had selected a large representative audience from marginal constituencies to confront each of the party leaders in separate sessions. Not since the rumbustious *Hustings* programmes of the 1959 election had any politician agreed to face the televoters; but fifteen years on, even the down-to-earth questioners from Granadaland raised few sparks. 'Public opinion was more than a little bored,' says Wilson. 'In the final days of the campaign the media gave great emphasis to arguments for a government of all the talents, which always have an appeal and are difficult to repudiate.'

In the end the election turned into an *un*popularity contest. The votes for all three parties dropped compared with February – but the Tories fell furthest. Labour achieved an overall majority of three, with a smaller share of the poll than any winning party since 1922. Ron Hayward, Labour's General Secretary, blamed the media for his party's relative failure: he said that television had treated the campaign with 'a trivialization that amounted to distortion'. But a subsequent research study by an academic whom Hayward appointed cleared both the BBC and ITV. Evidently in 1974 the more the electorate saw of its leaders on television, the less it thought of them – especially when they attempted to don new guises for the cameras. The 'new Wilson' and the 'new Heath' had failed to impress. The deeply-lying centre half and the national unitarian still seemed to resemble the same old pair who had been around for a decade. But neither man was to stay Leader for more than the next eighteen months. Heath was the first to go.

Within days of the election, the Tory blades were flashing. A group of the most senior backbenchers led by the Chairman of the 1922 Committee, Edward du Cann (later knighted), met at his City office in Milk Street to plot Heath's replacement. The 'Milk Street Mafia' eventually succeeded in persuading Heath to put himself up for re-election as Party leader. Under new rules, the winning candidate would need a lead of a clear 15 per cent of the electorate on the first ballot, or the contest would go to a second ballot. At this stage new candidates could enter the race: a provision that became known as the 'Cowards' Charter'. The first ballot was to be on 4 February, 1975 – between Heath, Margaret Thatcher and the rank outsider, Hugh Fraser.

Most Conservative MPs and almost every commentator felt at the start of the contest that Mrs Thatcher had no serious chance of winning. She had until recently seemed to share their view. 'I would not wish to be Prime Minister, I don't have enough experience for that job,' she had said as Education Secretary on television in 1973 and the following year had told reporters that she did not believe there would be a woman prime minister in her lifetime. But by the autumn of 1974, she had changed her mind. When she informed Heath in November that she intended to run against him, he replied bluntly: 'You'll lose.'

Ironically Heath himself had given Mrs Thatcher the opportunity that helped persuade Tory MPs she could lead the Party. After the October defeat, he had made her Treasury Spokesman, shadowing the Chancellor, Denis Healey. Her Commons performances had raised the first cheers of the Parliament from demoralized Tories: they cheered according to Frank Johnson in the *Daily Telegraph*, 'from genuine enthusiasm rather than the hope of distant knighthoods or peerages'. In a lacerating attack on Healey two weeks before the first ballot for the leadership, Mrs Thatcher responded to his jibe that she was 'La Pasionaria of privilege'. She wished she could say that the Chancellor had done himself less than justice, in fact he had done himself justice. 'Some Chancellors are micro-economic. Some Chancellors are fiscal. This one is just cheap.' It was the stuff of a Parliamentary triumph and could not have been better timed to impress the electorate of Tory MPs.

Both Heath and Thatcher agreed to take part in a filmed report on their campaigns made by the author and John Penycate for the BBC's *Midweek* on the eve of the first ballot. Asked if he found any irony in the fact that after ten years leading the party as a bachelor his main opponent was now a woman, Heath responded: 'No, I see no irony at all.' At the end of the interview, Heath's aides asked that it be filmed again, as he would produce better answers the next time. They wanted him to appear less abrupt and stress that women played a very important part in the Conservative party, in Parliament and in the constituencies. Even after ten years as leader he was still noticeably ill at ease in front of the cameras, and in thrall to his advisers.

Heath and his supporters sought to present Mrs Thatcher as a suburban woman of no international experience. Sir Ian Gilmour said that the Tories could not 'retire behind a privet hedge into a world of narrow class interests and selfish concerns', while Heath himself warned of the dangers of the party becoming a middle-class protection society. On *Midweek*, Mrs Thatcher was asked whether she would be able to attract back the Conservative votes lost in the North of England at the last two elections. 'It wasn't I who lost them, except by being a member of Mr Heath's administration and bearing the same responsibility as he does.' But it was suggested that as a middle-class lady representing Finchley she would not appeal to the North; as David Watt had put it in the *Financial Times*, 'to anyone north of the Trent she might just as well have come from Mars'. Mrs Thatcher responded sharply, 'I think it is a wholly false question. Mr Heath represents a South-Eastern seat and lives in Westminster.'

A revealing exchange took place in her room in the Commons when the interview was over.

THATCHER: Why is it that all you young men ask me about what I look like?

INTERVIEWER: Well, it may seem to people who work in a factory or a mill that you don't share or even understand their daily concerns.

THATCHER: Yes, all you young men ask me what I look like. I'm forty-eight so I suppose it is flattering that you concentrate on my appearance [she was in fact forty-nine].

INTERVIEWER: No, we are not asking what you look like as such, but we are asking about your political image.

THATCHER: Yes, why do you always ask what I look like?

INTERVIEWER, voice rising: You know perfectly well we are not asking about what you look like.

At which point Mrs Thatcher leaned forward and patted the interviewer gently on the knee and said: 'There, there, don't get upset, remember I was the one being asked the nasty questions.' The TV camera crew, delighted to see a front man discountenanced, burst into laughter. Mrs Thatcher was already showing her skills in dealing with the men from the media. And on the eve of the first ballot she turned an unlikely opportunity into a triumph.

She had agreed to give full access to her home and family to Granada's *World in Action* for a profile entitled, 'Why I want to be Leader'. It was a brave and risky decision. As the *Observer* commented, 'Since Mrs Thatcher probably ranks somewhere near the Chilean junta in *World in Action*'s scale of affection, it seemed possible they were examining her as a toxic phenomenon. Perhaps it was assumed that mere exposure would suffice.' In the event, Mrs Thatcher once again proved the old television rule that access breeds enchantment, even among the most radical of TV types. The programme was just what her television adviser, Gordon Reece, wanted.

'She came alive as never before for TV viewers last night – almost diffidently, frequently blushing, passionate but mild in affirming Conservative values,' enthused the *Daily Telegraph*. 'Mrs Thatcher is becoming an adept at helping a film crew to stage the fake candid,' Clive James noted in the *Observer*. 'The hang-up has always been the voice – the condescending, explanatory whine which treats the squirming interlocutor as an eight-year-old child with personality deficiencies.' One sequence in the *World in Action* programme showed Mrs Thatcher talking to men working on an industrial refuse dump. A worker was hesitant about the sort of things he had to collect: 'I clean up, er, how can I put it . . . ?' 'Refuse?' volunteered Mrs Thatcher. 'Refuse and people who die.' The Tory leadership contender was not struck speechless for more than three seconds: 'It's a job that has to be done and requires someone of quiet dignity to do it.'

World in Action was transmitted on the eve of the ballot. Many Tory MPs, normally rare viewers, crowded round sets in the Commons to watch it. Asked why Conservative MPs should vote for her, Mrs Thatcher responded: 'They know I don't flinch from attack. I can and do attack quite vigorously when it is needed.' 'Hear, hear,' harumphed her audience. 'Her family apparently think that television doesn't do her justice, but she has resourcefully picked it up and used it like a pistol,' wrote Nancy Banks-Smith in the *Guardian*. *The Times*' political correspondent reported that her charm and modesty came through strongly: 'Her supporters have always said that she is a much better television performer than Ted Heath.' It was a view that her *World in Action* performance seemed to support. Her son Mark found the programme excellent and felt it gave a boost to her campaign.

The result of the first ballot astounded MPs. Mrs Thatcher's campaign manager, Airey Neave, a skilled psychological warrior and Heath reject, had instructed his aides to go round the House deliberately looking glum, before the voting. His tactic was to play down her support in an attempt to encourage complacency in the Heath camp and attract a sympathy vote. In the event Mrs Thatcher won 130 votes, Heath 119 and Fraser 16. One of her backbench campaign team said: '*World in Action* was worth twenty votes to us: many MPs had never seen her like that before and did not know what she was really like.' Airey Neave predicted that she would win the second ballot as support for her grew in the constituencies due to the success of *World in Action*. Ironically the leader of the Tories' radical Right seemed to have hitched a ride towards victory in the favourite vehicle of television's radical Left.

When she heard the result of the first ballot, Mrs Thatcher held a celebratory press conference in a Commons' Committee room; television cameras, normally banned from the precincts, had managed to find their way inside. The dark horse had been transformed to the front runner. What the *Daily Mail* described as 'the hysterically elated Thatcher camp' quickly circulated a new joke: *Knock, knock.* Who's there? *Ted.* Ted Who? *See, you've forgotten already.*

'So, we got it all wrong,' said Heath when the result was brought to his room. However he looked at the figures, he could see no way of hanging on. Within two hours he had resigned as Tory leader. Mrs Thatcher and her supporters drank celebratory champagne in front of the TV cameras. Ted Heath felt every cork was aimed at him and remains bitter about the Thatcher campaign. 'I do not think it was conducted in the way of colleagues. When we had the original leadership election in 1965, we didn't carry on in great television and radio campaigns and press campaigns behind the scenes. You can say I was simple and taken unawares, but I am afraid I had standards. I think the other thing which upset me more was to find that after the elections there were celebrations with champagne. Now I really don't think that's a relationship between colleagues. It's something Reggie Maudling, Enoch Powell and I would never have dreamt of for a moment. It's an indication of the different attitudes right from the beginning.' Heath had evidently forgotten both his own celebrations on being elected Leader and the fact that eight years before that he had dined on game pie and champagne at the Turf Club with Macmillan on the night he beat Butler for the Premiership.

With Heath gone, four new challengers declared they were standing against Mrs Thatcher in the second ballot: Willie Whitelaw, Jim Prior, John Peyton and Sir Geoffrey Howe. Loyalty to Heath had kept them from running against him in the first round, but they were now depicted as indecisive, even cowardly. 'A whole crowd of faint-hearts left it to a courageous and able woman,' editorialized the *Daily Telegraph*. 'If they ganged up to deny her her just reward it would smell all the same.' The four men had the problem of trying to wheel-clamp the speeding Thatcher bandwagon. Whitelaw had long been considered Heath's heir apparent, but under the scrutiny of the TV cameras he came over as a waffler. He was filmed wearing an apron doing the washing-up. And when one Tory MP complained to Whitelaw that he was not tough enough and always seemed to agree with whatever the last person said, he boomed: 'I agree, I agree.'

On the weekend before the second ballot, Whitelaw was completely outmanoeuvred by Mrs Thatcher. Both were due to speak at the Young Conservatives' Conference, but they had agreed that neither would make campaigning speeches. Whitelaw dutifully plodded through his pre-arranged question and answer session on devolution: it was the most restrictive of opportunities. In contrast, Mrs Thatcher had to wind up the economic debate and produced a rousing affirmation of her beliefs. She attracted the cameras and a standing ovation that was all the more significant as the Young Conservatives had been Ted Heath's strongest supporters and were not seen as her natural allies.

The following day, Mrs Thatcher and her campaign managers pulled off their boldest media coup of all. She had agreed to appear with the other four candidates for separate interviews on *Panorama*. But on Gordon Reece's advice, she suddenly decided to pull out. Her campaign managers' line to the press was that she objected to the format of the programme: as it was proposed to pre-record the interview, Mrs Thatcher would not have the opportunity to reply to any criticisms of her policy her rivals might make. 'Many of her friends consider that she was perfectly right to show the BBC that politicians are not at its beck and call,' reported The *Daily Telegraph*. In fact the decision to withdraw, had nothing to do with *Panorama*'s format, which the programme makers offered to change by interviewing Mrs Thatcher live.

Reece calculated that without Mrs Thatcher, the other four male candidates would all appear much of a muchness – grey men quarrelling among themselves. By her absence, she would demonstrate her individuality. Additionally, her canvass returns put her well ahead among Tory MPs and a poor performance could cost her votes. Mrs Thatcher herself was unconvinced by Reece's reasoning and she had a series of fraught telephone calls with the *Panorama* producer, Roger Bolton. 'It was obviously a very tense and emotional time for her,' says Bolton, who felt Mrs Thatcher sounded near to tears on the telephone. 'She had given me her word and now she was advised that for tactical reasons it would be counter-productive for her to appear. But she found it extraordinarily difficult to pull out of the programme. We spent a long, long time on the phone.'

Reece's tactics worked. On *Panorama* the four men scarcely produced a spark between them. The next day, Mrs Thatcher won with a handsome overall majority. Reece was on his way to becoming her media guru. At a victory press conference, the new Tory leader faced rows of television and press cameras with total composure. She revolved her head slowly round so that each of them could have a perfect full-face picture. 'And now I am going to take a turn to the right, which is very appropriate,' she said. In a television interview with the author that night Mrs Thatcher explained how she felt to follow in such illustrious footsteps: 'My predecessors, Edward Heath, Sir Alec Douglas-Home, Harold Macmillan, Anthony Eden, then of course the great Winston, it is like a dream. Wouldn't you think so? I almost wept when they told me. I did weep.' The new Leader bit her lip and her eyes welled.

Mrs Thatcher felt she had no time to lose. Labour's Parliamentary position was so precarious, there could be another general election at any time. Fearing that Wilson might engineer one before she had any chance to build herself up with the voters, Mrs Thatcher decided to go on a series of tours across the country. She drew huge and excited crowds in the North of England and Scotland – areas assumed to be implacably hostile to her. A month after her election, she was due to make her first party political broadcast. She did not relish the prospect. 'Winston was never on television,' she said, 'certainly never interviewed on it.' Mrs Thatcher arrived at the TV studios carrying a book menacingly entitled 'Invective and Abuse', but she put on a cheery performance. The broadcast opened with scenes of her being mobbed on her tours: 'From Edinburgh to Eastbourne, the same scene – friendliness, enthusiasm, optimism,' ran the voice-over, 'a feeling among all groups of people that we can look for a new approach and new hope in the Leader of the Conservative Party.'

Mrs Thatcher then recounted her own Grantham version of an American presidential candidate's log-cabin-to-the-White-House story. She had lived above the shop for the first eighteen years of her life, gone to an ordinary state school and had had no privileges. Her father had taught her the virtues of thrift and self-reliance. She was very aware of her new responsibilities and a little apprehensive: 'Who wouldn't be when you think of the names that I follow? To be the first woman at it is quite a responsibility. But after all, you know, the men haven't made such a success of it all the time. So to yesterday's men, tomorrow's woman says "hello".'

But tomorrow's woman was far from happy with her appearance on the screen. She reacted to television like an African tribesman faced with a tourist's camera: she almost seemed to believe it would take her soul away. 'It's not really me you are seeing, because so far I don't feel natural on television,' said Mrs Thatcher a month after the leadership election. She was convinced both that television would be crucial for any long-term political success and that she faced special problems as a woman in broadcasting effectively. It was to make many protracted and agonizing sessions on closed circuit with Gordon Reece before her performances improved.

Harold Wilson began by treating his new rival dismissively: 'Some of us are rather old hands at these matters,' he informed Mrs Thatcher on her first appearance at the dispatch box. 'What the Prime Minister means is that he has been around for a long time – and it looks it,' she snapped back. It was a personal riposte that Heath would never have made. Wilson would clearly have to adapt his technique, if he was to see off his fourth successive Tory leader. But with his tiny overall majority, the Prime Minister was devoting almost all his energy to holding his increasingly fractious party together and ensuring his Government's survival.

As inflation surged out of control, Wilson claimed in a ministerial broadcast that the country was facing its gravest crisis since the war: the Government had to defeat 'the big battalions' on both sides of industry which were grabbing more than their share of the national wealth. But the Prime Minister would only fight one battle at a time. He felt he had first to dispose of the continuing controversy over Britain's membership of the Common Market. For a year since Labour's return to office, the Foreign Secretary, James Callaghan, had sought to renegotiate the terms of entry. In June 1975, the public were to vote in a referendum whether Britain should remain a member on the new terms. The referendum had been adopted as a device to hold Labour together in the early seventies; now the referendum campaign threatened to split the Party irrevocably and perhaps bring down the Government as Cabinet ministers paraded against each other across the television screens.

The pro-Marketeers had a majority in Cabinet and some – like Roy Jenkins and Shirley Williams – had committed themselves on television to resign if the referendum went against them; but a third of the Cabinet remained passionately opposed to membership. Wilson took the unprecedented decision to suspend the doctrine of collective Cabinet responsibility. For the duration of the campaign, ministers would not have to speak publicly with a single voice – they had a unique licence to put their opposing views. Wilson maintained the Government itself would remain neutral. He and the Foreign Secretary intended to present themselves as above the partisan battle. 'All our people are going to get so fed up with the screaming cacophony that they are going to put their fingers in their ears,' Wilson said in an ITV interview at the start of the campaign, 'the more they get confused the more they will listen to the voice of reason, which is how Jim Callaghan and I approach it.'

At first Wilson instructed that Cabinet ministers on opposite sides were not to appear together on the the the same television programme. He sought to prevent an edition of *Midweek* from featuring separate filmed interviews with the pro-Market Fred Peart and the anti-Market Peter Shore. But the Head of BBC Current Affairs, Brian Wenham, resisted the Prime Minister's pressure and transmitted the programme. Anti-Market ministers then lobbied Wilson to relax his no-debate rule for the final days of the campaign. Over tea at Number 10 the Prime Minister told Lord Swann, the BBC Chairman, that he had decided to agree to a unique confrontation on *Panorama*: Roy Jenkins *versus* Tony Benn, the leading Labour anti-Marketeer.

As they walked into the *Panorama* studio, Jenkins said to Benn: 'I had never realized you were so tall.' Benn replied, 'I don't think I've been measured since I was in the RAF – I was five foot eleven then, I believe.' It was almost as if the two men were strangers instead of having sat together around Cabinet and Shadow Cabinet tables for the past ten years. On the programme they maintained an elaborate show of courtesy, while arguing passionately against each other; the two members of the same Cabinet seemed to share none of each other's beliefs about the economy, the Labour party, or Britain's future. Benn appeared the more relaxed of the two and argued his case persuasively. But the Prime Minister himself had already belittled his own Industry Minister on television.

'Mr Benn has some of the qualities of an old Testament Prophet without a beard. He talks about the new Jerusalem,' Wilson had said on ITV, 'but after the referendum on 6 June, make no mistake about it, there will be one Cabinet with one Cabinet view.' Like Callaghan, Wilson had distanced himself from the pro and anti campaigns. He had complained that he was being kept off television and provoked invitations for interviews on both BBC and ITV. In them, he argued that after long debate and much hard work he had become convinced that a 'Yes' vote was on balance really in Britain's best interests. He had shifted from his earlier opposition to Heath's terms of entry and subsequent research showed he took a number of waverers with him.

The result of the referendum was a 66 per cent 'Yes' vote. Benn claims that Wilson's role in the campaign was decisive. 'If he had come out against the renegotiation, people would have voted "No". I regard it as the third election in which the Labour party was defeated and Wilson won.' This exaggerated the Prime Minister's importance; most voters seemed to take the down-to-earth view that once we were in, we might as well stay in. On 7 June, Wilson told the TV cameras on the steps of Downing Street that fourteen years of national argument were over. He went inside to drink champagne with Callaghan to a job well done. Then it was back to what his chief policy adviser, Bernard (later Lord) Donoughue, described as the 'lurking economic horrors'.

By the summer of 1975, wages and prices were rising by 25–30 per cent. The Prime Minister had returned from a trip to America just before the referendum campaign to face a major sterling crisis. 'We had to play for time,' says Wilson. He decided to make an immediate television appearance in an attempt to steady the pound. Seeking a suitable platform, the prime ministerial eye lighted on *Weekend World* – the Sunday morning programme presented by Peter Jay, the Foreign Secretary's son-in-law. Joe Haines rang the programme to offer an interview with the Prime Minister and was accepted immediately.

Weekend World had been created some two years earlier as a self-consciously new form of television journalism. Its aim was in-depth analysis (although its first edition had included an interview with the strip-teaser turned *Men Only* sex adventurer, Fiona Richmond). By the start of 1975, Peter Jay and John Birt, the programme's creator, had come up with their celebrated rationale of *Weekend World*'s existence. The inquiry commissioned by Labour's General Secretary into television coverage of the October general election had just been published. It cleared both BBC and ITV of bias. But Jay and Birt claimed there was indeed a bias on television – 'a bias against understanding'. They argued that constantly repeated news pictures of ministers going into Number 10 did nothing to increase viewers' understanding of the complexities of international liquidity just as endless film of terrorist outrages revealed nothing of the root causes of the Irish problem: indeed the emotive effect of the images worked directly against rational exposition and analysis.

The Jay/Birt solution was detailed lectures written by Jay and other *Weekend World* producers, followed by long studio interviews. The programme had became a great *succès d'estime*, although few viewers actually watched it: the Home Secretary, Roy Jenkins, felt it existed by levitation. But most senior politicians liked appearing on the programme – principally because the next day's newspapers normally carried lengthy extracts from their interviews, thanks partly to *Weekend World*'s speed in providing Fleet Street political editors with transcripts.

On *Weekend World*, Wilson and his pipe exuded imperturbability. He had been away for two weeks and in that time nothing had in fact happened. 'But I come back and find not only journalists, commentators, but some politicians rushing around like wet hens as though some devastating crisis has hit the country.' The Prime Minister blamed much of the trouble on a gloomy report about Britain on American television based on 'London cocktail circuit gossip'. His performance seemed to achieve its purpose. 'Dry old cock comes home to roost', 'I am at the helm,' said the newspaper headlines. 'It was a display of calm complacency and defensiveness that even he has never excelled,' reported *The Times*' political editor. '*Weekend World* was of course being used by Wilson,' wrote the programme's official historian, Michael Tracey. 'Many more people would have read about the programme than actually seen Wilson on it and in that sense it is a classic illustration of *Weekend World*'s emerging ability to inform and stimulate discussion while remaining two steps removed from the bulk of the population.'

Wilson admitted privately that the Government was living on borrowed time. He knew that before the summer was out he would have drastically to cut back wage rises if he was to avert economic disaster. He felt the Government's survival depended on reaching an agreement with the miners. 'But would the bailiffs in the form of the international financial community give us time to win the support of the miners?' he asked in his memoirs. The answer came on 30 June. Wilson was opening the Royal Agricultural Show at Stoneleigh in Warwickshire. He delivered a speech rejecting 'melodramatic measures and panic solutions' and was filmed eating strawberries by the TV cameras and press photographers. It presented a picture of complacency. 'I was depicted in an abdicatory posture eating strawberries while Rome was burning,' says Wilson. Sterling fell by five points, the biggest slide ever in a single day.

On his return by helicopter that afternoon from Stoneleigh to Downing Street, the Prime Minister was met by a familiar deputation: the Governor of the Bank of England, who had arrived by the back door to avoid the cameras, and the Chancellor, Denis Healey. They said the only way out of the crisis was through a statutory incomes policy. The Treasury had already prepared a Bill, incorporating many of the same phrases that Heath himself had used two years earlier. Persuaded by his Number 10 advisers that the Treasury was offering a prescription for political disaster, Wilson came up with an Irishism. There would be a new voluntary pay policy with sanctions – it was a prime ministerial version of the old army joke of the Sergeant Major nominating volunteers. Unions would be offered a flat across the board £6 a week increase and there would be sanctions on employers who paid more.

'Harold was determined to take an obvious lead in putting the message of restraint across to the country,' says Marcia Falkender. He successfully wooed the miners with a much heralded speech to their annual conference. And in August 1975 he made a ministerial broadcast, appealing direct to the viewers in lapidary, Churchillian style. 'Join the attack on inflation. Get involved. The next year is crucial. Living standards for many will fall. The harsh truth must not be disguised. This year justice will be rough, but justice there will be nevertheless. The prospects for our country if we were to fail would be grim indeed: that is why I ask that the next year be a year for Britain, for Britain by all of us – the people of Britain.' But the Prime Minister was not himself able to give a year for Britain. Within seven months he would be gone.

At first the £6 policy seemed to work; although it was piling up resentments and anomalies for the next Prime Minister to deal with, it bought time. Wilson set up a special publicity unit at Number 10, run by two senior figures seconded from the *Daily Mirror*, to promote the new policy on TV, radio and in the press. He happily sought to enlist television as a propaganda arm of his administration. But like other prime ministers, both before and since, he was obsessively concerned to keep the Government's decision-making process hidden from public view. A rare glimpse into how the Wilson Cabinet actually operated was provided by Granada with an innovatory programme about the Chrysler crisis at end of 1975.

In December the American car company threatened totally to shut down its British operation, unless the Government provided nearly £200 million in subsidies. Closure would mean the loss of thousands of jobs and Wilson feared there would be riots at Chrysler's main plant, Linwood in Scotland. 'The American car men acted like Chicago hoods making the British Government an offer it could not refuse,' says Bernard Donoughue. For weeks, Wilson admits, the Chrysler crisis dominated the Cabinet; eventually the Government gave in to the American company. Granada chose to reconstruct the agonized Cabinet debates by using political journalists to play the role of the leading Cabinet ministers involved. Each of the journalists, making use of his special access as a Lobby correspondent, sought to have himself privately briefed by the minister he was portraying. The Westminster air was thick with the unattributable grinding of axes.

The result was a riveting programme called *The State of the Nation*. In the eyes of some Cabinet ministers it was the nearest television had ever come to showing the way the Wilson Government took decisions. Granada was to repeat the exercise with different crises over the coming years to the dismay of both James Callaghan and Margaret Thatcher. Wilson himself was dismissive of the first programme: 'Media reconstructions of Cabinet discussions reached an all-time high in a Granada TV representation of a Cabinet meeting on the issue: it was an unrecognizable caricature of that or any other Cabinet meeting.' The Prime Minister's own contribution to public knowledge about the Chrysler crisis came when he banned one of the central players, Harold Lever, the Chancellor of the Duchy of Lancaster, who in Wilson's own words made 'a major contribution to the final decision', from giving evidence to a Commons Select Committee inquiring into the affair.

Chrysler was almost Wilson's last crisis. As Lady Falkender put it, 'we were entering a curious political no-man's-land, a sort of twilight period before the end'. Wilson had confided to her and a few other intimates in the autumn of 1975 that he was planning to retire the following spring, on his sixtieth birthday. His 'Kitchen Cabinet' was sworn to secrecy as the Prime Minister wanted his departure to come as a total surprise. He planned to use television as effectively to cover his exit as he had stage-managed much of his premiership. 'True to form, Mr Wilson the great news editor made known his departure by means of a "Shock Bombshell Sensation",' wrote Frank Johnson in the *Daily Telegraph* on 17 March. Wilson had summoned a sudden farewell press conference. Although he had only just managed the previous week to survive a vote of confidence over planned public spending cuts of £3 billion, Wilson claimed he was leaving the Government in good shape: 'They don't need me to stay on as a doctor or a healer,' he said, reverting to his favourite self-image. And looking round the assembled press and television reporters he added, like a Yorkshire pontiff, 'I forgive you all.'

Wilson arranged a farewell photocall for the press and TV cameras on the Chequers estate. The Prime Minister, his wife and his labrador, Paddy, dropped in for a Sunday lunchtime pint at the Bernard Arms. It was the end of a television era. Wilson was seen at the time as the most sophisticated small-screen practitioner British politics had yet produced. But today Joe Haines, for seven years his closest media adviser, takes a different view. 'Harold and I were a couple of TV amateurs. We were like the man with the red flag walking in front of the motor car compared with Mrs Thatcher's highly professional publicity advisers today. It was principally Harold, myself and Marcia – she was very good about the value of television; she watched much more than the rest of us, perhaps because she had less to do than the rest of us. But her voice was a very valuable asset. But we were one man and a dog. And I was the dog.'

It was appropriate that the last picture taken of Harold Wilson in Number 10 showed him singing 'Auld Lang Syne' with hands linked to Marcia Falkender and David Frost. He had signed up to do an exclusive series with Frost for Yorkshire Television, called *A Prime Minister on Prime Ministers*. Wilson was the first of them to have regarded the small screen as a central instrument of government. Recognizing its power, he had sought more eagerly to master televisual techniques and had fought more bitterly with the broadcasting authorities to control his coverage than any of his predecessors. As the longest peacetime Prime Minister this century, until Mrs Thatcher broke his record, Wilson had used the cameras in an attempt to project many different images of himself: the young dynamic Kennedy figure, the Churchillian bulldog, the family doctor, the Baldwinesque pipe-smoker and the football manager. Although he had been one of the most intellectually brilliant Oxford dons of his generation, he had become skilled at presenting himself as an ordinary bloke. But he had never managed to win the complete trust of the people. As Harold Wilson put it himself, in his last interview as Prime Minister with David Frost: 'Television has undoubtedly had a good effect on politics. All the people can hear the leaders of political parties and size them up. They can decide whether what is being said is for political effect or whether it's real.' And he added: 'Television is a cruel medium.'

CHAPTER 13

Crisis, What Crisis?

*'I rather liked a rude TV interviewer – because the public sympathy
would be on the side of the man being heckled rather than the
man doing the heckling.'*

James Callaghan

No one has ever become Prime Minister with more experience of television
than James Callaghan. He had been one of its first political stars. When the
BBC in the early fifties excluded Michael Foot and A. J. P. Taylor as too
left-wing from *In the News*, Callaghan was invited to sail on what was then
the current affairs flagship more often than any other politician. *The Listener*
noted his 'chin-thrusting fluency' and the *Daily Telegraph* in 1962 reported
'he packed a better television punch than practically anyone on the Labour
front bench'. His unique tenure of the three great offices of State before
the premiership had given him constant exposure and unrivalled studio
experience. As Chancellor of the Exchequer he had learned to use the
autocue and talk direct to the camera in his regular budget and emergency
economic broadcasts; he had kept up his high televisual profile at the Home
and Foreign Offices. On 6 April 1976, Callaghan arrived at Number 10
feeling he had little to learn about the small screen. And if he needed advice
on technique, he had to turn no further than to his immediate family: his
daughter Margaret worked for *Panorama*, his son-in-law Peter Jay presented
Weekend World. 'Jim was the supreme TV professional,' says Tom McNally
who worked as Callaghan's political adviser from 1974–9. It was ironic
therefore that Callaghan's downfall would come in part through a disastrous
misjudgement in his use of television.

He had shown his sophisticated understanding of television in the three-
week campaign to elect a successor to Harold Wilson. While the other
Labour leadership contenders – Roy Jenkins, Michael Foot, Tony Benn,
Denis Healey and Tony Crosland – had agreed to personal filming and
interviews with the news and current affairs programmes, Callaghan only
allowed coverage of his work as Foreign Secretary. He was filmed calmly
dealing with the great affairs of State or flying off to commune with other
world leaders. He rejected the pleas of his campaign managers to make
special appearances on television, reasoning he had more to gain by

projecting himself as the experienced statesman, aloof from such vulgar preoccupations as a leadership campaign: 'I told them I would prefer to give no interviews with press or television. In my view our fellow MPs who lived with us cheek by jowl, were fully aware of my strengths and weaknesses and were unlikely to be impressed by pictures of me on their TV screens dressed in a striped apron and pretending to wash up in the kitchen, as had happened during the Tory leadership election [with Willie Whitelaw].'

For all his television experience, Callaghan looked surprisingly ill at ease when he made his first broadcast as Prime Minister on the night of his appointment. It was a straight talk to camera; he had declined all requests for interviews. Callaghan at once made clear that his was to be a different style from Harold Wilson's: he was the solid, avuncular man to trust – a politician Dixon of Dock Green. This was his first engagement as Prime Minister, he began, 'and I want to share with you the people of Britain my thoughts'. His two overriding priorities were to bring down inflation and unemployment. Thanks to the co-operation of the unions, there had been good progress in the past year, but there was still a long way to go. 'No one owes Britain a living. There is no soft option . . . Well, that's a gloomy start. But it isn't all gloomy.' The country could have a great future if everyone joined together with honesty and fair dealing in a national effort. The Government had 'a special responsibility to take you into our confidence, to tell you the truth'. He claimed 'this new Labour Government' (which was almost identical with the old one) would 'trust the people' and create greater social justice. And he ended with a reassuring smile: 'Do you, like me, sometimes feel that we've been slipping? Then join me. Join all of us in a national effort to uphold our values and our standards.'

Television producers and reporters looked with scepticism at Callaghan's first prime ministerial broadcast. Many had been bruised in their encounters with him over the past years. Although he liked to adopt an amiable screen persona, his private dealings were sometimes heavy-handed and intimidatory. More than one producer was warned that his television career would not advance if he failed to heed Callaghan's requirements. 'He is very different from his screen image,' said Willie Whitelaw, the Conservative deputy leader, who had often appeared on discussion programmes with Callaghan. 'He is very petulant if things go wrong, very touchy and very quick tempered – as anyone who deals with him in a TV studio will know.' Callaghan often referred to the fact that he had left school at sixteen and had received no higher education; he seemed convinced that university-educated television people were always seeking to do him down or take him for a ride.

Tom McNally used to help Callaghan prepare for major studio interviews. The Prime Minister was determined that he would say what he wanted in the way that he wanted to say it, whatever his interviewer intended. Sometimes Callaghan told his adviser that he planned to become very angry if a particular sensitive subject was raised. 'And then in the studio he would bang the table and be indignant,' says McNally, 'but I don't think that is dishonest, I think that is the relationship of the good professional – he wasn't losing control but letting the audience know how he felt.' Callaghan also regarded the use producers made of television lights in the studio as something of a conspiracy against him. 'He felt sometimes he was strapped in his seat and left to fry under the lights for twenty-five minutes, so when the interview started he was noticeably perspiring,' says McNally. 'He wanted to be in control. He knew the techniques of television and he knew the atmosphere of a studio and therefore he was buggered if he was going to sit there baking and then the grand interlocutor arrived to sit comfortably and calmly to grill him. I think he was right to do that.'

Callaghan's early months as Prime Minister were ruled by the familiar trio: sterling, inflation and unemployment. In June 1976, as sterling fell to a new low, Mrs Thatcher put down a motion of no confidence claiming that Callaghan was presiding over 'debt, drift and decay'. He had decided to adopt a tone of paternal mockery towards Mrs Thatcher. 'Now, now, little lady,' he said in the debate, 'you don't want to believe all those things you read in the papers about crisis and upheavals and the end of civilization as we know it. Dearie me, not at all.' The Prime Minister had managed to round up enough minor party support comfortably to defeat the motion. But the plight of sterling continued to dominate his administration. The pound dropped by over 20 per cent during Callaghan's first six months as Prime Minister; by September the Government went cap in hand to the International Monetary Fund for the largest loan in its history.

To support the application, Callaghan delivered a jeremiad to the Labour Party Conference, partly written by his son-in-law, Peter Jay. 'We used to think that you could spend your way out of a recession and increase employment by cutting taxes and boosting government spending. I tell you in all candour that that option no longer exists.' There was no way out 'by printing confetti money to pay ourselves more than we produce'. The speech was aimed both at the delegates and at the Philippines where the IMF was holding its annual conference. Callaghan hoped his satellite appearance would help convince the international financiers of his Government's conversion to monetary rectitude. That same morning the Chancellor, Denis Healey, had set off intending to fly from Heathrow Airport to present the loan application in person to the IMF. But sterling had once again begun to plunge. On the telephone from Blackpool to the VIP departure lounge, the Prime Minister advised his Chancellor to cancel the trip and come straight to the Party Conference instead. TV and press pictures of the Chancellor's sudden airport U-turn produced the most graphic images of government funk. Callaghan himself now admits it was a mistake: 'Hysterical panic set in for forty-eight hours. The markets behaved with all the restraint of schoolgirls at a rock concert.' The Prime Minister felt he was 'case hardened' by his own experience at the Treasury, but his principal worry was 'the depression caused by the doom-laden headlines in the newspapers and the effect of the funereal tones of the radio and TV announcers on the public and on the nerves of some of my Cabinet colleagues'. He agreed to give his first interview as Prime Minister to Robin Day in an attempt both to steady the pound and his own ministers.

The interview produced a memorable exchange which exemplified the television style Callaghan had decided to adopt. Day asked whether the conditions attached to the IMF loan would result in a fall in the standard of living; the Prime Minister claimed they would make no difference.

DAY: I ask you the question, Prime Minister, because it has been suggested this morning that, as a result of the loan and tighter money which may result, people should be prepared for higher prices, higher mortgage payments, higher rates, higher VAT to curb spending, perhaps higher unemployment because of spending curbs. Now is this possible?

CALLAGHAN: When you say what's said this morning do you mean at Conference . . .?

DAY: No, no, no, no, no, in the press, in the press.

CALLAGHAN: . . . or did you mean on the front page of a daily newspaper?

DAY: Particularly on the front page of the *Daily Mail* but also in other newspapers.

CALLAGHAN: That's right, yes, yes, yes, yes, yes, I saw that, but that I think is pure newspaper speculation.

DAY: And no truth in it all?

CALLAGHAN: Speculation.

DAY: Is there any truth in it?

CALLAGHAN: Speculation.

DAY: Is there any possibility of it?

CALLAGHAN: Look, the only certainty in life is death. There will be a Budget next April; what will happen I don't know and I think it would help a great deal if the press were not to speculate about all the worst things that could possibly happen.

DAY: I was only asking you, Prime Minister . . .

CALLAGHAN: No, and I am not attacking you, Mr Day, on this.

Callaghan had thought long and hard about what his relationship as

Prime Minister should be on the screen with Robin Day, who had interviewed him many times over the previous twenty years. Harold Wilson had always attempted a matey approach and called Day 'Robin'. 'Jim decided on "Mr Day" – this was before the knighthood – because he did not want to give the appearance of a cosy old boys' club,' says Tom McNally: 'This was to be the British Prime Minister giving the people the truth about a situation. He was determined that what he wanted to say and how he wanted to say it would dominate the programme: it was not going to be the Robin Day Show.' Day himself described the most impossible interview he ever had to do as 'one in which Jim Callaghan decides to mix it, whatever you try to ask'. For his part, Callaghan says: 'I often used to say to the BBC when they wanted me to have an interview, "could it be Robin Day?" He was my favourite interviewer. I liked his tough manner of questioning and although he could be a bit of a bully if his victim seemed to flinch, I hardly ever found he took unfair advantage. I rather like a rude TV interviewer – I am not saying that is why I asked for Robin – because the public sympathy would be on the side of the man being heckled rather than the man doing the heckling.'

Inspectors from the IMF arrived in Britain in November to go through the Government's books. Callaghan held an unprecedented nine Cabinet meetings in three weeks, as ministers agonized over the terms of the loan. He knew that his survival as Prime Minister depended on cajoling the Cabinet expansionists like Tony Crosland and the siege economists like Tony Benn into agreement on heavy public spending cuts. Eventually Callaghan's emollient skills of chairmanship together with his threat of resignation persuaded the dissidents to accept cuts of £2.5 billion. The Prime Minister had succeeded in having his own way and keeping the Cabinet together. Granada found many eager ministerial moles when they reconstructed the agonized discussions for another *State of the Nation* programme.

Callaghan emerged from the IMF crisis as the Cabinet's dominant figure but he still faced the most difficult of situations. Labour had lost its tiny majority in Parliament and the Prime Minister was committed to carrying through an economic policy that was deeply unpopular both with his party's activists in the constituencies and with his left-wing MPs. 'We always needed the support of other parties for our legislation or on occasion for our very existence and this made for an exciting ride on the parliamentary switchback,' says Callaghan. He regularly used a potent threat to whip his own troops back into line: either they supported him or they would find themselves landed with Prime Minister Margaret Thatcher.

By 1977, Labour's bogeywoman was establishing herself as a formidable television presence. Current affairs producers discovered that her media adviser, Gordon Reece, would make special demands when Mrs Thatcher agreed to an interview. 'I was not a very experienced producer at the time but it came as a complete shock,' says Roger Bolton, then a producer on *Panorama*. 'Gordon Reece would ask what would be the colour of the set, would there be flowers – he thought that was necessary – what sort of chairs did we plan? Normally a party leader's press secretary would be wanting to know about the areas of questioning for the interview. But I suppose Gordon Reece was the first such person in British politics to do his job properly; he took what I would regard as the depressing view that the image was more important than the message and he concentrated on leaving an impression with the viewer of what Mrs Thatcher was like, rather than drawing attention to what she said in detail.'

Mrs Thatcher's first interview as Tory leader on *Panorama* in 1976 had left a lasting impression on her. She had been highly nervous and objected that the studio looked like a barn; she wanted it be more intimate – like the radio studio for the *Jimmy Young Show* where she enjoyed appearing. And she turned on Robin Day who was sitting surrounded by his notes. 'If he has notes then I want notes,' she said to Gordon Reece. 'Oh Margaret, I think it would be better if he is seen to speak with notes and you are seen to speak without them,' soothed her media adviser. 'All right,' she responded, 'but I want him to look at me when I answer, I will not talk to the top of a head that is reading notes.' The frigid atmosphere in the studio only began to thaw when the floor manager told Mrs Thatcher that they planned to record a shot of her for the programme's opening titles and she was looking rather fierce. 'You mean you want me to smile at Mr Day?' 'We wouldn't want you to do anything that you wouldn't do naturally,' responded Day sweetly. Mrs Thatcher gave a little laugh, but she complained afterwards that she felt that she had been brought not to a studio but to a KGB inquisition room.

Gordon Reece severely rationed Mrs Thatcher's appearances on the major current affairs programmes on both BBC and ITV. An 'enemies list' of interviewers whom Mrs Thatcher considered hostile or too pro-Labour was drawn up and she refused to appear with them. Reece feared an interviewer's aggression would draw out matching aggression from the Tory leader. According to Patrick Cosgrave, who was one of her advisers, Mrs Thatcher developed a fixed conviction that a minute's attention by the television news was worth almost a whole current affairs interview. She was to make an exception of *Weekend World* when the former Labour MP, Brian Walden, took over as its presenter in 1977. 'She likes Brian,' said Gordon Reece, 'but more important midday on Sunday is an excellent time. There is normally no political news on Sunday, so what Margaret says will make the news bulletins for the rest of the day and will be all over the front pages of the newspapers the next morning.'

After each of her early broadcasts as Leader, Gordon Reece had commissioned private opinion polls. The findings were conflicting. Many viewers said her voice was too shrill and upper class, her style too hectoring, her appearance too austere and school-marmish – yet they approved of the strength of her character and the evident sincerity of her convictions. Armed with this evidence, Reece would play video recordings of her interviews back to Mrs Thatcher. In the privacy of a closed circuit studio he gave the Tory leader what were effectively reverse elocution lessons to make her sound more ordinary. He also urged her to wear simpler, less fussy clothes on television and to soften her hair-style and make-up. And on the advice of the playwright Ronald Millar (later knighted), who helped write her speeches, Mrs Thatcher consulted a voice tutor from the National Theatre: she was given humming exercises to bring down the pitch of her voice.

Reece felt in a dilemma. He realized the danger of playing up Mrs Thatcher's femininity was that the strength of character and belief which the viewers admired might not come across. But he wondered how she could appear simultaneously as the fluffy and the toughie. Ironically it was the Tory leader's sworn enemies, the Russians, who provided the perfect synthesis. The Red Army newspaper reacted to a fiercely anti-Communist Thatcher speech by dubbing her the 'Iron Lady'. At first Mrs Thatcher rejected the label. 'I stand before you tonight in my chiffon evening gown, my fair hair gently waved – the Iron Lady of the Western world?' she innocently asked her Finchley constituents at the start of 1976. But then she and Reece began to see its advantages: Mrs Thatcher took to using the phrase in her own interviews and speeches: 'The Russians said I was an Iron Lady.' Pause. 'They were right.' Pause. 'Britain needs an Iron Lady.' Tumultuous applause.

Margaret Thatcher was taking the job of leading the Tories on to new television paths. She broke with the tradition that an Opposition leader should never go to a by-election for fear of being blamed for any defeat: she paid well-publicized and much-filmed visits and her party pulled off a string of spectacular victories. Mrs Thatcher also arranged to change the rules for the scheduling of Tory party political broadcasts. Until then the parties had insisted that each broadcast should be transmitted simultaneously on all channels to ensure a captive audience. But Mrs Thatcher reasoned that as she advocated greater freedom of choice for consumers, there should also be a choice of viewing and the broadcasts should be shown at different times on different channels. And, under the guidance of Gordon Reece, she considerably widened the range of television programmes where she would agree to appear.

At the start of 1977 the Tory leader appeared on *Jim'll Fix It* with Jimmy Saville (himself later to be her Christmas guest at Chequers) and a group of children who had asked to meet her. One little girl announced that her ambition was also to become Prime Minister. 'Wonderful – two generations,' enthused Mrs Thatcher, 'my dear, we must keep in touch and get the next fifty years sorted out together. When I was small I didn't think there ever could be a woman Prime Minister. But we hope you're going to fix it, Jimmy.' 'I already have done, privately,' responded Saville, 'but I didn't want everyone to know.' When Tory critics claimed that her appearance on the programme was demeaning, Gordon Reece responded: 'Rubbish. Did you notice how hard Denis Healey tried to get on *Jim'll Fix It* after she had appeared? I simply encourage her to appear everywhere she can to the best advantage. It's the most ludicrous intellectual snobbery to say that a politician should not appear on general interest programmes because the viewers are supposed to be on a lower level of humanity than the people who watch *Panorama*. They have votes too and if she talked down to them they'd soon rumble her. The others are just jealous because they couldn't do these programmes.'

Reece was deliberately seeking to aim Mrs Thatcher at the section of the electorate that the Tories' private polls identified would be decisive in the next election – better-paid workers and their wives. Mrs Thatcher's speeches were always carefully crafted to include a passage that would appeal to them and be picked up by the television news bulletins. Reece also encouraged her to be filmed doing everyday tasks like shopping and household work. In woman-to-woman interviews the Tory leader talked about her dress size, her use of face cream and whether she ever cried. 'It was all sham,' claims one of her biographers, Penny Junor, 'but favours in the media all came at a price.'

By the spring of 1977, Callaghan realized that he had to counter Mrs Thatcher's successes. Labour's private opinion polls showed that Tory support was rising rapidly among women and skilled workers. 'We had research which showed that virtually no working-class women watched the television programmes he normally appeared on,' says Tom McNally. 'We felt that he could reach this audience by going on *Nationwide*.' The programme had invited the Prime Minister to follow the example of President Carter in America and answer questions from viewers from all round the country. Apart from Harold Wilson in the October 1974 general election, no previous prime minister had ever been directly questioned on television by the voters. Callaghan and McNally considered how he should make a special pitch to women. 'When I saw the programme I was delighted to hear some of the phrases we had discussed in advance coming out,' says McNally.

'If we could stop prices going up there's nothing I'd like to do better,' Callaghan said on *Nationwide*. He admitted it was 'going to be horrid' for the next few months. 'Women do have a great problem, but if women can really see us through the next three or four months our expectation is that the price rates of inflation will start to diminish after mid-year.'

The Prime Minister sat facing a bank of monitors on which he could see his questioners in regional studios around the country. 'He was in homely, electorally charming mood,' according to the *Daily Telegraph*. 'We had a little chat about that in the Cabinet this morning,' said Callaghan when dropping a hint that the following week's budget might have some help for pensioners in trouble with gas bills. He had a smile and a wave for a woman in Cardiff, his constituency: 'I hope Cardiff is looking good today. Sorry I am not there.' 'May I call you Jean?' he asked a schoolgirl who wanted his advice on whether she should become a teacher. 'I beg you to do it, if you have a vocation.' The only heat came from an exchange with a man who had claimed billions were wasted on civil servants and disputed Callaghan's denial. 'Now please don't go on shaking your head,' said the Prime Minister, 'I tell you that's correct.' Finally a pools winner asked Callaghan what to do with his £4000 winnings. 'Congratulations, put it into bricks and mortar – always a good investment,' responded the Prime Minister conservatively. 'The Premier spent most of the programme acting as a Mr Fixit and a Marjorie Proops-type adviser,' reported the *Daily Mirror*.

'We were absolutely amazed by the post bag afterwards,' says Tom McNally, 'we had tapped into the working-class female audience which was almost almost totally absent from *Panorama*. And Jim was very good at it, once he had set his mind to doing a different kind of programme from the formal sombreness of a normal current affairs interview. I remember some criticism that this wasn't quite the thing. Looking back now it seems almost an age of innocence in terms of television and politics, as we have now moved so far away from the standard flagship programmes to more diverse political exposure.'

Callaghan appeared on *Nationwide* the day after he had transformed his minority Government's chances of survival: he had stitched up a parliamentary pact with the Liberals. To the frustrated rage of the Tories, the Liberal leader David Steel agreed his party would support the Government in exchange for consultation on major policy initiatives and for promises on Scottish devolution and the European Parliament elections. 'My correspondence is fifteen to one in favour of what has been done,' said Callaghan on *Nationwide*. 'Our active supporters really back my judgement on this.' He claimed it was the only way to see through his Government's policies even though he recognized at this half-way stage that he personally was 'probably very unpopular'. The Lib-Lab Pact had come just in time to thwart a fresh vote of no confidence which Mrs Thatcher had tabled. The Government survived by 322 to 298.

'The agreement with the Liberal party introduced a new stability by removing the prospect of an early general election and both the Opposition and the media became less feverish,' says Callaghan. At the same time the measures demanded by the IMF were starting to bring down inflation and strengthen the pound – at the cost of higher unemployment. On Fridays, the end of the Parliamentary week, Callaghan took to visiting successful factories. 'Every day I watch the television, I listen to the radio, I read the newspapers recounting their daily diet of industrial gloom,' he said on a visit to the Triplex windscreen factory and attacked the media belief that 'good news is no news'. The aim of the Prime Minister's visits was to provide the television news bulletins with upbeat pictures of his association with Britain's industrial recovery. 'But you could be absolutely sure that as soon as the visit was planned there would be an industrial dispute,' says Tom McNally. 'So when the Prime Minister arrived there would be a huge demonstration which all the media would film and it was associated very clearly with Callaghan. The demonstrators would melt away when the television cameras disappeared and it gradually dawned on us that these visits were not the best way of boosting his image, so we stopped doing it.'

Like Harold Wilson before him and Margaret Thatcher after him, James Callaghan became convinced that the TV companies were deliberately choosing to show film of his visits which put him in the worst light. His special target was the BBC. In July 1977 the Government had given the Corporation an increase in the licence fee well below the level of inflation. The rise was only for a single year and the BBC felt it made planning for the future impossible. The Corporation at once began lobbying for a further longer-term increase. At that year's Labour Conference, the Head of Current Affairs, Brian Wenham, found Tom McNally in unreceptive mood. 'There is always a feeling with Labour governments that the BBC is doing them down, misreporting them, angling it against them,' recalls McNally. 'I remember at the Conference having a real nose-to-nose with Brian Wenham. I said that if you go on treating us like this you can wait for your increase in the licence fee until hell freezes over. That was part of the bullying process that goes on all the time between Number 10 and the BBC, whoever is in power.'

Sir Ian Trethowan, who had become Director-General in September 1977, says: 'There was within the Callaghan Government some wish to dismember the BBC.' The Prime Minister's own attitude came out later in a barbed tribute he paid to Trethowan on his retirement. He had not been surprised that Trethowan had been made Director-General because he had always thought of him as one of those 'mild Conservatives without extreme views': exactly the sort of person who went to the top of the Corporation 'with a strong sense of principle and determined a Conservative government is going to win'. The view had grown in the Callaghan Cabinet that the BBC was hostile to workers and trade unions, that its producers and reporters were middle class and favoured middle-class values (which was not how Mrs Thatcher's Shadow Cabinet saw it). 'Callaghan said little in public about the BBC or indeed the media in general, but I always suspected this was rather deceptive,' wrote Trethowan in his memoirs. 'As Prime Ministers, Wilson and Thatcher would openly rage against the BBC's iniquities, but I suspect each of them held some affectionate memory of an earlier, benign BBC to which – if only its present leaders could be bullied into sense – it might return. Callaghan was more agnostic and less violently hostile on particular occasions, but there was a suspicion that he was not averse to taking a personal hand in an exercise that was clearly designed "to do something" about the BBC.'

When the Annan Commission, set up by Harold Wilson to inquire into broadcasting, published its findings in 1977, Callaghan seized his opportunity. He decided to chair the Cabinet Committee which would choose the parts of Annan it wanted to implement. Central to the resulting White Paper was a plan to give the Government much greater direct control over the BBC's output by inserting a new layer of management appointed by the Home Office. The BBC was horror-stricken, yet the plan brought no joy to its commercial rivals. The IBA's Director of Television described the proposal as 'government intervention on a scale previously unknown in Britain and far exceeding anything that would be considered tolerable if applied to the press'. The BBC mounted a highly effective resistance campaign. Trethowan briefed many of his friends in Fleet Street and the Government's White Paper was met with what he calls 'a barrage of hostility from virtually every newspaper in the country'. Callaghan decided discreetly to pigeon-hole his White Paper, without informing the BBC.

By the start of 1978, his Government had made a remarkable recovery in public support. Inflation was down to single figures, the pound was strong and the economy seemed to be recovering. A year earlier Labour had been sixteen points behind the Tories, now one opinion poll put them two points ahead. Callaghan also benefited from the start of regular radio broadcasting of Prime Minister's Question Time: he came over as well-briefed, avuncular and in control, while Mrs Thatcher often had to screech to make herself heard above the sound barrage. Gordon Reece remarked that the broadcasts had set his work on her image back two years. In February, David Steel wrote of Callaghan in his diary: 'He says he wants to play the next election as the leader of a left-wing party heading towards the centre while she is the leader of a right-wing party heading towards the Right.'

Mrs Thatcher had provided Callaghan with ammunition a fortnight earlier when she gave the most controversial television interview of her career as Opposition leader. The story behind the interview illustrated her developing technique in using television to appeal to working-class voters on 'gut issues'. On 28 January there had been a race riot in Wolverhampton when two hundred black youths responded to taunts from young whites by throwing bricks at the police and smashing shop windows. Mrs Thatcher gave an interview to a local Granada programme which was re-shown on *World in Action*. The first question was whether the Tories planned a severe cut-back on immigration. She responded that official statistics projected a black population of four million by the end of the century: 'Now that is an awful lot and I think it means that people are really rather afraid that this country might be rather swamped by people with a different culture. And you know the British character has done so much for democracy, for law and done so much throughout the world, that if there is any fear it might be swamped, people are going to react and be rather hostile to those coming in.' Her solution – which she repeated four times on the programme – was that 'you have to hold out the prospect of a clear end to immigration', otherwise 'my great fear is that if we get them coming in at that rate, people will turn round and we shall not have good race relations with those who are here.'

The interview, and in particular Mrs Thatcher's use of the word 'swamped' caused uproar: she was attacked by Cabinet ministers, bishops, much of the press and even members of her own party. In the House, Mrs Thatcher claimed 'the media raised it, not me. I have given my views and I have been bullied and intimidated.' Lobby journalists in London were briefed by her press advisers to say that Mrs Thatcher did not really mean it, that she had a tendency to 'shoot from the hip' and 'make policy off the cuff as she went along', supposedly due to her inexperience. 'This was all nonsense,' says Mrs Thatcher's biographer, George Brock. 'The line of the interview and the use of the word "swamped" had been discussed beforehand with advisers and in the Shadow Cabinet.' Mrs Thatcher's remarks had been carefully calculated to chime in with the findings of the Tories' private opinion polls. These showed that while the public supported the Government on its handling of inflation, unemployment and the unions, the Conservatives were ahead on immigration and other social issues, although some of their support was being siphoned off by the National

Front. At a meeting over the Christmas recess, the Shadow Cabinet had agreed to concentrate for the next five months on the social issues – starting with immigration.

Following *World in Action*, Mrs Thatcher received over ten thousand letters in support of her views on immigration, many from Labour voters. Her remarks had been well timed for the by-election in the Labour marginal seat of Ilford North at the start of March. Voters in the largely lower middle-class Essex constituency, with its 8 per cent black and Asian population, placed immigration at the top of the list of concerns. After a campaign which the National Front sought unsuccessfully to dominate, the Conservatives won the seat with a lead of 12 per cent. A poll on election day identified Mrs Thatcher's stance on immigration as the main reason former Labour voters switched sides. The Granada interview had been a prime instance of the Conservative leader's developing use of television. Often her studio rhetoric was significantly tougher than her subsequent policies. Her Government was not to be noticeably more restrictive about immigration than successive Labour governments, but Mrs Thatcher did not feel the same constraints about appealing to the electorate's gut instincts. And the public response to the interview helped convince her that she possessed what one of her critics derided as 'a direct line to the people'.

By the summer of 1978, the Prime Minister was becoming cautiously optimistic about Labour's election chances. 'The tide was coming in,' claims Callaghan. But he recognized that the sharp rise in the rate of unemployment was one of his biggest electoral problems. Gordon Reece, whom Mrs Thatcher had appointed the Conservatives' Director of Communications, made the most of it. He had hired the thrusting Saatchi and Saatchi agency to produce the Tories' advertising and party political broadcasts. In the late summer Saatchis plastered the country with posters showing what purported to be an unemployment queue – but subsequently turned out to be Hendon Young Conservatives – above the slogan: 'Labour isn't working'. The Tories' party political broadcasts repeated the theme. Speculation grew about an autumn general election.

That August the Prime Minister pondered the election date at his farm in Sussex. He had canvassed his Cabinet colleagues and most felt that it was worth soldiering on. He made his own calculations with the help of *The Times* election books and a private opinion poll. Eventually he decided on delay: 'Why run the risk of a very doubtful election result in October 1978, if we could convert it into a more convincing majority in 1979?' But he was not going to announce his decision until the Cabinet met again on 5 September. In the meantime he misled both the Trades Union Congress and the public about his intentions. Six top TUC leaders came away from dinner on the Prime Minister's farm on 1 September convinced he was planning an autumn election. The media regarded it as a certainty.

The following week Callaghan claims he sought to make his intentions clearer when he burst into an Edwardian music-hall song during his speech to the TUC. The song (which he purposely miscredited to Marie Lloyd, fearing the TUC and the TV news audience would not have heard of its true originator, Vesta Victoria) told of a bride left abandoned at the altar with just a note from her intended: 'Can't get away to marry you today, my wife won't let me'. The Prime Minister's light baritone brought the house down. His intended message was that he had promised no one an election date in October, but almost everyone interpreted him as forecasting that next month's election result would leave Mrs Thatcher in the lurch. Election speculation heightened and the *Daily Mirror*, the paper closest to Labour, confidently headlined 5 October as polling day. When Callaghan told his Cabinet two days later that there would be no early election, 'there was a moment's silence then every Cabinet minister fell off his chair,' remembers the then Transport Secretary, Bill Rodgers.

After the Cabinet meeting, Callaghan said he would make a five-minute ministerial broadcast that night. Only his senior colleagues knew what he planned to announce. By chance Mrs Thatcher had arranged drinks at the Commons that lunchtime for reporters who were to follow her during the campaign. 'I don't imagine he's making a ministerial broadcast just to say he *isn't* going to hold an election,' she smiled. Callaghan used the broadcast to continue his tease. For most of the five minutes, he rehearsed the reasons why he should call an election. The economy was looking up, the pact with the Liberals was over so the Government could not be sure of a majority. There were even those, he said with a look of hurt, who accused him of rigging an economic boom so that he could hold an election in the most favourable circumstances. Perish the thought. 'I am not proposing to seek your votes because there is blue sky ahead today.' It was only twenty seconds before the end of the broadcast that he stated specifically he would not be calling an election and the Government would be carrying on for the good of the economy and the country. 'He had enjoyed the mystery and the drama and especially misleading the press whom he held in even greater contempt than did Harold Wilson,' says Bernard Donoughue.

The Prime Minister had not only wrong-footed the media, but also the TUC – and that was soon to bounce back on him. According to Donoughue, the trade union leaders felt 'snubbed and betrayed as they had stage-managed their Congress as an election launch, working very hard to cover up various disputes in order to give the Prime Minister a united front: their irritation was important since it clouded their future attitudes to his pay policy.' Callaghan was proposing that there should be a fourth year of pay restraint with rises limited to 5 per cent. But no longer faced with an immediate election, the unions were not having it. All the pent-up anger that had built up over the rigidities and apparent injustices of the previous three years of wage controls now spilt out. Union leaders and shop stewards set about destroying Callaghan's strongest electoral card – his twin claim that he could handle the unions and that Mrs Thatcher would guarantee a return to the confrontation of the Heath years.

A series of strikes of increasing nastiness broke out in the autumn and winter, with the public service workers in the van. 'One of the most notorious excesses', says Callaghan, 'was the refusal of Liverpool grave diggers to bury the dead, accounts of which appalled the country when they saw pictures of mourners being turned away from the cemetery. Such heartlessness and cold-blooded indifference to the feelings of families at moments of intense grief rightly aroused deep revulsion and did untold harm to the cause of trade unionism, which I like many others had been proud to defend throughout my life.' It was against this background at the start of 1979, that Callaghan made the greatest publicity mistake of his political life.

He decided that he would fly off to a summit meeting on the Caribbean island of Guadeloupe. The main aim was to discuss with the leaders of the US, France and Germany the modernization of the West's nuclear weapons and the prospects of a treaty with the Russians to limit strategic arms. Callaghan also saw the benefit in what was bound to be an election year of projecting his image as an international statesman on a par with the American President. With the press kept at a distance from the substance of the talks, cameramen filmed palm trees, silver sands and topless bathers as well as the holiday-shirted leaders meeting in straw huts. The nightly pictures sent back by satellite from the sun-baked Caribbean formed a vivid contrast on the TV news bulletins with strike-torn, freezing Britain. And on his return, Callaghan was to make matters worse.

The RAF VC-10 flying Callaghan back from Guadeloupe was about two hours from Britain when it received a message: there were a great many reporters and TV crews waiting for the Prime Minister at Northolt airport, would he be prepared to give a news conference when he landed? On the plane with Callaghan was the Downing Street press secretary, Tom McCaffrey (later knighted), a cautious career civil servant who had followed him from the Home and Foreign Offices to Number 10. McCaffrey advised the Prime Minister against saying anything at the airport, there was a danger he would be caught cold, he had been away from home and did not have the 'feel' of the situation. Callaghan normally took McCaffrey's advice but his political adviser, Tom McNally, saw it differently. Here was the chance for the Prime Minister to use the television cameras to reassert his authority, to show on that night's news bulletins that he was in charge. Callaghan thought it over for twenty minutes and then told McNally he had decided to take his advice: 'I think Tom McCaffrey is wrong but he is not a politician like we are.' The Prime Minister planned to put Britain's problems in a world context and to take a swipe at the *Daily Mail* whose telescopic-lensed photographer had caught him swimming.

When the news conference started McNally's heart sank almost immediately. 'I knew in my bones he had got it wrong. The answer that particularly gave me a sinking feeling was to a question about going swimming; he was too light-hearted, too jocular.' Callaghan had replied with heavy irony: 'Do you know? I actually had a swim. Well of course, that is the most exciting thing of the visit, but no, I think you should put all that kind of criticism in perspective. One mustn't allow jealousy to persuade you from doing the right thing.' The Prime Minister was then asked what he planned to do about the 'mounting chaos' in the country: 'Well, that is a judgement that you are making and I promise if you look at it from outside – and perhaps you are taking a rather parochial view at the moment – I don't think that other people in the world would share the view there is mounting chaos.'

The *Sun*'s headline the next morning was 'CRISIS – WHAT CRISIS?' Although Callaghan had never actually used those words McNally felt it was a fair paraphrase. 'I think that was the impression he gave. His mind was still full of summitry: he had been talking in Guadeloupe about world peace and SALT 2 – the whole future of mankind – while Fleet Street had been trying to get a picture of him with a topless swimmer. And back home those industrial disputes, though serious, were manageable but were dominating everything. I watched the TV news that night and he came over as a guy who had come back from sunny climes and wasn't even sure that the streets weren't being de-iced in Oldham or people buried in Liverpool. It was a total disaster and some commentators said we never recovered from it.'

Following Callaghan's return from Guadeloupe the strikes grew worse. Television and newspapers carried accounts of cancer patients sent home to die from their unheated hospital wards and small children going without emergency operations. If Gordon Reece and Saatchi and Saatchi had been writing the script, they would not have been able to do better. The images of the 'winter of discontent' were to feature in virtually every Conservative party political broadcast for the following eight years and the next three general elections. During the 1987 election Mrs Thatcher arrived for her *Panorama* interview armed with 1979 newspaper headlines which she brandished at the camera. Bernard Donoughue says that he realized at the time, 'the nightly television pictures of violence and the brutal face of trade unionism were doing terrible damage to the Government and the trade union movement itself. The pickets were ensuring a future victory for Mrs Thatcher.'

On 17 January, a week after Callaghan's disastrous airport news conference, Mrs Thatcher used a party political broadcast to talk direct to camera. It was a cleverly pitched appeal for national unity. She began by picking up from the continuity announcer: 'Yes, technically this is a party political broadcast on behalf of the Conservative party, but tonight I don't propose to use the time to make party political points. I don't think you would want me to do so.' The situation was far too serious. Some of the things she had seen on television made her wonder what had happened to 'our sense of common nationhood, and even of common humanity. What we face is a threat to our whole way of life.' She proposed a threefold reform of the unions: the banning of secondary picketing, secret elections for union officials and the outlawing of strikes in essential services. She hoped the Prime Minister would go along with it, although of course the unions were Labour's paymasters so it would be very difficult for him. But, she concluded, 'we have to learn to be one nation again or one day we shall be no nation. If we've learned that lesson from these first dark days of 1979, we have learned something of value.'

It was a subtle, well-judged piece largely written by the head of the Conservative Research Department, Chris Patten, and the playwright, Ronald Millar. Mrs Thatcher had spoken in persuasive and reasonable style, the former hectoring tone was gone. She had accepted the last-minute suggestion that she change from the suit she was wearing into something less fussy and less governessy. Her advisers believe that nothing contributed more to consolidating the Tory advantage over Labour than that broadcast. 'We did not write the script for that broadcast,' says Tim Bell, then Managing Director of Saatchi and Saatchi, 'but we did produce it and give advice on how the material could be most effectively presented. Although I am not a political scientist my feeling is that this broadcast won her the election.' An opinion poll showed that 80 per cent of voters agreed with Mrs Thatcher's proposals for union reform.

Over the next month, as the worst Arctic gales in twenty years deposited a foot of snow on Britain and the increasing ranks of strikers grew more bloody-minded, the country shivered to a halt. It was difficult to tell which part of the misery was caused by the strikes and which by the weather. But the Government got the blame. Callaghan, who had become known as 'the keeper of the cloth cap' because he had based his whole political career on alliance with the trade unions, seemed paralysed into inactivity. 'We are prostrate before you,' he told the TUC. 'There was deathly calm in Number 10, a sort of quiet despair,' says Bernard Donoughue. Callaghan refused to go on television or make a speech, claiming he had nothing to say. But behind the scenes he sought desperately to patch up some sort of agreement with the unions. Eventually he came up with a so-called 'Concordat' – 'the bastard son of Solomon Binding', as Phillip Whitehead called it – and on 26 February, the day it was signed, the Prime Minister gave an interview to *Panorama*.

'We have had a basinful this winter,' admitted Callaghan, 'and I've been appalled at some of the things that have gone on. I have bitten my tongue more than once.' The Prime Minister was wearing a new pair of large-framed modern glasses and sought to give the impression he was still calmly in control of events. He objected when Robin Day asked him why he 'shrank' from bringing the law into industrial relations. He said he would never shrink from a fight if he thought it was right and called on Day to withdraw the word. 'God bless you, thank you,' said the Prime Minister when Day complied. From his experience imposing the law on trade unions only made things worse, said Callaghan, and it was better to solve disputes by voluntary agreement. 'We have now got a new agreement with the unions that they will help get the inflation rate down to 5 per cent in three years. Then this country really will be steaming.' Reviewing Callaghan's performance, the *Daily Telegraph* claimed that the Prime Minister had developed 'his impervious affability to such an extent that nothing less than Armageddon would disconcert him'. The Conservatives reacted angrily to the broadcast: while pointing out that the 'Corcordat' was having no effect on the chaos and violence in the streets, they demanded equal time for Mrs Thatcher from the BBC. They did not have long to wait.

Within a week the Government faced defeat in the Commons, not over the economy but over the issue that profoundly bored most of Britain – devolution. Callaghan had promised a measure of self-government to the Welsh and Scottish nationalist parties as the price for their support in Parliament. But at the start of March devolution was decisively rejected by the Welsh people in a referendum and failed to achieve the required 40 per cent of the electorate in Scotland. As devolution had been one of the Government's central policy promises, it appeared that the Prime Minister would be forced to resign. But Callaghan played for time. He made a ministerial broadcast offering all-party talks on what the Cabinet should do next. Mrs Thatcher, realizing that the opportunity to defeat the Government had come at last, exercised her right of reply. Gordon Reece gave her intensive coaching for the broadcast. She proposed to end it by calling on all the minority parties to support her planned motion of no confidence: in that way the House of Commons would 'reassert its historic right to say to the Government of the day – "enough is enough." ' But in rehearsal she had great difficulty in placing the right stress on the critical last three words. Mrs Thatcher went through many takes, but each time her voice would rise on the final 'enough'. 'It's a lowering not a raising,' cajoled Reece. On the seventh 'take' the Conservative leader succeeded. 'That's it, you've got it,' her media adviser exclaimed delightedly.

The outcome of the no confidence debate six days later was in doubt until the last moment. MPs from the minor parties were offered all manner of threats and bribes by those who claimed to speak for the Prime Minister and the Leader of the Opposition. After a tense and nervy seven-hour debate, the Speaker finally announced the result amid scenes of pandemonium peculiar to the Mother of Parliaments. The Government had lost by a single vote – 311 to 310. Callaghan's was the first Government since Ramsay MacDonald's half a century earlier to lose a vote of confidence. He was forced to call an election with the Tories well ahead in the polls. Labour's hope was that the pressure and heat of the campaign would tell on Mrs Thatcher and what they called 'Maggie's gaffe' would help them to victory. 'Whatever we do, this election is all about Mrs Thatcher,' Callaghan told Bernard Donoughue.

The Tory leader's campaign began in personal tragedy. A car bomb planted by an IRA splinter group, the INLA, killed Airey Neave as he drove from the Commons car park. He was Mrs Thatcher's Shadow Northern Ireland Secretary and closest political confidant. As a young barrister, she had been a pupil in his chambers and he had brilliantly managed her campaign for the Tory leadership. Neave was to have played a central strategic role in the general election campaign. 'Some devil has got him. They must never, never, never be allowed to triumph. They must never prevail,' a shattered Mrs Thatcher said that night on *Nationwide*. She postponed the start of her campaign until after Neave's funeral.

On the day before the assassination, the Prime Minister had made a ministerial broadcast announcing the election: it was a curious performance which set the pattern for the campaign. He said the country had to decide whether it wanted to risk 'tearing everything up by the roots' by changing governments. Like Harold Wilson in 1970, Callaghan was effectively offering the choice between a reliable conservative – himself – and a dangerous radical – Margaret Thatcher.

It seemed the campaign might feature for the first time in a British general election a direct studio confrontation between the two party leaders. Both the BBC and Granada had put up the idea in the summer of 1978. While Mrs Thatcher had been interested, Callaghan had said 'no'. But now he had changed his mind. When London Weekend Television, on prompting from Downing Street, wrote suggesting a confrontation, Callaghan agreed and his acceptance was leaked to the *Daily Mirror*. Every previous Prime Minister had turned down a face-to-face, unwilling to concede equality of status to the Opposition leader. But with Labour well behind in the polls, Callaghan saw no alternative. 'TAKE HIM ON, MAGGIE!', exhorted the *Sun* and that was exactly Mrs Thatcher's initial inclination. But Gordon Reece had other ideas.

Although she might beat Callaghan's arguments in the debate, he feared she could lose out by coming over as hectoring and aggressive – exactly the characteristics his private polls told him turned off the viewers. He succeeded in persuading Mrs Thatcher that she had more to lose than to gain. News coverage of the campaign would be dominated by stories of the party leaders' preparation for the confrontation. The Tories were well ahead in the polls, it was not worth risking everything on one television programme. A single slip of her tongue or even unfortunate clothes or make-up might have a disproportionately damaging effect. The Tory deputy leader, Willie Whitelaw, and the Party Chairman, Lord Thorneycroft, supported Reece. 'We wanted the election to be about the winter and not about a TV programme,' said one of them. Mrs Thatcher wrote to LWT turning down the invitation: 'We should continue with the traditional broadcasting arrangements. Personally I believe that issues and policies, not personalities, decide an election. We are not electing a President.'

Despite that disclaimer her campaign was to move closer to American techniques of packaging a presidential candidate and projecting an image than had ever been seen before in Britain. Reece had been to the US to study the media campaigns of Jimmy Carter and Gerald Ford during the 1976 presidential elections and had returned for the 1978 Congressional elections. He introduced for the first time into a British election the 'photo-opportunity' beloved by American presidential hopefuls. The idea was to place Mrs Thatcher in a 'telegenic' setting to provide novel pictures for the press and especially for the national and regional TV news bulletins. Mrs Thatcher was an eager and able subject. In Leicester she cut her own dress pattern, she had her heart and lungs electronically tested beside her husband in Milton Keynes and she coated chocolates at Bournville.

There was an important purpose behind the seemingly jokey 'photo-opportunities': to make Mrs Thatcher look and sound more in touch with 'ordinary people'. Gordon Reece had long since taught her to stop worrying and love the boom microphone – that it would feed hungrily on whatever snippets of conversation she offered. 'I find tea bags are so much more convenient,' she said confidentially to women workers at a tea factory in

Newcastle and to twenty million viewers on the TV news bulletins that night. When the writing journalists protested to Mrs Thatcher at yet another photo-opportunity which was providing them with no hard political news, she replied candidly: 'It's not for me, it's for the cameramen, they are the most important people on this campaign.'

In contrast, James Callaghan fought a campaign almost from a pre-television age. While reporters covering the Tory leader on what they called 'Thatchertours' paid £600 for seats in her hired campaign jet, those following the Prime Minister had to make their own way. Sometimes they failed to keep up with the prime ministerial Rover and when they did arrive Callaghan would often exclude the cameras altogether from his meetings with the faithful in Labour committee rooms. Alternatively he would insist on silent filming, with the boom mikes left outside. 'Jim's style was to treat his tour as a private affair between himself and the electorate, making no concession to the television-age razzamatazz adopted by the publicity men at Conservative Central Office,' said Michael Sullivan, the BBC reporter assigned to follow Callaghan. 'It's not my style,' the Prime Minister would say as he turned down yet another plea from the cameramen for an interesting picture, 'if I do, I'll seem as phoney as she does.' When he did eventually agree to a walkabout in a supermarket, the resulting TV pictures were largely of bewildered shoppers crushed by cameramen.

Mrs Thatcher's most incongruous photo-opportunity of the campaign came in Suffolk, where she posed for fifteen minutes clutching a new-born calf to her tailored executive outfit. 'This was a very unusual little news conference,' reported Michael Brunson of ITN wryly, 'the first perhaps ever given by a senior British politician sitting in a field stroking a twelve-hour-old calf.' At the time Mrs Thatcher told the author: 'The press and television have their job to do and I'm very conscious of it. They say "we don't just want another photograph of her with a hundred bullocks in superb condition." Instead there was this beautiful calf.' As his wife tightened her grip on the baby animal, Denis Thatcher muttered 'if we are not careful we'll have a dead calf on our hands'. The Prime Minister, who had himself allowed the occasional 'Farmer Jim' picture in the past, responded scornfully to Mrs Thatcher's bucolic photo-opportunity at his evening rallies. 'If you want to be photographed holding a calf the wrong way, she'll oblige. But ask them to discuss the issues and all you get is a deathly silence. The truth is in this election the Tories are being sold as though they were Daz or Omo.'

'The speeches objecting to soap-powder advertising techniques did not help the morale of the people trying to work for the Labour party,' says Tim Delaney, one of a discreet team of volunteers from the advertising world advising Callaghan on publicity. Labour's campaign managers saw the Prime Minister as their greatest asset and they attempted to present him as the assured, experienced statesman. They gave BBC and ITN access to film Callaghan calmly working at his desk in Number 10 with a large globe in the background. In one election broadcast he implied Mrs Thatcher did not have the required experience for the top job. What had struck him in his three years at Number 10 was 'how much alone you are as Prime Minister. It's upon your shoulders the weight finally rests: the buck stops here. I must say looking back over the years it has been the greatest help to me that I had experience beforehand of being Chancellor of the Exchequer, Home Secretary, Foreign Secretary in a rather long political life, because experience in those offices is of the very greatest value.'

But all the Prime Minister's experience had not prevented the winter of discontent, the Tories' election broadcasts reminded viewers. The second programme in the series featured shots of rubbish piled high in the streets, pickets outside hospitals, grave-diggers on strike, cancelled trains and planes. Eight times the Callaghan-like voice-over repeated: 'Crisis? What Crisis?'

Both Labour and Tory campaigns went largely to plan. Despite the predictions of bitterness, the 1979 election was lower key and better mannered than most since the war and there were virtually no unexpected intrusions from outside events. The worst moment for Mrs Thatcher, who led in every opinion poll throughout the campaign, came with the publication near the end of the campaign of a poll showing the Conservatives' lead cut to just 0.7 per cent – every other poll had showed them well ahead. Earlier in the day the Party Chairman, Lord Thorneycroft, had suggested that she should invite Ted Heath to share the platform with her at one of the final London press conferences in an attempt to widen the Tories' appeal. Mrs Thatcher understood Thorneycroft to be proposing that Heath share the final election broadcast with her – traditionally the preserve of the Leader alone. 'Margaret hit the roof,' says her sympathetic biographer, Penny Junor, 'she went white with fury, stood up from the table and stormed out of the room, leaving a group of astonished aides who couldn't understand why she had found the suggestion so offensive.'

The television climax of the campaign came with a programme from Granada called *The Great Debate* featuring Callaghan, Mrs Thatcher and David Steel. From 1959 to 1974, the leading politicians of all parties had refused to appear in the studio with voters, as a result of a collective folk memory of the BBC's rumbustious *Hustings* programmes during the 1959 campaign. But now all three party leaders were in the same studio on the same night – although not at the same time. Each had agreed to answer questions from a cross-section of voters from a marginal Lancashire constituency. As one leader finished and left the studio, the next arrived. According to an opinion poll after the programme, Mrs Thatcher came over by far the best of the three, with Callaghan a poor third. Partly this was because he had ignored one of his own first rules of television: he had not prepared himself for the programme.

The Prime Minister had arrived late, hot and flustered, and was still at the last minute fretting about whether he would appear or not. In the studio, his customary sang-froid deserted him. He was aggressive to his questioners, often starting his answers before they had finished speaking. When a young nurse sought to query his record on pay, he said sharply: 'What's wrong with that, love? It's no use shaking your head, love, these are the facts.' David Lipsey, a political adviser to Callaghan, felt the programme was loaded against the Prime Minister: 'There is no way a politician can argue on television if you have a pretty nurse of seventeen in the front row saying how little she is paid a week. It looks sweet, it is televisually appealing and even the most superb political performer in the world cannot argue against that kind of visual impact. I would never advise anyone I was involved with to go on a programme of that character again.' In the 1987 general election, Margaret Thatcher was to refuse to answer direct questions from the voters on both Granada and the BBC. But eight years earlier she was the star.

Partly this was because she had made the programme a top priority. While the Labour and Liberal campaign managers told Granada staff that they 'regarded it as just another date in an already full appointment book', Gordon Reece had long discussions with the producer about the lighting, the set and even the height of her chair. He also sought to ensure the camera would concentrate on Mrs Thatcher's 'good side' (her left). In an academic paper on the programme, Robert Self wrote 'she appeared relaxed, candid and quietly confident without giving the impression of condescending complacency.' Mrs Thatcher stuck a chord with her firm views on immigration and won the loudest applause for any of the three leaders with a ringing declaration of support for capital punishment. In an interview with the author at the time, she admitted that she had been afraid of television when she first became Leader, 'but I now realize that what you TV people want is a positive answer and that is what I always try to give'. Her relationship with the media had improved as the campaign had progressed while Callaghan's had deteriorated.

The Conservatives' final election broadcast featured Mrs Thatcher speaking in a low and reasonable voice. She used many of the key phrases that Saatchi and Saatchi's advertising research of the past fourteen months had identified as appealing directly to the Tories' main 'targets': C2 women, skilled workers and first-time voters. 'A lot of things we take for granted seem to be in danger of disappearing. Money that keeps its value; real jobs that last; paying our way in the world; feeling safe in the streets – especially if you are a woman; schools that gave children from modest backgrounds like my own the chance to get on in life as far as we were able.' She understood that some people still felt 'a little bit uncertain about the prospect of a woman Prime Minister', but she had always believed that what mattered about a person was not who they were or where they came from, but their convictions. Her own vision 'might seem like an impossible dream when you looked at the state of Britain today, but somewhere ahead lies greatness for our country again. This I know in my heart.'

In his final broadcast, filmed behind his desk at Number 10, Callaghan boldly suggested that the winter of discontent was actually a result of the unions pursuing Conservative free-for-all policies. His relationship with television had grown increasingly prickly throughout the campaign. It reached its lowest point at Cardiff City Hall on the eve of polling day when the Prime Minister gave his final interview about the campaign to David Rose of ITN. Rose concentrated on the so-called 'Concordat' with the unions to the Prime Minister's increasing tetchiness.

ROSE: On industrial relations and picketing, what about the TUC putting its house in order?

CALLAGHAN: The media is always trying to find what's wrong with something. Let's try and make it work.

ROSE: What if the unions can't control their own militants, are there no circumstances where you would legislate?

CALLAGHAN: I didn't say anything of that sort at all. I'm not going to take the interview further. Look here, we've been having five minutes on industrial relations, you said you would do prices. I am just not going to do this . . . This programme is not to go out. I am not doing the interview with you on that basis. I'm not going to do it.

Rose sought vainly to protest as Callaghan unclipped the microphone from his tie and stood up. 'Don't argue with me. I am not going to do it,' snapped the Prime Minister and stalked from the room. His staff immediately rang ITN in London and demanded an undertaking that neither the interview nor the walk-out be shown. ITN agreed and a fresh interview was recorded to which Callaghan did not object. The original interview would have been buried for ever had ITN not been feeding its recording simultaneously to the American television company, NBC. It ran the walk-out on the main nightly news bulletin and NBC's London correspondent claimed Callaghan's behaviour was evidence of his state of mind on hearing from Labour's private pollsters that he had certainly lost the election.

The next day, ITN issued an apology to the Prime Minister for not preventing the US showing of the interview. According to David Butler's and Dennis Kavanagh's study of the 1979 election: 'This incident shows very clearly both the deference of ITN and the means by which party politicians can effectively censor news material which does not accord with their requirements.' It also graphically illustrated a style of dealing with television James Callaghan had often adopted, although his remonstrations had normally been off-screen.

In the election, the Conservatives won a forty-four seat majority over Labour. Callaghan was gracious in defeat: 'For a woman to occupy that office is a tremendous moment in our history,' he told a news conference at Transport House. In his three years at Number 10, Callaghan had often been the most skilled and persuasive of political television performers. But he had been undone at the start of 1979 by his closest allies in the Labour movement and by his own ill-judged re-entry from Guadeloupe. As Prime Minister, Callaghan's relationship with both the BBC and ITV had grown increasingly fraught. The Corporation in particular breathed a collective sigh of relief that his plans for introducing a measure of direct government control were buried in the debris of Labour's election defeat. But the TV authorities now faced a new incumbent in Downing Street determined to lay siege to many of Britain's institutional centres of power – and television was near the top of her list.

CHAPTER 14

The Distorted Mirror

'The Home Secretary and I think it is time the BBC put its own house in order.'

Margaret Thatcher, 1979

Margaret Thatcher became Prime Minister with a keener appreciation of the political power of television than any of her predecessors. She had seen it help to fade out James Callaghan; she had diligently studied TV techniques and under the guidance of Gordon Reece had modified her voice, her hair and her clothes in the pursuit of a screen image that combined toughness with femininity; and she had approved Saatchi and Saatchi's deployment of modern commercial marketing methods for the purposes of political persuasion. After the most sophisticated media campaign until that time in British electoral history, the Iron Lady arrived in Number 10 absolutely convinced of what television could do for her and equally concerned what it might do against her. She was to fight many a bloody battle with the broadcasters.

In her first months as Prime Minister, Mrs Thatcher kept off the screen. She shared the view of Gordon Reece, who remained the Conservatives' Director of Publicity for her first eighteen months in office, that she had appeared often enough in the first part of the year. They both wanted to increase her televisual rarity value – to make a prime ministerial interview a major event and avoid what advertising men call 'the wear-out factor'. 'I can't even persuade her to do things which are axiomatic for a modern Prime Minister – like standing and waving on the steps of Number 10,' sighed Henry James, who served for the first three months as her Downing Street press secretary. Mrs Thatcher was cautiously playing herself into office: she knew how much in demand she was and determined that future screen appearances would be on her own terms.

At the BBC her election victory had been greeted with mixed feelings. Despite the relief that Callaghan's threats of greater government control had died with his administration, editorial nerve ends remained raw from an encounter with Mrs Thatcher some months before the general election. She had told the Director-General, Ian Trethowan, that she would welcome the chance to meet senior news and current affairs editors to discuss their problems. He had promptly invited her to a 'Grade A' BBC hospitality lunch with them. 'The lady arrived with all guns firing,' says Trethowan, 'she showed scant interest in, let alone tolerance of the editors' problems, and berated them on their failings over a wide area – in particular their coverage of Northern Ireland.' She had become Prime Minister at a time when the BBC most needed a sympathetic ear in Downing Street: the Corporation was facing bankruptcy. The Callaghan Government had only kept the BBC afloat by allowing it to increase its borrowing, but now the debts were being called in. The Corporation calculated it needed a substantial increase in the licence fee to last over a number of years and was preparing a detailed case to put to the Government. 'With a sceptical Prime Minister, logic suggested that the BBC should keep its relations with Number 10 on a calm, even keel,' wrote Trethowan in his memoirs. 'What it actually did was to get itself involved in two blazing public rows – both over Northern Ireland.'

In July 1979, the late-night current affairs programme, *Tonight*, filmed an interview with a masked gunman from INLA, the Irish National Liberation Army. Three months earlier the terrorist organization had been responsible for the assassination of Airey Neave, Mrs Thatcher's closest political colleague. Humphrey (later Lord) Atkins, the Northern Ireland Secretary, wrote to the BBC seeking to prevent the interview being shown, arguing it was 'ill-timed and unhelpful'. After some agonizing, the Director-General decided to reject Atkins' request. The transmission passed off virtually unnoticed late at night with relatively few telephone calls of complaint. It was only when Neave's widow, Lady Airey, wrote a letter of protest some days later to the *Daily Telegraph* that the political storm broke. The *Tonight* staff had tried but failed to warn her in advance of the programme. Lady Airey took particular exception to the gunman's allegation that her late husband was a 'torturer'. The BBC could scarcely have transmitted anything more wounding, she said. Tory MPs and much of the press vehemently attacked the BBC and were joined by the Prime Minister. 'Having seen a transcript of the programme, I am appalled it was ever transmitted. I believe it reflects gravely on the judgement of the BBC and those who were responsible for the decision,' Mrs Thatcher told the Commons and announced that the Attorney-General was considering whether legal action should be taken against the BBC under the Prevention of Terrorism Act.

The editor of *Tonight* was Roger Bolton. He held an almost missionary belief that television journalists had a duty to try to report and seek to explain what was happening in Northern Ireland. 'Mrs Thatcher sees herself at war with the IRA and does not understand why any journalist should go on talking to them or their supporters,' says Bolton. 'She is trying to implement certain policies; she is trying to change things. We are trying to report things as they are. In those circumstances an element of conflict is inevitable with any prime minister but particularly with one who believes so passionately that what she is doing is right.' The BBC's senior figures publicly supported Bolton over the INLA interview.

In a letter to the *Daily Telegraph* Trethowan admitted that the BBC had clearly misjudged the emotional impact of the interview, but defended its transmission. The Chairman of the BBC Governors, Sir Michael (later Lord) Swann, said the decision to show it had been taken 'in the genuine belief that the public interest would be served by people in Britain being reminded of the intransigent and murderous nature of the problem'. Ian Trethowan says the 'the bludgeoning' which the BBC and he personally received went on for almost a fortnight. 'With the benefit of hindsight,' he asks rhetorically, 'was I wrong to allow the INLA interview to be broadcast? Almost certainly, yes.'

For both the broadcasters and the Prime Minister, worse was to follow. In August the Provisional IRA murdered Lord Mountbatten in Ireland. The blowing-up of one of the most senior and popular members of the Royal Family caused profound national shock. Mrs Thatcher's reaction characterized the televisual style of her premiership. She flew immediately to Ulster and visited the Parachute Regiment at Crossmaglen, the most dangerous border area of the Province, where she was filmed wearing a regimental flak jacket and red beret. The Northern Ireland Office warned her that such garb would inflame Catholic opinion: 'if anything this advice made her more determined to dress as the Paras wished her to,' wrote her one-time adviser Patrick Cosgrave. The Prime Minister was using the visual power of television to demonstrate the Government's response to the murder. 'Mrs Thatcher is an extremely effective screen figure who uses actions as an alternative to words,' says the former Editor of ITN, Sir Geoffrey Cox. 'She did not concentrate on a great passage of prose to condemn the killing of Lord Mountbatten – although she did condemn it – but by suddenly appearing on the spot in Ulster she demonstrated her own personal authority and her Government's determination to face up to terrorists.'

Immediately after Mountbatten's murder, Ian Trethowan wrote to assure the Home Secretary, Willie Whitelaw, that the BBC planned no interviews with the IRA in the foreseeable future. 'From now on so far as Northern Ireland is concerned,' he told his senior colleagues, 'we are in a different ball-game.' A few weeks later, the Director-General suffered a mild heart attack and was to follow the next convulsive clash with the Government from his hospital bed.

Panorama, under its new editor, Roger Bolton, had decided to make a programme about the IRA. 'We wanted to try to explain why people should be behaving in this way,' says Bolton, 'and to explain that the IRA were able to continue operating in a part of the United Kingdom because a significant number of Catholics in the North support the IRA – at least as far as not trading them in.' In Dublin, Bolton's team made contact with Provisional Sinn Fein and then received an anonymous telephone call suggesting they drive to the village of Carrickmore, north of the border. There they saw ten masked IRA gunmen, who were staging a road block. The crew filmed for half an hour, then left the village and reported the incident to the security authorities the next day. The film remained in the can; but three weeks later the *Financial Times* carried a short report on the bottom of page 8 about the filming.

The Prime Minister had a new press secretary, Bernard Ingham, a red-haired Yorkshireman and former *Guardian* industrial correspondent who had journeyed to the Right. He prepared a meticulous daily press digest for the Prime Minister and on 8 November drew Mrs Thatcher's attention to the *Financial Times* report. She erupted. By chance both the Cabinet and the BBC Board of Governors were meeting that morning. 'Mrs Thatcher sent Willie Whitelaw, the Home Secretary, out of the room to phone the BBC Chairman,' wrote Michael Leapman in his *Last Days of the Beeb*. 'Whitelaw gave Swann a vivid description of the Prime Minister's anger and told him that some public act of contrition would have to be made to pacify the Cabinet. "It looks ugly," Whitelaw confided.'

The Governors rushed out an ambiguous statement which was immediately taken by Conservative MPs as an admission of BBC guilt. And that afternoon the London *Evening Standard* carried a fanciful account of the incident. It stated that the village had been taken over by no less than 140 masked gunmen armed with a rocket-propelled grenade launcher – and that the whole thing had been set up as a stunt for *Panorama*. This was nonsense. The film shows ten gunmen stopping cars in a road block – similar IRA road blocks had been filmed and transmitted before – and the Editor of *Panorama* subsequently won libel damages from the *Daily Telegraph*, which had suggested that there had been collusion between the programme and the IRA in setting up the road block. But the lurid *Standard* version immediately became gospel among Tory MPs in the House of Commons. By the time the Prime Minister arrived for questions that afternoon, MPs were baying for BBC blood.

'It seems to me to be at least a treasonable activity,' claimed the Leader of the Ulster Unionists, James Molyneaux. Amid cheers the Prime Minister replied: 'This is not the first time we have had occasion to raise similar matters with the BBC. The Home Secretary and I think it is time the BBC

(Gibbard, *Guardian*)

put its own house in order.' At the regular weekly meeting of the BBC's senior journalists five days later, David Holmes, the BBC's Political Editor, said it should be recognized that the pressure from the Government was not simply a naked political one. Anything concerning Northern Ireland was special as far as the Prime Minister was concerned; it was one of the areas in which she was on a short fuse.

'To say that this latest incident will sour the BBC's relations with Mrs Thatcher would be to understate the position significantly,' commented the *Financial Times*. It seemed there would have to be a BBC sacrifice to appease the Prime Minister's wrath. Roger Bolton was chosen. The acting Director-General sacked him as Editor of *Panorama*. But five days later after concerted protests from many of the BBC's senior managers and from its journalists, Bolton was reinstated. Mrs Thatcher saw the climb-down as a further example of the Corporation's preference for defending its men rather than putting its own house in order. She did not forget it. Ian Trethowan returned to Broadcasting House with the view that the *Panorama* team had been naïve to go to Carrickmore without checking and should have reported rather sooner to the authorities what they found. But, he says, 'that behaviour could not justify the sensational response of very senior politicians and the rather febrile attitude of the BBC's Governors: no film had been shown when the balloon went up and to condemn in such violent terms the recording of a piece of film seemed a ludicrous over-reaction.'

Northern Ireland represented the most difficult and touchy of political subjects that the television companies had to cover. Over the years there has been a long list of programmes either delayed or shelved by both BBC and ITV at Government instigation. The motive force for suppression was the entirely comprehensible official desire not to give publicity to those people who murder innocent civilians and seek to shoot British soldiers in the back. At the same time the British Government has been attempting to reconcile Catholics and Protestants through a democratic, political process – and free reporting is a normal feature of a democracy. There were no easy answers.

The INLA and Carrickmore affairs served to strengthen the Prime Minister's profound dislike and distrust of the Corporation. 'What are we going to do about the BBC?' she had asked on her first formal visit to the Home Office as Prime Minister. The BBC represented almost everything she was against. It was a public corporation that made programmes: she favoured private enterprise that made profits. It was an established institution of the kind that aroused her deepest misgivings: over the years the Foreign Office, the Church of England, the Civil Service as well as the BBC would feel the thunk of the Thatcher handbag. And, perhaps most important, politically the BBC seemed to stand for everything that the Prime Minister despised. If it was not a bunch of Marxists and Trotskyists – as her husband believed – it was at best a collection of well-meaning liberals who favoured consensus, compromise and fudge. Mrs Thatcher had based her whole appeal on a deliberate rejection of such politics. In a speech during the election campaign, she had declared: 'The Old Testament prophets did not say, "brothers I want a consensus". They said "this is my faith, this is what I passionately believe. If you believe it too, then come with me." ' The Corporation as a bastion of consensus politics had to be sapped. The time would come – and would no doubt have come sooner were it not for Willie Whitelaw, the Home Secretary, who was in charge of broadcasting. He was an ally of the BBC, yet his total loyalty to the Prime Minister enabled him to curb her more radical instincts. And Mrs Thatcher also had her hands full dealing with supporters of the derided consensus even nearer to home – those ministers who formed a majority within her own Cabinet.

Many of her senior colleagues were not true believers: they neither shared her faith in a rigid control of the money supply nor her total animosity to the trade unions. Jim Prior, the Employment Secretary in charge of union reform, favoured the 'softly softly' approach, while Mrs Thatcher wanted a radical reduction of union power. At the start of 1980, she agreed to give her first major interview as Prime Minister to Brian Walden of *Weekend World*. The former Labour MP and the Tory leader formed a mutual admiration society. Walden had given a number of laudatory interviews about Mrs Thatcher: she was very warm, with a fine set of brains, entirely trustworthy, a warrior and the British people were very lucky to have her. In turn, the Prime Minister regarded him as her favourite interviewer.

'The seriousness and effort attached to an interview with the Prime Minister', wrote Michael Tracey in his official history of the programme, 'is indicated by the fact that *Weekend World* took a complete mobile outside broadcast studio and fifty-five people to Number 10. This included four cameras and eight cameramen, a director and his PA, a vision mixer, a production manager, make-up people, a lighting man, a sound man and someone to lay cables. What the other thirty or so were up to is lost to history.' Fifty-five was roughly double the number the BBC needed. Yet until her third term in office the Prime Minister was prepared to turn a blind eye to the built-in overmanning and restrictive practices at ITV that she was determined to remove from the rest of British industry.

Walden has been granted more interviews by the Prime Minister than anyone else. He describes the preparations vividly: 'A horrible aura of snobbery rolls over the whole proceedings. Everybody tends to be a bit nervous. All the blokes who normally come in unshaved, wearing old pullovers, have got to put suits on. The PAs get all trembly. Everybody gets worked up and it tends to produce a rather strained atmosphere. I do my damnedest to avoid this, because Margaret is at her worst when she is strained and I do my best to jolly her along and go and chat with her beforehand which is something I never normally do. I don't talk to her about the interview, because that's fatal – that's running your race in the stable. But I try to get it to flow because she is at her best when she is relaxed and flowing. I was never in awe of her, that would make her more tense. She's tense as it is. She needs to be relaxed. As for the interview itself, many women respond to tone. If the tone is wrong Mrs Thatcher freezes and won't tell you anything.'

In her interview on 6 January, Mrs Thatcher produced a ringing defence of the virtues of her monetary policies. She had prepared for the interview with Gordon Reece, who had been a Christmas guest at Chequers, and the playwright, Ronald Millar, had suggested some telling lines for her. 'No one would have remembered the Good Samaritan if he had only had good intentions, he had money as well,' the Prime Minister told Walden. She confirmed that more public spending cuts were on the way and insisted that Britain had to earn its keep. 'It's part of what you would call the Thatcher experiment. There isn't a pot of gold to draw on. There is either your own extra effort, working machinery better, or you are taking something from your fellow citizens. Pennies don't come from heaven. They have to be earned here on earth. There are plenty more pennies to be earned, but get on and earn them because that is the way to increase prosperity.'

On the plans to reform the unions, the Prime Minister suppressed her gut instincts for dramatic and radical changes. Prior's proposed Bill was 'modest and sensible': there would be consultation with the unions and time to get it right. Mrs Thatcher soft pedalled on two measures which she and the Tory right wing favoured, but which Prior opposed. There would be no immediate legislation to deal with the problems of secondary picketing and she was 'not very enamoured at the moment' of the idea of docking money from social security payments to strikers. *The Economist* quoted the verdict on the interview of one of Mrs Thatcher's Cabinet opponents: 'Margaret put in a really good TV performance at the weekend. She seemed relaxed and very moderate on the unions after a brilliant briefing by Jim Prior.'

But even as the Prime Minister spoke, events in the streets were powerfully reinforcing her profound distrust of Prior's approach. For the first time in fifty years the steel workers had decided to go on strike. In what looked like a re-run of the winter of discontent, mass picketing returned to the TV screens. In mid-February, as thousands of secondary pickets succeeded in closing a private Sheffield steel works which was not involved in the strike, the Prime Minister felt herself under siege. Her strongest supporters insisted that she had to take immediate action to outlaw secondary picketing and cut State benefits to strikers. 'It may be no exaggeration to say the coming week will seal the fate of the Thatcher administration,' agonized the *Daily Telegraph* while the *Daily Express* warned the Prime Minister: 'If you don't act now the writing will be on the tombstone of the Tory Government.' But her Employment Secretary was totally opposed to heat-of-the-moment legislation.

Prior ignored an instruction from Bernard Ingham, the Prime Minister's press secretary, telling him not to give an interview to Robin Day and he skilfully lobbied his ministerial colleagues. In a Cabinet show-down Mrs Thatcher lost the argument, to her intense anger. The Prime Minister began referring contemptuously to ministers who opposed immediate hard-line reforms as 'wet' – ironically a term originally used by Heath about doubting colleagues. The Wets were born. Mrs Thatcher determined to take them on in public. She decided to give a major TV interview and chose Roger Bolton's distasteful *Panorama* – any studio in a storm.

On 12 February, the weekly meeting of the BBC's senior journalists had bemoaned the fact that Number 10 had repeatedly declined *Panorama*'s overtures and Bolton reported that it was unlikely the Prime Minister would appear on the programme for the foreseeable future. But a week is a long time in television politics and on 19 February, John Gau, Head of TV Current Affairs announced that the Prime Minister had suddenly agreed to appear on the following Monday's *Panorama*. He added that it represented not so much a U-turn as another example of the custom of prime ministers to accept invitations when they thought it best served their interests.

In her *Panorama* interview, Mrs Thatcher denied the Cabinet was in disarray: 'If I had a Cabinet of yes-men and sycophants, Mr Day, you would be the first to attack me. I expect us to argue and, when we come to a decision, to defend it loyally outside.' Yet the Prime Minister was prepared to use the interview to make public her own scepticism about the Cabinet decision to back Prior's 'softly softly' approach. She admitted that his Bill 'went some way, but not all the way' to fulfilling the Conservative's manifesto pledge to protect firms from secondary picketing. For the time being, she was prepared to go along with Prior's strongly held views: if it worked, 'well and good'. But if not, 'there was a lot to be said for going further' and legislating to end trade union immunities (although the Employment Secretary had warned in Cabinet this could lead to a general strike).

Day then asked the Prime Minister about leaked remarks from Prior that had indicated the Government's lack of confidence in the Chairman of British Steel and his handling of the strike: should she not have sacked Prior for what he had said? 'I think it was a mistake and Jim Prior was very, very sorry indeed for it; but you don't just sack a chap for one mistake.' The interview enraged Prior. His friends told political journalists that the Prime Minister seemed to be undermining Prior personally as well as his Bill. 'The Cabinet Room and not the *Panorama* studio is where future policy should be discussed,' said one Wet minister. But it was not to be the only occasion that the Prime Minister would use television to outbid her own Cabinet. 'She would set herself up in opposition to the policy of her own Government,' wrote Jim Prior in his memoirs, 'she was Boadicea hammering away at those wicked people seeking to carry policies alien to her trusted beliefs and nature.'

Knowing television's strength as a medium of impressions, Mrs Thatcher had taken particular care with her appearance for *Panorama*. Her hair had been done that morning and a young woman from Joan Price's Face Place had spent an hour before the interview making her up; wearing a black velvet jacket with a white silk blouse, pearl earrings and a diamond brooch, the Prime Minister appeared glamorous and self-assured. Roger Bolton noted that Mrs Thatcher had invented her own way of dealing with questions: 'Don't take a breath, or halt at the end of sentences. This means the interviewer can't get his question in or seems to be rudely interrupting if he is. If the programme is live the time soon runs out and accountability is evaded.' Robin Day said after the interview that Mrs Thatcher was much more relaxed than when he had last interviewed her in Opposition, she had developed the confidence and experience of power: 'It's a question of being in *that* position.'

The following month, Mrs Thatcher sought for the first time since becoming Prime Minister to explain her policies direct to viewers, when she devoted the whole of a party political broadcast to a bracing progress report. 'We didn't promise you instant sunshine,' said the Prime Minister. Her government was successfully beginning to overcome 'years of make-believe' although she admitted it was painful and in the short term things would get even worse. 'But after almost any major operation you feel worse before you get better. But you don't refuse the operation when you know without it you won't survive.' Margaret's medicine was proving too much for many of her patients. After a year in office, there were record post-war levels of unemployment, cost inflation and company bankruptcies. 'It's all very well to talk of industry rising like a phoenix from the ashes, but what if all we are left with is the ashes?' lamented the Chairman of the West Midlands CBI on *Panorama*.

Faced with a catalogue of economic doom, according to Patrick Cosgrave even the Prime Minister was adrift: 'It seemed the Thatcher experiment was crumbling to disaster.' There was continuous pressure on the Prime Minister to change course from industrialists, from Tory supporters in the country and from within her own Cabinet. For her final speech to that autumn's party conference, Ronald Millar produced a line aimed at the Wets that was guaranteed to lead the TV news bulletins. 'To those of you waiting with baited breath for that favourite media catchphrase "the U-turn", I have this to say: "You turn if you want to, the Lady is not for turning." ' The rapture the line evoked in the conference hall was matched by the scepticism outside.

Mrs Thatcher might have been in a great deal worse trouble politically had the Labour party not spent most of its time since the election on a favourite pursuit – fighting against itself. The election of Michael Foot to the leadership following James Callaghan's retirement in October brought no ceasefire. And in television terms, the oratorical darling of the Tribune Group was a disastrous choice. Although in the early fifties Foot had been an *In the News* panellist, his rambling style was ill-suited to modern political leadership. While Mrs Thatcher had learned some of the most sophisticated American methods of image projection, Foot himself had not been to America for thirty years. Asked to pose for pictures on the night of his election, Foot said: 'I am not Ronald Reagan.' His long white hair, his thick glasses and his walking stick did little to present the image of an alternative Prime Minister. He was to be astonished at the press fuss when he was seen on television wearing what looked like a donkey jacket for Remembrance

Sunday at the Cenotaph. Unlike Mrs Thatcher, the man *Private Eye* now christened Worzel Gummidge had given no thought to his appearance on the small screen.

The Prime Minister showed how diligently she had studied television techniques in an interview she gave to Angela Rippon for a BBC programme called *The Image Makers*. How important had Saatchi and Saatchi been in selling the Tories to the viewers? 'If you have got a good thing to sell,' replied the Prime Minister, 'use every single capacity you can to sell it. It is no earthly use having a good thing and no one hearing about it. And in television interviews we are up against people like your good self and the Robin Days and the Brian Waldens. You're professionals. I am not. We know how professional you are, but when people judge a party political broadcast they see how much more amateur we are. So you've really got to have your professional cameramen and people who know something about television.'

Angela Rippon asked what part Gordon Reece had played in modifying Mrs Thatcher's voice and appearance. 'No one can give you an image you don't possess. I think my hair probably is a little better because it's less fussy. You know that when you're nervous as a woman your voice goes higher pitched and what you learn is: bring it down, bring it down. You have to think for the first time in your life not only about the impression that you make in the flesh but what is it going to look like on the news on television. Are they going to get you at a bad angle? And you notice that sometimes they do. But it's all in connection with "I must put over the message and policy of my Party and not self at all".'

By the end of 1980, Gordon Reece had concluded that for the time being his pupil had learned enough from him. He accepted a lucrative offer to go to work in California for Armand Hammer, the wizard of Soviet-American trade deals. In a brief interview before he left, Reece played down his image-making achievements: 'It was a question of making her come over as she really is, rather than the image of her when I got to her. She is a wonderful person and that had to come over – and I think it did.' The *Guardian* put it less blandly: 'There was once a warrior Leaderene who frightened her followers almost as much as the enemy. Her tongue was a lash, her eyes chips of ice, her hair as stiff as an aardvark's bristle. Then one day she met a humble TV producer and a miracle occurred.' Reece, who was to receive a knighthood for his services to the prime ministerial image four years later, flew off to the Los Angeles sun, promising Mrs Thatcher could call on him whenever she felt the need. He was to turn up at her side at crucial political moments in the coming seven years – the first time, within six months.

By the start of 1981, it looked as if Mrs Thatcher's monetarist experiment had dismally failed. Public spending had risen not fallen – partly because unemployment had almost doubled in eighteen months – while industry felt crushed beneath soaring interest, inflation and exchange rates. A secret report commissioned by her own economic advisers in Number 10 told the Prime Minister that the Treasury had chosen the wrong methods to squeeze the money supply. On top of all this in February the miners voted by a large majority for a national strike to prevent pit closures. Mrs Thatcher recognized she could not fight on all fronts at the same time and, after weighing the odds, decided on a quick surrender to the NUM. According to Sir Ian MacGregor, later to become Chairman of the National Coal Board, it left her feeling humiliated and deeply embarrassed. Her Trade Secretary, John Biffen, candidly admitted on television that the Government had given in to 'industrial muscle'. Press commentators saw the retreat as the first of many U-turns that Mrs Thatcher would have to make as she inevitably followed in the path of Ted Heath. The Prime Minister had other ideas. In an interview on Thames Television she reaffirmed 'the direction in which we are going: we will go full steam ahead in that direction'.

The Opposition was in no shape to make the most of Mrs Thatcher's difficulties. Less than three months after Michael Foot's election as Labour leader, the assorted talents of Roy Jenkins, David Owen, Shirley Williams and Bill Rodgers had combined to found the Social Democratic Party – amid much media ballyhoo. Labour had now publicly split apart, while Mrs Thatcher's fiercest Tory critics still shared her Cabinet table. 'I am the Cabinet rebel,' the Prime Minister insisted. She remained determined to ignore the plangent calls for reflation from industry, the Conservative press and much of her own Cabinet.

In March the Chancellor, Sir Geoffrey Howe, followed the bidding of Number 10. His sharply deflationary budget, which the Prime Minister was later to claim marked the decisive turning point in her first administration, effectively raised both direct and indirect taxes. It had been prepared in total secrecy and most of the Cabinet only learned the contents on the morning of Budget day. 'It is not too much to say that we were all reduced to a state of catatonic shock,' said one Wet minister. At the meeting Jim Prior, Peter Walker and Sir Ian Gilmour attacked the Budget – but it was too late.

In a televised speech at a lunch the next day, Mrs Thatcher aimed her fire directly at the dissidents. Her press office had warned BBC news and ITN in advance of the key passages. 'Now what really gets my goat is this,' declaimed the Prime Minister, 'it's very ironic that those who are the most critical of the extra tax are those who were the most vociferous in demanding the extra expenditure. And what gets me even more is that having demanded the extra expenditure they are not prepared to face the consequences of their own action and stand by the necessity to get some of the tax to pay for it. And I wish some of them had a bit more guts and courage than they have.' Her targets could not have been clearer. Following a Lobby briefing at Number 10, the press, radio and television had identified the ministers who had opposed the Budget. On the TV bulletins that night the Prime Minister was seen waging war on her own Cabinet colleagues.

The Wets had long warned that Mrs Thatcher's economic experiment was testing Britain to destruction. Graphic evidence to bolster their case burst on to the television screens the month after the Budget. The riots of the spring and summer of 1981 first started in Brixton, the district with the highest black population in London. They followed a high-profile police operation codenamed 'Swamp 81' – an echo of Mrs Thatcher's televised warning of people's fears of being swamped by immigrants. TV pictures of gutted buildings, looting by blacks and whites, blazing cars and vicious confrontations with the police just a mile from Westminster caused profound political alarm. 'Nothing, but nothing, justifies what happened,' said Mrs Thatcher on television and denied that unemployment was the primary cause of the riots.

The following month Mrs Thatcher sought to put a human face to the Government's policies. She agreed to answer direct questions from viewers on *Nationwide*, the current affairs programme with the largest working-class and young audience. 'Unemployment is the most difficult problem I face,' she admitted, 'it is unacceptably high.' A Bristol housewife asked how Mrs Thatcher reacted on a personal level to the suffering and hardship caused to families by her political theories: was her conscience troubled? 'I do not find any pleasure in having to deal with a situation in which over the last five years the country had paid itself 100 per cent more for producing 2 per cent less,' replied the Prime Minister, 'but that is what I am faced with. I do feel deeply concerned when I have people who want jobs and can't get them. But I can't conjure them out of thin air. Of course I feel deeply about it: I wouldn't be human if I didn't.' What could she do to prevent a repeat of the Brixton riots? 'They were a tragedy. It was a dreadful evening – dreadful as we saw those scenes on television and saw how marvellous our police were. I think we have done everything we can by law and there is a great deal of money being made available to try to stop this kind of thing happening again.' But worse was soon to follow.

Over the first weekend of July there was a ferocious new outbreak of rioting in the Toxteth district of Liverpool and the West London suburb of Southall – both areas with a high immigrant population. The following day the Prime Minister kept a long-standing engagement to visit the Royal

Agricultural Show at Stoneleigh in Warwickshire. Six years earlier Harold Wilson had been filmed at Stoneleigh eating strawberries and cream as sterling slid and the complacent image pushed the pound down further. Now Mrs Thatcher was interviewed wearing an all-white outfit topped by a white pill-box hat with feathers: she looked and sounded out of touch. Gordon Reece had flown back that day from California to advise her on a party political broadcast she planned to make later that week. When he saw the Stoneleigh interview he was horrified. His pupil seemed to have forgotten what he had taught her about the impressionistic nature of television. 'When I saw the Prime Minister I advised that she should never be interviewed wearing a hat again.'

In her party political broacast two days later, Mrs Thatcher looked tired and nervous: 'Nothing can condone the appalling level of violence we have all seen on television. We all know that violence will destroy everything we value. That is why the violence must be stopped. The law must be upheld. People must be protected. Then we can put these terrible events behind us, repair the damage, and begin to rebuild confidence.' According to *The Times* the Prime Minister failed to raise the tone of her remarks to the level of events and even as she spoke the rioting was spreading throughout the country. Violence broke out in almost every large city, from Leeds down to Portsmouth, as well as in normally quiet places with very low immigrant populations like Cirencester and Aldershot. As nightly television reports showed petrol bombers taking on police armed with CS gas, one Dry Cabinet minister remarked: 'the riots have gone political fast'. The Prime Minister demonstrated her identification with the police by spending eight hours through the night of 9 July at Scotland Yard and Brixton police station. Four days later she paid a much-televised visit to Toxteth.

There was considerable press speculation about the role that television played in encouraging 'copy-cat rioting'. The veteran clean-up TV campaigner, Mrs Mary Whitehouse, sent a telegram to the BBC and ITN on 11 July: 'Massive television coverage of acts of vandalism and violence is contributing to the spread of riots. It creates excitement, teaches techniques and encourages intimidation.' It was a belief widely shared by the press. At the end of a week of rioting, the Prime Minister gave her own view in a speech at a dinner to mark the centenary of the Parliamentary Press Gallery. She delivered her credo on the power of television and the duties of the programme-makers.

The riots, said Mrs Thatcher, were a challenge to all of those who were responsible for setting the tone and standard of society. Television broadcasters were very high on that list and, if they valued the freedom of broadcasting, they had the responsibility to discharge their roles as opinion formers with due regard to the effects their activities had on the quality of society. 'There can be no escape from that responsibility in the concept of "detachment" and "balance",' declared the Prime Minister. 'None of us can be detached from the quality of the society we live in or be balanced on the issue of freedom. Television has all the power and impact of a visual medium. It has national and continuous coverage.' We were now living with the first television generation – a generation of adults brought up for twenty or twenty-five years on continuous television – some of them watching it for four or more hours a day. Television images inevitably came to represent the norms and aspirations for viewers. How could some young people, who had been brought up to watch television for several hours a day, do otherwise than absorb some of the values to which they were exposed by it? How could they fail to be affected in their attitudes and conduct by the attitudes and behaviour they saw portrayed on the screen?

Looking directly at the television reporters in her audience, the Prime Minister continued: 'You have of course to report the sort of events we have been recently witnessing. You have a duty to show the disfigurations of society as well as its more agreeable aspects. But may I put the point to you in the way it was put to me by one of your colleagues in television? If the television of the Western world uses its freedom continually to show all that is worst in our society, while the centrally controlled television of the Communist world and the dictatorships show only what is judged advantageous to them and suppress everything else – how are the uncommitted to judge between us? How can they fail to misjudge if they view matters only through a distorted mirror? Our democracy can only be damaged if we distort, whether by neglect or intent.'

It was clear from her speech that the Prime Minister endorsed the view that television had helped spread the violence from one city to another by its immediate transmission of the methods and weapons used by the rioters. But a study by the British Film Institute claimed there was no evidence of the rioters being affected by the coverage of the riots or of their being encouraged by the presence of the cameras. (At times it seemed the opposite was true as television crews were attacked and their equipment smashed.) 'The youngsters spend their time on the streets, influenced by rumours of something going on. Most of them do not even watch the television news,' claimed the BFI report. The Prime Minister would return over the years to her charge that television acted as a distorting mirror – from which she and her Government suffered.

Then, almost as suddenly as they had started, the riots died down: the short, hot summer was over.

But Mrs Thatcher still felt a prisoner in her own Cabinet. That September saw action. In a major Cabinet reshuffle she dropped prominent Wets, like Sir Ian Gilmour, and exiled James Prior to Northern Ireland. In his place the hard-line Norman Tebbit became Employment Secretary. The Prime Minister had stormed her own Cabinet. But many political commentators believed the Tories were heading for a defeat, when the general election eventually came, of 1945 proportions or worse. It was a view bolstered by the opinion polls, which showed Mrs Thatcher to be the most unpopular Prime Minister since records began. There were Tory whispers of a Westminster Palace coup to replace her.

At the start of 1982, unemployment reached three million and the SDP-Liberal Alliance led the opinion polls with the Tories third. The Prime Minister agreed to give a studio interview to Thames Television's *TV Eye*. A special chair had been flown in from Sweden for Mrs Thatcher: she had approved the design but not the colour of the one Thames had planned to use. In the interview Mrs Thatcher poured particular scorn on the SDP: 'They are the people who hadn't the guts to fight when they were in the Labour party, they put us under the thumb of the trade unions, they took us to the IMF – they are the self-same people.' Her interviewer, Llew Gardner, suggested that one way of bringing down unemployment would be to reflate the economy. '*Reflate?*' repeated the Prime Minister in the manner of Lady Bracknell. 'Of course we can't reflate – it would be totally wrong. Let us get one thing clear: anyone who says we should reflate is asking the Government to be dishonest with money.' In the *Observer*, Clive James reported that the Prime Minister sounded as if she was telling 'an assembled school of not very bright children that no responsible adult could possibly *think* of reflating. She made it sound like a synonym of flatulence – something which rude small boys did and only the sillier girls giggled at.' Gardner asked how long Mrs Thatcher wished to remain Prime Minister. 'Until I am tired of it.' How long would that be? 'Oh, I do not get tired very easily. I am not suffering from any fatigue – so long as Britain needs me, I will never be tired of it.'

To mark the impending retirement of the BBC's Director-General, Sir Ian Trethowan, Mrs Thatcher came to lunch at Broadcasting House. She noticed a bust of Lord Reith. 'Ah, there was a great man,' exclaimed the Prime Minister, 'they don't make them like that any more.' Trethowan did not take it as a compliment and records in his memoirs that he learned later that Mrs Thatcher had found his manner rather odd. 'Well, Prime Minister,' said one of her aides, 'Reith was the BBC's first Director-General.' 'No, no, he was Chairman.' 'No, Prime Minister, he was Director-General.' 'Oh,' responded the Prime Minister. Trethowan subsequently paid a farewell visit to Downing Street and Mrs Thatcher had only one question to ask about his chosen successor, Alasdair Milne: 'Is he one of us?' According to Francis Pym that question was put regularly by the Prime Minister and meant: 'Is he completely free of any doubt as to the utter rightness of everything we are doing?' Mrs Thatcher was soon to discover for herself the answer in Milne's case. He did not take office until July 1982, but in the preceding months he was to have one of the bloodiest initiations to the top that any Director-General ever had. On 1 April, came the event that would totally transform Mrs Thatcher's political fortunes and lead to the most rancorous of public clashes between the Prime Minister and the Corporation. Argentina invaded the Falklands.

For the Iron Lady – the champion of strong defence for Britain – the invasion was a catastrophe. Two nights earlier, when she first received intelligence of General Galtieri's intentions, the Prime Minister had hastily summoned senior ministers and Chiefs of Staff to her room in the Commons. 'If the Argentines invade and we cannot do anything about it, my Government will fall,' she told them. That weekend she announced the despatch of the Task Force. It caught the tide from Portsmouth on a wave of maritime patriotism, with bands playing and the ships' decks crammed with military hardware for the world's TV cameras to see. While some critics saw it as a classic instance of gesture politics, the Prime Minister evoked imperial echoes.

'There is no possibility of defeat,' the Prime Minister told BBC and ITN, 'I am talking about succeeding in a very quiet, I hope, British way.' She was recycling the words of Queen Victoria that Winston Churchill had kept on his desk throughout the Second World War: 'We are not interested in the possibilities of defeat, they do not exist.' Mrs Thatcher had seen the apophthegm on a visit to Churchill's bunker beneath Whitehall in 1981, little supposing that she was herself soon to become Britain's first war leader in an electronic age. Yet, as she admitted during the general election campaign of 1983, there had been every possibility of defeat for the Task Force.

The Falklands War faced the Government and the broadcasters with peculiar problems. It was not total war nor did it threaten Britain's national survival. Opinion polls in the early days reflected what researchers call 'cognitive dissonance': a majority favoured the despatch of the Task Force yet a majority opposed military action to end the conflict. And a quarter of the population continued in its disapproval of the Government's actions throughout the war. While television programmes sought occasionally to reflect the view of this minority, the Prime Minister felt she was fighting to retrieve the national honour and national broadcasting organizations should suspend questioning and fall into line behind the Government.

As the Task Force set sail there had been a fierce battle between the Navy and Number 10 over publicity. The Navy, with its tradition as the Silent Service wanted no reporters, but the Prime Minister and her press secretary intervened to ensure that a small contingent from the BBC, ITN and Fleet Street would be aboard. 'The impression we got', says ITN's Task Force reporter, Michael Nicholson, 'was that Mrs Thatcher expected us to report the "good news war". You remember how Gaumont British News used to put it: "and there goes Tommy climbing over the trenches and he's going to give the Argies another black eye" and up comes the music. I thought that is the kind of thing the PM is expecting us to do.' Nicholson's view was confirmed aboard HMS *Hermes* by a Ministry of Defence press officer: 'You must have been told when you left you couldn't report bad news. You knew when you came you were expected to do a 1940 propaganda job.'

Mrs Thatcher graphically demonstrated how she saw television's role in the conflict on 25 April. That afternoon she received a signal that British troops had landed on the island of South Georgia. Four hours later, as ITN's main evening bulletin was about to go on the air, Bernard Ingham alerted the editor to have his camera unit in Downing Street ready to transmit. In mid-bulletin, the director went live to Number 10. On cue, Mrs Thatcher and the Defence Secretary, John Nott emerged. The Prime Minister announced to the camera: 'The Secretary of State for Defence has just come over to give me some very good news and I thought you would like to hear it immediately.' Mrs Thatcher watched proudly as Nott read part of the rousing signal from the Task Force Commander which ended: 'Be pleased to inform Her Majesty that the White Ensign flies alongside the Union Jack in South Georgia. God Save the Queen.' As the Prime Minister turned to walk back inside, the assembled reporters shouted, 'What happens next?' 'Are we going to declare war on Argentina?' Mrs Thatcher glared at them: 'Just rejoice at that news and congratulate our forces and the Marines. Good night, gentlemen.' She disappeared into Number 10 pausing only to deliver a further 'Rejoice!' over her shoulder.

Although the news of the capture of South Georgia had been given peak viewing, evidence was mounting that the Government was suppressing bad news for political rather than security reasons. Those television programmes which felt their function was to report rather than rejoice came in for further prime ministerial wrath. On BBC's *Newsnight* a week later, Peter Snow sought to analyse the conflicting military claims of the two sides: 'We cannot demonstrate that the British have lied to us but the Argentinians clearly have,' said Snow. 'Until the British are demonstrated either to be deceiving us, or to be concealing losses from us we can only tend to give a lot more credence to their version of events.' For Mrs Thatcher and her supporters this was carrying detachment too far. 'Those words from an organization that is called the *British* Broadcasting Corporation will cut a scar for ever,' says Norman Tebbit. During Suez twenty-five years earlier, with the nation split down the middle, the BBC had driven Eden to apoplexy by providing a platform for the Opposition and reporting doubts about the whole venture. In the interim television had become both more influential and less trusted by governments. Mrs Thatcher was determined to keep national and international opinion firmly on her side. But it appeared that once again 'those Communists at the BBC' – in Eden's phrase – were showing their true colours.

A Conservative MP, John Page, attacked *Newsnight*'s coverage as 'totally offensive and almost treasonable' and in the House of Commons the Prime Minister agreed that many people were very concerned that 'the case for our British forces is not being put over fully and effectively. I understand there are times when it would seem that we and the Argentines are almost being treated as equal.' This gave offence to many people and caused great emotion.

George Howard, the Chairman of the BBC, answered the Prime Minister. The large and colourful owner of the sumptuous Castle Howard, the TV setting for *Brideshead Revisited*, was an old friend of the Home Secretary. In 1980 Willie Whitelaw had managed to persuade Mrs Thatcher to appoint Howard Chairman even though he was politically a Whig grandee rather than 'one of us'; she felt he was at least preferable to the best-qualified candidate, the Vice-Chairman Mark Bonham-Carter – a Liberal. Howard's riposte to the Prime Minister came in a public speech: 'It needs saying with considerable vigour that the BBC is not and cannot be neutral as between our own country and an aggressor.' But in a free country people wished to be told the truth, however unpleasant it might be. 'Strong supporters of the Government side will expect the BBC to be, as it were, "on our side", and will accuse us of treason if we are more neutral. Doubters will look for the neutral tone and accuse us of jingoism and warmongering if we adopt any other. We are not in the business of black propaganda or distortion of the truth. All we can do is to proclaim the truth so far as we can.' And the BBC's Managing Director of Radio, Dick Francis, added: 'Whatever reputation the BBC may have does not come from being tied to the Government's apron-strings'.

In that first week of May what had been presented as a *Boy's Own Paper* escapade suddenly turned real with the sinking of the *Belgrano* and HMS *Sheffield*. Both the BBC and ITN carried film from Argentina of grieving relatives of the *Belgrano* dead, but it was the Corporation which remained the subject of Tory attacks. On 9 May, Robert Adley MP claimed that the BBC was becoming 'General Galtieri's fifth column in Britain'. The following night's *Panorama* seemed to many of his Tory colleagues to confirm Adley's view. It began with an interview with the Argentine representative at the UN. Then followed a report, made by the author, on parliamentary misgivings about a military solution; it included interviews with two Conservative MPs who had the temerity to express publicly doubts which others were revealing privately – the BBC's Political Editor, John Cole, calculated that some twenty per cent of Tory MPs had reservations about the circumstances in which the Task Force would be used. The programme ended with an interview with Cecil Parkinson, Chairman of the Conservative Party and a member of the War Cabinet. Dressed to go out for dinner, Mrs Thatcher sat watching *Panorama* 'transfixed' – according to Bernard Ingham – on the edge of her armchair in her flat at Number 10. That night the BBC switchboard lit up with complaints and John Cole was advised by a Government Whip to wear his steel helmet when he ventured into the MPs' Lobby. 'Sure enough the flak from the Tory right-wingers was fierce,' says Cole.

At Prime Minister's Question Time the next day, Mrs Sally Oppenheim, one of Mrs Thatcher's ex-ministers, described the programme as 'an odious and subversive travesty which dishonoured the right of freedom of speech in this country'. Mrs Thatcher replied: 'I share the deep concern that has been expressed on many sides particularly about the content of yesterday's *Panorama* programme. I know how strongly many people feel that the case for our country is not being put with sufficient vigour in certain – I don't say all – BBC programmes. The Chairman of the BBC has said in vigorous terms that the BBC is not neutral on this point and I hope his words will be heeded by the many who have the responsibility for standing up for our Task Force, our boys, our people and the cause of democracy.' The Director-General designate, Alasdair Milne, felt he had seen it all before. Twenty-six years earlier as a young current affairs producer he had been indirectly in Eden's Suez firing line. Now he said: 'I always thought the Government would turn on us, once there were losses and they came under pressure. But it happened several days later than I expected.'

With Sir Ian Trethowan away in America, George Howard and Alasdair Milne agreed to attend a meeting of the Tory backbench media committee in an attempt to assuage feelings. Over a hundred MPs poured into Committee Room 13 on 12 May. It was a hot night and the Chairman was soon sweating profusely and mopping his brow. Faced with a barrage of hostile questions, Howard sought unavailingly to explain the BBC's case. Many of the MPs belonged to the new breed of self-made Thatcherites and had no time for lectures from a Whig grandee. And Alasdair Milne had little opportunity to display his Wykehamist logic. 'The first time I spoke,' remembers Milne, 'they barked "can't hear you", so I said I'd speak up. It was like being in the Star Chamber. When they got really angry they started waving their order papers and growling like dogs.' Milne sat hunched and silent as Winston Churchill the younger derided the BBC's claim of trying to live up to its World War II standards: Goebbel's propaganda machine had not been given equal time. One young Tory MP jabbed a finger at Howard as the meeting ended – 'You, sir, are a traitor.' 'Stuff you,' responded the BBC Chairman.

As they left the meeting, MPs offered colourful accounts. 'They went for their throats.' 'There was blood and entrails all over the place.' And the ex-minister, Sir Hector Monro, said 'It was the ugliest meeting I have ever attended in my twenty years as an MP.' The two BBC men went discreetly for a drink with Willie Whitelaw, who told them: 'It had to happen.' Some ministers shared the Home Secretary's view that the attack on the BBC represented a useful ritual blood-letting while the War Cabinet planned the next moves in the South Atlantic. Certainly the Prime Minister declined an invitation to escalate the conflict with the Corporation at Question Time the following day, remarking only that everyone was entitled to free speech. But Derrik Mercer, in his book *The Fog of War*, says the public row stemmed from a deep Government suspicion about the BBC which pre-dated the Falklands. One member of the War Cabinet recalls: 'I was absolutely disgusted with the BBC. Oh God, yes we all were – from Mrs T. down.' And another said: 'At a War Cabinet meeting there was a general hate of the BBC whom we reckoned to be biased and we were pro-ITN who we reckoned were doing much better. One minister said: "We give all this information to the bloody BBC and what do they do with it? We don't help ITN enough." '

Compared to *Newsnight* and *Panorama*, ITN had decided to adopt a noticeably more supportive and unquestioning tone. Michael Nicholson's gung-ho reports from the Task Force contrasted sharply with the deliber-ately unemotional style of the BBC's Brian Hanrahan. And *News at Ten* would end each night with a brief patriotic editorial from Alastair Burnet. Mrs Thatcher rewarded ITN with an interview at the end of May. Asked what she now thought of the media's coverage of the war, she admitted: 'I had one or two rather acid things to say about certain programmes. May I say since then it is very much better. It was our decision, you know, to put correspondents on board the ships and some of them have been very, very helpful indeed and given very, very vivid accounts and helped us all to know what is going on.'

273

(John Kent, *Daily Mail*)

Those helpful accounts had been delivered without the aid of pictures. Mrs Thatcher told the BBC's senior management the following year that television had lost America the Vietnam War (a finding disputed in many academic studies). The Royal Navy shared her view and was unwilling to arrange the speedy transmission of film back to London. While video cassettes of the Cup Final were on the Task Force ships within forty-eight hours, TV film of the fighting on the Falklands took three weeks to arrive in London, longer than William Howard Russell's despatches about the charge of the Light Brigade in the Crimean War had taken to reach *The Times*. But Mrs Thatcher and the War Cabinet grew increasingly concerned that the Government was losing the propaganda war as the television companies, starved of film from the Task Force, made use of film from the Argentinians.

The Thames programme, *TV Eye*, secured an interview with General Galtieri – given as a compensation for its crew being kidnapped by thugs on a Buenos Aires street corner. The Prime Minister and her War Cabinet discussed in horrified disbelief the company's intention to transmit the interview. Willie Whitelaw was despatched to lean on the Director-General of the IBA. Sir Brian Young then insisted on watching the interview in advance but passed it for transmission with minor amendments. The Argentinian military dictator failed to set the Thames on fire. 'The idea that the sight of

Galtieri speaking could create a mass collapse of national morale was a great nonsense,' says Sir Ian Trethowan, although he admits that broadcasters were 'occasionally insensitive to the fearful pressures on those who had to make the crucial decisions, particularly the Prime Minister herself. But politicians in their turn showed an alarming lack of confidence in the emotional sturdiness of the public on whose behalf they claim to govern.'

The Prime Minister was determined to break the news of the final military victory herself. On 14 June Downing Street imposed a complete news blackout on reporters in the Falklands – for nine hours they were unable to file any story to London. In the middle of *News at Ten*, Mrs Thatcher stood up in the Commons to announce that White Flags were flying in Port Stanley. It had been a remarkable feat of arms; it had vindicated the Prime Minister's nerve and skills as a war leader; and it had transformed her political prospects. Mrs Thatcher's personal opinion poll rating rose from an all-time low of 24 per cent at the start of the year to 60 per cent at the end of the war. Her authority as Prime Minister was unchallengeable. As she put it in a television interview with Fred Emery the following year: 'Before we had the Falklands, people were always asking "when are you going to make a U-turn?". We never get those questions now.' And Mrs Thatcher told an American TV interviewer that she had applied exactly the same principles in the Falklands as she had to the economy. 'People saw the kind of results it produced in the Falklands and I think they began to realize it was the right way to go at home as well. I think people like decisiveness, I think they like strong leadership.'

The slogan for that October's Party Conference was 'The Resolute Approach'. The Wets had all but evaporated: their contribution was limited to heavily coded speeches at fringe meetings. To evoke memories of the South Atlantic, the backdrop for the Conference had been designed to resemble a grey battleship and the widow of Colonel 'H' Jones VC, hero of Goose Green, took a seat on the platform alongside the Prime Minister. The man responsible for the look of the conference was Harvey Thomas, an ebullient born-again Christian and public relations expert. He had worked for years staging rallies for the American evangelist, Billy Graham. Now he was using the same techniques for the Tories.

To put the audience in the right emotional state to receive Mrs Thatcher's final conference speech, Thomas arranged that an organist would play 'Rule Britannia' and other patriotic music in the build-up to the leader's triumphal entry. 'I think it's terribly important that an evangelist – whether it is Billy Graham or Margaret Thatcher – should not have to waste vital minutes trying to get the attention of the audience,' says Thomas. 'They should be able to go straight in with the vital message.' He saw his prime task as creating maximum television impact for the Prime Minister's final conference speech. Thomas supervised the lighting and ensured that the cameras had a clear shot of Thatcher speaking against a blue background, with no distractions behind her. 'When the Prime Minister makes that speech, we only get a few seconds on the TV news and we have got to make sure that those few seconds are absolutely pure as far as the message is concerned,' says Thomas. He had also coached Mrs Thatcher in the use of a special speaking device new to British politics.

The Prime Minister had seen President Reagan using a Head Up Display Unit at Westminster Hall earlier in the year and decided she had to have a HUDU of her own. It was a sophisticated electronic autoprompt system, virtually invisible to the audience and the TV cameras. It enabled Mrs Thatcher to deliver her speech without appearing to be reading and while looking straight at her audience. In television terms it gave her the distinct advantages of eye contact with viewers – HUDU was known as 'the sincerity machine'. For her final speech, the Prime Minister's appearance and diction had subtly altered. Her hairstyle, which Sir Ronald Millar said looked as though a swan could nest in, was now less elaborate. And she had spent early morning sessions in the dentist's chair since the capture of Port Stanley having her teeth capped.

'The spirit of the South Atlantic was the spirit of Britain at her best,' the Prime Minister proclaimed to the conference. 'It has been said that we surprised the world, that British patriotism was rediscovered in those spring days.' Pause. 'Mr Chairman, it was never really lost.' Applause. Her Cabinet colleagues had been instructed to leave the Falklands for Mrs Thatcher's final speech. But she did not dwell on the military triumph. She did not need to: the Prime Minister was the Falklands Factor made flesh.

At the start of 1983, Mrs Thatcher suddenly flew amid the tightest secrecy to the Falklands. There was no doubting her desire to pay tribute to the courage of the armed forces, yet she could not ignore the domestic political advantage in the visit. For security reasons there had been no advance notice of the trip – even Mrs Thatcher's Cabinet had not been told – and only the BBC happened to have a television TV crew on the islands; ITN had rejected a cryptic suggestion from the Ministry of Defence to send one. The BBC took exclusive film of Mrs Thatcher's arrival among the cheering people of Port Stanley. The Prime Minister paid tribute to the armed forces and one islander replied: 'You didn't do such a bad job yourself.' At Government House an army officer called out 'three cheers for the PM'. It seemed the whole population of the islands responded. These were the 'photo-opportunities' that public relations men dream on. Mrs Thatcher's press secretary, Bernard Ingham, who had flown with her to the Falklands decided that the film should be seen on all four television channels in Britain.

Ingham rang the BBC's Assistant Director-General, Alan Protheroe, in London to insist that the BBC must 'pool' its film with ITN. By chance a radio ham in the Falklands recorded the conversation, which forms an authentic record of how Number 10 can pressurize the broadcasting authorities. Ingham pointed out that the BBC crew had only stayed on the islands thanks to a heavy hint from the Army and he threatened the Corporation with 'incalculable consequences' if Protheroe did not agree to pool its material with ITN. Protheroe responded that he would have appreciated prior consultation: 'I really find it very difficult to accept that Number 10 can just declare a pool when necessary, Bernard.' But the BBC man undertook to consult his colleagues. The Prime Minister then authorized her press secretary to play the card that had been used so effectively during the war itself – the Government's total control of communications from the island. 'No filming is coming out tonight unless I have your absolute assurance it will be made freely available to ITN and IRN,' warned Ingham. Protheroe protested that he felt the BBC was being used for the Government's own purposes. But after many more hours of telephone argument Protheroe eventually capitulated. Ingham rang his Downing Street press office in triumph: 'I've won.'

For the next five days the Prime Minister's triumphal process through the islands was shown at peak times on BBC and ITV. Mrs Thatcher appeared windswept on a hillside battleground, taking the salute on board ship, genial with grateful villagers, firing a 105mm gun and tearful as she placed wreaths on the graves of fallen soldiers. 'The hushed reverential tones adopted by the TV announcers, the expensive seconds of television time spent establishing pictorial frames for her patriotic tableaux, the constant references to her troops, all proclaim this is a royal visit,' wrote the late David Watt in *The Times*. And Mrs Thatcher's biographers, George Brock and Nicholas Wapshott, claimed it provided some of the most potent pre-election help the Prime Minister was likely to receive from the small screen.

Although Parliament still had eighteen months to run there was insistent press speculation about an early general election, which Mrs Thatcher and her ministers did nothing to quell. For the previous year, Saatchi and Saatchi had been engaging in 'qualitative' research, about voters' attitudes. Their surveys revealed a powerful nostalgia for imperialism, thrift, duty and hard work which chimed in with the Prime Minister's own beliefs (similar findings by another advertising agency had inspired the cobble-streeted TV commercials for Hovis). On her return to England from the Falklands, Mrs

Thatcher endorsed 'Victorian values' on *Weekend World*. 'Those were the values when our country became great, not only internationally but at home.'

In a sure sign that an election was on the way the Prime Minister suddenly began making herself and Number 10 accessible to television. She was following the example of the two Harolds, Macmillan and Wilson. For the first three and a half years of her Government not a foot of film had been shot further inside 10 Downing Street than the entrance hall, aside from set-piece interviews. Now Mrs Thatcher gave a lengthy guided tour to her old friend the mystic anthropologist, Sir Laurens van der Post, for an ITV documentary – *The Woman at Number Ten*. In the Blue Room, Mrs Thatcher told how she had replaced the Italian paintings at Number 10 with portraits of great English heroes, Clive of India, Nelson, Wellington. 'I thought of Wellington very much during the Falklands.' In her private study she showed van der Post a statuette of the paratroopers raising the flag at Port San Carlos. 'I think it just portrays everything that is marvellous about the British soldier: the dignity, the calm and the kindliness.' And in the Cabinet room, never filmed before, the Prime Minister sat in the chair 'where Winston used to sit' as well as the first prime minister of all, Sir Robert Walpole: 'it's a great comfort to us that he stayed for twenty-one years,' she smiled.

'No one can have shown off an official residence with such proprietorial chic since Jacqueline Kennedy,' wrote Philip Purser in the *Sunday Telegraph*. 'Mrs Thatcher came across as a formidable charmer: it was a cordial occasion with the Prime Minister facing not an interviewer but a friendly elder lobbing woolly balls.' According to the *Sunday Times* the programme amounted to 'a lengthy plug for Mrs Thatcher's ideas and values'.

Six weeks later she called the election. Jock Bruce-Gardyne, one of her Treasury ministers, described the art of successful parliamentary government as making the painful changes early enough to bear fruit in good time to impress the voters. In this the Prime Minister had succeeded: inflation was forecast to drop below 5 per cent for the first time since the sixties and earnings were rising at nearly double that rate – the classic formula for winning elections. Mrs Thatcher had felt most vulnerable over the three and a quarter million unemployed, but to her pleasant surprise Saatchi's research revealed that the majority of voters blamed the unions, management failures and the world slump more than the Government. Further to defuse opposition attacks, Saatchi came up with an election broadcast which showed the faces of successive Labour prime ministers dissolving into each other and the legend: 'Every Labour Government there has ever been has increased unemployment.'

That message was to be repeated in all the Conservative election broadcasts and by the Prime Minister in television interviews. 'It's the same as advertising a product, you just say something more and more frequently and people will eventually understand and say it themselves,' explained the Conservatives' Director of Marketing, Christopher Lawson (later knighted). Lawson was an old friend of the Party Chairman, Cecil Parkinson, and had spent years in America marketing packaged snacks for the Mars chocolate company. Now he applied sophisticated techniques of persuasion to the Tories' election campaign. On the advice of behavioural psychologists, Lawson had installed alternative backdrops for the Prime Minister's daily televised press conferences at Central Office. His purpose was to change the mood from day to day. The dark blue backdrop indicated robust resolution and light blue the relaxed, informal approach.

Also back from America for the election campaign was Gordon Reece. Although four years in Number 10 had greatly strengthened Mrs Thatcher's confidence on television she still admitted to feeling nervous when the red light glowed on the camera. Reece, with his ability to charm and relax the Prime Minister, provided reassurance: he was her TV talisman. When she worried at the end of the first week of the campaign about an answer she had given delighting in her 'headmistress image', Reece soothed her doubts. 'The more the media concentrates on the strong personality of the Prime Minister, the more we reckon the public likes it,' was his line.

It seemed that 1983 would finally see a televised confrontation between the two major party leaders. Brian Walden had put the suggestion personally to Mrs Thatcher and believed he had secured her agreement. Gordon Reece, who had been against the idea in 1979 was now in favour, convinced that the Prime Minister would trounce Michael Foot. But both the Home and Foreign Secretaries saw dangers: Willie Whitelaw and Francis Pym deployed the traditional argument against raising the Opposition leader to equal status with the Prime Minister. Mrs Thatcher was persuaded. She turned down both Walden's proposal and two others from ITV and BBC, arguing that she had no wish to turn the election into an American presidential contest. Yet the Tory campaign was once again to be more personalized and presidential than in any previous election.

'We came to the view that Mrs Thatcher was obviously our key weapon and how she used the three weeks was absolutely critical and that was the core of our campaign,' says Cecil Parkinson. 'We took a lot of trouble with her tour, making sure she would be saying something at the right time for the news bulletins and that there would be the right pictures.' Tory officials had spent months scouring the country for suitably telegenic venues. The Prime Minister's tour was no longer centred on marginal seats, indeed she avoided Labour marginals altogether. They were in urban seats and offered the prospect of anti-Thatcher demonstrations and chanting. 'There is no percentage in showing her on television to be unpopular in certain parts of the country,' said Parkinson. Her tours concentrated on Tory seats. The only advance warning of her arrival was given to local Party headquarters so they could round up a group of loyalists to cheer for the cameras. The Prime Minister would arrive at a factory selected to provide images of prosperity and new technology, almost in the manner of the last Tsar of Russia inspecting a Potemkin village.

With the help of President Reagan, Mrs Thatcher managed to turn her mid-campaign flying visit to the world summit in Virginia into an international photo-opportunity. The President effectively acted as the Tories' American campaign manager, paying fulsome tribute to the Prime Minister in an interview for British television and waiving the summit rules so that she could hold her own televised press conference before it ended. The Conservatives then used the news film of Mrs Thatcher with the President and other world leaders in an election broadcast. Britain had once again become a world leader, claimed the voice-over, 'because of one woman who believed that our country, our people could do more than we dreamed possible for many, many years'.

The Prime Minister's rallies resembled American presidential conventions, with warm-up music and Union flags thoughtfully provided for each member of the audience to wave. They were ticket-only affairs. 'Hecklers are now geared to TV coverage, why should we provide them with free publicity?' asked Harvey Thomas. The overriding aim was to ensure that the extracts from the Prime Minister's speech on the TV news programmes would show her in powerful and confident form. According to the Oxford Research Fellow, Max Atkinson, in his book *Our Masters' Voices*, Mrs Thatcher had learned techniques of rhetoric and body language for triggering applause. And the passages with applause were invariably those that the TV news bulletins chose to run. The Prime Minister appeared on the screen to be speaking without a script and looking straight at her audience, which could scarce forbear to cheer. She was using her sincerity machine to its best advantage. In contrast, Michael Foot's undoubted skills as an orator were ill-suited to a modern election.

He had spent forty years speaking without a note, but he hooked himself to a prepared text for the campaign. Foot would run one paragraph into another and scarcely ever produced a self-contained section for the news bulletins. Nor did he use techniques to provoke applause. The televised extracts from his speeches that would follow Mrs Thatcher's on the news would show the Labour leader hunched over his lectern, obviously reading and being received in total silence. That the Prime Minister clearly saw the need to elicit applause is revealed in her daughter Carol's diary: 'Chain-munching biscuits and drinking tea, Mum went through her speech complaining that it didn't read well and contained too few claplines.'

The Tories saw Michael Foot as one of their major election assets. But Mrs Thatcher had vetoed a suggestion from Gordon Reece that Saatchi run an advertisement featuring a photograph of the Labour leader walking his dog on Hampstead Heath with the caption 'as a pensioner he'd be better off under the Conservatives'. She was content to let Labour do the Tories' work for them. As Jim Prior puts it: 'Labour kicked the ball through their own goal with almost unnerving accuracy and regularity.' In contrast with Margaret Thatcher, Michael Foot had learned none of the techniques for a television election. One of Foot's Shadow Cabinet colleagues derided his leader's 'oxy-acetylene welder's glasses and the fact that on TV he looked like a lizard who had just stumbled out into the sun'. For his press conferences Foot was given a bright red backdrop, technically the worst colour for television as it 'bled' into his white hair. 'It looked like Mephisto-pheles and his gang with the whole thing about to burst into flames,' claimed Cecil Parkinson.

Roy Jenkins, the so-called 'Prime Minister designate' of the Alliance, fared little better than Foot. The plan of the Alliance tacticians was for Jenkins to have the grandiloquent title, while the Chairman of the Campaign Committee, David Steel, would do the television. But the scheme backfired. The TV companies kept asking for 'the Prime Minister designate'. Jenkins had always felt uncomfortable with television: his orotund speaking style was ill-suited to the informality of the small screen. Towards the end of the campaign, David Steel staged a minor coup to make himself the TV voice of the Alliance, as had been intended all along. But it was too late. By then Jenkins had done almost all the big interviews.

The televisual shortcomings of Roy Jenkins and Michael Foot mattered more in 1983 than in any previous campaign. Having failed to set up a Thatcher/Foot confrontation, the weekly BBC and ITV current affairs programmes discarded analysis or reporting of the election and looked to their own status: they each arranged separate studio interviews with the party leaders. From a total of seven editions featuring party leader interviews in 1979, the number rose to sixteen in 1983 – virtually one per day of the campaign, in addition there were regular lengthy interviews on the news. But none of the top interviewers was a match for the Prime Minister. According to Martin Harrison in *The British General Election of 1983:* 'She dominated Robin Day, Alastair Burnet and Brian Walden in turn, leaving at least two of the three feeling they had failed to make the best of the occasion.'

'Don't interrupt me now, I am in full flow,' she admonished Brian Walden on *Weekend World*. Walden agreed to hold his tongue, no doubt hoping for a moment of revelation: he received a familiar recitation. 'Mum came over superbly,' Carol Thatcher confided to her diary: '"Brilliant," said Dad and rushed to congratulate her.'

And in a novel variation of prime ministerial ploys for dealing with Robin Day in her *Panorama* interview, Mrs Thatcher seemed to have forgotten that he had received a knighthood on her recommendation two years earlier: she referred to him throughout as 'Mr Day'. 'You seem to have stripped Sir Robin of his knighthood,' were Gordon Reece's first words to her at the end of the interview. 'Oh dear, Robin, you don't mind, do you?' soothed the Prime Minister. The broadcasting knight was gallant: 'You called me Mr Day about eight times. Never mind, it's not important. It doesn't matter to me, but the viewers will notice.' Sir Robin had himself apologized on air at the end of the interview for occasionally interrupting the Prime Minister. 'That's all right,' she responded, 'I can cope with you.' It was a verdict shared by Day himself in a moment of public self-excoriation: 'I thought I handled it badly. I failed to ask a number of important questions to which the viewers were entitled to have answers.' In all her set-piece studio encounters the top interviewers scarcely succeeded in laying a glove on the Prime Minister. She said what she had come prepared to say and no more. But there was one exception.

Mrs Diana Gould was a doughty, grey-haired geography teacher from Cirencester. She was chosen from thousands of viewers who had written to *Nationwide* to put live questions to the Prime Minister for its *On the Spot* election feature. Mrs Gould asked Mrs Thatcher why, during the Falklands War, she had ordered the sinking of the Argentine cruiser, the *General Belgrano*, when it was outside the exclusion zone. The Prime Minister began on the wrong foot. In the Commons she would normally insist that the precise position of the cruiser was irrelevant; now Mrs Thatcher claimed that she ordered the sinking because it was sailing towards the Task Force. Mrs Gould seized on the discrepancy. 'Keep going, you've got her rattled,' whispered one of the other prospective questioners in the studio to Mrs Gould, who sharply pointed out that the official position of the *Belgrano* showed it sailing *away* from the Falklands. The Prime Minister changed tack: 'When it was sunk it was a danger to our ships – you accept that, don't you?' 'No, I don't,' responded Mrs Gould. 'No professional interviewer would have challenged a prime minister so bluntly and – precisely because she was answering an ordinary voter – Mrs Thatcher had to bite back her evident anger,' wrote Martin Harrison. In the view of the *Guardian* Mrs

Gould emerged as a rank outsider to claim the crown as Britain's champion heavyweight political interviewer.

After the programme, the Thatcher family were united in condemnation. 'Only the BBC could ask a British Prime Minister why she took action to protect *our* ships against an enemy ship that was a danger to our boys,' seethed Mrs Thatcher. Her husband virtually acted out the *Private Eye* parody of his view of the BBC as 'a nest of long-haired Trots and wooftahs'. And Carol Thatcher described *On the Spot* as 'an example of the most crass nastiness and discourtesy shown to a Prime Minister on a television election programme'. The Editor of *Nationwide*, Roger Bolton, no stranger to the prime ministerial lash from his INLA and Carrickmore experiences, says: 'By the time of the election, Mrs Thatcher had become very confident in her ability to deflect television interviewers in order to put across the points she came to put across. But Mrs Gould was not a person to be deflected: she saw no reason to shut up and kept on chasing the Prime Minister. To some extent I thought Mrs Thatcher was on both sides of the camera at the same time.'

The parties' own election broadcasts took less prominence than in previous campaigns. Partly this was because there were now four channels and the broadcasts no longer went out simultaneously; partly because 15 per cent of the population now had video recorders and could miss the TV election altogether; and partly because the current affairs interviews with the leaders so dominated the television coverage. The Tories had also decided to reduce the length of their election broadcasts from ten to five minutes. Saatchi and Saatchi argued that anything that could be said in ten minutes could be said just was well, if not better, in five and the shorter the programme the less the chance of alienating viewers.

The Tories' broadcasts featured fast-moving graphic images with few shots lasting more than ten seconds. They were linked by a professional actor who looked like a clean-cut TV reporter. Cabinet ministers, except Margaret Thatcher, were reduced to bit-part players. Only Cecil Parkinson, Norman Tebbit and Michael Heseltine appeared and none for more than a minute. The politicians who complained about television's snippety treatment were producing the bittiest programmes of all. Apart from occasional shots, Mrs Thatcher spoke only in the last programme.

'May I suggest to every citizen of our country,' she concluded, 'every man and every woman of whatever political persuasion, that on Thursday you pause and ask yourself one question – who would best defend our freedom, our way of life and the much-loved land in which we live? Britain's on the right track, don't turn back.' There was more than nostalgia for the dear, dead broadcasts beyond recall, commented Martin Harrison tartly, 'in the feeling that British politics was not the healthier for a situation in which only the Prime Minister was deemed capable of sustaining four consecutive minutes' talking to the voters.'

As the climax of the Conservative campaign, Central Office laid on four helicopters to fly the press and the Prime Minister to the Isle of Wight. She landed against the backdrop of the country's biggest Union flag, that was emblazoned on the hangar doors of the British Hovercraft Corporation. Mrs Thatcher was much filmed with her arms outstretched in front of the flag. She then made an amphibious landing on another part of the island, standing moulded like Britannia to the foredeck of the military hovercraft. The final photo-opportunity of her election campaign had combined leadership, patriotism and advanced technology.

The Prime Minister's last set-piece rally was staged for the TV cameras by Harvey Thomas and featured 'Britain's Youth Strong and Free'. He provided three thousand Young Conservatives, decked out in 'I love Maggie' T-shirts, hats and badges, with streamers and balloons. First they cheered the rock bands. Then Thomas built up the suspense with a parade of blond super athletes and show business celebrities – among them Bob Monkhouse, Jimmy Tarbuck, Steve Davies and Kenny Everett. 'Let's bomb Russia,' joked Everett, 'let's kick Michael Foot's stick away.' The crowd loved it. At last came the triumphal entry of Everett's 'megachick' – the Prime Minister. The bands played their loudest, the Young Conservatives went wild. Looking straight at them through the sincerity machine, Mrs Thatcher asked: 'Could Labour have organized a rally like this? In the old days perhaps, but not now. For they are the Party of Yesterday. Tomorrow is ours.' Margaret Thatcher was re-elected Prime Minister by a landslide – broadcasters were in for their roughest ride from a Prime Minister since the start of the age of electronic politics.

CHAPTER 15

The Oxygen of Publicity

---

*'It was President de Gaulle who said: "They have the newspapers,
I have television." Why should Mrs Thatcher have both Fleet
Street and the BBC?'*

Aubrey Singer, Managing Director BBC TV, 1982–5

The parliamentary majority of 144 intensified the convictions of a Prime
Minister who was not prone to self-doubt. 'I am absolutely in tune with how
people feel, because of what they feel in their pockets, but – more than that
– what they feel in their bones, in their bloodstream, in their heart of hearts,
in their minds,' Mrs Thatcher told Brian Walden in her first long television
interview after the election. Around the world, she continued, other
governments were following her economic lead: 'They are all Thatcherites
now.' Yet to her chagrin, the Prime Minister recognized pockets of resistance
at home that were untouched by the Thatcher revolution: among them
stood the citadels of television. Her next years in office were to be
characterized by the fiercest assaults that a government had ever directed
against the broadcasting authorities – starting with the BBC and moving on
to ITV. At the same time the attempts by both the incumbent and alternative
Prime Ministers to use television to project favourable images of themselves
were to reach new levels of sophistication.

But from the start of its second term Mrs Thatcher's Government ran
into political trouble. During the election campaign Francis Pym, then
Foreign Secretary, had warned on television of the dangers of a large
majority. Dismissed from office, he saw his prediction coming true as
ministers slithered from one banana skin to another. The most spectacular
faller was Cecil Parkinson. The aftermath of his affair with his secretary,
Sara Keays, was played out in front of the cameras at the October party
conference. The midnight resignation and dawn departure from Blackpool
of the architect of election victory eclipsed Mrs Thatcher's final speech. In
its first six months back in power, the Government seemed to lose its sense
of direction. And in the spring of 1984 came the confrontation that the
Prime Minister had long feared could remove her from office.

Arthur Scargill called a national miners' strike. Mrs Thatcher had felt
personally humiliated by her earlier tactical surrender to the NUM in 1981;

this time she wanted a fight to the finish. Her views were shared both by Scargill himself and by the man he dubbed the 'geriatric American butcher', Ian MacGregor (later knighted). The newly appointed Coal Board Chairman and the Prime Minister were convinced that Scargill was a revolutionary seeking to use the miners as shock troops in a class war aimed at overthrowing the Government. It was a conviction the NUM President did nothing to dispel. The Prime Minister felt that television would have a decisive part to play in any prolonged coal strike. And she recognized in Scargill a formidable array of skills at manipulating the electronic media.

It seemed in the first weeks of March 1984 that Scargill's strike tactics were succeeding. He had decided to enforce solidarity not by a ballot – the traditional NUM method – but by organized flying pickets, who would arrive in coachloads to persuade doubtful miners. The NUM President would augment the message with finger-pointing fluency in a succession of television interviews. At first the Government left the talking to MacGregor and maintained the public line that the strike was a matter for the Coal Board alone. There were no ministerial speeches or television interviews in the early months of the dispute. The sole exception was the Prime Minister. She agreed to answer some questions on the strike in the course of a *Panorama* interview on 9 April.

The interview assumed such importance that it took precedence over other affairs of state. President Mitterrand of France was due to arrive in Britain on the same day for the formal inauguration by the Queen of a joint European jet project. At a press conference in Paris the previous week Mitterrand said he hoped to see the Prime Minister to try to resolve Britain's budget dispute with the Common Market. But Mrs Thatcher's press office briefed journalists that she would be too busy that Monday to meet the President. Not publicized was her main engagement for the day: the Prime Minister had arranged for a lengthy dry run of the *Panorama* interview – with Bernard Ingham, her press secretary, playing the role of Sir Robin Day. Together they would seek to compose the most persuasive responses to the predicted line of questioning.

The aim was to avoid driving doubtful miners into Scargill's arms by politicizing the strike. Above all the Prime Minister should appear reasonable. Harvey Thomas, the Tories' staging expert, supervised the lighting for the interview. He insisted on back-lighting Mrs Thatcher to help produce what he called 'a softer and more attractive picture'. To check the results, Thomas asked her to sit in some forty-five minutes before the interview began, instead of the normal ten. He discountenanced Day by depriving him of a desk to put his papers on. Thomas had decided that Mrs Thatcher came across more effectively if there was no physical barrier between her and the interviewer: Day was left to balance his clip-board on his knee.

The line that the Prime Minister had worked out with Bernard Ingham came through strongly on *Panorama*. No government had done more for the coal industry than hers; the miners had been deprived of the right to ballot on the strike; the police were doing a wonderful job on combating picket line violence. 'Most of us who have watched scenes on television have only the highest praise for the police. They indeed have kept the right of miners to go to work open and they've done it marvellously.' What did the Prime Minister say to the charge that the police were acting as strike-breakers for the Government? 'I believe the police are upholding the law, they're not upholding the Government. This is not a dispute between miners and the Government, this is a dispute between miners and miners.' For the first months of the strike that remained the Cabinet's public stance.

Mrs Thatcher was determined not to repeat Ted Heath's 1974 experience. She kept herself from public involvement in the conduct of the dispute. But behind the scenes in Whitehall, she chaired a special Cabinet Committee, which received regular reports from a specialist monitoring agency on what the strike looked like on television. As she got up each morning, the Prime Minister deputed her husband to monitor breakfast television from his bed. His anguished roar would tell her of another appearance by the NUM President.

By July the Prime Minister was becoming convinced that the Coal Board was losing the television propaganda battle and that Scargill's constant depiction of her Government as callous, inflexible and dogmatic was having its effect. Not since before the Falklands War had her personal rating in the opinion polls fallen so low. And for the first time Labour, under its new leader, had moved ahead of the Tories.

Neil Kinnock, who had succeeded Michael Foot, owed almost everything to television. He had never held ministerial office at even the lowest level, but he had been one of the repertory company of political talking heads to which television producers always turn. As he prepared for his first appearance on *Weekend World* after his election to the leadership in October 1983, one of his advisers offered him a suggestion. 'You don't need to tell me what to do,' responded Kinnock, 'I got to be Leader of the Labour Party by being good on television.' After Foot almost anyone was an improvement, but Kinnock was bringing new sophistication to the electronic techniques of promoting a political leader.

His first party political broadcast had set the style: a heroic montage of Kinnock saluting the party faithful with both arms, hugging his wife, talking concernedly with nurses and playing rugby – all cut to music by Brahms. The Conservatives' private polls showed the new leader was pushing up

Labour's support, particularly among young voters. He had appeared on a pop video with Tracey Ullman and performed 'Singin' in the Rain' under a multi-coloured umbrella for the TV cameras. Mrs Thatcher attempted to play Kinnock at his own game.

At the start of 1984 she had appeared in a sketch with the stars of her own favourite television programme, *Yes Minister*. Mrs Thatcher had agreed to present an award to the programme and wrote the sketch with the help of Bernard Ingham. The Prime Minister and her press secretary did not resist the temptation to put Whitehall's best-known Permanent Secretary firmly in his place. Mrs Thatcher, playing herself, wanted Sir Humphrey to abolish all economists from the Government service and forced him to admit that he was himself one of the dreaded breed.

PM (*soothingly*): Capital, my dear Sir Humphrey. You'll know exactly where to start.
SIR HUMPHREY (*bleakly*): Yes, Prime Minister.

One of the programme's regular scriptwriters, Jonathan Lynn, congratulated Mrs Thatcher on her excellent timing as an actress; the other, Anthony Jay, commended the sharpness of her writing and suggested she join them. Instead the Prime Minister recruited Jay to the informal team that advised her on television techniques and helped write her speeches and political broadcasts. That summer Mrs Thatcher's advisers decided she should make another excursion into TV show business in an attempt to counter the Scargillite image of her.

'I was talking to a group of people in Liverpool,' she told the *Sunday Mirror*, 'and they said you are not a bit like what you seem on TV, when you seem rather hard and tough. And here you are talking naturally to us. I said that didn't they realize that on television one is often put into a belligerent position: you are asked questions in a belligerent way, I tend to fight back.' Number 10's search for the least belligerent of interviewers located Michael Aspel, who had just started a new programme. In July 1984, Margaret Thatcher became the first serving prime minister ever to appear on a chat show. 'This is a different sort of question time from what you are used to,' began Aspel. She was so busy, how did she find time to come on the programme? 'I've just got to get out, I must, so I was very grateful when you gave me the invitation.'

The Prime Minister offered glimpses into her personal life. She remembered how shocked she had been when her gynaecologist had informed her in the delivery ward that she was about to give birth not to a single baby but twins. 'The doctor said: "I think there are two there", and I remember saying, "Well, I hope you can get both of them." ' At Downing Street, each day began at six in the morning listening to the news and the farming programme on the radio; breakfast was a Vitamin C pill in sparkling water. She laughed at an impression of herself by Janet Brown but said she could not bear to watch her real self on television. The exception was when she had to check a recording of a party political broadcast – 'very dull, aren't they? Sometimes I think we could do without them.'

The only political question came when Aspel asked if she would ever at the end of a day say to the Labour leader 'you were on good form today, Neil.' Straight-faced, the Prime Minister replied: 'I don't think I've ever had occasion to say quite that.' While admitting to many faults, she declined to list them as Mr Kinnock might be watching. She revealed herself as mistress of the unwitting *double entendre*. As a junior minister, she recalled brandishing fresh statistics and proclaiming to the House: 'I've got the latest red-hot figure.' Now at Number 10, she said, 'I am always on the job.'

The Prime Minister came over as friendly, attractive and nicely self-mocking. The fans of the pop singer Barry Manilow, who made up the other half of the bill, were entranced: 'She was wonderful.' 'Not at all an old stick-in-the-mud.' But while the Prime Minister was seeking to counter Scargill's portrayal of her as a callous harpy, she was at the same time determined to show that politically there was no softening in her line on the coal strike. On the day of recording the Aspel programme, she addressed an end of session meeting of the 1922 Committee of Tory backbenchers.

'In the Falklands we had to fight the enemy without,' proclaimed the Prime Minister. 'Here the enemy is within. And it's much more difficult to fight and just as dangerous to liberty.' Her views were chorused by ministers as the Government launched the whole weight of its publicity machine against Scargill. For three months the television companies could not get a minister to come on: now they could not keep them off. Peter Walker, Norman Tebbit, Nigel Lawson, Tom King, Leon Brittan and the Party Chairman, John Selwyn Gummer, all took to the airwaves or made speeches furiously denouncing Scargill. And the Prime Minister agreed to appear on *Newsnight*.

She plugged a single theme: Scargill had replaced the ballot box with his bully boys. 'I think if any government gave in to the violence and intimidation of the kind which has disfigured our screens, there would be no future for democracy, or for any other union or for any moderate trades unionist in this country . . . You always expect the NUM to have a ballot – they have been renowned for that throughout the years . . . One never expected to see some miners threatened by violence and intimidation. Never . . . It is the work of extremists. It *is* the enemy within . . . Violence and intimidation must never be seen to pay. Never. Liberty doesn't have any future if you give in to that.' She was seeking both to encourage strikers to defect and discourage other unions from coming to the aid of the NUM.

Mrs Thatcher's was a powerful message and it was strongly reinforced by the television pictures from the picket lines. There was daily coverage of the worst scenes of civil violence ever in modern Britain. For the most part the striking miners were responsible for initiating the clashes with the police. Television strengthened that impression as TV news crews tended to film from behind police lines for their own safety. The miners would attack crews that filmed with them – even at one stage beating up an NUM video crew by mistake.

The violence cost Neil Kinnock dear. Privately he had nothing but contempt for Scargill, whom he had referred to as the Labour movement's nearest equivalent to a First World War General – destroying the coal industry single-handed. But Kinnock judged it tactically unwise to provide Scargill with an alibi for any eventual defeat by condemning his violent tactics outright. So for six months the Labour leader mealy mouthed. That autumn Scargill turned both the Labour and TUC conferences into vast gatherings of his fan club. Yet while the delegates at the two conferences voted to support him, in practical terms he received virtually nothing.

By now the Prime Minister had dropped the claim that she was not involved in the strike. At the end of August, when some dockers struck in support of the miners, she cancelled her tour of Malaysia and Singapore arranged for mid-September. Her reason was simple. Mrs Thatcher had no intention of following the example of James Callaghan and being shown on television enjoying herself in exotic, hot countries while the nation was enduring the miseries of a strike. The 'Crisis, What Crisis?' airport news conference now held pride of place in the folk memory of prime ministerial video nasties.

By the autumn Mrs Thatcher was growing increasingly worried about MacGregor's disabilities on television. The low point had come at the start of September when TV cameras filmed the NCB Chairman arriving for talks with Scargill at a supposedly secret venue in Edinburgh. MacGregor decided to indulge in the most dangerous thing for a public figure – a little joke. 'It probably fell flatter than almost any antic I have pulled in my life. I got out of the car and, taking a Harrods' bag which had some of my wife's knitting in it, held it up in front of my face and said: "Gentlemen, don't you know this meeting is so secret it is not actually taking place? Can't you see I am not here?" ' In Downing Street the scene caused incandescent rage, especially as it ran repeatedly on the TV news bulletins.

During the Tory Party Conference the following month, the Prime Minister was again infuriated to see MacGregor outwitted by Scargill. The latest round of talks had broken down – and the NUM President was immediately on the *Nine O'Clock News* denouncing the Government and the Coal Board for its intransigence. There was no sign of MacGregor. A message from the Prime Minister's advisers eventually reached the Chairman insisting that he appear on the breakfast programmes to seek to undo the damage. MacGregor duly did his interview, but his message was lost in the blast that shattered the Tory Conference that night.

At three in the morning a bomb planted by the IRA in the Grand Hotel exploded. The Prime Minister had just finished working on her closing speech. 'The windows and the curtains blew out into the street, there was a great whoosh of air and dust,' says Mrs Thatcher. 'I was very, very conscious we were in an acutely difficult situation and must stay absolutely calm and think about the best thing to do.' Detectives, with their guns out, led the Prime Minister in a dressing-gown over her nightdress along the hotel corridor and took her to Brighton police station. 'Business as usual', was her message to waiting television reporters at five in the morning. At that stage Mrs Thatcher did not know that there had been five deaths in the explosion – only that her Cabinet had survived.

Determined that nothing would stop her end of conference speech that afternoon, the Prime Minister knew she needed the help of Harvey Thomas. The Conference organizer had had a miraculous escape. He was trapped beneath tons of rubble for two and a half hours before firemen rescued him. At eight in the morning he gave a television interview wrapped in his hospital blanket: 'When I heard the explosion, I didn't quite know what was happening. At first I thought it was an earthquake. Then I thought – not in Brighton, not during a Tory Party Conference.' Thomas says that even as he lay in his hospital bed he was worried about 'the television image and presentation' of the Prime Minister's Conference speech. He insisted on discharging himself and went straight to the Conference centre. 'Harvey Thomas, bless his golden heart, came into the room,' says Mrs Thatcher, 'and I was just so thankful that someone who had been through all the last terrible hours could still be remarkably cheerful and keep going.'

The Leader's speech was always the climax of the conference. 'Our initial thought was to play "Rule Britannia",' says Thomas. 'Let's fly the flag and show the terrorists that you can't bomb away democracy. But on reflection that was the wrong mood: you didn't have to add artificial excitement to help get people excited.' Mrs Thatcher says: 'I decided no organ music at the beginning because it was inappropriate. And I cut out all the highly combative party political parts from the speech.' She also decided not to use the autocue or 'sincerity machine' to deliver the speech. 'The question was not would the Prime Minister be speaking from the heart,' says Thomas, 'but would she be *seen* to be speaking from the heart? It was most appropriate just to let it happen.'

The nation faced probably the most testing crisis of our time, declared the Prime Minister in her speech – the battle between the extremists and the rest. She was talking about the miners' strike; she might as easily have been talking about the bombing. 'We have seen in this country the emergence of an organized revolutionary minority who are prepared to exploit industrial disputes, but whose real aim is the breakdown of law and order and the destruction of democratic parliamentary government.' But, she concluded, 'this Government will not weaken; this nation will meet that challenge; democracy will prevail.' For once her traditional standing ovation mingled tears and cheers in equal measure.

From early dawn the Prime Minister's strength of spirit had been on display to the TV cameras. 'I can think of no other medium than television that could have brought home so vividly to people her character and reaction under such acute stress,' says the former editor of ITN, Sir Geoffrey Cox. A week after the bombing. Mrs Thatcher's ratings in the opinion polls had risen ten points. But she feared that MacGregor's handling of the miners' strike could bring it tumbling back down.

'You have to realize that the fate of the Government is in your hands, Mr MacGregor,' the Prime Minister told the Coal Board Chairman immediately after the Brighton conference. On a visit to Yorkshire later that month, she was forcibly reminded by loyal Tory workers of MacGregor's inadequacy at matching Scargill on television. They implored her to do something about it. MacGregor was taking publicity advice from Tim Bell, the Saatchi and Saatchi Chairman, who was one of the Prime Minister's most trusted television consultants. But beyond suggesting that MacGregor wear light suits so that his dandruff would not show up on camera, Bell found there was little he could do to alter the septuagenarian's screen *persona*.

That October both men privately conceded that the Coal Board's public relations had been a disaster. MacGregor accepted part of the blame and agreed that the Board needed a new spokesman for television. Bell studied videotapes of different Coal Board area managers and recommended the Yorkshire area manager, Michael Eaton. He had a reassuring manner, a Yorkshire accent and blinked less often than others – a low blink rate is thought to be a sign of sincerity on television. Mrs Thatcher approved when her press secretary reminded her that she had met and quite taken to Eaton three years earlier. Meanwhile, Scargill committed his gravest publicity blunder, when it was revealed that he had been soliciting money from Colonel Gaddafi. Public memories of the Libyan shooting of a woman police constable in St James's Square earlier in the year were still fresh.

The strike was beginning to crumble. The Coal Board strategy of offering miners strong financial inducements to return to work, coupled with persuasive newspaper advertisements drawn up by Bell, was beginning to work. On the TV news bulletins each night the number of 'new faces' reporting for work grew. By the start of 1985, it was clear that Scargill had lost. He had long promised General Winter would come to the miners' rescue; instead general disillusion arrived.

The Prime Minister had won a famous victory. She had ignored the received wisdom that no government should ever take on the NUM. There was virtually no public sympathy for Scargill: the opinion polls showed that 84 per cent felt that he had mishandled the strike. At the start of February Mrs Thatcher gave a long interview to Peter Jay on Channel 4's *A Week in Politics* to mark the tenth anniversary of her election to the Tory leadership. She explained why she had called Scargill and his followers 'the enemy within': 'People could see the violence, they knew the intimidation. Oh, they knew, they knew. They were watching it on their screens.'

But the political dividends to Mrs Thatcher from her victory over the miners were by no means as clear-cut as she hoped. Sixty per cent of the electorate had disapproved of the Government's handling of the strike and among her political opponents, Mrs Thatcher's own reputation for strident inflexibility was strengthened. Peter Jay picked up the question of her reported intolerance of dissent. What did she mean when she asked of people, 'are they one of us?' Mrs Thatcher supplied her definition: 'Are they hard-working, do they believe in personal responsibility, do they believe in endeavour, do they believe in the voluntary spirit? Do they believe fundamentally the same philosophy I believe in?'

Three years earlier, the Prime Minister had asked whether Alasdair Milne, then the newly appointed Director-General of the BBC was one of us. Now she had become convinced that he was not. And having taken on and defeated one institution which conventional wisdom told her could not be beaten, she was determined to turn her attention to another: the BBC.

The man she had appointed to succeed George Howard as Chairman of the Corporation of 1983 was proving a severe disappointment. Stuart Young was a millionaire accountant from Mrs Thatcher's Finchley constituency. 'It's great to be Young and even greater to be well-connected,' commented the Opposition Home Affairs Spokesman, Peter Snape – a remark that seemed even more apt the following year when Young's brother David became one of Mrs Thatcher's Cabinet ministers. But Stuart Young was not living up to prime ministerial expectations. When she had first appointed him a BBC Governor in 1981, he had shared her view that the BBC should take advertising. Like Tony Benn and Harold Wilson twenty years earlier, the Prime Minister believed this was an essential means of breaking the power of the monolithic Corporation. In 1984 the Conservatives' advertising agency, Saatchi and Saatchi, had published its own analysis of the case for advertising on the BBC. But the Corporation had lobbied back. Downing Street despaired that Stuart Young had emulated some of his predecessors in the BBC Chair and gone native.

He came out against advertising and to the considerable annoyance of the Government spearheaded a public campaign for a large increase in the licence fee. Young and Milne called a press conference to launch the campaign under the slogan 'the Best Bargain in Britain'. The Prime Minister spoiled its chance of being adequately reported. On the day of the press conference, her press secretary, Bernard Ingham, briefed the Lobby correspondents on the Prime Minister's views of the BBC: over-committed, overstaffed and inefficient, it should no longer be protected from the fresh winds of market forces. Advertising was the answer.

There followed an acrimonious semi-public battle. Young claimed that as an accountant he had fully costed the request for the increased licence fee: the BBC was not spendthrift nor wasteful and every penny of the claim was fully justified. The Government was not convinced. It kept the Corporation on short rations and announced it was setting up an inquiry to review alternative methods of finance. To the fearful BBC it appeared that the Prime Minister was packing the Commission with hired guns. The Chairman was Professor Alan Peacock, a monetarist economist; other members included Sam Brittan, an influential monetarist commentator and brother of the Home Secretary, Leon Brittan. For the conspiracy theorists – and there were many of them in the corridors of Lime Grove and Broadcasting House – it was all pat: the Prime Minister would receive the answer she wanted.

But the Peacock Commission was to take over a year to produce its report. No sooner had it begun collecting evidence than the BBC stumbled into the most bitter of confrontations with Mrs Thatcher. It came over the subject that aroused passions in the Prime Minister that were understandably even fiercer after the Brighton bombing: television's coverage of terrorism. She saw terrorism as armed propaganda and a particularly vivid example of the use gunmen made of the airwaves to promote their cause was on display in July 1985.

The Beirut hijacking of a TWA jet by a Shi'ite Moslem group and the subsequent playing out of the hostage drama on television – with the apparent connivance of the US networks – profoundly alarmed the Prime Minister. America was being held to ransom in prime time through a new form of terrorvision. In a speech to the American Bar Association in London on 15 July, Mrs Thatcher said that terrorist acts made good copy and compelling viewing. The hijacker and the terrorist thrived on publicity. 'They see how acts of violence and horror dominate the headlines and the TV screens and they exploit it.' To rousing applause, she declared: 'We must try to find ways to starve the terrorists of the oxygen of publicity on which they depend.' Later that month it seemed to her that the BBC was supplying free oxygen masks to the IRA. The *Real Lives* affair marked a new low point in relations between the Prime Minister and the BBC and led to the gravest internal crisis in the Corporation's history.

The *casus belli* was a film made by the BBC's documentary department featuring two Ulster extremists, who had both been elected to the Northern Ireland Assembly and to Londonderry City Council. One was Gregory Campbell from Ian Paisley's Protestant Democratic Unionist Party; the other was Martin McGuinness of Sinn Fein, who had reportedly been the IRA's Chief of Staff between 1970 and 1982. As an elected representative of the IRA's political wing, McGuinness had done a number of previous interviews both on BBC and ITV. But *Real Lives: At the Edge of the Union* was a different kind of film. It was made in the 'fly on the wall' style where the participants spoke for themselves; there was no commentary and no challenge to their views from a reporter. The producer, Paul Hamann, believed in giving his subjects plenty of rope. His aim was to show the irreconcilability of extreme views in Northern Ireland; the security forces had co-operated with the filming.

But none of this was known to the Government when the crisis broke. It was sparked off by the Prime Minister's answer to a hypothetical question from a *Sunday Times* reporter. The newspaper had learned about the planned transmission of the programme and asked Mrs Thatcher, who was on a visit to Washington, how she would react if a British TV station – say the BBC or ITV – were to broadcast an interview with a leading terrorist, like the IRA Chief of Staff. Scarcely surprisingly the Prime Minister said she would 'condemn them utterly' and added: 'the IRA is proscribed in Britain and in the Republic of Ireland. We have lost between 2000 and 2500 people in the past sixteen years. I would feel very strongly about it and so would many other people.' The *Sunday Times* had their story and their headline; 'THATCHER SLAMS IRA FILM'. But the ironies were ignored. First, Sinn Fein was not a proscribed organization; second, as an elected Northern Ireland Assemblyman, McGuinness was entitled to a salary from the British Government; and third his previous television interviews as an elected Sinn Fein representative had passed without protest.

Back in London the following day, the Home Secretary, Leon Brittan, took his cue from the Prime Minister. He issued a press statement deploring the planned broadcast and then wrote a public letter to the BBC Chairman, Stuart Young. Brittan began by claiming that as the minister responsible for broadcasting he respected the BBC's independence and would not attempt to censor it; but as the minister responsible for fighting terrorism, he said the programme – which he admitted he had not seen – would materially help the terrorist cause. 'Even if the programme and any surrounding material were as a whole to present terrorism in a wholly unfavourable light,' he added, 'I would still ask you not to permit it to be broadcast.' Recent events had shown that terrorism thrived on the oxygen of publicity. It was a none too subtle intimation that he was speaking with his leader's voice.

Brittan's request had a convulsive effect on the BBC: it split the Governors apart from the Managers. Although the Director-General, Alasdair Milne, was away on a trout-fishing holiday in Finland, his fellow members of the Board of Management watched the film. They unanimously recommended to the Governors that it be transmitted and warned about the effect on the BBC's perceived independence of banning the film.

When the Governors met in emergency session the following morning they were in the deepest of binds. Should they defer to the Prime Minister and the Home Secretary – with the danger of appearing to be bowing to political pressure? Or should they follow the advice of their professional managers and put the onus on Brittan to use his emergency powers to ban the film outright?

It had long been a guiding principle in the Corporation that the Governors should not watch programmes before transmission; to do so would make them *parti pris* and deprive them of their status as independent guardians of the public interest after transmission. Once before the Governors had watched a programme in advance: but *Yesterday's Men* was scarcely the most auspicious of precedents. Yet this time, they felt they had no alternative. Almost all were horrified by what they saw. Led by William Rees-Mogg, the Vice-Chairman and former Editor of *The Times*, they condemned the programme. 'It made the men of violence out to be nice guys, bouncing babies on their knees,' claimed Stuart Young. It was a 'Hitler loves dogs' programme said another Governor tersely. By nine to one they voted to ban the film. There was an immediate storm of protest.

The Opposition parties as well as most of Fleet Street claimed the Governors had kow-towed to the Government. State-controlled broadcasting stations around the world had a field day. Radio Moscow and Libyan radio chortled that the decision proved what they had said all along: the BBC was Thatcher's mouthpiece. The former Director-General, Sir Hugh Greene, said on *Channel 4 News* that it had been one of the most fateful days in the Corporation's history. 'It is a case of giving in to Government pressure. I cannot imagine any BBC Board in the past giving way to such pressure.'

Other critics of the Governors' decision claimed that it resulted directly from Mrs Thatcher's politicization of the Board of Governors. She had not begun the process – Harold Wilson had done that – but she had taken it further than any other prime minister: no previous Chairman of the BBC had a brother in the Cabinet, nor had both the Chairman and Vice-Chairman ever before been known Conservatives – as Stuart Young and Rees-Mogg were. Senior BBC executives saw almost all Mrs Thatcher's other gubernatorial appointees as safe, conservative-minded figures; they instanced the fact that John Mortimer, the playwright, and Moira Shearer, the ballet dancer and left-wing wife of the broadcaster Ludovic Kennedy, had been vetoed by Number 10. As Mrs Thatcher had put in her own choices, the character and mood of the Board had gradually changed. Alan Protheroe, then Assistant Director-General, puts it succinctly: 'The Governors tended to think that if you worked for the BBC you must be a bit of a prick; going to meetings with them had become a kind of ritual crucifixion.' He felt there was now only one Governor with a straightforward set of liberal values, the others were much more hardline. And Stephen Hearst, the former Head of Radio 3 and special adviser to successive Directors-General, says: 'That particular mix of Governors did take the view that the television service was not under proper control and that the producers needed to be reined in. Mrs Thatcher felt the same.'

By chance, the Prime Minister had a long-standing agreement to appear on *Newsnight* on the evening of the Governors' meeting. Had they acted differently, she might not have felt able to keep the appointment. As it was, Mrs Thatcher denied on the programme that there had been any illicit pressure on the Governors, while readily acknowledging they had come to their decision in the light of her own comments. 'I do not believe that any great body like the BBC should do anything which might be construed as furthering the objectives of terrorists. And I feel extremely strongly about it.' Every single person in Northern Ireland had the vote and should reject the bullet and the bomb. She had not seen the film but the IRA was a pro-scribed organization operating against democracy itself. Her interviewer, Donald MacCormick, pointed out that the Provisional Sinn Fein was not a proscribed organization and McGuinness was one of its elected representa-tives. Should the broadcasters put him in quarantine? Mrs Thatcher replied that people like McGuinness had no difficulty in putting their views; they had seats on local authorities, they had votes, if they wished to speak out there were democratically elected bodies in which to do so.

She went on: 'The BBC in my view – because we don't censor, never do, we request – sometimes – should never show things which help anyone who wishes to further their cause by the use of violence. And that is why we said: "have a look at it again". The BBC and the Governors who are ultimately responsible to the public did have a look at it again and have made their decision and I am very pleased with it, and I believe that most people will applaud their decision. But let me make it quite clear: yes, I do say things to the media, I do request them. But I am never going to put censorship on – we are not that kind of Party. But we say, "you use freedom, please recognize your tremendous responsibilities to the continuation of that freedom, and consider that in making your decision." ' *The Times*, no lover of the BBC, commented in a leading article the next day that however much the Prime Minister and the Home Secretary emphasized the absence of censorship, 'Mr Brittan's quasi-dictat is scarcely distinguishable from it.' Aubrey Singer, who had been Managing Director of BBC Television until earlier in the year, put it more bluntly: 'It was de Gaulle who said: "they have the newspapers, I have television": why should Mrs Thatcher have both Fleet Street and the BBC?'

The BBC's much-vaunted independence of government looked even thinner just a fortnight after the *Real Lives* storm broke. The *Observer* revealed that a retired brigadier, Ronnie Stonham, worked inside Broadcasting House in liaison with MI5 to vet all senior journalistic appointments. This came as a surprise to many Conservative MPs who had long seen the BBC as a 'nest of Trots'; they squared the circle by condemning the inefficiency of the MI5 vetting. Milne's public embarrassment at the revelation contributed to the impression that the Corporation was falling apart.

But the BBC was not alone in its troubles: Mrs Thatcher's own party colleagues were reporting growing criticism of her – even from Tory supporters. The dominant issue was her style. The Tories' private polls in the first months of 1985 showed that her popularity had fallen sharply. The majority felt she was out of touch and tended to talk down to ordinary people. Only 21 per cent believed that she understood the problems facing Britain. But according to the BBC's Political Editor, John Cole, 'Mrs Thatcher's own self-confidence as a broadcasting propagandist was unsurpassed.' Certainly she had been both triumphalist and virtually unstoppable in her *Newsnight* interview with Donald MacCormick. 'Yes, let me blow our own trumpet. Highest standard of living ever, highest output, highest investment, highest retail sales, highest ownership of houses, highest expenditure on health, highest number of doctors and nurses, highest amount spent per pupil on education. Please will you remember that sometimes?'

What of the charge that she was inflexible? The Prime Minister's response echoed Senator Barry Goldwater's celebrated view that extremism in defence of liberty was no vice. 'Inflexible? I am inflexible in defence of democracy, in defence of freedom, in defence of law and order and so should you be, so should the BBC be and so should everyone else be.' Would there be any change in her style towards a more compassionate side? 'I know what I would expect of a prime minister,' responded Mrs Thatcher. 'Strong leadership, clear leadership, doing what you believe to be right. That I have done, that I must continue to do. It is the only way I know how.'

The psychiatrist, Dr Anthony Clare, wrote about the interview: 'Given half the chance she would have led poor MacCormick and the camera crew in a chorus of "Rule Britannia" before the credits rolled. She is the most outrageous female performer since Edna Everage, she positively exults in getting whatever Buggins is unfortunate enough to have his turn in the ring and clouting him round the head, and kneeing him in the groin and all the time she smiles that damnable smile.' But the Prime Minister's advisers were growing increasingly concerned about the electoral effects of her triumphalist style. Tory MPs were starting to fear that the Prime Minister was becoming an election liability.

In common with her predecessors Mrs Thatcher was suffering from the fragility of a TV image: like the delicate adjustment of focus on a camera the public perception of a prime minister can subtly alter. Just as the unflappable Macmillan came to appear complacent and out of touch, and the razor-sharp Harold Wilson turned into a gimmicky temporizer, so Mrs Thatcher's celebrated conviction politics began to blur into bossiness and blind faith.

Tory publicity men calculated how they should best counter the charge that the Prime Minister was harsh and uncaring. They arranged for her to visit new hospitals and talk to patients. In September 1985, they invited TV cameras to cover Mrs Thatcher at a home for handicapped children. Her advisers confirmed they wanted to project the Prime Minister's tender side in the period before the next election: but her visits to the injured in hospital following air and sea disasters aroused some misgivings. Hugo Young suggested in the *Guardian* that such missions might be better left to the Royal Family as cynics would remember her image-making forays in the past: 'Nobody who at her handlers' request has adopted as many poses as she has before the cameras can expect the memory of such studious contrivances to vanish when real life makes the pose recur.'

The autumn of 1985 saw another rather different way of softening the Prime Minister's public image. Well before the *Real Lives* crisis, the Downing Street press secretary, Bernard Ingham, had rung the BBC's

Parliamentary Correspondent, Christopher Jones, at his home. Jones had made a reverential television series about the Houses of Parliament called *The Great Palace*. Now Ingham told Jones that Number 10 had first become the Prime Minsiter's official residence in 1735. Would he like to make a film to commemorate its two hundred and fiftieth anniversary? Jones could have the run of the place and film the Thatchers at home in their 'flat above the shop'. Ingham knew the BBC would never knowingly allow an anniversary to go uncelebrated. The resulting programme included a series of prime ministerial charades.

At school Mrs Thatcher had wanted to become an actress; now her ambition was fulfilled. At dawn she was filmed in her kitchen making instant coffee for her breakfast in a black dress with pearls. She did not appear to know where things were kept. 'I have always longed for a really lovely kitchen, which I have never had. I want one with a patio where you can have breakfast.' The Prime Minister revealed details of the frozen foods she cooked to save time in the kitchen – shepherd's pie and lasagne from Marks & Spencer. Later she sat on a sofa going through her list of engagements with a rather grumpy husband. 'Shan't be here – I'm working that day,' growled Denis Thatcher. She was kindness itself to the small children who had come to watch Trooping the Colour from Number 10. Then she helped her staff arrange the place settings for an official banquet. 'Peter, would you fetch my splendid gold salver? We can put it at the end.' The *Daily Telegraph* reported: 'It had all the illicit appeal to viewers of being allowed to eavesdrop on occasions to which most could never hope to be invited.' 'And Mrs Thatcher doesn't look the teeniest bit frazzled by midnight – not fair,' complained the *Daily Mirror*.

The Prime Minister was following the tradition of offering television controlled access to Number 10 in the hope of a sympathetic programme. 'Mrs Thatcher was very co-operative,' said Christopher Jones. He was even allowed to film for the first time the start of a Cabinet meeting. Although ministers had been carefully rehearsed and said nothing of substance, the scene marked a minor break-through in television's coverage of politics. And it seemed that autumn the cameras would gain a rather more significant entrée.

The Prime Minister had long been an opponent of allowing television into the Commons. Now she appeared to have changed her mind. In the first debate she had heard on entering the Commons twenty-six years earlier, the Labour left-wing leader, Aneurin Bevan, had proposed the admission of the cameras, arguing that in a democracy the electors had a right to see and hear what was being done in their name. But this was not the argument that had now appealed to the Prime Minister.

During the summer Mrs Thatcher's publicity advisers, notably Gordon Reece, sought to persuade her that televising the Commons would work to her political advantage. She was more than a match for Kinnock at Question Time and television would show her as the resolute leader standing up to the mindless assaults of the Left. The image of the woman alone at the Dispatch Box putting down the ruffians of the Opposition would be worth half a million votes. In the run-up to a general election she and other ministers would be seen to be making positive announcements while the Opposition merely sniped.

It seemed the Prime Minister was persuaded: the serious newspapers carried stories of her conversion. But Neil Kinnock's performance at the Labour Party Conference that October gave her third thoughts. He was widely acclaimed as having come over brilliantly on television with his speech attacking Derek Hatton and the Militant Tendency in Liverpool. Mrs Thatcher and her Party managers now feared that televising the Commons would provide the Labour leader with a twice-weekly platform at Prime Minister's Question Time that would show him as at least her equal. It was a view Kinnock himself shared. In the week of the debate Michael Jones of the *Sunday Times* reported that Mrs Thatcher told her Cabinet colleagues that she was worried. She felt television might be suitable for big occasions, but feared the Opposition's 'destructive abilities' being relayed to a mass audience.

Although there was to be a free vote, a group of Tory backbench opponents of the cameras organized a last-minute lobbying operation. 'Please do not think you will be helping the Government or the Prime Minister by voting for television,' they wrote to their colleagues and played on anti-BBC sentiment. TV producers were only interested in screening spicy, anti-Govenment footage, they claimed, and instanced the intensive coverage a year earlier of Harold Macmillan's maiden speech in the televised House of Lords. In his new guise as the Earl of Stockton, the former Tory Prime Minister had commended the miners during their strike and condemned Mrs Thatcher's privatization policy as 'selling off the family silver'. On the eve of the debate on televising the Commons, the press carried inspired stories asserting that after uncharacteristic dithering Mrs Thatcher had changed her mind once again and now opposed the cameras. But no one could be certain.

In the debate Mrs Thatcher's estranged predecessor, Ted Heath, argued that although he had sometimes been frustrated and infuriated by television, Britain's was the best and fairest in the world. Televising the House would help to guarantee freedom of the individual by allowing the public to judge what the politicians were really like. But the Labour MP Joe Ashton claimed the cameras would turn Parliament into a political soap opera, trivialized to attract mass audiences. 'It would be reduced to the "Maggie and Neil Show" or "Scrap of the Day" – an everyday story of people having a bash at each other.'

The debate ended in farce. There was a procedural mix-up and the vote had to be retaken. But it became clear from the first division that the Prime Minister had come out against admitting the cameras. 'The word passed quickly to the creeps and sycophants,' said one jubilant Tory anti, who saw a number of his colleagues now following their leader into the 'No' Lobby. The Prime Minister's example and the stirring of anti-BBC sentiment had their effect. The antis won by 275 votes to 263. 'To be perfectly honest, I did it just to kick the BBC in the goolies,' one Tory admitted. Mrs Thatcher smiled broadly at the announcement of the result, as MPs waved their order papers amid scenes of jubilation. She wanted her television appearances to be on her own terms. And a week after the vote her preferred image was on the screen.

Two years after receiving the invitation, Mrs Thatcher had agreed to give an interview to Dr Miriam Stoppard for a Yorkshire Television programme called *Woman to Woman*. the Prime Minister's manner, her make-up and her hair style were all noticeably softer than for a normal political interview. She talked of her humble origins in 'a very small home with no mod cons and an outside toilet'. Highlight of her week was the Saturday morning visit to the library for two new books, one novel and one on current affairs, that she and her father would read and discuss. Occasionally she would sally forth with her mother to buy new settee covers, 'a great experience and a great event'. Later there was marriage to Denis – 'this was the biggest thing in one's life now sorted out' – and then the Miracle of Birth – a phrase she invoked several times.

At one stage the Prime Minister nearly broke down in tears. She was talking about her father, whom she clearly worshipped – 'the best-read man I've ever known, he gave me the education he had never had'. Miriam Stoppard asked what example her mother had set. 'Oh, Mummy backed up Daddy in everything as far as you do what was right. She would say to me: "Your father had a very difficult day in Council standing up for his principles." ' But he was eventually forced to resign from the Council. 'Did your mother protect him?' asked Miriam Stoppard. Mrs Thatcher ignored the question: 'Yes, I remember my father making his speech when he was turned off the Council. Very emotional: "In honour I took up this gown and in honour I lay it down." ' Her eyes moistened. It was a much less prosaic, more affecting version of her father's departure from office than appeared in her numerous biographies.

Much of the press was cynical: 'There was a handkerchief before you could say onions,' wrote Nicholas Shakespeare in *The Times*. 'It would have been more honest to label the programme a party political broadcast and be done with it,' claimed the *Daily Express*. The *Daily Telegraph* was judicious: 'Her performance on camera is likely to be applauded by her admirers as revealing her softer side; her less than iron-clad appearance will have won her new sympathy and be criticized by her detractors as displaying her ability to manipulate a medium she understands intimately.' The programme ended with Mrs Thatcher saying she did not think of herself as the first woman Prime Minister: 'I am still thrilled to be the *person* who is there at Number 10.' But two months later she believed she was in imminent danger of being replaced by another person.

1986 began with the most damaging public row to hit her Cabinet since Mrs Thatcher became Prime Minister. At first, the Westland affair had looked no bigger than a distant helicopter on the horizon. But the whirring blades became so lethal that they cost Mrs Thatcher two of her most prominent ministers and brought her to the brink of resignation. The clash within the Cabinet over the future ownership of a medium-sized West Country helicopter factory escalated into public warfare over the Prime Minister's style of government. Leading the charge against her was the pin-striped Tarzan – Michael Heseltine, the Defence Secretary. For the preceding weeks Heseltine had carried on an increasingly public feud with the Industry Secretary, Leon Brittan. It was not an even match.

The telegenic Heseltine was a skilled media manager, while Mrs Thatcher had moved the less well-favoured Brittan from the Home Office soon after the *Real Lives* affair, partly because he was not good on television. In mid-December Heseltine had defied specific instructions from Bernard Ingham not to appear on a BBC programme: he had given an interview calling for joint European ownership of Westland in direct contradiction to the plan favoured by Brittan and Mrs Thatcher for an American take-over. Over Christmas and the New Year the Defence Secretary continued to ensure the press, radio and television carried his case – to the Prime Minister's growing anger.

At a Cabinet Meeting on 8 January, she sought to silence Heseltine by asking all her ministers to agree that they would offer any planned statements to the Cabinet Office in advance for vetting. Heseltine demurred. 'I must leave the Cabinet,' he said picking up his papers. He paused in the washroom to comb his hair and straighten his Brigade of Guards tie before walking out of Number 10. The press and television photographers who had filmed the Cabinet arriving an hour earlier had all gone for coffee; only a BBC news cameraman was left. 'I have resigned from the Cabinet,' the blond bombshell announced to the camera, 'I will be making a statement later this afternoon.'

In the concourse of the Ministry of Defence, where Harold Wilson had held his sudden resignation press conference ten years earlier, Heseltine produced for the press and television the most damaging indictment of the Prime Minister. He accused her of double-dealing and of autocratically imposing her will on the Cabinet. And he complained about the mysterious leaking to the press of a letter from the Solicitor-General that was highly damaging to Heseltine's case. The leak became a central issue in the affair. It quickly emerged that the letter had been written at Mrs Thatcher's request and leaked by Brittan's ministry with the acquiescence of Bernard Ingham and other Number 10 officials. But what was at issue was the Prime Minister's exact role: whether she had instigated the leak herself and had then covered up.

Investigative journalists desperately sought a smoking gun. Normally anonymous civil servants received brief notoriety as television news programmes identified members of Mrs Thatcher's Number 10 staff. One of them, Charles Powell, confided that he felt like an Arab terrorist when he saw himself freeze-framed and ringed standing behind Mrs Thatcher. For three weeks after Heseltine's resignation, the Prime Minister was shielded from the questions of television and press reporters on her rare forays outside Westminster. Inside the Commons she came under fierce assault and her first long statement on the affair was widely regarded as incredible. It was met by howls and jeers from the Opposition and sullen silence from many of her own supporters.

Leon Brittan resigned and Mrs Thatcher's own political survival seemed to depend on the outcome of an emergency debate called for 27 January. Weeks earlier Mrs Thatcher had agreed to appear on Channel 4's *Face the Press* on what would now be the eve of the debate. It seemed certain she would cancel. But the programme's producer correctly predicted: 'She'll do it, she needs the Shires.' The *Face the Press* presenter, Gillian Reynolds, had consciously decided to 'out-frock the Prime Minister', as she put it, and had brought an expensive new grey outfit. Mrs Thatcher arrived for the interview also in grey: 'Ah we're all colour co-ordinated, I see,' she remarked. 'Yes,' responded Reynolds, 'and you're wearing that nice blouse you wore at the Party Conference.' The Prime Minister looked daggers.

Edgy and drawn, she turned the interview into a filibuster. Refusing to answer almost every direct question on Westland, the Prime Minister insisted that the Commons had to hear first. Her repeated line was that the problems had been caused by Heseltine – he was a member of the team but had not played as a member of the team. If that was the case, why had she not dismissed him earlier? 'If I had done so, you would have been the first to call me bossy boots.' One of Mrs Thatcher's interviewers, James Naughtie of the *Guardian*, said that many people found her statement – that she had not known the details of the leak of the Solicitor-General's letter for sixteen days – hard to believe. 'Truth is often stranger than fiction,' responded the Prime Minister.

It was an apt comment on the most hazardous domestic crisis of her six and a half years in Downing Street. As Mrs Thatcher prepared the following day for the emergency debate, she admitted to a colleague: 'I may not be Prime Minister by six o'clock tonight.' Television carried live sound coverage of the debate – but as is often the case with much ballyhooed Westminster occasions, it turned out an anticlimax. Neil Kinnock failed to rise to the occasion. The Prime Minister produced a judicious statement of regret for the leak and Heseltine jumped up to support her – much to Labour's derision. Michael Foot recalled Churchill's words 'It's all right to rat, but you can't re-rat.' Although the Tories beamed their relief at the ex-Defence Secretary, Westland cost the Prime Minister dear.

Her opinion poll rating fell to 24 per cent. She agreed to give her one major interview of the affair to *Panorama* on 11 February. Mrs Thatcher had learned, according to David Butler and Dennis Kavanagh in *The British General Election of 1987*, that some of her more trusted senior ministers and their wives were talking of the need to replace her. With both her Cabinet and her party in turmoil, her *Panorama* interview was seen as one of the most important television appearances of her career. Her interviewer, David Dimbleby, had worked out a technique which he hoped would be productive. Instead of a combative approach, he planned to incorporate Mrs Thatcher's known response in his questions, hoping thereby to elicit something fresh. It did not work out like that: she tended to repeat the lengthy premise of the question with the result that Dimbleby sometimes appeared less an interlocutor than a friendly counsel.

Mrs Thatcher's line was to play down the significance of the Westland affair. 'It wasn't a crisis of the kind that Falklands was or of the kind that the coal strike was; this was not a crisis in any sense – save that we had two ministerial resignations.' She did not think it had a great effect on her personal authority as Prime Minister, nor did she feel that her style of running the Government would change very much. Was she running short of Cabinet ministers? 'Oh, my goodness me, no, no, no.' She intended to lead the Party into the next election. There was no question of her standing down as Tory leader: she was still walking up the hill and there was quite a long way to go.

The interview marked the return of the self-confident Mrs Thatcher showing all her old resilience, reported the *Financial Times*. At their weekly meeting, the BBC's journalistic hierarchy agreed. Given the battering she had received in recent weeks, said the Head of Radio Current Affairs, John Wilson, her performance had been amazing; if he had to put his money on any leader at the next election, it would go on Mrs Thatcher. Alan Protheroe, the Assistant Director-General, felt that the Prime Minister had shown astonishing self-confidence: she was the classic exponent of the art of deciding beforehand what she wanted to say and then saying it, regardless of the interviewer's questions.

Her *Panorama* interview staved off any immediate crisis of confidence in the Prime Minister. One Tory MP, Sir Anthony Meyer, who was on record as saying he was prepared to support a challenger for the leadership, watched her performance with other backbench colleagues and said he now believed 'the fire had been put out'. But a series of other débâcles immediately followed Westland: the revelation of secret Government plans to sell off Land-Rover to the Americans, the backbench Tory revolt against the Sunday Trading Bill and Mrs Thatcher's decision to back the American bombing of Libya from bases in Britain without consulting the whole Cabinet. The Party Chairman, Norman Tebbit, claimed that Westland and the other controversies were doubly damaging because 'they disappointed the public expectation of unity and competence in Conservative governments'.

In the spring of 1986, the Conservatives were third in the polls behind both Labour and the Alliance. Mrs Thatcher's own rating had fallen to record low levels: in the party's private polls she was identified as at once overbearing and ineffectual. Inside Number 10, the Prime Minister was becoming an increasingly embattled figure, convinced that television coverage was biased against her and even the press had turned sour. It would need little short of a miracle for the Prime Minister to reverse the public perception of her and to win the forthcoming election. But Mrs Thatcher and her media advisers were working on it.

CHAPTER 16

'The TBW Factor'

'In today's world selective seeing is believing and in today's world, television comes over as truth.

Margaret Thatcher, 1986

Margaret Thatcher summoned her senior ministers and media advisers to Chequers on 13 April, 1986, to review the chances of winning the next general election. With the Tories third in the opinion polls and the Prime Minister's popularity rating at its lowest level, her own television image was a central and highly delicate question on the agenda. John Sharkey, the Managing Director of Saatchi and Saatchi, produced the agency's research findings. He began by playing video extracts to the meeting of in-depth interviews with small representative groups of voters on what they thought of Mrs Thatcher and of life in Britain today.

Saatchi had done comparable interviews four years earlier after the Falklands. Then the message was all in favour of Mrs Thatcher's strong leadership. But now, according to Sharkey, 'the findings were only too clear: people felt the Government had lost its way and run out of steam.' The victories over inflation and the trades union bosses were taken for granted. 'With the lack of new battles to fight the Prime Minister's combative virtues were being received as vices: her determination was perceived as stubbornness, her single-mindedness as inflexibility and her strong will as an inability to listen. It was these findings I had to present to the Prime Minister at Chequers – not without some nervousness.' Mrs Thatcher listened, her face setting harder by the minute, as Sharkey pointed out that now she was perceived as the least forward-looking of all the party leaders. 'That went down like a ton of bricks,' recalls one participant. 'But the message was listened to,' says Sharkey, 'the messenger I am glad to say was not shot – at least not mortally.'

Mrs Thatcher was far from pleased with the Saatchi message. But it was confirmed at the following month's local elections as Tories on the doorsteps cited what they called 'that bloody woman' as their reason for defecting. In Conservative Central Office this had become known as 'The TBW Factor'. On TV-am, David Frost was brave enough to put the words direct to the Prime Minister: it led to a memorable exchange.

FROST: Some people talk about 'The TBW factor' . . .

THATCHER: The what? TVW? I've never heard of it.

FROST: I am afraid it means, if you'll excuse me . . .

THATCHER: What? Television?

FROST: Not quite, it means actually – 'That Bloody Woman'.

THATCHER: Oh dear, how dreadful!

FROST: Isn't it awful. But you see they don't tell you these things . . .

THATCHER: They don't tell me. I think they don't tell me because they know it isn't true. And recently I just stopped shouting in the House of Commons at Question Time. And they always make a noise when I get up and I try to make my voice rise over it. And then I thought, well why should I? If you want to hear what I am saying, you can keep quiet. And they say, 'Oh she's softened'. And that's not so at all. I'm just the same as ever I was. What they are cross about is that they've built up an image and now they're cross that I don't match up to the image they've built up.

The Prime Minister reluctantly accepted that interviewers might say the unspeakable to her on television. Her own Cabinet ministers were another matter entirely. The weekend after the local elections, John Biffen, Leader of the House and formerly one of her loyalest acolytes, went on *Weekend World* and committed what might be called *lèse*-Maggiesté. He suggested that in the general election the Conservatives would do better with joint leadership, or a balanced ticket, rather than relying on Mrs Thatcher alone. And he gave intimations of her mortality by saying that nobody seriously supposed she would be Prime Minister throughout the next term. Mrs Thatcher was livid. 'Thinking aloud on television that morning was the end of Biffen,' commented Peter Jenkins. Biffen became an unperson until he lost his Cabinet post the following year. The Prime Minister was feeling herself increasingly beleaguered: the prisoner of Downing Street. She developed the belief that television news coverage, by its very nature, was increasing her unpopularity.

'Television', her press secretary told Lobby journalists at an unattributable briefing that summer, 'suffers from the egg syndrome. All they want is a picture of someone throwing an egg at the Prime Minister. Or one or two boos when she gets out of her car.' Mrs Thatcher built up the critique in a speech to the Conservative party's annual Council meeting, the equivalent of a small-scale party conference. 'Why aren't we better at getting our message across?' asked the Prime Minister and answered her own question.

'We live in a television age and television is selective,' said Mrs Thatcher. 'One camera shot of a pretty nurse helping an elderly patient out of an empty ward speaks louder than all the statistics in Whitehall and Westminster. Never mind that the hospital is being closed because it is out of date. Never mind that a few miles away a spanking new hospital is being opened with brighter wards, better operating theatres and the very latest equipment. In today's world, selective seeing is believing and in today's world television comes over as truth. I remember myself opening a beautiful new hospital. Virtually the only publicity was a demonstration outside – about cuts.'

Saatchis' in-depth research had identified the Health Service, education and unemployment as the three top 'caring issues', on which Mrs Thatcher was seen to be doing substantially worse than the other three party leaders. Her advisers wanted to show that she cared. In a speech to the Scottish Conservative Party Conference in May, she devoted a passage designed for the TV news bulletins to caring. She used the word eight times in one minute. Her opponents were never slow to proclaim a monopoly of care, but caring was what you did, not just what you said: the Government cared about the old, cared about the disabled, cared about unemployment, cared about drug addiction, cared about Britain's world reputation: and it was doing something positive about all of them. 'We need no lessons in care from other parties.' But the Prime Minister was taking lessons in presenting a caring image from her own party professionals.

That August *The Times* reported that the Prime Minister was to be projected in 'a softer and warmer light'. Voters needed to be shown 'the other side of the Iron Lady'. First evidence of the new image came on the BBC and ITN when a King Charles spaniel named Polo was filmed running along a Cornish beach with the Prime Minister in tow. Polo belonged to her Chief of Staff, Sir David Wolfson, in whose seaside bungalow Mrs Thatcher was taking a week's holiday. 'I would love a dog', panted the Prime Minister, 'but my job won't allow it.' Mrs Thatcher's publicity advisers were delighted with the television and newspaper coverage of her canine photo-call; two more dogs would play bit parts in her image-building in the months to come. The effort to present the Prime Minister in her more informal moments as a mellow woman of the people continued that autumn. She agreed to open her wardrobe up to the television cameras.

The writer, Angela Huth, was making a BBC documentary about English women and their clothes. Mrs Thatcher readily agreed to take part. Angela Huth and her producer, Ruth Jackson, were invited to lunch at Number 10 before filming. 'Mrs Thatcher's vitality and enthusiasm on the subject of clothes was astonishing,' says Huth. 'She kept going into the bedroom and bringing out piles of clothes throughout the lunch and arranging them on a rack: "There you are – they are all colour-graded for you." '

In *The English Woman's Wardrobe*, the Prime Minister was seen rummaging through the rack and pulling out different outfits: 'This is what I wore for Polaris . . . This came through the Falklands War all right.' Her thrift and inherited skills as a dressmaker's daughter were also on display. She told how she had her clothes altered to keep them in fashion; several outfits she had been wearing for years. But she always had to think how a dress would come over on television. 'I sometimes have to say "no" because it will look terrible on camera . . . This dress I couldn't wear any more, it looked so blobby on camera.' But underneath, the Prime Minister was just like every other woman: she bought her underwear – 'from Marks & Spencer, of course, doesn't everyone?' According to Alan Rusbridger in the *Observer*, she evidently hoped to come over as 'sympathetic, concerned, ordinary and popular'. Admittedly there was a risk it would not work, but 'by the time snippets of the programme have been trailed *ad nauseam* on breakfast, daytime, dusk and evening telly, you've done a pretty good Saatchi'.

While Mrs Thatcher was seeking to use the media, her Party Chairman approached the problem of the Government's unpopularity in a characteristically hard-nosed way. Norman Tebbit swivelled his guns towards the messengers. In June he announced he was setting up a special unit to monitor all news and current affairs programmes on television for anti-Conservative bias. He was responding, he said, to an overwhelming demand from Tories in the consistuencies. For the previous few months the Party's own newspaper, *Newsline*, had been stoking up the campaign. A typical letter to the Editor attacked 'those Reds at the BBC and ITV, whose bias year in and year out is sickening and frightening'. Another letter on the front page of the paper in June 1986 made the reasons for Tebbit's campaign clear. It came from Miss Beryl Goldsmith OBE; readers were not made aware that she was Tebbit's secretary in the House of Commons.

'Television in particular can win or lose the next election for us because it brings into everyone's home the biased and distorted views of the Left,' wrote Miss Goldsmith. Conservative supporters should jam the switchboards of the TV companies with their complaints: 'Unless these channels are hammered consistently and with absolute determination by us all then we shall carry as great a responsibility as the presenters themselves.' Tebbit promised to produce his Unit's findings that autumn and made clear that his particular target was the BBC. The Tory Chairman believed the Corporation was in the hands of a Marxist Mafia. He joked privately that he did not think there was a conspiracy to do down the Government seven days a week – 'just five or six, and I do not exclude Sundays'.

The Prime Minister shared her Chairman's view. Like her predecessors at Number 10, she had become increasingly intolerant of the alternative power centre she felt the Corporation represented. 'The Thatcher Government regards the BBC as editorially unsound, financially profligate and run by second-rate managers,' wrote Simon Jenkins in the *Sunday Times*. The Prime Minister believed all these ills flourished in the cosy incubation of guaranteed public funding. What Mrs Thatcher had most wanted – and the BBC most feared – when she set up the Peacock Commission in 1985 was the recommendation that the Corporation should take advertising. The chill winds of commercial competition and the disciplines of the market place were to bring the BBC into line.

But, in that respect at least, Peacock was a dead duck. The Commission rejected advertising on the BBC. Its report, published in July 1986, recommended instead that the licence fee be linked to the retail price index for the next decade. This would remove a potent weapon from Mrs Thatcher's hands. The actual or implied threats of successive prime ministers to withhold a licence fee increase unless the BBC mended its ways could be made no more. Even though the BBC argued that costs in broadcasting rose faster than the RPI, indexation would at least offer the Corporation a guaranteed income. Alasdair Milne had won a rare victory. According to one account, the Director-General wore the uncontrollable smile of a man who had shut his eyes, bet the deeds of the plantation on an inside straight and opened them again to see a huge pile of blue chips being slowly shovelled towards him. The BBC congratulated itself on a successful lobbying operation that had been deftly organized by its Director of Television Programmes, Brian Wenham. Admittedly Peacock had also recommended that the BBC should considerably step up its intake of programmes from independent producers over the next decade – and after that subscription or pay-as-you-view should replace the licence fee. But a decade is a lifetime in television. 'We have won on the short-term recommendations and the long term never tends to happen anyway,' exulted one BBC executive. The Government reluctantly accepted Peacock's no advertising proposal and tied the licence fee to the cost of living until 1991. The Prime Minister had other ideas on what should happen after that.

In the meantime, there was a sudden opportunity to influence the Corporation directly. Its Chairman, Stuart Young, died at the end of August. As the Prime Minister considered his replacement, the BBC came under a series of attacks. The right-wing Freedom Association published an allegation from the playwright, Ian Curteis, that the Corporation had dropped a play he had been commissioned to write about the Falklands War, because he refused to portray Mrs Thatcher in an unsympathetic light. Tory MPs and columnists drew the contrast with a drama series that was transmitted: *The Monocled Mutineer*, they claimed, was left-wing, anti-patriotic propaganda. The Prime Minister saw the two cases as further evidence of the need to bring the BBC under control. Her first idea was to replace Young with the Chairman of British Airways, Lord King.

He was her favourite businessman and seen at the BBC as an obsessive profit seeker with no sympathy for the idea of public service broadcasting. One of her confidants informed the Prime Minister over lunch that the Corporation was 'getting its knickers in a twist' at the prospect of Lord King. Smiling at the indelicacy, not something she would normally do, the Prime Minister noted on a card 'BBC – John King – in a twist'. But to the disappointment of both King and Prime Minister, he was not available. Much as he relished the challenge of knocking the BBC into shape, Lord King felt he had to stay on to oversee the forthcoming privatization of British Airways.

Instead Mrs Thatcher appointed Marmaduke Hussey, the former Managing Director of Times Newspapers. His reputation for toughness resulted from his shut-down of the *The Times* for a year in an abortive attempt to curb the print unions. 'Duke' Hussey said he belonged to no political party. Those who knew him well saw him as a high Tory: his wife was a lady-in-waiting to the Queen and the guest list for his annual cocktail party was filled with Palace people. Hussey was a rumbustious, clubbable man, who still suffered pain from the leg he had lost at Anzio: 'Damned stump is playing up'. Mrs Thatcher liked men with a good war record and believed he could bring discipline to the Corporation. The word from Norman Tebbit's office was that Hussey was appointed 'to make it bloody clear that things have to change: he is to get in there and sort it out – in days and not months'. Tebbit immediately began to fill the new Chairman's agenda.

A week after Hussey's appointment, Tebbit laid into the BBC at the Conservative Party Conference. He said his officials had carried out a rigorous examination of a BBC story and compared it to treatment given to the same event by ITN. 'They will be hearing from us soon,' he added ominously. Tebbit waited to deliver his evidence until a libel case brought over a *Panorama* programme, *Maggie's Militant Tendency*, by two Conservative MPs was ended.

For two and a half years Alasdair Milne and Stuart Young had stood by the programme, which had alleged links between far Right organizations and the Conservative party. But the Corporation's commitment to defend *Panorama* seemed to die with the Chairman. Four days into the Court hearing, which was expected to last ten weeks, the Governors ordered the BBC management to settle. The two MPs each received damages of £20,000, plus their costs and a full apology. Roger Bolton, the Editor of

'Mr. Hussey? – with the Prime Minister's compliments, Sir . . .' (Gale, *Daily Telegraph*)

Thames Television's *This Week* and a former editor of *Panorama* – although not responsible for the programme – claimed: 'the BBC got the worst of all worlds. It settled too late to prevent the prosecution from making its case in public, too soon to allow the defence to be heard.' There was Tory jubilation at the BBC's climb-down and calls for the heads of those responsible for the programme from the Director-General's down to the author's.

The following week, with the Corporation's senior executives lying spread-eagled, Tebbit came up with his new charges. In April, America had bombed Libya and Mrs Thatcher's decision to allow US bombers to take off from British bases had been highly controversial and had added to her unpopularity after Westland. Now Tebbit blamed the BBC for having stirred up – or, as his report put it – 'conditioned' the audience against the bombing through a combination of inaccuracy, innuendo, imbalance and uncritical carriage of Libyan propaganda in its news bulletins. The Tory report was put into the hands and on the screen of ITN even before the Governors of the BBC to whom it was addressed had received it. This was, claimed Peter Fiddick in the *Guardian*, 'a gesture of cold spite worthy of Harold Wilson at his Beeb-loathing worst'. While many Tory backbenchers cheered their Chairman's efforts, Tebbit's analysis was rebutted both by the BBC and by eminent individuals such as Lord Denning and William Rees-Mogg; the latter (who had no love for the Corporation) said it appeared that Tebbit wanted to appoint himself as news editor of the BBC.

It seemed that Tebbit's aim was to soften up the BBC in the run-up to a general election. The Liberal leader, David Steel, claimed that the Tory Chairman was seeking 'to suppress criticism of the Government line and to ensure a supine media which backs up Mrs Thatcher, whether she is right or wrong'. Tebbit denied this: his only aim was to get the BBC to live up to the standards it laid down for itself.

In both the libel case and the Libyan controversy, Mrs Thatcher had refused publicly to join in the attacks on the BBC, confining herself at Prime Minister's Question Time to saying they were matters for the BBC Governors. Her previous experience had shown that it was often counter-productive for her to take on the BBC in a frontal assault. Although her determination to cut the Corporation down to size was in no way diminished, for the time being she was playing Miss Nice to Norman Tebbit's Mr Nasty. She was also making a dramatic recovery in the polls, that might have been harmed by too harsh a partisanship on her part.

From its low point in the summer of 1986, the Government's poll rating had been rising steadily and was boosted by the Tory Party Conference that autumn. The theme of the Conference was The Next Move Forward: every minister had been told to produce a positive package of measures and plans. For the first time, Saatchi and Saatchi were involved in staging and designing the conference to give it maximum impact on television; the agency even helped draft ministers' speeches. And Mrs Thatcher was given advice on exactly where to sit on the platform for the best camera angles of her rapt look of attention during her colleagues' speeches. But the successful conference did not by itself account for the turn-round in the Government's fortunes.

The Tories were benefiting from an Opposition that was divided not just into two but many parts. The Alliance had split over defence while many Labour councils did their best to live up to their image in Tory demonology as the 'Loony Left'. Against that a £20 million television advertising campaign was promoting one of the Thatcher Government's central policies. The commercials for the privatization of British Telecom caught the popular imagination and were, in effect, the most expensive party political broadcasts ever. But the central factor in the Government's recovery in the polls was the continuing economic boom. 'The standard of living is higher than it has ever been,' Mrs Thatcher told ITN at the end of November. The Chancellor had even been able to conjure an extra £10 billion for extra spending on health, education and jobs in his autumn statement. For years the Government had been saying that you could not solve problems by throwing money at them but, as Peter Jenkins remarked, this did not apparently apply to general elections.

1987 seemed almost certain to be an election year, with the sensitivities of Number 10 and the broadcasters even more acute than usual. The first clash between the two sides was not long in coming. After hearing the views of the Ministry of Defence, Alasdair Milne decided to drop a film about the secret Zircon spy satellite project. BBC Scotland had made the film as one of a six-part series called *Secret Society;* the presenter was Duncan Campbell of the *New Statesman*, who specialized in embarrassing the authorities over security matters. His film alleged that the Government had illicitly kept details of the £500 million Zircon project from Parliament. Pushed hard in the Commons, Mrs Thatcher eventually admitted: 'the Government prevented the showing of the film' and gave national security as the reason. The front bench Labour spokesman, Robin Cook, claimed it was 'blatant political interference: the reason the Government leant on Milne had nothing to do with security and everything to do with its own political embarrassment'.

To the Government, the Zircon film was proof posititive that under Milne the Corporation was out of control. Mrs Thatcher failed to understand how the BBC could have made the programme at all – let alone use a reporter who, as she put it, 'significantly, works for a Left-wing organ and ferrets out secrets for personal gain' (a fine definition of what any journalist should be doing, claimed the *New Statesman*). But she felt it typical that only at the last moment had the BBC management informed the Governors of the film.

At the end of January, with all the finesse of the Keystone Cops, Special Branch men raided the BBC's headquarters in Glasgow and took away three van loads of documents and film about all six programmes in the *Secret Society* series. Although the aim was to identify the source of the leak to Campbell about Zircon, the raid seemed to show the Government's low regard for the independence of the BBC. 'A shabby, shameful, disgraceful state-sponsored incursion into a journalistic establishment,' fulminated Alan Protheroe, the BBC's Assistant Director-General. And Neil Kinnock claimed the raid was prompted 'by an obsession to save Mrs Thatcher's face'. The Prime Minister indignantly denied that she had a hand in authorizing the raid. But there was no word from Milne. He was Director-General no longer. Two days earlier, he had been unceremoniously dismissed by Duke Hussey, with the approval of the Board of Governors. 'When I heard the announcement, I went catatonic – just froze,' says Alan Protheroe, 'it was a mind-bending experience to realize the Kremlin gets rid of its leaders more elegantly than the BBC.' Milne had received a premonition of his fate six weeks earlier from Mrs Thatcher. At a BBC reception following the memorial service for Stuart Young, she had cut Milne dead.

News of Milne's departure was greeted with unconcealed glee by many Tory MPs. He had been their target since his defence of the Corporation's reporting during the Falklands War. His own ennui with politicians and his habit of finishing people's sentences for them – not always in the way they intended – had not helped him. But no previous Director-General had been subjected to such a continuous campaign of political intimidation. 'The Tory vendetta against the BBC is real and dangerous,' remarked the *Sunday Telegraph*. In the van of the *revanchistes* was Mrs Thatcher. She had appointed Hussey to sort out the Corporation. He had not wasted much time. Ironically Tebbit's attacks over the Libyan coverage had given Milne a stay of execution. But after an interval scarcely long enough to be decent, Hussey had struck. Milne's sacking had no precedent in peacetime; Sir Hugh Greene's semi-voluntary departure eighteen months after Harold Wilson's appointment of Lord Hill was the nearest parallel. With the Governors all by now her appointees, Mrs Thatcher had a greater indirect influence on the choice of the Corporation's next chief executive than any previous prime minister.

In the Commons, a Tory MP asked Mrs Thatcher to support the candidacy of someone 'who could curb the treasonable tendencies of the BBC and with the Herculean qualities to clean up its Augean stables'. The Prime Minister seemed to accept the diagnosis: although the appointment was a matter for the Governors, she was sure that the remarks would be noted in the appropriate quarters. The Board of Governors in turn rejected the most creative figure in British television, Jeremy Isaacs. 'You don't seem like a man who takes kindly to discipline,' one Governor reproachfully told Isaacs at his interview. Isaacs agreed. The Board chose instead the most numerate of the contenders. Michael Checkland mirrored Mrs Thatcher in his modest social origins: the son of a shopkeeper, he had become an accountant after grammar school and Oxford. Asked what he hoped the BBC would be like after his time as Director-General, Checkland responded: 'smaller'. It was an ambition he shared with the Prime Minister but few producers saw it as an inspiring declaration of creative leadership.

Checkland was soon joined by a new Deputy Director-General. John Birt came from London Weekend Television where he had created Mrs Thatcher's favourite current affairs programme, *Weekend World*. His brief was to transform the BBC's political coverage. The Corporation's top management was now in the hands of a DG who had never made a programme in his life and his deputy who many people in Lime Grove believed had never made an interesting programme in his life. Overnight life changed in the BBC. With the odds now firmly on a June election, the

(John Kent)

new mottoes were heads down and safety first. These seemed unlikely to produce much in the way of daring or innovative campaign coverage.

Before Mrs Thatcher announced the election date, both she and Neil Kinnock planned foreign trips to boost their electoral chances. The contrast between the two visits – and the way they came over on the screen – could not have been greater: in the Labour leader's case disastrously so.

Mrs Thatcher's visit was to the USSR. Nearly thirty years earlier, Harold Macmillan's white fur-hatted entry into Moscow had prefigured a British general election campaign. Now another Tory Prime Minister's advisers shrewdly perceived the public relations advantages that *glasnost* offered. Mrs Thatcher had struck up a rapport with Mikhail Gorbachev two years earlier, when he had briefly visited Britain before becoming Soviet leader. 'He is a man I can do business with,' the Iron Lady had announced. Her immediate business was to demonstrate that she was the West's most respected and experienced leader.

The Prime Minister's Russian trip turned into a peak-time television spectacular. Before she arrived, an official at the British Embassy in Moscow admitted that the visit was about pictures: a series of telegenic locations had been arranged. Top of the list were Mrs Thatcher's meetings in the Kremlin with Gorbachev. The official Soviet spokesman claimed there was 'a physical chemistry' between the two leaders – and the television film of their encounters seemed to provide evidence.

In all, Mrs Thatcher had eleven hours of meetings with Gorbachev, culminating in a private dinner with brandies by the fireside at a Moscow villa. The contrast with the occasions when Western leaders would sweat until the last minute as to whether they would even be allowed even to see a top Soviet leader at all could scarcely have been greater. But the visit clearly suited both Gorbachev – who had developed a remarkably sophisticated feel for the media – and Mrs Thatcher.

Away from the official meetings, she made very effective televisual use of her time. Sometimes it almost appeared as if the Prime Minister were fighting a by-election in Moscow North. She shopped for the cameras at a Soviet supermarket, buying local cheeses and rye bread. On a visit to a model housing estate in a Moscow suburb, she used her politician's instincts and plunged into the crowds. Shaking hands enthusiastically, Mrs Thatcher offered a few words in pidgin Russian: 'Ochen priatno' – Pleased to meet you. 'Do svidanya' – see you later. The Muscovites recognized star presence and realized this was an officially sanctioned performance: 'God bless you,' they responded, 'May you live a long time.' Beneath her brown fur hat, the Prime Minister beamed with pleasure.

It was a measure of the change in the Soviet Union that Mrs Thatcher was able to include previously forbidden areas on her itinerary – although she was careful not to push too far. Her attendance at a church service, where she lit a candle at the altar, made powerful television pictures. She also had meetings with the dissident leaders Andrei Sakharov and Josef Begun. In deference to the Kremlin, she would not be filmed with either of them, but Begun came out and told the waiting TV cameras, 'the English people should be proud of Margaret Thatcher'.

Like Macmillan, Mrs Thatcher appeared on Soviet television. But she insisted on being interviewed – 'instead of just looking through a cavernous camera', as Macmillan had nearly thirty years earlier. And she was given not five but fifty minutes. Gorbachev doubtless calculated that a dose of Thatcherite home truths might help him in his Kremlin battles. She in turn backed up his domestic reforms as the most exciting she had heard for a long time – 'fantastic'. Wearing the same blue outfit she had for her speech at the previous autumn's Tory Party Conference, the Prime Minister had done her own make-up and faced three top Soviet journalists. They proved no match for her.

'One at a time, your turn will come,' she instructed the TV troika. 'Why does the West fail to take disarmament seriously?' asked one of her questioners. 'If you take that view why do *you* have so many nuclear weapons?' riposted Mrs Thatcher. As the interviewer sought to reply, she cut him short: 'One moment. You have more intercontinental ballistic missiles than the West. You started intermediate nuclear forces. You have more short-range missiles than us. You have more than anyone else.' The Soviet Union knew that nuclear weapons had kept the peace for forty years and that deterrence worked. 'Doesn't the bully go for the weak person rather than the strong?' Her questioners, like many before them, were reduced to silence.

'After the Central Committee watches that interview', remarked one Soviet journalist, 'there will be training courses in how to conduct TV interviews set up all over Moscow.' The Russians had never before seen anything like it on their screens, claimed the *Guardian*'s Moscow correspondent, Martin Walker: 'Her style, her appearance, her frankness on security matters made her appear like a creature from another planet – and they found her terrific.' Extracts from the interview were replayed on the television news programmes in Britain. The image of the strong leader unafraid to speak her mind came over powerfully.

For nearly a week reports of Mrs Thatcher's triumphal trip led the BBC News and ITN: Muscovites cheered, Cossacks danced, dissidents paid tribute and the Gorbachevs received her royally. The Kremlin had redesignated the Iron Lady – its former hate figure – 'the Lady with Blue Eyes'. It was all a British election campaign manager's dream come true. The *Observer* put it down to her press secretary, Bernard Ingham: 'the Eisenstein of the photo-opportunity had pulled off the big one – the most successful exercise in public relations Downing Street has mounted for years'. Each day Ingham's Number 10 office fed him and the Prime Minister in Moscow a 2000-word summary of British TV and press coverage of the visit. Mrs Thatcher slapped down a BBC reporter who suggested that she was making domestic political mileage out of the trip: 'I am here on an historic mission representing my country – enlarge your view.' But *The Times* reported, 'the Prime Minister got what she came for in election year: as a television show and a contrast to Neil Kinnock's experience in Washington last weekend, it could scarcely be bettered. And Mrs Thatcher looked marvellous in those fur hats.'

The Labour leader's visit to Washington the previous weekend was at best a débâcle. If Mikhail Gorbachev acted as Mrs Thatcher's Moscow campaign manager, Ronald Reagan continued in his role as her man in Washington. The point of Kinnock's visit was to try to persuade the US Administration to take his Party's unilateralist nuclear disarmament policy seriously and to project the inexperienced Labour leader as a man who walked with presidents. Reagan, however, could spare Kinnock less than half an hour of his time: the exact number of minutes became a matter of heated dispute, but shrank to insignificance compared with the eleven hours of the Thatcher-Gorbachev communion. The White House did not even allow the TV cameras to film the two leaders together, which was part of the point of the trip. And Reagan's press secretary produced a disparaging briefing afterwards. Kinnock would have done better to have stayed home in Ealing.

Moscow gave Mrs Thatcher's popularity a substantial boost. The first opinion polls taken after her return showed the Tories at their highest level for three and a half years. 'Mrs Thatcher's Soviet visit seems to have gone nicely from a re-election point of view,' noted her former Number 10 adviser, Ferdinand Mount. Two weeks after her return to England the Tories made full use of the Moscow footage in a party political broadcast. The theme was the country's transformation under Mrs Thatcher. Before she came to power, ran the voice-over, 'we weren't Great Britain, we were second-rate Britain; but in 1979 we chose a leader with the courage to take on the big bosses of the unions and win.' Film of Arthur Scargill was followed by Mrs Thatcher on Soviet television: 'And in Russia we've not been shy to tell the truth. Mrs Thatcher represents the new spirit of Britain – together we share the feeling it's great to be great again.' A fortnight later the Prime Minister called the general election for 11 June and scenes of the Moscow visit featured in her election broadcasts. A montage of Mrs Thatcher's foreign trips, depicting her as the leader the superpowers looked up to, was cut to triumphal music specially composed by Andrew Lloyd-Webber. *The Times* described it as subliminal television: words were superfluous, the images said more and the contrast with Kinnock's lack of experience did not need to be made explicit.

The Conservatives went into the campaign with a winning hand. The tax cuts in Nigel Lawson's March Budget were due to come through in the week before polling day. Earnings were rising nearly twice as fast as prices and most people were much better off than they had been four years earlier. Norman Tebbit seemed to have no doubts about the election result. 'We'll walk it,' he boasted in the House of Commons. It was a view echoed by the Prime Minister in her first television interview of the campaign.

John Cole, the BBC's Political Editor, asked if this was going to be her last election. 'I would hope not, this is only the third time we are asking, there is quite a long way to go.' Mrs Thatcher's sights were clearly set on the millennium. 'We are going to be rather lucky to be living at a time when you get the turn of the thousand years and we really ought to set Britain's course for the next century as well as this . . . Yes, I hope to go on and on.' She was breaking the first rule of campaigning: don't take the voters for granted. The Tories' private polls immediately registered the public's dislike of such hubris and the Prime Minister stated her ambitions noticeably more modestly in later interviews. The campaign turned out to be far from the clear run for the Tories that the final result suggested: there was much doubt, hesitation and pain in Number 10 – and at one stage fear that everything was lost.

Partly this was because of the tension at the top between the Prime Minister and her Party Chairman. Once her favourite, Tebbit had slipped down the ladder of favour. Just before she announced the election date, Mrs Thatcher installed her new 'trustie', Lord Young, in Conservative Central Office to help the Chairman. But she went into the campaign without anyone in the role that Gordon Reece had played in the two previous general elections. The post of Director of Communications was unfilled, as Mrs Thatcher had been unable to accept any of the potential candidates. Reece himself was to take no public part in the campaign, in case Labour sought to make political capital from the fact that he had given publicity advice to the Guinness company, although he was not implicated in the Guinness scandal. Responsibility for the Tories' television campaign was divided between a number of inexperienced hands – with no one in sole charge. But in 1987 television's role in the election was greater than ever.

Rather than covering it, in many ways television *was* the campaign. Mrs Thatcher's day would begin with a dawn viewing. A new video cassette machine had been installed in Number 10 and at six o'clock each morning a half-hour tape of the previous night's election highlights was sent round from Central Office to Number 10. The Prime Minister felt the need to see how she had come over and what she was up against. In 1983, she had found it unnecessary to watch what Michael Foot was doing, as his campaign had been a complete television shambles. But now Labour had geared everything to the cameras. Bryan Gould, the campaign organizer, had been a television reporter and the publicity director, Peter Mandelson, was a former TV producer. Mandelson boasted that Labour's campaign would be better organized than ever and more professional than Saatchi and Saatchi – not that Saatchi, which had lost Tim Bell, its crucial conduit to Mrs Thatcher, any longer enjoyed pride of place in the Prime Minister's esteem.

In Parliament on the day after Mrs Thatcher announced the election, Kinnock challenged her to a face-to-face debate on television. She declined: 'I fear that such a debate would generate more hot air than light.' Labour MPs chanted 'Frit, frit, frit', the Lincolnshire dialect word meaning 'frightened' which the Prime Minister had once used herself to describe Michael Foot. 'The Right Honourable Gentleman will find his own platform,' she went on, 'I shall not give him one.' She was also determined to avoid direct confrontations with voters in the television studios.

Mrs Thatcher wanted to confine herself to appearing with professional interviewers, whom she felt she could handle. Memories of her clash with

Mrs Diana Gould over the sinking of the *Belgrano* on the BBC's *On the Spot* in the previous campaign had not been erased. Central Office turned down invitations to the Prime Minister from *On the Spot* and the *Granada 500*, indicating it would reject similar requests from *Channel 4 News* and the BBC's *Election Call*. The fear was that ordinary electors with their licence to question in ways that television interviewers would not dare might elicit abrasive and seemingly uncaring responses from the Prime Minister.

The image Mrs Thatcher preferred was on *News at Ten* three days after she announced the date of the election. She had given ITN exclusive access to Number 10 for a personal profile. As on the Cornish beach nine months earlier, the Prime Minister had a canine co-star. This time Chancellor Lawson's King Charles spaniel was pressed into service. 'Hello Tigger, lovely spaniel, aren't you?' exclaimed the Prime Minister. As she walked up the stairs of Number 10, the mistress of inconsequential small talk for the boom microphone told her husband: 'It's going to be a lovely weekend by the looks of things'. Then she showed Denis Thatcher a photograph album of her Moscow visit. 'And this is at the Bolshoi ballet – Mr Gorbachev, Mrs Gorbachev. Aah, that was opening the British Trade Centre, we hope to do a lot more trade with them.'

This was the Prime Minister's only special television appearance in the first ten days after announcing the election date. She and her advisers had decided on a late start. 'Three weeks is long enough for a campaign,' said Mrs Thatcher. 'I know that people get fed up to the back teeth with only politics to look at on the television.' Her party's research indicated that she should be used in small doses: she was at once the Government's greatest asset and its biggest liability. Few people were neutral when that familiar face loomed onto the screen. But the Tories' planned sluggishness gave Labour the chance of a flying start to the campaign.

Kinnock believed that television had made him Labour leader and could now make him Prime Minister. Labour had cast aside its old disdain for the techniques of commercial advertising. Peter Mandelson, the chief of publicity, had test marketed the party's new symbol of a red rose as if it were a consumer product. Kinnock's campaign rallies were stage-managed down to the last petal. The Labour leader bounded up the steps to flaunt his youth and his wife. He wanted to project the image of a winner: his arms were either aloft or punching the air like Boris Becker. His campaign tours were organized with the aim of showing him on the screen surrounded by adoring crowds, while the Prime Minister – partly because of immensely tight security – appeared more aloof and distant. Labour sought to present Kinnock and his wife as the perfect couple: idealistic, compassionate and attractive. The Party's first election broadcast exchanged Walworth Road for Madison Avenue.

It might have been called: 'Neil 'n' Glenys: The Movie' – a Vaseline-lensed biography of the Labour leader, with musical accompaniment. The director was Hugh Hudson, who had not only made *Chariots of Fire* but over one hundred television commercials. Hudson understood the techniques of selling and persuasion. His film began with a heart-tugging montage from the Valleys of Kinnock, the young family man, remembering the death of his parents. His surviving relations paid folksy tribute to him. Contrasting images showed the Labour leader smilingly informal in a sweater, speaking with wide green-eyed sincerity, then working statesmanlike behind his large Westminster desk. Kinnock and his wife walked hand-in-hand by a cliff top to the specially adapted sound of Brahms. Older Labour politicos like Barbara Castle and James Callaghan endorsed the Welsh *Wunderkind*. 'There's real steel at the heart of that young man,' said Mrs Castle. Callaghan compared Kinnock to William Pitt who had become Prime Minister at the age of twenty-five and had answered his critics: 'Yes, I know I am young and inexperienced but it is a fault I am remedying every day.' Next came a clip from a conference speech. Why, hyperbolized the Labour leader, was he the first Kinnock in a thousand generations to go to university (a line that was soon to be cribbed by an American presidential candidate). Was it because his predecessors who could sing and play musical instruments, write and recite poetry and make beautiful things with their hands and dream dreams were thick or weak or did not have the talent? 'Of course not. It was because there was no platform on which they could stand.' The violins surged and the last words were Barbara Castle's: 'Neil Kinnock's greatest asset is his youth, because he is bringing a freshness to the sad state in which our society is today. They want someone who will change all that and he has the youth, the vision and the vigour to do it.' The broadcast ended with the caption not 'Labour', but 'Kinnock'.

The programme was nearer to an American presidential commercial than any previous election broadcast in Britain: it made Saatchi's efforts seem old hat. 'As an ad for toilet paper it might have appeared over the top: as a party political broadcast it appeared near revolutionary,' wrote Simon Hoggart in the *Observer*. Kinnock himself pronounced it an 'unremitting success' and decided it should be repeated in response to requests from his own party supporters.

The Tories became seriously worried by the apparent success of the Labour campaign. After the first week Kinnock's personal rating shot up by 16 per cent – admittedly from the very low level it had reached after the Washington débâcle – although his party's rise was much less marked. Mrs

Thatcher launched into the kind of attacks that had been regularly made against her since the arrival of Gordon Reece and the brothers Saatchi. 'Had *I* been packaged in Cellophane and tied up in ribbon, the media would have been the first to criticize me and say that I was being sold like some detergent,' she told ITN. But in an interview after the election with Rodney Tyler she back-handedly acknowledged the effectiveness of Kinnock's campaign. 'We realized that some people weren't actually seeing it was a con. And that's when we had to turn round and show it up. I mean you have a positive duty not to let people get into power on the basis of concealing things. It was the age-old con trick. You present yourself with a nice smile and beautifully turned out and people say "Ahhh, what a nice guy".' The Conservatives had to reveal, said the Prime Minister in a speech during the campaign, 'the reality behind the soft sell and the tinsel image'.

The Tories' television counterblasts used the same manipulative techniques as Labour, although the emotion they tapped was fear. One Conservative election broadcast produced, in the *Daily Mail*'s description, 'a blood-curdling picture of the hard Left crouching like an alien beast in the wings ready to dethrone Kinnock in the event of a Labour victory'. It featured Bernie Grant, Ken Livingstone, Arthur Scargill *et al.*, complete with unflattering pictures, doomy music and damaging quotes. In their workers' revolution, the police, the Army and the Royal Family would be the first victims. Another broadcast made freedom its main theme. While Labour had brought in Brahms, the Tories enlisted Gustav Holst. 'I Vow to Thee My Country' provided the sound-track for none too subtle intercutting of Battle of Britain spitfires with Nazi rallies and Mrs Thatcher with miners' picket lines. The broadcast ended with the Union flag flying as the music swelled over the slogan: 'It's Great To Be Great Again'. 'Mrs Thatcher is claiming credit for winning the Second World War,' mocked the SDP leader, Dr David Owen.

The clear message of the Tory broadcasts was that Labour would leave Britain undefended: a charge that Neil Kinnock knew from his Party's private research he had to defuse. Yet on television he provided the Conservatives with even more potent ammunition than they could lash up in an editing suite.

In the TV-am studio early on Sunday morning, 24 May, David Frost asked Kinnock if his unilateralist policy did not face Britain with the choice between extermination or surrender. That was the classical choice, agreed Kinnock, but he claimed the only way out was 'to use the resources you've got to make any occupation totally untenable'. He did not spell out how. But his opponents soon filled the gap for him. 'We've struck gold,' exclaimed Norman Tebbit when he read the transcript of the interview belatedly provided by the media monitoring unit at Conservative Central Office. Saatchi and Saatchi produced their most telling poster of the campaign: a soldier with his hands held up in surrender captioned 'Labour's Policy on Arms'. For three successive nights, attacks on Kinnock's policies led the TV news bulletins.

First came Mrs Thatcher's contemptuous dismissal of Kinnock's 'policy for defeat, surrender, occupation and finally prolonged guerrilla fighting'. Next day from across the Atlantic, Mrs Thatcher's partner-in-arms did his bit. In an interview with ITN, President Reagan talked of Kinnock's 'grievous error'. On the third day Mrs Thatcher reinvoked the Falklands Factor. Kinnock's was the policy of the White Flag. 'During my time in Government White Flags have only once entered our vocabulary. That was the night at the end of the Falklands War I went across to the House of Commons to report "the White Flags are flying over Port Stanley". That signified the victory of our troops over the army of occupation.' A Labour Party survey after the election identified defence as one of its principal vote-losers.

Although David Owen produced the most telling crack against Kinnock's defence policy – 'he wants Dad's Army back and Captain Mainwaring's return to the colours' – it did little good to the Alliance, which was itself publicly split on defence. The election campaign had begun with many predictions that the Alliance would finish in second place to the Tories and perhaps hold the balance of power. David Owen's and David Steel's original campaign strategy was always to appear together on television: the aim was to present a perfect picture of unity. It did not work out like that. 'We are not a Tweedledum and Tweedledee act,' admitted Steel, who believed they came over looking like two garden gnomes. In mid-campaign the two Davids decided they should appear separately, but it was too late. The voters had little idea of what the third force stood for and seemed to prefer a straight choice between Labour or Conservative to the twin hosts of the half-way house.

Both the Alliance and Labour had followed the Tories' 1983 example and set up their own media monitoring units. By polling day each party had amassed 500 four-hour tapes. Throughout the campaign the parties kept up steady pressure on the broadcasters for control of the election agenda: which spokesman should appear and what issue would they discuss? Most politics on television requires a degree of complicity – studios need bodies, reporters need film, so politicians try to set terms for their participation. Sometimes in the 1987 campaign, the party leaders found they were pushing at open doors in seeking to mould television coverage to their liking. At his morning press conference a week before polling day, Neil Kinnock brought up the case of a ten-year-old boy prevented from having a vital hole-in-the-heart operation by Health Service cuts. The lunchtime news bulletins carried moving interviews with the boy and his family. The Labour party had provided the boy's name and address in advance and the TV crews had completed their filming before Kinnock had spoken. A comparable event came the next day when the BBC and ITN were invited to film the Prime Minister on her campaign bus.

As filming began, Mrs Thatcher took up the telephone and appeared to be hearing for the first time some very good news. Putting the receiver down, she announced to the cameras that she had just heard of the release of a British diplomat who had been kidnapped and held by militants in Iran. In fact she had received the news some time earlier and her telephone conversation was play-acting – to the bemusement of the Central Office secretary on the other end of the line. But after eight years at Number 10, Mrs Thatcher knew that television producers love 'natural prime ministerial sound'. This had been a key element in the 'photo-opportunities' which she and Gordon Reece had introduced to British election campaigns. Eight years on, the Prime Minister was still regularly putting on her hard hat and her white coat. One highlight of her election tour was a visit to a training school for guide dogs for the blind to have her face licked by an Alsatian. It was an evident attempt to play up her human side and Kinnock's organizers quickly arranged a similar visit for the Labour leader.

While the overall purpose of Thatchertours '87 was to show 'the regeneration of Britain', Kinnock's photo-opportunities were geared to providing the television news bulletin with pictures to illustrate Labour's theme for each day. On Health Service day, he would have breakfast with nurses: on pensions day he would dance with residents of an old people's home. 'No words here,' his press secretary Patricia Hewitt would say to the disgruntled writing journalists. Newspaper reporters travelling with the Prime Minister fared little better. 'Could we have the camera crews and photographers on one bus and the people who just write go on the other,' one of Mrs Thatcher's tour organizers would request less than tactfully. The grim demands of security made the Prime Minister more restricted than ever to pre-arranged events and rallies staged solely with the eye to how they would appear in the living room. The campaign styles of both party leaders reinforced television's tendency to depict general elections as gladiatorial contests – as did Labour's decision to concentrate much of its attack on the Prime Minister personally.

One Labour election broadcast featured a man suffering from the same painful hand condition as the Prime Minister had the previous year. 'It's known as Dupeytren's contracture, but you could call it Thatcher's contracture,' said the man. He had been waiting five years for the operation that she had immediately had privately: the camera showed his finger had set rigid into a hook. 'How can Mrs Thatcher say the Health Service is safe in her hands, when she doesn't trust her hands to the Health Service?' asked the voice-over. Labour's campaign organizer, Bryan Gould, admitted that one of his main aims was 'to make the Prime Minister wobble'. He succeeded. Mrs Thatcher became increasingly unnerved by the Labour attacks on her. Much as she disliked to acknowledge it, she was politician enough to recognize the potential strength of 'the TBW Factor'.

Until the last week of the campaign, Mrs Thatcher was far from the commanding figure she had been in 1983. She sought to avoid giving any intimations of mortality to the viewers and put on her glasses as rarely as possible in public. This meant having to dispense with her 'sincerity machine', as she now had difficulty in reading her speeches off it without them. Most of the celebrated 'gaffes' in the Tory campaign were hers – from her opening 'on and on' interview to her pronouncement that she had private health insurance to enable her to go to hospital 'on the day I want, at the time I want and with the doctor I want'. For much of the campaign the Prime Minister was suffering from a painful and enervating tooth abscess and, in a rare admission to journalists travelling with her, she said: 'I have been under considerable strain, sometimes.' Mrs Thatcher had also been at odds with Norman Tebbit.

'I cannot be expected to be Prime Minister, leader of the Party *and* Chairman of the Party at the same time,' she complained. Although the Tory position in the polls remained remarkably steady, the odd poll showed Labour closing the gap. The Prime Minister took to consulting advisers from her previous election triumphs: Gordon Reece, Tim Bell and Cecil Parkinson. Mrs Thatcher described them as 'my communications group in exile', while Tebbit privately likened them to a buzz of courtiers round the Queen each vying with the other to say, 'I bring bad news back from the front.' The worst news came on 4 June, the day that Tebbit calls 'Black Thursday'.

With just a week to go before polling, Gallup showed that Labour had narrowed the gap to within four points of the Tories. Suddenly the fearful spectre loomed of Prime Minister Kinnock and Chancellor Hattersley. At a series of crisis meetings between Mrs Thatcher and Norman Tebbit's campaign team, much blood spilled on the carpets at Central Office and Number 10. 'She was highly emotional, not at all her usual rational self that day,' says one Cabinet member drily. The Prime Minister complained bitterly of the Tories' lacklustre campaign and called on Saatchis to rework their advertisements for the final week.

Mrs Thatcher was particularly concerned at Labour's depiction of herself as 'uncaring'. It was agreed that her final election broadcast should include a lengthy extract from her 1985 conference speech, where she stressed her compassion for 'the child crying for help, the elderly couple in need of protection and the youngster hooked on drugs'. Accompanying violins would heighten the message. The Prime Minister also decided that she would make an unprecedented series of television appearances in the last week and show by what she said that she did care. She finally accepted invitations to answer questions from viewers on the BBC's *Election Call* and on *Channel 4 News*, in addition to four other long interviews she had already agreed to give. But she did not look forward to any of the programmes.

'Do I enjoy television broadcasting?' Mrs Thatcher asked rhetorically in an interview at the end of the campaign, 'in retrospect, sometimes, yes: but in prospect, I'm – one doesn't have nerves of steel, you know – one is frightened to death that one won't do as well for your cause as you should. Frightened isn't quite the right word to use. You are very anxious to do the best for everything you believe in and worried you might not do justice to your cause.' The Prime Minister was distinctly on edge before the first of her series of interviews in the last week of the campaign – with Jonathan Dimbleby on *This Week*. When Mrs Thatcher came on to the set she insisted that the table placed between herself and Dimbleby be removed. But on air, she produced a confident performance. Often she turned the questions back on her interviewer – as when he put it to her that the majority of people could not afford private health insurance. 'What I think you are saying, Mr Dimbleby, is that if everyone can't have it, then no one shall have it. If you take that view there'll be no progress at all. That's the Socialist – it's the Communist argument.' As she left the studio, the Prime Minister was asked what she felt about such interviews. 'I hate them, I hate them, I hate them,' was her fervent response.

Mrs Thatcher had been deliberately kept away from the television studios in the early stages of the campaign. But, to blunt the attacks on her as harsh and uncaring, she now decided to admit her faults more often on the screen in five days than she had the previous eight years. 'I think I must have made quite a lot of mistakes. I'm just as human as anyone else. I too make mistakes,' she told a panel of voters from marginal constituencies on *Channel 4 News*. They gave her a hard ride. 'Could I *just* say one more thing,' Mrs Thatcher pleaded at one stage in the tone of a plaintiff seldom allowed to utter in public. But the audience roared back 'No'.

Mrs Thatcher was noticeably gentler with voters than with professional interviewers. On *Election Call*, according to *The Times*, she answered as if she were narrating a pleasant children's bedtime story. 'We have Mr Ariza of Surbiton on the line,' announced Robin Day. 'Good Morning, Mr Ariza of Surbiton,' beamed the Prime Minister, as if he were as familiar a figure as Mr Bun the Baker. When the ordinary voter bluntly interrupted to challenge the Prime Minister's familiar statistics on Government health spending, she responded sweetly: 'I don't want a shouting match. I have that every Tuesday and Thursday in the Commons.'

The Prime Minister saw her interview with Robin Day on *Panorama* as her most important chance to influence the voters. It was to be recorded at lunchtime on 8 June and she had arranged to have a massage and go early to bed on the night before it. But that did not happen as she was up until midnight recording her last election broadcast. Written and re-written by many hands, including the co-author of *Yes, Prime Minister*, Anthony Jay (knighted six months later), Tim Bell and Sir Ronald Millar, it proclaimed the election was about 'the heart and soul of Britain'. The Prime Minister said she wanted to appear 'homely': only after fourteen takes was she satisfied.

Mrs Thatcher arrived for her *Panorama* interview the next morning armed with newspaper headlines from the winter of discontent in 1979. To the charge of having divided the nation, she brandished the headlines at the cameras. The greatest division this country had ever seen was under a Labour Government. The trade unions were holding the country to ransom. 'You want division, you want conflict, you want hatred – there it was. It was that which Thatcherism tried to stop.' Day vainly tried to put a question but the Prime Minister ploughed on. Eventually he objected: 'This is not a party political broadcast. It must depend on me getting a question in occasionally.' 'Yes, indeed,' she responded graciously, 'but you asked what I know you call "the gut question".'

What of the accusation that she was insensitive to the needs of ordinary people on the Health Service? 'No, along with five million other people, of whom I know many are in the media, I pay my way for private health . . . I pay three times: I pay my whack in taxes, I pay personally when I go to a doctor and I also forgo 20 per cent of my salary which falls back into the Treasury.' Day asked how she reacted to the charge that she was a hard woman, uncaring and out of touch with the feelings of ordinary folks? It was a measure of how damaging the Prime Minister had found Labour's attacks on her that she now cited her own private work for charity. 'Denis and I spend a great deal for our own favourite causes – my own the National Society for the Prevention of Cruelty to Children'. It was not something Mrs. Thatcher had ever mentioned publicly before.

Her performance on *Panorama* delighted her campaign advisers. John Sharkey, the Managing Director of Saatchi and Saatchi, said he would never forget it. *The Times* agreed, calling it the most effective appearance by any politician in the whole campaign. 'If you missed the show but can happen on a record of Marlene Dietrich in the Café de Paris in 1955, you may get the feel of it,' wrote Allan Massie, 'the real stars have real authority. It would not convert those for whom she is She Who Must Be Obeyed and the Wicked Witch of the West rolled into one, but it must have stiffened a few sinews and brought thousands of the faint-hearted back into the fold.'

The Prime Minister said after the campaign that she believed the concentrated blitz of media interviews in the last week was the single most important weapon in the Tory victory. 'From the time of the Jonathan Dimbleby interview onwards, that was when the tide turned. Those interviews were the most influential thing of all.' But there was one interview that had greatly worried her.

It was her eve of poll encounter on *BBC News* with David Dimbleby. In three different ways he asked about her image and why she did not show more sympathy for the unemployed and the underprivileged. What mattered, she responded, was what you did rather than what you said. Rehearsing the Government's record, the Prime Minister made great play with the defeat of 'the militant wreckers' who had engineered the coal strike. And she summed up with a phrase that produced by far the most revealing exchange of the whole election campaign: 'But please, if people just drool and drivel that they care, I turn round and say: "Right, I also look to see what you actually do."'

DIMBLEBY: Why do you use the words: 'Drool and drivel that they care'? Is that what you think saying you care about people's plight amounts to?'

MRS THATCHER (*after a pause*): No, I don't. I am sorry I used those words. But I think some people talk a great deal about 'caring' but the policies that they pursue – and I am sorry I used those words – do not amount to what they say.

DIMBLEBY: Mrs Thatcher, it's a personal question but a political one as well and perhaps you have just embodied it by the way you put that and then withdrew it. Isn't one of the difficulties for the Tories that your way of governing and talking about government gets up the nose of a lot of voters?

MRS THATCHER: Well, I am sorry if it does, it's not intended to. I am very sorry if it does.

Dimbleby ended the interview by asking if there were any lessons the Prime Minsiter had learned in the campaign. 'Perhaps you have taught me one,' she responded contritely, 'it's not enough actually to do things which result in caring, you also have to talk about it.'

The interview had been recorded at ten in the morning and the Prime Minister walked out of the Central Office studio bitterly angry with herself and convinced that the BBC would make the most of it. Tebbit shared her concern. Dimbleby hugged himself: it had been exactly the kind of magic moment that most professionals feel television is about. As Dimbleby himself had defined it at the start of election: 'You've got somewhere a revealing moment when the viewer sees something unexpected – a train of thought, a reason for a policy, the gut instinct that lies behind it, an attitude to society.' The interview fulfilled all four of these criteria. Dimbleby rang to communicate his excitement to the hierarchy at *BBC News*. But the management decided to keep the interview in the can for as long as possible to minimize its impact on the election campaign.

It did not run on the *One O'Clock News*, nor on the *Six O'Clock* but only on the *Nine O'Clock*. The argument was that in the early bulletins there was no room for the whole interview and there was no way of balancing the clip with comparable extracts from the other party leaders: there were no comparable clips. So the Prime Minister was buried deep within the *Nine O'Clock News*. Her interview went out as the last item of a fifty-minute programme – too late for Opposition comment. Mrs Thatcher, who had expected the BBC to make much more of the exchange, was delighted. It seemed that the browbeating of the past year had worked. The Prime Minister rewarded *BBC News* with the first long interview after the campaign: in previous elections this had been given to ITV. She came to the studios, ended the interview with the words 'my pleasure' and stayed for lunch.

The drool and drivel incident apart, Mrs Thatcher had come back strongly on television in the last week of the campaign. She benefited from the paradoxical impression that she gave viewers: most found it difficult to like her or feel that she cared. But they grudgingly admired her as the strong leader who said what she meant and delivered the goods. Living standards were unprecedentedly high and the Conservatives won the election by a majority of over a hundred. Labour's campaign, which had started so powerfully, fell apart under pressure. The glossiness of Kinnock's presentation seemed counter-productive in the end as Labour's opponents effectively depicted his policies as impractical, hypocritical or extreme. 'The electors can smell a dead rat whether it is wrapped in a red flag or a bunch of roses,' was Norman Tebbit's characteristically douce verdict.

At three in the morning after the election, Mrs Thatcher told her staff inside Central Office: 'You can have a marvellous party tonight, clear up tomorrow and on Monday we have a really big job to do in the inner cities. Politically we must get right back in there because we want them, too, next time.' That autumn the Prime Minister paid a series of visits to inner-city areas, which had been conspicuously absent from her campaign itinerary. After strolling across an industrial wasteland for the cameras in Cleveland, the county with the highest unemployment in Britain, Mrs Thatcher, told reporters that she had 'no easy, quick magic wand'. The hat trick of election victories had given new assertiveness to her television style. The normal conventions of interviewing were stood on their head: she asked the questions. When the BBC news reporter in Cleveland wanted to know if private rather than public capital really was the key answer to unemployment, Mrs Thatcher demanded: 'How else are you going to do it? Now just tell me. How else are you going to create jobs?' By Government investment? volunteered the reporter. 'And where does Government investment come from? Come on, let's work it through.' As the reporter vainly tried to put another question, the Prime Minister interrupted him: 'No, no, no, no. It comes from taxing successful industry and commerce – tell me any other source.' But the Government was spending millions for instance on the unemployed. 'Yes indeed, what do you want me to do, leave them without any income? Now I asked you a question, because you are asking facile questions of me. I want to get at the truth.' It was all in marked contrast to her humility on the screen during the last week of the election campaign.

In his first interview with the Prime Minister after the election, Robin Day returned to the 'on and on' theme. Did Mrs Thatcher intend still to be Prime Minister at the turn of the century, a youthful seventy-five in the year 2000? 'You never know. I might be here; I might be twanging a harp.' Before that happened, the Prime Minister had great plans for twanging the terrestrial television authorities.

For a change, ITV was first in line. On 20 September, the Prime Minister held an unprecedented seminar at Number 10 with the heads of all the ITV companies and the BBC as well as television industry experts. Michael Grade, John Birt, Jeremy Isaacs, Paul Fox and a dozen others faced the Prime Minister, the Home Secretary, Douglas Hurd, and the Industry Secretary, Lord Young. The Chancellor, Nigel Lawson, puffed his way into the meeting in the Cabinet room after it had started. 'Those who come from the nearest place always seem to be late,' remarked Mrs Thatcher.

The Government was planning new legislation radically to change the structure of television in Britain: the ostensible aim of the meeting was to consult the industry. But the ITV executives reeled under a prime ministerial onslaught. Television, she told them, was 'the last bastion of restrictive practices in British industry'. She focused on the ITV trade unions' so-called 'Spanish customs': overmanning, ghost workers, rigid demarcation and huge overtime payments – a replica of pre-Wapping Fleet Street. Like many politicians, the Prime Minister saw more television crews than she saw television. She had not failed to notice the disparity between the numbers that came to interview her from ITV compared with American television: 'a long crocodile files in, while the Americans do it with a two-man team'. Mrs Thatcher urged the ITV executives to purge the industry of irresponsible union practices. And a few months later, to encourage the management of TV-am to break a strike by ACTT technicians, the Prime Minister gave the station an interview, which the management transmitted itself.

'Stand up for free enterprise, Mr Isaacs, won't you,' Mrs Thatcher had told the new head of Channel 4 at a Downing Street reception to mark its launch in 1982. Five years on, a quarter of the channel's output came from newly formed small independent production companies. As Isaacs himself put it: 'Channel 4 has released market forces so dear to the Government's heart. Mrs Thatcher, whose government brought us into being, plainly knew much more than I did of what was to come.' But at the 1987 Downing Street meeting Mrs Thatcher berated the ITV companies for obstacles they were creating for the independent producers seeking access to their network. 'I don't want the big boys threatening the little boys,' said the Prime Minister. 'I urge you to embrace competition.' The clear message was that if they failed to do it voluntarily the Government would do it for them.

All the Prime Minister's free-market instincts were to open British television up to competition from extra broadcast channels as well from cable and satellite. She had been advised and accepted that advances in technology meant there could be as many as thirty different channels available within ten years. But at the Number 10 meeting there was an evident contradiction between what could be called the Milton Friedman side of Mrs Thatcher's brain and the Mary Whitehouse side. Although she welcomed the prospect of free competition, she was also concerned that the viewers might face an unrestricted barrage of sex and violence. 'I must say there is too much violence on television,' she had said earlier in the year. 'I believe that watching this night after night on the TV screen – though the TV people will tell you there is no evidence to support this theory – *must* have some effect on young people: they will imitate.' The indiscriminate gunning-down of civilians by Michael Ryan in Hungerford the month before the Downing Street meeting had intensified the Prime Minister's convictions.

'I am a regulator,' she told the broadcasters, 'it is the Government's duty to restrict too much violence and pornography. We must get the framework right.' The Prime Minister forcefully suggested that advertisers who supported pornographic or excessively violent programmes beamed on to British television screens should face criminal prosecution. When Michael

Grade pointed out that too narrowly legalistic a definition of violence would make those who transmitted *King Lear* potential criminals, Mrs Thatcher did not demur. Gloucester's eyes being gouged out on a television set six feet away was also a problem, she said. As well as legal controls, she said, there should be a new Broadcasting Standards Council.

The Downing Street meeting lasted three hours and the TV executives stayed for lunch. It was clear that television faced its biggest ever shake-up. The old relationships between Number 10 and the duopoly of BBC and ITV would be radically altered. The Prime Minister was herself chairing the Cabinet Committee preparing the legislation. Sir Denis Forman, Deputy Chairman of Granada, wondered about the Government's true aims. 'Political intervention can always be justified by high motives – to end a monopoly, to shake up an industry, to give the advertiser a fair break – but it is just possible the purity of intent may sometimes have in it the smidgin of another motive: desire for revenge, to get even with those insufferable broadcasters and at last to silence their ill-informed and biased criticism.'

The gulf between the Prime Minister and the broadcasting organizations was very publicly on display in the spring of 1988. At an IRA funeral in Belfast two British Army corporals had been dragged from their car, beaten by the Republican mob and then shot to death. Both BBC and ITN had shown the early part of the attack, and the murders caused a wave of anger and revulsion in Britain. In the hope of identifying the killers, the Royal Ulster Constabulary asked the broadcasting organizations to hand over any untransmitted film they had. Both the BBC and ITN refused, saying that they had no film of an evidential nature and it was their firm policy not to hand over untransmitted material to the police. To do so could brand camera crews as informers and put their lives at risk. The refusal outraged Tory MPs: 'the BBC has sunk beneath contempt,' claimed one backbencher and at Prime Minister's Question Time on 22 March, four days after the murders, Mrs Thatcher declared: 'Either one is on the side of justice in these matters or one is on the side of terrorism.' Everyone, including the media, had 'a bounden duty to do everything that he could to see that those who perpetrated the terrible crimes that we saw on television and that disgusted the whole world are brought to justice'.

In vain did the broadcasters argue that it was the very presence of the cameras which had allowed the crimes to be seen on television and if the broadcasting authorities were seen as an extension of the RUC video unit, then the only filming would be what the security forces or the terrorists allowed. Television would then lose the ability to report what was happening in Ulster. The following day RUC officers arrived at the BBC and ITN offices in Belfast and threatened senior executives with arrest unless they handed over the film. They did so. Mrs Thatcher announced that she was satisfied with the outcome. But an even sharper clash with the television authorities the following month left her incandescent with rage.

On 28 April, Thames Television planned to put out a programme called *Death on the Rock*. It was a *This Week* investigation into the shooting in Gibraltar some seven weeks earlier of three IRA terrorists by the SAS. The terrorists had been planning to blow up British soldiers and civilians at a Gibraltar military ceremony. At issue was the Government's account of the shootings. Sir Geoffrey Howe, the Foreign Secretary, had told the Commons that the terrorists had been shot dead rather than arrested because they appeared to be going for their guns when challenged. Mrs Thatcher indicated that there was no need for an inquiry beyond the normal inquest and the soldiers were to be congratulated. She seemed to be expressing the gut feelings of most people in the country and the Government had basked in the glow of a job well done. But some uneasy questions had remained: was Sir Geoffrey's account complete and accurate, or had the Government decided to fight terror with terror and operate an undeclared shoot-to-kill policy? *This Week*, now edited by ex-*Panorama* editor Roger Bolton, promised 'startling new evidence' on exactly how the terrorists met their death.

Mrs Thatcher, recalling the storms over Bolton's previous Northern Irish programmes, feared the worst. Two days before the planned transmission, she encouraged Sir Geoffrey Howe to lean heavily on the IBA. Although Government lawyers had failed to find any grounds for an injunction against the programme as the British courts' jurisdiction did not extend to Gibraltar, the Foreign Secretary sought to stop its transmission. On the telephone to the IBA Chairman Lord Thomson, Sir Geoffrey insisted the programme could prejudice the inquest on the IRA bombers due in Gibraltar at a date not yet fixed.

Lord Thomson, a former Labour Cabinet minister, claimed later that in his nine years at the IBA he had never been put under such pressure by the Government: but he resisted. He and his top officials watched the programme, then gave Thames the go-ahead. *Death on the Rock* flatly contradicted the Government's account. The reporter Julian Manyon and producer Chris Oxley had come up with new eye-witnesses undiscovered by the Gibraltar police. One of them claimed the terrorists were shot with their arms up in surrender. *This Week* saw Mrs Thatcher's hand behind the SAS operation: she was shown vowing after the Enniskillen bombing the previous autumn that there could be no hiding place anywhere in the world for the IRA and, ran Manyon's commentary, 'she must have had on her desk the details of how an IRA unit had been detected in Spain'.

The programme caused the Tory party to erupt into fury. Jerry Hayes, a normally restrained backbencher (who lists one hobby in *Who's Who* as 'slumping in front of the TV with my wife'), accused Thames of 'raking through the gutters of Gibraltar to find people to rubbish our security forces'. And Sir Geoffrey Howe claimed the transmission was 'a gross and wholly improper thing to do': it could 'contaminate' the evidence before the inquest. Lord Thomson responded that the IBA did not believe the programme would prejudice the inquest and to have shelved it would 'have given the terrorists even more oxygen of publicity'.

The Prime Minister was less than delighted to hear her own phrase turned against her. She was officially described as being 'beyond anger'. In a television interview on the day after transmission Mrs Thatcher said, 'It's not a question of being furious – it is much deeper than that. The freedom of people depends on the rule of law and a fair legal system. The place to have trials is in a court of law. If you ever get trial by television or guilt by accusation, that day freedom dies.'

In Lord Thomson's view the Government was 'going overboard about the programme, as they had done on other things. It is not trial by television at all. That's a fallacious phrase. Thames journalists were not engaged in being judge, prosecution and witnesses. It was a normal piece of current affairs journalism.' Thames was doing no more than the newspapers had done since the Gibraltar shootings. 'The trouble is that politicians – and I know because I was one – do tend to over-react to the broadcasters.'

The following week, Mrs Thatcher returned to the attack. By questioning witnesses in advance of the Gibraltar inquest, both Thames and the IBA had failed to live up to the high sense of responsibility required of them, the Prime Minister told the Commons. 'One of the proudest bastions of liberty is that the rule of law is inviolate – that is what is at stake.' The television authorities had considerable freedoms under the law, they also had a responsibility to uphold the rule of law and not try to substitute their own system for it. But there were many eminent judicial figures who questioned the Prime Minister's appeal to the rule of law. Lord Scarman pointed out that there was no trial planned in the UK which could be prejudiced by the broadcast, nor any public inquiry planned or even promised. The right to be informed and comment on matters of public interest was vital to the working of a democratic society. 'It would be sinister indeed', added Scarman, 'if a government could impose restraint on a broadcasting authority acting within the law, unless able to establish to the satisfaction of the High Court a sufficient ground for an order to that effect.' Such pronouncements emboldened the BBC to transmit – after considerable agonizing – a report on the Gibraltar shootings in a local Northern Ireland programme, but not in mainland Britain.

Even some of the Prime Minister's normal supporters among the press felt she had gone too far over *Death on the Rock* and suspected they knew the reason. The *Spectator* claimed the Government's prime interest was in coming unscathed out of a potentally damaging situation. Behind all the Government's complaints could be heard 'the rattle of skeletons in the cupboard: why should the Prime Minister "be beyond anger" unless she had something to hide?' And the *Sunday Times*, while attacking the Thames programme, editorialized: 'Mrs Thatcher wants to control what viewers can watch both in terms of moral tone and when broadcasters threaten to expose or embarrass the Government.' It added that when, as promised by the Prime Minister, British television was transformed from 'a state-supported cosy cartel' into an industry with an unlimited number of largely privately-owned channels, 'it would become increasingly difficult for governments to lean on the broadcasters as Mrs Thatcher's has done in the past ten days'.

At the start of 1988, Mrs Thatcher had celebrated becoming Britain's longest-serving prime minister this century with a photo-call. Delaying the start of a trip to Africa to ensure she would be at Number 10 the day Asquith's record fell, Mrs Thatcher and her husband emerged on cue to wave triumphantly for the press and TV cameras. 'When I first walked through that door – and many of you were with me photographing me then – I little thought that we would become the longest-serving prime minister of this century,' confided the record-breaker. In 1979 the country was suffering from the British disease; now it was known for having the British cure. 'The eight years and 244 days have gone very quickly indeed and there is so much more still to do.' Her homily led all BBC news and ITN bulletins that night – the BBC dressing it up into a three-minute encomium: she was the Prime Minister who thought solely of the good of the nation, worked tirelessly, and even the sun shone for her photo-call.

The producers of *Panorama*, who had the temerity to publicize in advance some disobliging remarks by one of her ex-ministers in a generally favourable survey of her record tenure, were berated by the Number 10 press office – the Prime Minister was very disappointed to have her great day soured in that way. But the transmitted programme found the favour of both Conservative Central Office and Mrs Thatcher. She gave a full-length anniversary interview to *Panorama* two weeks later.

The interview was notable because she chose to deflect attacks over the state of the Health Service by announcing to David Dimbleby that she was herself chairing a fundamental review into its financing. This news was a complete reversal of her previous public line and came as surprise to most ministers, who were forced to chase up video cassettes of the programme to discover exactly what government policy now was. After the interview, the Prime Minister took a hand in casting the following week's *Panorama* on the Health Service. Reminding the producers of the BBC's duty under its Charter to be impartial, Mrs Thatcher asked which Government minister the programme planned to interview. She was told that all the DHSS ministers had declined to appear and the programme had filmed an interview with Norman Tebbit, now a backbencher, instead. Mrs Thatcher told *Panorama* to resubmit the invitation to John Moore, the Social Services Secretary: she felt sure he would accept. He did, and the BBC agreed to the condition that Moore would appear in a lengthy uncut interview at the end of the programme. In the past *Panorama* had always strongly resisted such conditions by ministers. However, the Prime Minister found the Commons and even some Tory MPs less amenable than the Corporation at the start of February.

MPs were for the eleventh time in twenty-two years debating whether to allow the TV cameras into the Chamber. This time Mrs Thatcher made her opposition clear in advance. 'I don't think that televising the House of Commons would enhance its reputation,' she said in a BBC news interview after the 1987 general election: 'I've thought about it very deeply. The Commons is a small, intimate chamber; those heavy lights, the heat, I think would be dreadful. Also I don't think the House of Commons has improved since it was sound broadcast. Indeed, if anything, the rules of order have been even more difficult for the Speaker to implement.' Mrs Thatcher led a campaign against the cameras, aided by her Whips. At getting-to-know-you tea parties with new Tory MPs the Prime Minister put her arguments: left-wing MPs would abuse parliamentary privilege and name security chiefs or allegedly crooked financiers, confident they would be splashed all over the news bulletins; there would be more publicity-seeking, and possibly violent demonstrations in the spectators' gallery; and the cameras would encourage even rowdier behaviour by the Opposition. 'Televised debates would merely provide a platform for hooligan elements in the Commons,' claimed Mrs Thatcher's Parliamentary Private Secretary, Archie Hamilton, in a rare public speech.

Supporters of televising the Commons suspected the Prime Minister's resistance had other causes – primarily that she believed it would work against her. Mrs Thatcher had learned that since the introduction of cameras to the Canadian Parliament, no Government had been elected for more than a single term. Even the position of the sun during Prime Minister's questions, she was told, was not in her favour: it would bathe the Opposition in a golden glow, while the Government benches would look dark and drab. Her advisers also feared she would come over as shrill and hectoring and the unfamiliar sight of her wearing glasses would be a disadvantage.

John Biffen, the former Leader of the House who had been dismissed by Mrs Thatcher after the 1987 election, was in favour of admitting the cameras. Pointing out that the Prime Minister had chosen *Panorama* rather than Parliament to announce the NHS review, Biffen argued that the Government now routinely used television news and current affairs programmes to outflank the Commons. The existing arrangements, he claimed, strengthened the executive at the expense of backbenchers. 'Prime Ministers like to be seen above the dust of battle, loftily speaking for the nation,' said Biffen, 'they prefer to be seen meeting Chancellor Kohl or reviewing the Boys' Brigade or opening hospitals. Margaret Thatcher has a lot to lose by being seen in the rather vulgar arena of Question Time, the only arena she has in the Chamber, being answered back in a sharp and rude fashion. The disrespect would intensify. That's not good for the Prime Minister.'

Theoretically the House was to reach its decision in a free vote – without the Whips on. But for many backbenchers, when their leaders make their own views clear, there is no such thing as a free vote. Both Margaret Thatcher and Neil Kinnock left no one in any doubt at Prime Minister's Question Time just before the debate. The Labour leader asked what reasonable cause there could be for not televising the House, given that it was already broadcast in sound: 'What is the Prime Minister afraid of?' 'My concern is for the good reputation of this House,' responded Mrs Thatcher to Labour's conditioned response of 'frit, frit, frit [frightened]'. 'I do not think that television will ever televise this House. If it does televise it, it will televise only a televised House, which will be quite different from the House of Commons as we know it.'

In the debate that followed, the Tory MP, Anthony Nelson, said: 'The Prime Minister has everything to gain and little to lose from the televising of Parliament.' Neil Kinnock's selflessness in wanting the cameras was astonishing, as he could not hope to be more than best supporting actor while Mrs Thatcher played the lead role. But the Shadow Leader of the House, Frank Dobson, claimed that the Prime Minister was opposed because she saw the Commons as a place where mishaps could occur; where she would be questioned 'not by complacent interviewers made pliable by knighthoods or the promise of knighthoods, but by people on both sides of the House with knowledge, commitment and passion'. They were not manageable as television was. The present compromise of sound and no vision suited Mrs Thatcher very well: the polls showed that most listeners believed she gave her lengthy and detailed replies from memory. And Dobson concluded: 'Television would show the truth that she recites these replies not from memory but from her briefing folder.'

However, the Leader of the House, John Wakeham, said that Mrs Thatcher had been advised that televising the House would probably work in her favour: 'Her opposition was that it was no good for the House of Commons.' In the division, it appeared that Mrs Thatcher's campaign of persuasion had largely worked on her own side: the great majority of Tories – more than on the previous occasion eighteen months earlier – followed their Leader and voted against the cameras. But a skilled lobbying campaign by the BBC and ITN, with demonstrations at Westminster of remote-controlled cameras and the low lighting needed, had stilled some fears on both sides of the House. The Labour vote was almost entirely in favour: combined with the smaller parties and dissident Tories it produced a majority of fifty-four for a six-month experiment.

Although Mrs Thatcher looked rueful as the result was announced, the *Daily Telegraph* claimed 'she cannot be wholly sad as she gets the star role' and *The Times* reported that 'she was determined to turn the cameras to the Government's advantage'. What seemed certain was that television, with its tendency to intensify impressions, would work both ways for the Prime Minister. For some, she would come out as the indomitable battler standing firm against a mob of baying men: she would probably adapt her present technique of seeking to out-shout the Opposition and would learn to stand silent at the despatch box during the noise. But for others the 'TBW factor' would be more in evidence than ever.

In her years at Number 10 Margaret Thatcher had played many parts on the small screen: tearful mother, Iron Lady, wide-eyed *ingénue*, war leader, simple housewife and world statesman. She had been taught to move her weight from one buttock to another to appear more interesting while answering questions in a studio and she had become an expert in the art of hijacking interviews. Robin Day joked that he planned to begin his next interview: 'Prime Minister, what is your answer to my first question?' She had won three elections partly by exploiting television's complicity in its coverage of politics: there would be no photo-opportunities and prime ministerial charades if there were no cameras. A medium that in any case tends to magnify personalities had been faced with a giant-sized one. Although the Prime Minister's screen presence sent some viewers screaming from the room, she spoke a populist language that could turn on many more.

Mrs Thatcher had been Leader of the Tory Party for over a quarter of television's lifetime. She had profoundly transformed the relationship between television and Number 10 – partly by reshaping the citadels of broadcasting. The Government's decision to set the licence fee well below the level of the BBC's costs together with a continuous campaign of political pressure had injected new caution into the Corporation. 'The licenced gadfly on the body politic' – as Sir Hugh Greene had seen the BBC's role – seemed to have been exterminated.

A similar timidity had affected many ITV companies. Their chief executives had felt the lash of the prime ministerial tongue at the September 1987 Downing Street meeting and feared for their franchises, due for renewal in 1992: better to play it safe than be sorry. For in the coming years Mrs Thatcher had made clear she planned to revolutionize the structure of British broadcasting.

In 1930 Ramsay MacDonald had installed a prototype TV set in Number 10. Nearly sixty years on there were no less than thirteen sets in the building: those in the Prime Minister's flat and private office were cabled and already received a cluster of satellite channels. 'Television is the most powerful form of communication known to man,' Mrs Thatcher had told the broadcasting chiefs at the Downing Street meeting. She had learned better than any of her predecessors how to harness its power to her purposes. And the Prime Minister had every apparent intention of going on and on doing so in the brave new multi-channel world she was calling into existence.

Bibliography

Alexander, Andrew, and Watkins, Alan, *The Making Of The Prime Minister*, Macdonald, 1970

Arnold, Bruce, *Margaret Thatcher*, Hamish Hamilton, 1984

Atkinson, Max, *Our Masters' Voices*, Methuen, 1984

Benn, Anthony Wedgwood, *Diaries 1963-7*, Hutchinson, 1987

Black, Peter, *The Mirror in the Corner*, Hutchinson, 1972

– *The Biggest Aspidistra in the World*, BBC, 1972

Blumler, Jay, Gurevitch, Michael, and Ives, Julian, *The Challenge Of Election Broadcasting*, University of Leeds, 1978

Bosanquet, Reginald, *Let's get through Wednesday*, New English Library, 1980

Boyle, Andrew, *Only the Wind Will Listen – Reith of the BBC*, Hutchinson, 1972

Briggs, Asa, *The BBC – The first fifty years*, Oxford University Press, 1985

– *Governing the BBC*, BBC, 1979

– *The History of Broadcasting in the United Kingdom*, Vols 1-4, Oxford University Press, 1961-79

Bruce-Gardyne, Jock, *Mrs Thatcher's First Administration*, Macmillan, 1984

Butler, David, Kavanagh, Dennis, King, Anthony and others. *The Nuffield Studies of British General Elections from 1950 to 1987*, Macmillan, 1951-88

Butler, David and Kitzinger, Uwe, *The 1975 Referendum*, Macmillan, 1976

Callaghan, James, *Time and Change*, Collins, 1987

Castle, Barbara, *The Castle Diaries*, Weidenfeld and Nicolson, 1980

Clark, William, *From Three Worlds*, Sidgwick and Jackson, 1986

Cockerell, Michael, Hennessy, Peter and Walker, David, *Sources Close to the Prime Minister*, Macmillan, 1984

Cole, John, *The Thatcher Years*, BBC, 1987

Colville, Sir John, *The Fringes of Power, Downing Street, Diaries, 1939-55*, Hodder and Stoughton, 1985

Cosgrave, Patrick, *Margaret Thatcher – A Tory and her Party*, Hutchinson, 1978

– *Thatcher – The First Term*, Bodley Head, 1985

Cox, Geoffrey, *See it Happen*, Bodley Head, 1983

Crewe, Ivor, and Harrop, Martin, *Political Communications – The General Election Campaign of 1983*, Cambridge University Press, 1986

Crosland, Susan, *Anthony Crosland*, Jonathan Cape, 1982

Crossman, Richard, *Diaries of a Cabinet Minister*, Vols I–II, Hamish Hamilton and Jonathan Cape, 1975-7

Curran, Charles, *A Seamless Robe*, Collins, 1979

Curran, James and Seaton, Jean, *Power Without Responsibility*, Methuen, 1985

Day, Robin, *Television*, Hutchinson, 1961

– *Day by Day*, William Kimber, 1975

Dimbleby, Jonathan, *Richard Dimbleby*, Hodder and Stoughton, 1975

Donoughue, Bernard, *Prime Minister*, Jonathan Cape, 1987

Eden, Anthony, *Memoirs*, Cassell, 1960

Egremont, Lord, *Wyndham and Children First*, Macmillan, 1968

Evans, Harold, *Downing Street Diary 1957-63*, Hodder and Stoughton, 1981

Falkender, Marcia, *Downing Street in Perspective*, Weidenfeld and Nicolson, 1983

Frishchauer, Willi, *David Frost*, Michael Joseph, 1972

Golding, Peter, Murdoch, Graham, and Schlesinger, Philip, *Communicating Politics*, Leicester University Press, 1986

Grisewood, Harman, *One Thing at a Time*, Hutchinson, 1968

Hastings, Max, and Jenkins, Simon, *The Battle for the Falklands*, Michael Joseph, 1983

Haines, Joe, *The Politics of Power*, Jonathan Cape, 1977

Harris, Robert, *Gotcha!*, Faber and Faber, 1983

– *The Making of Neil Kinnock*, Faber and Faber, 1984

Heath, Edward, *Sailing*, Sidgwick and Jackson, 1975

Hetherington, Alastair, *News, Newspapers and Television*, Macmillan, 1985

Hill, Lord, *Behind the Screen*, Sidgwick and Jackson, 1974

Hooper, Alan, *The Military and the Media*, Gower, 1982

Howard, Anthony, and West, Richard, *The Making of the Prime Minister*, Jonathan Cape, 1965

Hurd, Douglas, *An End to Promises*, Collins, 1979

Hutchinson, George, *Edward Heath*, Longman, 1970

– *The Last Edwardian at Number 10*, Quartet, 1980

Jenkins, Peter, *The Battle of Downing Street*, Charles Knight, 1970

– *Mrs Thatcher's Revolution*, Jonathan Cape, 1987

Junor, Penny, *Margaret Thatcher*, Sidgwick and Jackson, 1983

Keegan, William, *Mrs Thatcher's Economic Experiment*, Penguin, 1984

Kellner, Peter, and Hitchens, Christopher, *Callaghan – the Road to Number 10*, Cassell, 1976

Kettle, Martin, and Hodges, Lucy, *Uprising*, Pan, 1982

Kleinman, Philip, *The Saatchi and Saatchi Story*, Weidenfeld and Nicolson, 1987

Leapman, Michael, *The Last Days of the Beeb*, Allen and Unwin, 1986

– *Kinnock*, Unwin Hyman, 1987

Linklater, Magnus, and Leigh, David, *Not With Honour – the Westland Scandal*, Sphere, 1986

Macmillan, Harold, *Memoirs*, Macmillan, 1988

Margach, James, *The Abuse of Power*, W.H. Allen, 1978

Mayer, Alan J., *Madam Prime Minister*, Newsweek Books, 1979

Mercer, Derrik, Mungham, Geoff, and Williams, Kevin, *The Fog of War – the Media on the Battlefield*, Heinemann, 1987

Mitchell, Leslie, *Leslie Mitchell Reporting*, Hutchinson, 1981

343

Money, Ernle, *Margaret Thatcher, First Lady of the House*, Leslie Frewin, 1975

Murray, Tricia, *Margaret Thatcher*, Star, 1978

Norden, Denis, Harper, Sybil, and Gilbert, Norma, *Coming to you Live!* Methuen, 1985

Prior, James, *A Balance of Power*, Hamish Hamilton, 1986

Pym, Francis, *The Politics of Consent*, Hamish Hamilton, 1984

Quicke, Andrew, *Tomorrow's Television*, Lion Publishing, 1976

Reith, Lord, *Into the Wind*, Hodder and Stoughton, 1949

Riddell, Peter, *The Thatcher Government*, Basil Blackwell, 1983

Roth, Andrew, *Heath and the Heathmen*, Routledge and Kegan Paul, 1972

– *Sir Harold Wilson – A Yorkshire Walter Mitty*, Macdonald and Jane's, 1977

Schlesinger, Philip, Murdock, Graham and Elliot, Philip. *Televising 'Terrorism'*, Comedia, 1983

Seaton, Jean, and Pimlott, Ben, *The Media in British Politics*, Avebury, 1987

Smith, Anthony, *Television and Political Life*, Macmillan, 1979

Stephenson, Hugh, *Mrs Thatcher's First Year*, Jill Norman, 1980

Thatcher, Carol, *Diary of an Election*, Sidgwick and Jackson, 1983

Thomas, Harvey, *In the Face of Fear*, Marshalls, 1985

Tracey, Michael, *The Production of Political Television*, Routledge and Kegan Paul, 1978

– *A Variety of Lives – A biography of Sir Hugh Greene*, Bodley Head, 1983

– *In the Culture of the Eye – Ten Years of Weekend World*, Hutchinson, 1983

Trethowan, Ian, *Split Screen*, Hamish Hamilton, 1984

Tyler, Rodney, *Campaign! – The Selling of the Prime Minister*, Grafton, 1987

Wapshott, Nicholas, and Brock, George, *Thatcher*, Futura, 1983

Wenham, Brian, and others, *The Third Age of Broadcasting*, Faber and Faber, 1982

Whale, John, *The Half-Shut Eye*, Macmillan, 1969

– *The Politics of the Media*, Fontana, 1977

Wheen, Francis, *Television*, Century, 1985

Whitehead, Phillip, *The Writing on the Wall*, Michael Joseph, 1985

Wigg, Lord, *George Wigg*, Michael Joseph, 1972

Wilcox, Desmond and Rantzen, Esther, *'Kill the Chocolate Biscuit'*, Pan, 1981

Williams, Marcia, *Inside Number 10*, Weidenfeld and Nicolson, 1972

Wilson, Harold, *The Labour Government 1964-70*, Weidenfeld and Nicolson, 1971

– *Final Term*, Weidenfeld and Nicolson and Michael Joseph, 1979

Williams, Philip, *Hugh Gaitskell*, Jonathan Cape, 1979

Wilson, Des, *Battle for Power*, Sphere, 1987

Worcester, Robert and Harrop, Martin, *Political Communications – The General Election Campaign of 1979*, George Allen and Unwin, 1982

Worsley, T.C., *Television: The Ephemeral Art*, Alan Ross, 1970

Wyndham Goldie, Grace, *Facing the Nation*, Bodley Head, 1977

Wyatt, Woodrow, *Confessions of an Optimist*, Collins, 1985

Young, Hugo and Sloman, Anne, *The Thatcher Phenomenon*, BBC, 1986

Index

ACTT, 333
Adley, Robert, 272
Airey, Lady, 254
Alexander, Andrew, 150, 202
Alliance, 281, 314, 325
Allsop, Kenneth, 59
Annan Commission, 155, 180, 238
Ashton, Joe, 301–2
Aspel, Michael, 79, 288–9
Associated Rediffusion, 28
Astor, Lord, 90
Atkins, Humphrey, 254
Atkinson, Max, 280
Attenborough, David, 39, 136
Attlee, Clement, 6, 8, 26, 27, 32–3, 40, 109
ATV, 73, 89, 109

Baird, John Logie, 1
Baker, Stanley, 166, 167, 197, 210
Baldwin, Stanley, 1, 3, 60
Banks-Smith, Nancy, 206, 217
Barber, Anthony, 111, 172
Barnes, George, 8
Barratt, Michael, 160
Baverstock, Donald, 34
BBC: first transmissions, 1–2; and the General
    Strike, 3; Second World War, 4–6; early
    news programmes, 7–8; 1950 election, 8–9;
    and the Fourteen Day Rule, 8, 18, 37, 40,
    41, 51; first party political broadcasts, 10–14,
    16–18; and the Coronation, 19–20;
    televises party conferences, 21–2, 41–2;
    opposition to creation of ITV, 24, 25–6;
    Party Manners row, 24–5; refuses to allow
    ministerial broadcasts, 27–8; 1955 election,
    28–37; ministerial broadcasts, 38–9,
    115–16; Suez crisis, 45–52, 271; Rochdale
    by-election, 58–9; interviews Macmillan, 61;
    1959 election, 68, 69, 73–4; Macmillan's
    'report to the people', 77–8; 25th anniversary
    of television, 78–9; Macmillan's Common
    Market address, 83–4; satirical programmes,
    85–6, 98–9; and Kennedy's assassination,
    99; 1964 election, 102, 103–9; Wilson
    clashes with, 114–16, 120–7, 129–30,
    131–7, 140–5, 150–3; licence fee, 116,
    133–4, 237, 254, 294, 311, 340; 1966
    election, 125–7, 128–30; Wilson boycotts,
    141–3, 183, 205–6; Annan Commission,
    155, 238; 1970 election, 157, 158, 159–61,
    163, 167–9; Yesterday's Men row, 176–80,
    183, 296; Complaints Commission, 180; and
    The Question of Ulster, 181–3, 184; Heath's
    relations with, 188–90; February 1974
    election, 197, 198, 201–2; Wilson complains

about Steptoe and Son, 207–8; October 1974
    election, 211, 214; EEC referendum, 221–2;
    Callaghan's relations with, 237–8; 1979
    election, 246, 249, 253; Mrs Thatcher's
    relations with, 253–4, 258, 293–8, 309,
    310–16, 340; financial problems, 254,
    293–4, 311; Northern Ireland programmes,
    254–8; Falklands War, 270–3, 276–7; 1983
    election, 279, 281; Peacock Commission,
    294, 311; Real Lives affair, 295–8; and the
    proposed televising of the Commons, 302,
    339–40; Tebbit monitors, 6–7, 310, 312,
    313–14, 316; Milne sacked, 315–16; Secret
    Society row, 315; 1987 election, 250, 326,
    328, 330–1; refuses to hand over film,
    334–5; see also individual programmes
BBC News, 330–1
BBC Scotland, 315
Beatles, 102
Begun, Josef, 318
Beirut hijacking, 294–5
Belgrano, 271–2, 282–3, 322
Bell, Tim, 244, 292–3, 321, 327, 329
Benn, Tony, 58, 100, 140, 209, 228, 232,
    293–4; sees importance of television, 32–3;
    1955 election, 34–5; 1959 election, 70–2;
    Wilson's relations with BBC, 133; plans
    reform of BBC, 134; attacks BBC, 142;
    February 1974 election, 196, 199; EEC
    referendum, 221–2
Bernstein, Sydney, 206
Bevan, Aneurin, 33, 65, 300
Bevins, Reginald, 85
Biffen, John, 264, 308, 339
Birch, Nigel, 57, 91
Bird, John, 117
Birt, John, 176, 223, 316
Bishop, Freddie, 77
Black, Peter, 20
Blackler, George, 197
Bligh, Jasmine, 1
Bolton, Roger, 219, 233, 254–5, 256, 257, 260,
    283, 312–13, 335
Bonham Carter, Mark, 271
Bonham Carter, Lady Violet, 21
Booker, Christopher, 145
Boothby, Bob, 9–10
Bosanquet, Reginald, 43, 44, 60, 159
Boyne, Harry, 146
Bradley, Clive, 104, 106
British Army, 334
British Film Institute, 267
British Steel, 260, 261
British Telecom, 314
Brittan, Leon, 289, 294, 295–6, 298, 303–4